METHODS IN EDUCATIONAL RESEARCH

METHODS IN EDUCATIONAL RESEARCH

From Theory to Practice

Marguerite G. Lodico, Dean T. Spaulding, Katherine H. Voegtle

JOSSEY-BASS
A Wiley Imprint
www.josseybass.com

Published by Jossey-Bass
A Wiley Imprint
989 Market Street, San Francisco, CA 94103-1741   www.josseybass.com

Jossey-Bass books and products are available through most bookstores. To contact Jossey-Bass directly call our Customer Care Department within the U.S. at 800-956-7739, outside the U.S. at 317-572-3986, or fax 317-572-4002.

Jossey-Bass also publishes its books in a variety of electronic formats. Some content that appears in print may not be available in electronic books.

Library of Congress Cataloging-in-Publication Data

Lodico, Marguerite G.
  Methods in educational research : from theory to practice / Marguerite G.
Lodico, Dean T. Spaulding, and Katherine H. Voegtle.
       p. cm.
  Includes bibliographical references and index.
  ISBN-13: 978-0-7879-7962-1 (alk. paper)
  ISBN-10: 0-7879-7962-7 (alk. paper)
  1. Education—Research—Methodology. I. Spaulding, Dean T. II. Voegtle,
Katherine H. III. Title.
  LB1028.L586 2006
  370'.7'2—dc22

                                                                    2005023416

Printed in the United States of America
FIRST EDITION
HB Printing   10 9 8 7 6 5 4 3 2 1

CONTENTS

To our partners, Jim, Phil, and Chip, for their constant encouragement and for putting up with us over the past year as we worked to make this book a reality.

TABLES, FIGURES, AND EXHIBITS

Tables

Figures

Exhibits

PREFACE

Methods in Educational Research: From Theory to Practice is pedagogically based: written from the fundamental perspective of how one learns in general and, more specifically, how one learns through research. In this book, we have tried to apply the techniques and instructional practices underlying "good teaching" to teaching people about educational research. Furthermore, we have paid attention to the metacognitive processes associated with *how* one *learns* about research and *how* one develops and becomes a more active participant in the educational research community.

Today's political climate of No Child Left Behind, "scientifically based" research, and school accountability has certainly changed the face of education as well as the knowledge and research skills needed by educators in the 21st century. In addition to building these competencies, this book hopes to empower teachers to take an active role in conducting research in their classrooms, districts, and the greater educational community—activities that are now not only expected but required of all teachers.

Therefore, the purpose of this book is to assist students, primarily graduate students, in the area of education or related fields (administration, school psychology, or school counseling) in developing competencies and skills in educational research. More specifically, the purpose of this book is to provide an understanding of such competencies that is both broad and deep. Breadth of understanding is established in the student who demonstrates general knowledge as to the characteristics and properties of all the quantitative, qualitative, and mixed-methods research approaches. In doing so, the student should be able to identify and distinguish between the various types of research approaches: their underlying philosophies, purposes, and methods. Depth of understanding is established through the student determining a need for a particular type of research approach and developing a research proposal around that idea, including a review of literature that supports the study and a proposed methods section that complements the research problem.

We pilot-tested the chapters in our own classes and, after many revisions, arrived at a final ordering and integration of concepts that seemed optimal for both our teaching and our students' learning. In educational research courses, it is always challenging to cover the information needed by students "in time" for them to use the information in their research and writing for their proposal. The increasing complexity of research approaches and data analysis in educational research today makes teaching this course for master's-level students an especially difficult task. Some of the practical tools in this book, such as the article summary sheets in Chapter Two, have been designed to make this process less confusing and intimidating for our students.

The book includes a number of special features designed to assist the teaching and learning processes:

• Research vignettes illustrating research that is tied to practice and used to make decisions about educational practices open each chapter on specific research approaches and are discussed throughout the chapters.

• The book focuses on both conceptual understanding and practical aspects of conducting research.

• Research issues and concepts relevant to the accountability movement and data-driven decision making are discussed throughout the book.

• Developmental processes involved in researching and writing a research proposal are emphasized.

• Research proposals using both qualitative and quantitative approaches are included along with annotations on the key criteria for evaluating a proposal.

• Key concepts students should know are highlighted in each chapter.

Suggested readings are provided at the end of each chapter to extend the discussion of general issues raised in the chapter and provide citations for sample studies that illustrate the type of research discussed.

• Discussion questions are provided to stimulate thinking about the issues raised in the chapter or encourage students to apply the concepts presented.

ACKNOWLEDGMENTS

Any textbook on educational research owes a debt to numerous people who have built the rich and varied literature in this field. In some sense, this book grew out of the conversations and relationships we have had with colleagues over many years, especially at meetings of the American Educational Research Association and the American Evaluation Association. Although we cannot name all of these persons, we certainly could not have begun to think about this book without the stimulation of many people in these vibrant educational communities.

However, many people closer to home also made this book possible. The College of Saint Rose and especially our former dean, Crystal Gips, provided substantial support for our work by granting us course reductions, providing funding for conference presentations and support services, and making available to us capable graduate assistants. The idea for the book began with a survey of all members at our college who taught research courses, and our colleagues generously provided ideas and input into what was needed. We are especially indebted to Steve Black, one of our college librarians, who has a background in education and teaches courses in educational research for our department. Steve shared with us his innovative ideas on strategies for searching the literature and using library resources effectively. Many of his ideas are reflected in Chapter Two of this book. Members of our department consistently encouraged us in our writing, and our present and past department chairs, Richard Brody and Ismael Ramos, always managed to get people to cover courses as needed each semester. Our colleagues who are practicing educational researchers, James Allen, Aviva Bower, Donna Burns, Ron Dugan, and Heta-Maria Miller, each contributed his or her own special expertise and pedagogical ideas to the book. In addition, Kathy's partner, Jim Fahey, a professor at a nearby university, helped us to "get our philosophy right." Jim created the organizing tables on the philosophical frameworks, and his precise prose is responsible for the crystal clarity of the section on philosophical frameworks in Chapter One.

Elizabeth Gerron, a former student and graduate assistant of ours, returned to work for us as an editor of early versions of the book. Her keen eye for detail and passion for clear and well-organized writing considerably strengthened the early chapters of this book. Kathy and Marguerite's graduate assistant, Jessica Gillis, spent hours online and in the library locating resources that would be helpful and interesting for students. Dean's graduate assistant, Jian (Ken) Geo, provided invaluable assistance in finding resources, checking references, and formatting the book. He always got us what we needed, even at times when we were hysterically trying to meet impossible schedules. We are also certainly grateful to the staff at Jossey-Bass, including Andy Pasternack, Catherine Craddock, Seth Schwartz, and Susan Geraghty for the opportunity to make this dream come true. Input by Catherine and Susan greatly improved the book.

We also thank the students from our educational research classes who patiently read through often-imperfect drafts of the book, providing feedback and suggestions. Many of them allowed us to include samples of their work in this book to help us fulfill our goal of making courses on educational research more comprehensible, relevant, and useful to future generations of preservice educators.

Writing a book also results in a great deal of clutter and requires quite a bit of physical space. We would like to thank our colleagues who share our office pod for their patience and good humor in putting up with our frequent group meetings in the pod's common space. As they have told us, they will be glad to see the book completed.

Finally, on a personal level, we thank our partners, Jim Fahey, Phil Lodico, and Chip McCarthy, who kept us sane, well fed, and entertained throughout the often-hectic job of creating this book.

M.G.L., D.T.S., and K.H.V.

ABOUT THE AUTHORS

MARGUERITE G. LODICO, ED.D., received her doctoral degree from the University of Houston and is a professor at The College of Saint Rose where she teaches child development and educational research. In addition to her teaching responsibilities, she has served as chair of the Educational and School Psychology department and as interim dean. Her recent research interest has focused on students in urban environments. She is the coauthor of the casebook *Child and Adolescent Life Stories: Perspectives from Youth, Parents, and Teachers,* published in 2004. She is currently copresident of the Teaching Educational Psychology Special Interest Group for the American Educational Research Association.

DEAN T. SPAULDING, PH.D., received his doctoral degree from the State University of New York at Albany in 2001 and is currently an associate professor at The College of Saint Rose where he teaches educational research and program evaluation. His research and program evaluation work has focused on technology, after-school and enrichment programs, and environmental education in K-12 settings and in higher education. He is currently the chair for the Teaching Evaluation Topic Interest Group for the American Evaluation Association.

KATHERINE H. VOEGTLE, PH.D., received her doctoral degree from the University of Cincinnati and is currently an associate professor at The College of Saint Rose where she teaches courses in human development, educational research, and educational psychology. She is coauthor of *Child and Adolescent Life Stories: Perspectives of Youth, Parents and Teachers* and has conducted qualitative and quantitative research projects on creative language development, school-based ally groups, technology training for preservice teachers, mentoring programs, and arts-based educational programs. She is currently copresident of the Teaching Educational Psychology Special Interest Group for the American Educational Research Association.

METHODS IN EDUCATIONAL RESEARCH

CHAPTER ONE

INTRODUCTION TO EDUCATIONAL RESEARCH

Chapter Objectives

After reading this chapter, you should be able to

1. Describe the role of research in the educational accountability movement
2. Describe key aspects of the No Child Left Behind (NCLB) Act, including

    the role of educational research in implementation of the act and

    the potential effects of NCLB on the future of educational research
3. Explain the differences between inductive and deductive reasoning
4. Articulate the key differences between knowledge-oriented philosophical frameworks for educational research (scientific realism and social constructivism) and action-oriented approaches (advocacy or liberatory and pragmatism) and *begin* to define your own framework
5. Explain the differences between and provide a simple example of
    * quantitative and qualitative methods of data collection and
    * basic and applied educational research
6. For each research approach discussed,
    * describe the key elements of that approach and
    * provide an example of a research study using that approach

Educational Research Today

At the beginning of the 21st century, the educational research community is again responding to the call for increased accountability in our nation's schools. This call for accountability comes from both within and outside the educational community. Educators, parents, students, communities, and politicians are hopeful that the new accountability will result in increased achievement for America's students. As discussed in Box 1.1, the No Child Left Behind (NCLB) legislation holds schools accountable for monitoring and reporting student progress based on test scores. Monies for schools are being made available for programs that are "scientific and reliable," although the federal government's definition of scientific research is very narrow (see Neuman, 2002).

Meeting NCLB requirements makes knowledge of educational research an essential component of professional preparation for all educators. However, to promote creative, innovative, yet sound solutions to current educational problems, future educators must become knowledgeable about a multitude of research approaches that reach beyond those techniques defined as "reliable" under the NCLB legislation. It is our hope that this book will enable students to participate in ongoing debates about the status and future of education on both national and local levels. We also hope that you will develop skills and knowledge to take part in a much longer and broader tradition: using scientific research to identify and develop effective educational practices.

Box 1.1 No Child Left Behind Act

Although the current movement for accountability began at the end of the 20th century, the No Child Left Behind (NCLB) legislation passed by the U.S. Congress in 2001 has brought accountability to a new level. NCLB is the reauthorization of the Elementary and Secondary Education Act, passed in 1965, which resulted in large federal expenditures to help improve education for children from disadvantaged communities. According to the U.S. Department of Education (2005b), since 1965 the federal government has spent over $300 billion to educate youth from low-income families. However, the government also reported that only 32 percent of fourth-graders could read at grade level and most of those who could not read were ethnic minorities. Believing that the money spent was not improving education, the Bush administration passed the NCLB legislation as a mechanism to increase accountability of individual schools and states and ultimately reform education.

What this legislation effectively does is to significantly increase the role of the federal government in education and set into place regulations that reach into virtually all public schools in this country. In short, the legislation requires (U.S. Department of Education, 2005a):

a) *Annual Testing*—By the 2005–06 school year, states must begin testing in grades 3–8 annually in reading and math. By 2007–08 states must develop tests to measure science achievement at least once in elementary school, middle school, and high school. All tests must be aligned with state standards and be reliable and valid measures. Additionally, a sample of the 4th and 8th graders must participate in the National Assessment of Educational Progress testing program every other year in the content areas of reading and math.

b) *Academic Progress*—States are responsible for bringing all students up to a level of proficiency by the 2013–14 academic school year. Each year, every school must demonstrate "adequate yearly progress" toward this goal. If a school fails to meet this goal for two years in a row and receives Title I funding (federal dollars), the state must provide technical assistance, and families must be allowed a choice of other public schools (assuming there is available space and that the other schools are making adequate progress). If a school fails to meet the defined level of proficiency for three years in a row, it must offer students supplemental educational services, which could include tutoring.

c) *Report Cards*—All states must prepare individual school report cards on all schools. These report cards must be made public and must demonstrate progress in reaching the state standards.

d) *Teaching Quality*—Currently, the federal government provides money to states and school districts to improve the quality of their teaching forces. Under the NCLB legislation, the federal government has indicated that it will provide greater flexibility in the spending of that federal money.

e) *Reading First*—NCLB offers new competitive grants called Reading First that will help states and school districts to set up scientific and reliable research-based reading programs for children in kindergarten through grade three. School districts in high poverty areas will be given priority for these grants. According to the U.S. Department of Education (2005a), the key characteristics of reliable research are:

1) a study that uses the scientific method, which includes a research hypothesis, a treatment group, and a control group,
2) a study that can be replicated and generalized,
3) a study that meets rigorous standards in terms of its design, the methods used and the interpretation of the results, and
4) a study that produces convergent findings, e.g., findings are consistent using various approaches.

These guidelines have significant implications for the way research is conducted in education. Specifically, the legislation calls for researchers to conduct studies with scientific rigor. According to Neuman (2002), NCLB's definition of scientific rigor is consistent with **randomized experimental designs,** study designs in which persons are randomly assigned to groups that are treated differently. Randomized studies certainly are one approach for establishing causality but may not be appropriate for all research questions. Almost everyone would agree that research studies should be rigorous and scientific. However, the narrow definition of scientific rigor as randomized experimental studies has the potential for greatly limiting the scope of educational research. Furthermore, according to R. D. Davies (2003), "devoting singular attention to one tool of scientific research jeopardizes inquiry efforts into a range of problems best addressed by other scientific methods" (pp. 4–5).

Educational Research: Using the Scientific Method

The NCLB initiative is certainly not the first effort to apply scientific methods to educational practices. Since the beginning of formalized education, research has been used to help improve education and to determine how education works in a wide range of situations. Through scientific research, educators hope to obtain accurate and reliable information about important issues and problems that face the educational community. Specifically, **scientific educational research** is defined as the application of systematic methods and techniques that help researchers and practitioners to understand and enhance the teaching and learning process. The steps used in the scientific process are shown in Figure 1.1.

FIGURE 1.1 THE SCIENTIFIC PROCESS.

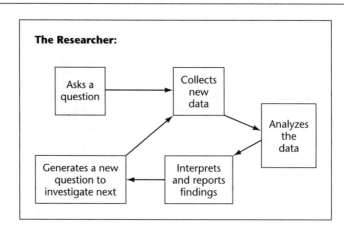

Much like research in other fields, research in education uses two basic types of reasoning: **inductive reasoning** and **deductive reasoning**. Inductive reasoning is often referred to as a "bottom-up" approach to knowing in which the researcher uses particular observations to build an abstraction or to describe a picture of the phenomenon that is being studied. Inductive reasoning usually leads to inductive methods of data collection where the researcher (1) systematically observes the phenomena under investigation, (2) searches for patterns or themes in the observations, and (3) develops a generalization from the analysis of those themes. So the researcher proceeds from specific observations to general statements—a type of discovery approach to knowing.

In contrast, deductive reasoning uses a top-down approach to knowing. Educational researchers use one aspect of deductive reasoning by first making a general statement and then seeking specific evidence that would support or disconfirm that statement. This type of research employs what is known as the **hypothetic-deductive method**, which begins by forming a **hypothesis**: a tentative explanation that can be tested by collecting data. For example, one might hypothesize that small classes would result in a greater amount of student learning than large classes. This hypothesis would be based on a **theory** or a knowledge base composed of the results of previous research studies. A *theory* is a well-developed explanation of how some aspect of the world works using a framework of concepts, principles, and other hypotheses. For example, a humanistic theory of education might emphasize strong teacher-student relationships as part of effective learning. Previous research studies may have shown that such relationships are more common in small classes. Therefore, based on the humanistic theory and these previous studies, the researcher in our example may have hypothesized that small class sizes will result in better student learning based on humanistic theory and previous studies. The next step in the hypothetic-deductive approach is to collect data to see if the hypothesis is true or should be rejected as false. The researcher might compare student learning in classrooms of 15 or fewer students with those of 25 or more students. If students in the smaller classes show a greater amount of learning, the hypothesis would be supported. If the students in the smaller classes do not show a greater learning, then by deductive reasoning, the hypothesis is shown to be false. To summarize, the researcher (1) began with a theory and a knowledge base and used them to form a hypothesis, (2) collected data, and (3) made a decision based on the data to either accept or reject the hypothesis or prediction.

The inductive and hypothetic-deductive approaches to knowing represent two general routes to knowledge used in educational research. Inductive reasoning is most closely associated with **qualitative** approaches to research, which collect and summarize data using primarily narrative or verbal methods: observations, interviews, and document analysis. Qualitative researchers are often said to take inductive approaches to data collection because they formulate hypotheses only *after* they begin to make observations, interview people, and analyze documents. These hypotheses are examined and modified by further data collection rather than being accepted or rejected outright. Qualitative researchers believe that full understanding of phenomena is dependent on the context, and so they use theories primarily after data collection to help them interpret the patterns observed. However, ultimately qualitative researchers do attempt to make claims about the truth of a set of hypotheses.

The hypothetic-deductive method is most closely associated with **quantitative** approaches, which summarize data using numbers. Hypotheses and methods of data collection in quantitative research are created *before* the research begins. Hypotheses or theories are then tested, and when supported, these hypotheses or theories are typically considered to be **generalizable**: applicable to a wide range of similar situations and populations. Quantitative researchers may also use inductive reasoning as they look for similar experiences and results and form new ideas, concepts, or theories.

Philosophical Frameworks for Educational Research

Educational research today is beginning to move away from a hard and fast distinction between qualitative and quantitative research methods. Researchers can, however, be separated into groups based on their philosophical frameworks, identified in terms of the assumptions they make about the nature of the reality being studied, claims about what we can and cannot know, and the ways in which they utilize theories and findings. Each framework also makes assumptions about whether qualitative or quantitative methods are most appropriate for extending our knowledge about education. As a beginning researcher, it is important that you consider which approach best captures your own assumptions about how the world works.

Scientific Realism

Scientific realism is a term applied to the framework used by most researchers who take a purely quantitative approach to research. Quantitative research is characterized by a desire to answer research questions by producing numerical data that represent various **constructs** and **variables**. A construct is a hypothetical concept that is typically developed from a theoretical framework. Although constructs are names for things that cannot be seen (e.g., intelligence, motivation, self-esteem), they are assumed to be real characteristics that influence educational outcomes. When constructs are measured in educational research, they are known as *variables*. Like the constructs they represent, variables are defined as attributes, qualities, and characteristics of persons, groups, settings, or institutions, such as gender, social skills, socioeconomic status, exclusiveness, or achievement. Scientific realists strive to establish cause-and-effect relationships where possible, using data collection methods such as questionnaires, tests, and observational checklists to produce quantitative data.

The philosophical underpinnings of the scientific realism approach can be found in the positivist arguments developed primarily to describe knowledge generation in the physical sciences. The first assumption made by scientific realists is that there is a real social and psychological world that can be accurately captured through research. In other words, there is an objective reality that research aims to describe. Scientific realists further assume that the social and psychological world can be studied in much the same way as the natural world by breaking complex phenomena and problems into smaller parts (constructs and variables). The major job for the researcher is to identify the most important parts or variables and accurately describe how these are related to each other in the real world. However, because humans are fallible and social scientists study human characteristics, reporting that reality must be done with a certain degree of probability. Scientific realists "see knowledge as conjectural" (Phillips & Burbules, 2000, p. 29) and therefore subject to possible revision. All hypotheses are tested using statistical tests that establish the level of confidence that one can have in the results obtained. Scientific realists do recognize that because educators study human behaviors and characteristics, research may be influenced by the investigator. For an investigator to maintain clear objectivity, he or she must play a **detached role**, where there is little opportunity for interaction with the participants under study. Scientific realists believe that inquiry can be value-free and that a researcher who strives to eliminate any personal bias can reliably determine findings. Although they borrow rigorous scientific techniques from the natural sciences, they recognize that in education and psychology, true scientific experiments are not always possible. Scientific realists concede that different persons might have different perceptions of reality; however, they assume that experiences overlap to a large degree and that a good researcher can take these different perceptions into account in providing the best possible explanation of reality.

Social Constructivism

Traditionally, purely qualitative research is often done by persons who hold a framework referred to as interpretive, constructivist, or naturalistic. (We will use the term **social constructivism** to refer to this approach.) Social constructivists challenge the scientific realist assumption that reality can be reduced to its component parts.

Instead, they argue that phenomena must be understood as complex "wholes" that are inextricably bound up with the historical, socioeconomic, and cultural contexts in which they are embedded. Therefore, they attempt to understand social phenomena from a context-specific perspective.

Social constructivists view scientific inquiry as value-bound and not value-free. According to Lincoln and Guba (1985), this means that the process of inquiry is influenced by the researcher and by the context under study. This philosophical perspective argues that reality is socially constructed by individuals and this social construction leads to multiple meanings. Different persons may bring different conceptual frameworks to a situation based on their experiences, and this will influence what they perceive in a particular situation. In other words, there is no one "true" reality, nor can one assume that the experiences that people have had will overlap to a large degree. Rather, we construct reality in accord with the concepts most appropriate to our personal experiences. Therefore, the researcher must attempt to understand the complex and often multiple realities from the perspectives of the participants. The acceptance of the existence of multiple realities leads social constructivists to insist that a set of initial questions asked in a study will likely change or be modified as these multiple realities are uncovered or reconstructed during the process of conducting research. The only true way to accomplish this understanding is for the researcher to become involved in the reality of the participants and interact with them in deeply meaningful ways. This provides an opportunity for mutual influence and allows the researcher to see the world through the eyes of the participants. "The inquirer and the 'object' of inquiry interact to influence one another; knower and known are inseparable" (Lincoln & Guba, 1985, p. 37). This approach, then, requires that researchers use data collection methods that bring them closer to the participants using techniques such as in-depth observations, life histories, interviews, videos, and pictures.

Advocacy or Liberatory Framework

Researchers taking an **advocacy** or **liberatory** framework for research also assume that there are multiple possible realities that are dependent on social, political, and economic contexts. However, they go beyond the social constructivist claim that researchers' values can influence research by insisting that moral values should form the impetus for research and that research should seek to improve the lives of persons who have little social power and have been marginalized by more powerful groups in their societies. In essence, the goal of advocacy or liberatory researchers is liberation through knowledge gathering. Paulo Freire (1921–1997), a literacy worker from South America and author of *Pedagogy of the Oppressed*, based his philosophy of research on these principles and argued that research should provide freedom from oppression and debilitating living environments. Working on literacy skills with poor and oppressed Chilean workers in the 1960s and 1970s, Freire asserted that research should be conducted in a collaborative manner with community members participating in the selection and analysis of themes during data analysis. This collaboration requires that the researcher engage in respectful dialogue with the study participants and understand reality from the perspectives of the community. According to Freire and other advocacy-liberatory investigators, research should not only use inductive processes to gather information but engage in research as a form of social advocacy. Whereas this type of research usually uses qualitative methods of data collection, it might use quantitative methods constructed in collaboration with participants if these data will help the people achieve social changes in their society. The type of data collected is less dependent on philosophical assumptions than by their potential to illuminate experiences and facilitate action to achieve a better life. In other words, research should be used not only to educate and produce knowledge but also to empower people to take political action and use their political voice to change and improve their place in society.

Pragmatism

Pragmatism is the framework that has been most developed by American philosophers. Unlike the other frameworks, pragmatism is not concerned with whether research is describing either a real or socially constructed world. Instead, for pragmatists, research simply helps us to identify what works. Of course, we might ask our pragmatists what they mean by what works. They are likely to reply that knowledge arises from examining problems and determining what works in a particular situation. It does not matter if there is a single reality or multiple realities as long as we discover answers that help us do things that we want to do. A pragmatist might insist that a good theory is one that helps us accomplish a specific goal (or set of goals) or one that reduces our doubt about the outcome of a given action. Most pragmatic researchers use a **mixed-methods approach** to research; for example, they use both qualitative and quantitative methods to answer their research questions. Pragmatic researchers propose that even within the same study, quantitative and qualitative methods can be combined in creative ways to more fully answer research questions. Campbell and Fiske (1959) are often thought to be among the first researchers to introduce the notion of using both qualitative and quantitative techniques to study the same phenomena. In current research, pragmatic frameworks are used by both professional researchers and researchers who are primarily practitioners (e.g., teachers, counselors, administrators, school psychologists).

The assumptions underlying the philosophical frameworks described above are summarized in Table 1.1. We turn next to a discussion of the specific research approaches used in education.

Types of Approaches Used in Educational Research

Philosophical frameworks describe the assumptions that underlie research. To some extent, your philosophical framework will guide your selection of the type of research approach you will use. The specific approaches used in educational research can be further classified according to (1) the extent to which the findings are applicable to educational settings (e.g., basic vs. applied research), (2) the methods used to design the study and to collect data (e.g., qualitative vs. quantitative approaches), and (3) how the information is shared (e.g., the dissemination of the findings).

Basic Versus Applied Research Approaches

The goal of **basic research** is to design studies that can test, refine, modify, or develop theories. As an example of basic research, Marcia's (1966) research on adolescent identity led to a refinement of one stage of Erik Erikson's psychosocial theory of development. Marcia's goal was not to create a program to address practical ways to help adolescents but, rather, to extend and support the theory. **Applied research** studies examine the effectiveness and usefulness of particular educational practices. Here the goal is to determine the applicability of educational theory and principles by testing hypotheses within specific settings. For example, Schmitt-Rodermund and Vondracek (1998) examined whether parenting behaviors predicted the amount of adolescent identity exploration as described by Marcia.

Both basic and applied methods of research have their place in the educational research field. To some degree, the approach selected depends on whether the findings are utilized and result in a change in practice. In basic research, the overarching goal is to develop and modify theory. These theory-based studies, while critical to the formulation of applied research, often have low utilization and do not result in systemwide change. Whereas the goal of applied research is to demonstrate the usefulness of theories in practice, the reality is that applied research studies often take many years to stimulate change, even though the findings are disseminated to large groups of individuals through applied research journals. Two approaches that do result in more immediate change are program evaluation and action research, which are discussed below.

TABLE 1.1 FRAMEWORKS AND ASSUMPTIONS UNDERLYING EDUCATIONAL RESEARCH.

	Scientific Realism	Social Constructivism
Knowledge-oriented approaches	• Research aims to describe an objective reality that most or all people would agree is real • Educational settings and problems can be studied by empirical analysis of component parts • Research should be value-free • Researchers should be detached from participants and strive to be objective • Theories and hypotheses are formed and then confirmed or disconfirmed through collection of data	• Reality is historically and culturally constructed so there are multiple possible realities • Educational settings and problems must be understood as complex wholes • Researchers must continually strive to be aware of and control their values • Researchers should become actively involved with participants in order to understand their perspectives • Theories and hypotheses are generated during data collection and achieve meaning through human interactions
	Advocacy-Liberatory	**Pragmatism**
Action-oriented approaches	• Reality is socially constructed and influenced by social, political, and cultural inequalities • Although qualitative methods are preferred, educational settings and problems can be studied using any methods that truly represent the experiences of the participants • Research must be based in values and should empower marginalized groups to improve their lives • Researchers should collaborate with participants as equal partners • Theories and hypotheses should provide action plans to achieve a better life	• The immediate reality of solving educational problems should be the focus of educational research • Educational settings and problems can be studied using any method that accurately describes or solves a problem • Research should strive to find ways to make education better • Researchers should collaborate with participants to fully understand what works • Theories and hypotheses are useful tools in helping to improve education

Quantitative Research Approaches

All quantitative research approaches summarize results numerically. However, the approaches differ in their goals and the procedures used to collect data.

Descriptive Survey Research. *Descriptive survey research* aims to describe behaviors and to gather people's perceptions, opinions, attitudes, and beliefs about a current issue in education. These descriptions are then summarized by reporting the number or percentage of persons reporting each response. The survey is the primary method used to gather such data or information from people. Although more and more technology and Web-based surveys are being used in research, the long-standing paper-pencil survey continues to be the main mode of data collection. A commonly held misconception is that descriptive survey research is an easy method, requiring simple questions and answers. This just is not so. Good descriptive survey research requires thoughtful and careful planning. Like experimental research, this approach is quantitative, and surveys are typically administered to a random sample of the population to which the researcher wants to generalize the survey results; however, in contrast to experimental research, there is no manipulation of variables, and data are not gathered to test a hypothesis. Therefore, descriptive survey is considered a nonexperimental approach. Rather, demographic items (designed to obtain background information on participants) and survey questions are developed through an extensive review of the literature in the area of study, and conclusions are drawn based on participant responses. Items are subjected to a series of preliminary tests, or piloting, which is essential in order to "work the kinks out" of the survey. Descriptive survey research is the most widely used method of research in education, with an estimated 70% of research falling into this category.

Experimental Research. The goal of experimental research is to test hypotheses to establish cause-and-effect relationships. For decades, experimental research has been a major approach used in quantitative research, and indeed, the manner in which NCLB defines "reliable research" may result in an increased use of this method. Often when people think about research and what research is, they commonly associate it with characteristics typical of experimental research. The overarching purpose of experimental research is to determine whether a particular approach or way of doing something is "better" than the "older" or more traditional approach that has served as the standard practice. (Keep in mind that sometimes experimental research is conducted with hopes that no difference will be found between the two methods or approaches under investigation.) So experimental research is about studying the effect or the impact of an approach under stringent and controlled conditions to make statements of causality. Sometimes, these conditions involve **random selection** of study participants from a larger group known as the **population**. The population is the larger group to which the researcher would like the results of a study to be generalizable (e.g., fourth graders or high school girls). Random selection is a procedure where each and every person in the population has an equal and independent chance of being selected for the study. The randomly selected participants constitute the **sample**. People in the sample are then assigned to one of two or more groups that are treated (**manipulated**) with regard to a specific educational approach or practice or are exposed to different treatments at different points in time. These differential treatment conditions are called the **independent variable**, which precedes and is assumed to cause a change in behavior referred to as the **dependent variable**. For example, a researcher might ask, "Does instructional strategy in reading (phonics or whole language) affect reading achievement of fourth graders?" In this study, reading achievement would be the dependent variable, and instructional strategy would be the independent variable. The sample would be a group of fourth graders randomly selected from the population to which the researcher wants to generalize the study results (e.g., fourth graders in an entire school district). Students would be randomly assigned to receive either phonics or whole language, and reading achievement would be measured. The final component of an experimental study is to control **extraneous variables**. An *extraneous variable* is any variable, other than the independent variable, that might influence the dependent variable. In any experimental study, there are many possible extraneous variables. In the study of phonics versus whole language, one would need to consider if the teachers for each class were equally good teachers. The amount of time spent on reading instruction might also be an extraneous variable. Differences in student abilities before the instruction begins are an extraneous variable that is controlled through random assignment. Many other ways to control extraneous variables are discussed in Chapter Eight.

Causal-Comparative Research. *Causal-comparative research*, or ex–post facto research, is a research approach that seeks to explain differences between groups by examining differences in their experiences. Like experimental research, it examines the effect of an independent variable (the past experience) on a dependent variable while also trying to control extraneous variables. However, unlike experimental research, the independent variable (the past experience) has either already occurred or it would be unethical to manipulate. For example, let us say that you are interested in what causes the differences in the readiness skills of kindergarten students. After reading past research studies, you decide to examine preschool attendance as an independent variable that might have "caused" a difference in kindergarten readiness (the dependent variable). Preschool attendance has already occurred or happened; as a researcher, you cannot control or manipulate it. If you were to conduct such a study, you will simply identify two groups, one group that attended preschool and one group that did not, and then measure and compare school readiness scores. If the groups differ on their readiness scores, the researcher infers that preschool attendance caused the readiness scores to differ. However, caution is warranted. Because no random assignment occurred, the two groups being studied could be very different to begin with, which might mean that other factors and not preschool attendance caused the difference in readiness scores. For example, there may be differences in family income or parental levels of education (or both). Therefore, making sure that the two comparison groups are as similar as possible on all other extraneous variables (other than the independent variable) is a critical part of designing a causal-comparative study.

Correlational Research. *Correlational research* is a quantitative method designed to show the relationships between two or more variables. Correlational research is similar to descriptive survey in that it is nonexperimental, consisting of only one group of individuals (e.g., fifth-grade students) and two or more variables that are not manipulated or controlled by the researcher (e.g., reading scores and IQ). The variables are examined to determine if they are related and, if so, the direction and magnitude of that relationship. Simple correlational research does not seek to show causality (that one variable is causing a change to occur in another). Rather, the main purpose of correlational research is to determine, through application of a quantitative statistical analysis, whether a relationship exists between the variables under investigation. One might make predictions based on these relationships, but not statements of causality. For example, if such a relationship does exist, the strength and the direction of the relationship are reported numerically in what is referred to as a **correlation coefficient**. Scores from this analysis fall somewhere along the correlation coefficient's range of negative 1.00 to positive 1.00. Note that negative and positive do not have any "moral value" attached to them in this context. A highly negative relationship is not a relationship that is bad but one that results from scores on two variables moving in *opposite* directions: an increase in one variable is accompanied by a decrease in the other variable being studied. For example, as absentee rates increase, student achievement decreases.

Meta-Analysis. Research studies using meta-analysis tend to pose a dilemma for students new to the area of research. This may be because when it comes right down to it, this type of research statistically summarizes the results of other studies. Now perhaps you see why so many consider it to be confusing. The purpose of a meta-analysis is to ask a research question and use past quantitative studies as data to answer the question. The data from these studies are reanalyzed using an appropriate statistical analysis, and a typical result, usually referred to as an effect size, across all studies is reported.

Qualitative Research Approaches

Qualitative research approaches collect data through observations, interviews, and document analysis and summarize the findings primarily through narrative or verbal means.

Case Study. *Case study* is one of the most common qualitative approaches. Although they are wide ranging in their scope and sequence, case studies typically focus on small groups or individuals within a group and document that group's or individual's experience in a specific setting (see next section on ethnographic research). In addition, the gathering of this information or data through multiple sources and perspectives is another key characteristic of the case study approach. For example, on the topic of parental involvement, a researcher could do a case study on a family or several families who are non-native-English speakers and determine how they are working with the school district and the teacher to help improve their child's academic performance. Some interesting questions the researcher might think about exploring as she or he approaches the study are how do the parents (who are not proficient in English themselves) interface with the school in supporting and working with their child? Do they feel that the school is assisting them, or do they view the school as an obstacle? How do teachers perceive the parents' efforts to help their child? Researchers working in case studies tend to use interview, observation, and document analysis as their primary tools.

Ethnographic Study. *Ethnographic studies* are often included in the same category as case studies, and for good reason. Where case study researchers focus their energies on the interactions of individuals or small groups in specific settings, ethnographic researchers tend to investigate how interactions in a cultural group are influenced by the larger society. Like cases, ethnographic studies also gather information about the phenomena being investigated from multiple perspectives. However, in addition to gathering data, ethnographic researchers "filter" or assess the information gathered through the setting, recognizing that the setting itself has a role and a function in the study. Ethnographic studies also require that the researcher gain the perspective of the participants, to some degree, by becoming part of the group being studied. For example, an ethnographic researcher decides to examine a school building within a large urban district and document how the school is trying to deal with issues of diversity. Specifically, the school has been working to increase student awareness of diversity, to heighten student tolerance toward individual differences, to create a learning community, and to infuse multicultural issues into the curriculum. A researcher who clearly knows the setting and culture and the participants in the setting gathers this information by using interviews, observations, and some document analyses. However, the researcher also recognizes that she or he has to be aware of alternative settings or issues that need to be considered (e.g., diversity of curriculum mandated by the school; interaction between minority students, the police, and the larger community; the interaction between the religious community and the school; and legislation). Whereas the researcher is examining only one building, the larger school district, the community, and possibly the state and nation may play a role in describing "the overall picture."

Grounded Theory. In grounded theory research, the researcher uses data gathered through qualitative techniques to develop a theory based on the data. In essence, the researcher builds a theory from the "ground" or from the narrative data produced in the study. Taking the example just used for ethnographic research, a grounded-theory researcher might take the findings of the study and develop a theory of how schools in general might effectively deal with issues of diversity. Let us say that the data suggested that there were four basic components essential to an effective diversity program: developing identity, tolerance training, understanding differences, and building learning communities. The theory then could be based on these principles, and from these principles the researcher would begin to develop a theoretical framework. As the theory begins to emerge, the researcher returns to collect more data to either confirm or challenge the initial findings. In some ways, the grounded theory researcher is attempting to use the findings generated in a particular context and develop a theory that could be generalized to other contexts.

Phenomenological Study. Like case studies, phenomenological studies are also a common qualitative approach. Phenomenological studies attempt to capture the "essence" of the human experience. Like other qualitative researchers, phenomenologists are interested in recording the individual perspectives of the participants in the study. However, phenomenology stresses the importance of each individual and his or her respective view of reality. To encourage these perspectives to emerge, phenomenologists use open-ended interviews as their primary data collection tool. The phenomenologist's role is to "give voice" to those perspectives. Consider the following: Take a look at the person sitting next to you in class. You both are sitting in the same course, at the same college, with the same professor; yet, the way you perceive the reality of this graduate experience is quite different. You each bring a history of personal experiences, attitudes, behaviors, and emotions, all of which will influence how you view this shared experience. For an example of a published study that used phenomenological methods to study the experiences of women in dance therapy, see Mills and Daniluk (2002).

Research Approaches Using Qualitative or Quantitative Approaches (or Both)

Several approaches to research are more flexible in their use of quantitative and qualitative methods. Two of these, program evaluation and action research, may use either qualitative or quantitative approaches or use both in a single study. Mixed-methods approaches, by definition, use both quantitative and qualitative methods.

Mixed-Methods Research. Mixed-methods research collects both quantitative and qualitative data because these researchers believe that a combination of approaches results in a more complete understanding of educational problems. Although one approach might be emphasized more than the other, both types of data are considered essential to the study. One type of data may be collected first, followed by the other, or both quantitative and qualitative data may be collected simultaneously.

For example, Jones and Kafetsios (2005) studied the effect of war on the psychological well-being of adolescents by collecting quantitative data from a trauma questionnaire and qualitative data through in-depth interviews. The use of two types of data enabled the researchers to better understand both the degree of trauma and the meaning of the wartime experiences to their youth. Widespread use of mixed-methods research is relatively new, and several designs (described in Chapter Twelve) have been developed.

Action Research. Action research is designed to enhance and improve current practice within a specific classroom, school, or district. Typically, it is a type of research undertaken by practitioners who have identified problems they wish to solve or who would simply like to find ways to enhance their own teaching or student learning, or both. For example, Pasko (2004) studied her own third-grade classroom to see how the students connected mathematical concepts to literature that they read independently. Her results provided support that her interdisciplinary approach to teaching was working for her students and suggested new ideas that she might try to improve her approach.

In general, there are two types of action research, **critical action** and **practical action** research. Critical action research, as described by Freire (1970) is research that is collaborative and is implemented to improve the lives of those who are being studied. Practical action research is conducted in classroom or school settings and provides practitioners the opportunity to identify and solve their own educational problems.

Whichever type of action research is pursued, all action research generally includes a three-step process: (1) identification of the problem(s) through careful observation and reflection, (2) planning and taking appropriate action (the study), and (3) using the findings to improve teaching and learning. This type of research continues to grow in use because educational practitioners find it an empowering and collaborative activity.

Program Evaluation. The field of education is filled with programs designed to improve both learning and teaching. Examples of these programs include a reading-intervention program designed to help struggling readers or a teacher-training program designed to help teachers integrate technology into lessons. Program evaluation is designed to attempt to determine the level of success or failure of such educational programs and to make decisions about such programs. Although program evaluation uses quantitative and qualitative methods, its overall purpose is different from most other types of research. Whereas quantitative and qualitative researchers certainly study programs, findings from such studies typically are slow to change or improve the programs themselves. In program evaluation, however, findings are often used for ongoing or short-term decision-making purposes, and programs can be changed or "improved" based on the results of a single evaluation. In some extreme cases, a program might even be eliminated based on such evidence. Most program evaluation approaches use two types of feedback loops for reporting findings: **formative feedback** and **summative feedback**.

Formative data are collected and provided to program developers as the program is occurring, with the hope that such evidence will support the needed changes. For example, if one is evaluating a new reading program and the instruction is not being delivered according to the program's specific goals, the evaluator would provide this information to the program director so that the instruction could be improved. Although some quantitative researchers use formative feedback loops, *it is the potential for action to be taken on the feedback* that makes program evaluation distinct from quantitative approaches. For example, experimental or quasi-experimental researchers would not dream of altering the program or treatment (the independent variable) as it was being studied. After all, if the study showed an increase in student performance, to what could the results be attributed? The program before the improvements? The program after the improvements? A combination of the two? In addition to collecting and providing formative feedback, program evaluation researchers attempt to collect summative data. Summative data focus on determining whether a program's goals were met. Examples of summative data are changes in students' reading scores, number of people served by the program, and job satisfaction ratings. Program evaluators tend to use both formative and summative information in identifying areas in need of improvement and in determining a program's success or failure.

Chapter Summary

Despite the narrow definition of "reliable" research embodied in the NCLB legislation, you can now see that multiple methods are available for investigating issues in education. Whereas NCLB focuses on quantitative research using experimental study designs (designs in which persons are randomly assigned to groups that are treated differently with regard to variables of interest), in this chapter we have discussed a number of other research approaches, which fall into the broad categories of quantitative and qualitative research. These approaches have grown out of differing philosophical views, but all focus on systematically endeavoring to answer questions about what works in education, and therefore, we would argue, all have value in the ongoing debate about how to go about improving education. The research approaches we have described have evolved out of philosophical frameworks that demonstrate widely divergent views on: the nature of reality, how we come to know that reality, and even if we need to concern ourselves with such ponderings as long as we can figure out what works and what does not! The philosophical viewpoint to which you personally subscribe will, in many ways, determine what research you are willing to undertake or accept as meaningful.

Despite whatever the current accountability environment might be, as a professional in the field of education you will be challenged on a daily basis to create and sustain an effective learning environment for yourself and your students. An understanding of educational research and its philosophical underpinnings is vital to making informed decisions about what research you will use to support your everyday practice.

Key Concepts

randomized experimental designs

scientific educational research

inductive reasoning

deductive reasoning

hypothetic-deductive method

hypothesis

theory

scientific realism

social constructivism

advocacy or liberatory

pragmatism

qualitative

quantitative

generalizable

constructs

variables

social constructivism

mixed-methods approach

basic research

applied research

random selection

sample

independent variable

dependent variable

extraneous variable

nonexperimental research

correlational research

causal-comparative research

correlation coefficient

ethnographic research

case study

grounded theory

phenomenological research

mixed methods research

critical action research

practical action research

program evaluation

formative feedback

summative feedback

Discussion Questions or Activities

1. NCLB and the accountability movement emphasize testing students and setting required benchmarks for student progress. Explore the tests and benchmarks used in your state or school district and discuss the factors that might influence whether schools meet their mandated goals.
2. Pick a philosophical framework that is closest to your personal belief about how knowledge is generated, and find a student in your class whose preferred framework is different from yours. Debate the pros and cons of each framework as a guide to research.
3. Pick an educational problem or topic, and discuss how it could be explored using one quantitative and one qualitative approach.

Suggested Readings

Onwuegbuzie, A. J. (2000). *Positivists, post-positivists, post-structuralists, and post-modernists: Why can't we all get along! Towards a framework for unifying research paradigms.* Paper presented at the annual meeting of the Association for the Advancement of Educational Research, Ponte Vedra, FL.

Peterson, P. E., & West, M. R. (Eds.). (2003). *No child left behind? The politics and practice of school accountability.* Washington, DC: Brookings Institute.

Popham, J. W. (2004). *America's "failing" schools: How parents and teachers can cope with No Child Left Behind.* New York: RoutledgeFalmer.

CHAPTER TWO

IDENTIFYING AND RESEARCHING A TOPIC

Chapter Objectives

After reading this chapter, you should be able to

1. Summarize the steps for identifying a topic and developing a focused research question and statement of purpose
2. Discuss how independent, dependent, and extraneous variables are used in quantitative research and how themes, processes, and meanings are used in qualitative research
3. Distinguish between the types of sources that can be used in a research paper and identify strategies for identifying sources as primary versus secondary sources, empirical research reports, opinion pieces, and how-to or experiential reports
4. Develop competence in finding research studies on a topic using several different strategies, such as locating a review of literature, searching databases, following citations, using people as sources, and finding and evaluating Internet sources
5. Develop skills in summarizing information from articles using an article summary sheet

Getting Started

Are you feeling a little overwhelmed with all the new concepts and strategies that are involved in studying educational research? Well, you are not alone! One of us (D.T.S.) has described student experiences in taking a course in educational research as similar to learning to drive at 200 mph. Especially when students begin to read studies published in professional journals, they often feel like there are just too many strange new concepts, too much information, and too many different types of research to expect anyone to navigate successfully without getting lost. This chapter presents some ideas to help you in your early travels through the professional literature. We cannot tell you everything you need to know before you "hit the road." But we can give you some tools to help you develop ideas for research studies, find information on research topics, and begin to understand and question studies as you read. We will start at the beginning by considering how to select or generate a research topic.

Developing Ideas for Research Studies: Possible Topics

The first task in developing a research study is coming to some decision about a possible research topic. For some students, this can be an exciting process: finally being able to pursue a topic that you have been interested in all your life but have never had the time or the opportunity to pursue. (Not that you have a whole lot of time now that you are in graduate school, but at least you can't say you don't have the opportunity.) For other students, coming up with a topic can be a horrible, painful experience: torn between several topics, one more interesting than the next, wanting to explore everything, leaving no stone unturned, and believing that it might be this study (or maybe the one right around the corner) that will somehow ultimately change the world . . . , if you could only wait one more day before having to decide. And then there are the students, many of whom are new to research, who are keenly interested in a certain broad topic but know little about it or the current research supporting it and who have no idea how to begin a study on it. Most graduate students in an introductory course to educational research are in this final group. So relax, take a deep breath, and let it out slowly. This is exactly where you should be right now in this process, and it is a wonderful place to be: ready for adventure and exploration.

Most students in a research course begin by initially deciding on a couple of broad research topics. In educational research, these broad research topics can be wide ranging, including—but by no means limited to—the following examples:

emergent literacy, technology integration, strategies in educational leadership, or counseling intervention practices. It should be noted that many students have the common misperception about educational research that it must take place within the context of a school building or classroom. This is a limited view of educational research, and although most educational research does indeed take place more or less within such a setting, many studies are done in nontraditional educational settings outside the brick-and-mortar infrastructure of the school building. For example, research conducted on how companies train new employees using distance learning and other technology hardware and software would certainly be considered in the realm of education-related topics and suitable for study in an educational research course. Educational research also includes research on programs and activities in after-school settings and in the communities surrounding schools.

Although there is no specific formula or proven method for selecting a topic to pursue, students and most professional researchers gravitate toward a specific topic for one of three reasons: past experience, theory testing, or replication of previous research (see Figure 2.1).

Experience. For most students in a research course, past experience is one thing that drives their interests in pursuing a particular topic. Past experience can also be a strong motivational factor for professional researchers, who sometimes devote their whole life to pursuing a certain area of study. For those in a graduate course on educational research, experience may be related to their current career as a teacher in the classroom, a school psychologist, counselor, or as a school administrator. In those situations, individuals should ask themselves questions such as

- I wonder if we did it this way, rather than the old way, would that make a difference?
- I wonder if I taught the class using an activity first, followed by an explanation of the content, would that make a difference in my students' understanding and increase their performance on the next chapter test?
- I wonder what intervention would be best for a student with multiple disabilities?
- I wonder what that new teacher in fifth grade is doing to keep her students so attentive during class?

All of these questions are cornerstones to developing a more comprehensive, researchable research topic. Keep in mind that researchers do not always pursue a topic of interest because they had a positive experience with it in the past. In fact, many researchers pursue topics based on a past negative experience for the sole purpose of improving practices and making them better for the next gener-

FIGURE 2.1 WAYS TO GENERATE A RESEARCH TOPIC.

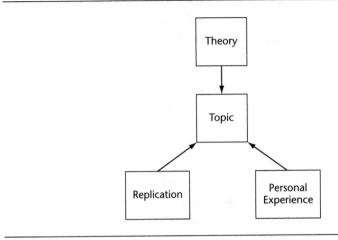

ation of learners. For example, one of our students explored student experiences in gifted education programs in her proposal because she experienced significant problems within her own high school gifted education program.

Theory. Research studies can also be developed based on theory, as discussed in Chapter One. For some researchers, a single theory might provide the focus for most of their research. For example, Robbie Case (1992) conducted many studies of Piagetian theory. These studies eventually led him to construct his own theory that blends Piaget's original stages with concepts from information-processing theory. Students might use theories presented in any of their classes as the basis for a research study. For example, several of our students have examined implications of a well-known theory of parenting styles (Baumrind, 1967) in relation to educational issues, such as student achievement, discipline problems, and attention disorders.

Replication. The third approach to doing a study is through what is referred to as *replication*. Although this approach may sound complicated, in essence, it is a "do over but do better" approach. Typically, a researcher conducts a replication by first selecting a research study that she or he recognizes (or learns through others' reviews of studies) as flawed; that is, it either uses poor methods to collect the data or sample participants or is poorly designed in other ways that will be discussed later in this book. Some of these issues may be directly related to poor planning and practice by the researcher. Aware of these methodologic limitations, the researcher conducts the study again, paying careful attention that such oversights do not repeat themselves. Other times, an existing study is replicated not so much because of methodological flaws per se but because the researcher wants to redo the study with a slightly different population (e.g., using fifth graders instead of fourth graders) to see if the findings are the same. For example, one of our students replicated a classic study of the benefits of preschool programs, but he included measures of attitudes toward school as well as student achievement and extended the follow-up for more years. Some other sample research topics from our students' proposals that were based on either experience, theory, or replication are listed in Box 2.1.

Box 2.1 Sample Topics for Research Proposals

- Student perceptions of school violence
- Approaches to classroom management at the middle-school level
- Involvement of single parents in their children's education
- Development of new instructional strategies for students with reading problems
- Divorce and students' school performance
- Attention deficit hyperactivity and strategies to improve behavior
- The principal's role in training new teachers

From Topics to Questions

After a topic has been selected, the next step in the process is an initial review of the literature. This initial review may consist of reading only a handful of research studies, literature reviews, and other articles on the topic. You are in the "exploratory" stage of your study where your goal is to simply increase your knowledge on your selected topic. Specifically, as you read, you should pay close attention to the issues and questions that are addressed within your topic. For example, you select a topic that involves the following: successful urban schools and teachers. Certainly a broad topic! You might begin your investigative process by selecting a few articles that focus on successful urban schools and teachers and find that the following issues are identified:

- Teaching urban students
- Issues related to teaching diverse populations
- Characteristics of quality urban teachers
- Training quality urban teachers

Your initial review has identified some of the major areas of investigation around the topic of successful urban teachers and students, which should help you to identify your research question(s).

Research studies typically are the result of a lot of planning and preparation, both in developing and refining the research question and carrying out the study. Generally research studies stem from a **research question** (or in some cases, a series of questions). One mistake that many students make when selecting a topic is to think that they need to generate a final, detailed research question at the exact moment they come up with their topic. In general, we recommend that students start with a general question that can be further developed after they begin to read the literature related to it. Students should not avoid a topic just because they cannot think of a research question to ask. Sophisticated research studies can begin with simple questions that are refined repeatedly as one reviews past research. Because the research question is the seed from which the study will eventually grow, it is imperative that the question be what is often referred to as *researchable* or doable. Researchable questions can be answered through the systematic collection of data and clearly meet ethical guidelines. Although the issues of ethics will be discussed in detail elsewhere in this text, all human research should protect participants from harm, provide confidentiality, and include informed consent. Researchable questions should also clearly define the variables (quantitative research) and identify themes, processes, and meanings (qualitative research) being investigated.

A **variable** is a characteristic or attribute that varies! This definition is the ultimate circular definition. As is, it does not tell us much. Let us back up and consider a few important elements that will help us to understand the term variable(s). In education and psychology, we are often confronted with constructs. A **construct** is a hypothetical concept that cannot be directly observed. For example, intelligence is a construct. We hypothesize that intelligence exists, but we cannot see it. We cannot surgically open up someone's brain and locate intelligence. However, based on theory, we know that that person has intelligence. Some of us have more intelligence, and some of us have less intelligence. To measure constructs, they must be **operationally defined**, that is, defined in terms of how they will be measured. The operational definition allows researchers to identify the variables that are being used to measure the construct. So if we operationally define intelligence as a score on the Stanford Intelligence Test, other researchers understand that in our study, intelligence is conceptualized as the ability to successfully complete the items on the test. Of course, operational definitions are limited, and the construct of intelligence is much broader and more complex. Therefore, some researchers might also include a more conceptual definition of intelligence, such as intelligence is the ability to solve complex problems.

As discussed in Chapter One, researchers using experimental, causal-comparative, and correlational approaches all measure or manipulate variables. Research questions for these types of quantitative research are often stated in terms of variables. Let us say that you are interested in tutoring in reading and its influence on reading performance. Your initial review of the literature might identify several variables related to reading performance, such as a parent's reading to a child, instructional methods used by the teacher, or gender. This review might also provide examples of how the variables were operationally defined, measured, or manipulated. If you decide to pursue an experimental or causal-comparative approach, your research question will need to identify the independent and dependent variables. Later in the proposal, you would design a study that would control for the effects of the extraneous variables identified in your review of the literature. If you decide to do a correlational study, your research question will need to identify the variables that you expect to be related.

Unlike their quantitative counterparts, qualitative researchers begin with a research question that does not identify specific variables. Instead, they identify a group or setting that they wish to study in depth. Qualitative researchers are concerned with **meaning,** which essentially is the unique way people make sense of their lives. Meaning is always described from the perspective of the participants, those who are being studied. For example, what are the perspectives of parents on the essential components of a quality education? What do they take for granted as a part of a good education? What resources do they assume will be available for their children?

Additionally, qualitative researchers will be concerned with **processes** (descriptions of how education is practiced) rather than **outcomes** (end results of those practices). Qualitative researchers are likely to focus on processes in their research questions. For example, in the study described previously the outcome of the study is reading performance. A qualitative researcher would be more interested in the processes that were used during the tutoring program. What materials were used by the instructors? How did the students and instructors interact during the tutoring sessions? How did the students feel about their participation in the tutoring sessions? When data from qualitative studies are analyzed, the researchers abstract and describe general **themes**—major, recurring issues, or concepts that they use to summarize their interpretations of their data. Themes from previous studies may help a beginning researcher start to develop a focus for his or her research question.

As you begin to explore the research on your topic, make note of the variables, themes, processes, and meanings that are reported in the studies. You will likely include some of these in your research question.

Developing a More Focused Research Question

With your research question in hand, you begin the process of further in-depth review of the literature by reading more research on your question. Students often ask: "What am I supposed to be doing while I am reading these studies?" A common misconception is that students are looking for one study that will completely answer their research question rather than simply exploring the issues and types of research done on their topic. Many students are uncomfortable with the idea of exploring for exploration's sake, and they have had little experience with this method through their previous school training. For those who are anxious about such investigative work, here are some questions that students should be asking themselves as they read and complete the first round of research studies and articles:

Are there any themes, processes, issues, or variables that seem to be appearing across the studies and articles I have read so far in the literature? If so, what are they? As you continue to conduct your review of literature or talk to experts about your research question, you will begin to focus on a smaller set of issues, variables, or problems, and this may lead you to revise your research question based on your new knowledge. This refined question then leads to a more in-depth review of the literature by focusing attention on these specific areas and finding studies that examine them.

Although there is some variation between quantitative and qualitative researchers, one would next conduct an exhaustive search of the literature. Some students might also call this an exhausting search as well because it is time-consuming and labor-intensive. Foremost, one begins to develop new knowledge on the topic, including what themes or issues recur, what settings or groups have been studied, and what the results of previous studies have been. Students should also continue to analyze the studies, identifying themes or issues that seem important and gaps or questions that have not been addressed. After each round of collecting and reading relevant research, students should be able to ask a more appropriate and researchable research question and to begin to generate ideas about a possible study that could be proposed. The research question will be continually refined down to a much more specific question and a statement of the purpose of the study. See Figure 2.2 for a summary of this process.

FIGURE 2.2 DEVELOPMENT OF A RESEARCH QUESTION.

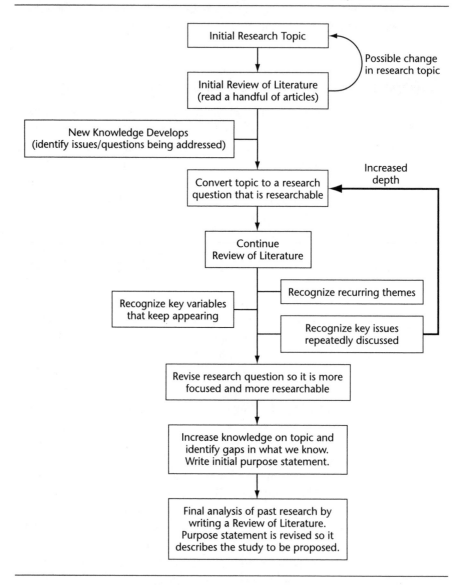

Looks complicated, doesn't it? However, remember that it will take several weeks to arrive at your final research question and statement of purpose. All you need to begin your search of literature is a topic to explore!

Searching the Literature

Every topic and every literature search is different, but all involve a substantial commitment of time and energy. In an age of expanding electronic resources, many of the tools used in searching the literature are computer based and digital. However, we urge all students to plan to spend a substantial amount of time in their college libraries for two reasons. First, reference librarians are experts in information literacy and are often the most knowledgeable technologists on college campuses. They can guide students in the use of ever-changing electronic resources and are often familiar with the terms used in databases of professional literature. Most libraries offer one-on-one consultations for students conducting literature searches, and the library staff are available at the reference desk at hours that far exceed the office hours of all three of the authors of this book combined! So use the librarians whenever you have a problem but especially early on in your search. Second, many of the sources needed in a research proposal are not online. So if you try to conduct a literature search using only online sources, you will miss critical information.

Types of Sources

Whether sources are online or print based, there are many different types of sources that can be used in a review of literature, including the following:

- Articles in professional journals
- Government and technical reports
- Conference proceedings and papers
- Reference books
- Monographs
- Books (general circulation)
- Master's and doctoral theses
- Web sites
- Magazines and newspapers
- Personal communications: information from interviews, presentations, lectures

A good researcher knows when and how to use each type of source most effectively. Sources for a research proposal are considered strongest if they are **peer reviewed**, meaning that a panel of researchers (considered your peers!) has reviewed the articles and rated the quality of the methods used in them. Articles in professional journals and some conference papers are the sources most likely to be peer reviewed. However, all of the sources listed above may be useful in some way, and not all articles in professional journals or conference proceedings are peer reviewed.

Another criterion used to evaluate sources in a review of literature is whether the sources are mostly **primary sources** that describe **empirical research**. A primary source is an article that describes original research conducted by the author of the article. By contrast, a **secondary source** is any article written by someone who is describing research done by others, so the description is second-hand. Empirical research is a term applied to studies in which a research question has been examined by *systematically* collecting and analyzing data. These articles usually (but not always) include a section labeled as the *method section* in which are described the persons or groups participating in the study and the methods used to study them. A secondary source, such as a book, may describe empirical research, but it usually gives less information on the research methods and so is usually considered to be a weaker type of source. Professional journals include both primary and secondary sources as well as empirical and nonempirical sources. One useful type of secondary source is a **review of literature** in which the author provides a comprehensive overview and critique of prior research studies on a given topic. Reviews of literature are useful sources when students are beginning their search of literature, and strategies for finding and using reviews of the literature are discussed below. Most empirical research articles provide a brief review of literature before their method sections, and articles that are solely reviews of literature have more comprehensive references but do not include a method section. **Theoretical articles** also provide overviews of empirical research, although the studies reviewed are selected based on their relevance to the theory examined.

Nonempirical articles frequently found in journals include **opinion pieces** or **commentaries** in which experts discuss their ideas or conclusions based on previous research, and **"how-to"** or **experiential reports** in which practitioners discuss how to implement an educational practice based on their own experiences. Whereas opinion pieces can be useful in identifying issues of debate in an area, the quality of the information will depend on the credibility of the expert. Experiential reports may provide creative ideas for educational practice, but because there is no systematic collection of data and results are based on the experience of just one practitioner, they do not provide strong evidence.

It is often difficult to tell if a source will be an empirical or nonempirical source based on just the abstract. Nonempirical sources are more likely to discuss the general issues related to a topic whereas empirical sources are more likely to describe the groups studied and the methods used in the study (e.g., surveys, observations). Exhibit 2.1 provides a comparison of sample abstracts for an experiential report and a primary, empirical study.

Books, monographs, and references books may also provide overviews of research, although these are likely to be several years older than comparable reviews from similarly dated journal articles. For some topics, government and technical reports may be useful sources, especially if the agencies or persons involved are professional researchers. Web sites provide sources that can vary enormously in

EXHIBIT 2.1 DISTINGUISHING BETWEEN TYPES OF RESEARCH: EXPERIENTIAL REPORT VERSUS AN EMPIRICAL STUDY.

Empirical Study

Praisner, C. (2003). Attitudes of Elementary School principals toward the inclusion of

students with disabilities. *Exceptional Children, 69*, 135-145.

Abstract: A survey of 408 elementary school principals found about 1 in 5 had positive attitudes toward inclusion while most were uncertain. Positive experiences with students with disabilities and exposure to special education concepts were associated with positive attitudes toward inclusion and more positive attitudes were related to less restrictive placements. (Retrieved April 18, 2005, from ERIC database.)

> Indicates measure used
> and size of sample

Experiential Report

Tooms, A.K. (2003). Bring in Mac. *School Administrator, 60*, 22-25.

Abstract: Describes how an executive coach nicknamed Mac helped a beginning principal develop her leadership skills. Also provides list of questions to ask oneself before hiring an executive coach. (Retrieved April 10, 2005, from ERIC database.)

> Based on one person's experience. Goal is
> to provide practical advice. No mention of
> methods of data collection.

quality. Remember that anyone anywhere can put information on the Web, so any information from the Internet should be cited with caution. Many Web sites for governmental agencies, educational institutions, and professional organizations provide useful information, although one must always carefully evaluate any information obtained from a Web site for potential bias and accuracy. The types of Web sites that are especially useful to students in educational research are discussed in Box 2.2. More detailed discussion of using and evaluating Web-site information is discussed later in this chapter.

Box 2.2 Useful Web Sites for Finding Information and Sources for Reviewing the Literature

Web sites of governmental organizations, professional associations, and research organizations often provide resources for both practitioners and researchers. Look for links that are labeled *Research, Publications,* or specific topics. The following are some sample Web sites that may be useful.

- Governmental organizations
  Centers for Disease Control and Prevention:
  http://www.cdc.gov
  National Center for Education Statistics:
  http://nces.ed.gov
  U.S. Census: American Factfinder:
  http://factfinder.census.gov
  U.S. Department of Education:
  http://www.ed.gov/index.jhtml
- Sample professional associations
  American Educational Research Association:
  http://www.aera.net
  American Psychological Association:
  http://www.apa.org
  American Association of Colleges of Teacher Education:
  http://www.aacte.org
  Association for Qualitative Research: http://www.latrobe.edu.au/aqr/
- Sample research organizations
  Center for the Study of Testing, Evaluation, and Educational Policy:
  http://www.csteep.bc.edu

Finding Sources

Finding sources typically entails the use of several different strategies. The strategy that works best will depend in part on how focused your topic is and whether there has been extensive research on it. Many students begin with a general topic, such as learning disabilities or child neglect and abuse, and have trouble initially thinking about how to focus or narrow it down. For some topics, it may be helpful to simply browse through a journal that focuses just on that topic. For example, the *Journal of Child Abuse and Neglect* and the *Journal of Learning Disabilities* are journals dedicated to those topics. If you are interested in these areas, you could read through the abstracts of the studies in one of these journals and select a couple of articles to read. Reading articles in the most recent issues of a journal might provide ideas about a particular issue or problem that could form the focus of a research proposal. It is also a quick way to locate specific articles on your topic and to identify some of the key researchers on a topic. We suggest that you browse through a couple of years of journal issues until you feel that you have a clearer idea of the topic that you want to research. Then it is time to move on to another strategy because it is unlikely that a single journal will provide all of the current information on a topic.

Locating a Review of Literature on a Topic. Although your ultimate goal is to find primary sources on your topic, many students find it useful to begin their literature search with a review of the literature. As noted above, this is a secondary source, but a good review of the literature will help acquaint you with the current issues, authors, research methods, and problems for a particular topic. The good news is that it does a lot of your work for you! The bad news is that current reviews of literature simply do not exist for all topics.

Important research areas are frequently summarized every couple of years in reference books, such as encyclopedias and handbooks. These are typically located in the reference section of the library, and topics are usually indexed alphabetically. Several journals also specialize in reviews of literature. Note that reviews in encyclopedias and handbooks may well be outdated because these reference books are published only periodically. Reviews in journals that specialize in reviews of literature are more likely to be up-to-date, but a more limited range of topics will be covered in each issue. Box 2.3 lists the most commonly used reference sources and journals for finding reviews of literature. Another approach to finding a review of literature is to use the words *review of literature* as one of your terms in searching databases, a strategy discussed in the next section.

Box 2.3 Journals and Reference Books for Finding Reviews of Literature

- *Encyclopedia of educational research*
- *Encyclopedia of human development and education*
- *Handbook of educational administration*
- *Handbook of educational psychology*
- *Handbook of research on curriculum*
- *Handbook of research on teacher education*
- *Handbook of research on teaching*
- *Handbook on social studies teaching and learning*
- *International encyclopedia of education: Research and studies*
- *International handbook of early child education*
- *National society for the study of education yearbooks*
- *Psychological bulletin*
- *Review of educational research*
- *Review of research in education*

Database Searching. When one of the authors of this book, K.H.V., was an undergraduate at Northwestern University (Evanston, Illinois), she had to do a research paper for a sociology class. Her professor said to read mainly primary sources in sociological journals, but he did not teach the students how to locate articles on a topic within the journals. K.H.V. quickly discovered that there were dozens of sociological journals in the library, but the articles were not in any particular order. She spent hours looking through journals for articles related to her topic, noting relevant references in each article, and then tracking down those articles in other journals. No one told her (and she was too shy to ask for help) that the research in most academic areas is organized into databases that make the process of finding articles on a particular topic faster and more efficient. Most databases for topics in education are computerized, and if your college offers off-campus access through the Internet, you may be able to use this strategy at home or work as well as at school.

A database is a collection of information on articles and materials that have been published, presented at conferences, or created by various educational groups or individuals. The most commonly used databases in education are listed in Table 2.1, along with a description of what these databases include.

A database will include information about an article, such as the author, title, number of pages, where it was produced or published, and an abstract or sum-

TABLE 2.1 COMMONLY USED DATABASES IN EDUCATION.

Database Name	What It Includes	Additional Features
ERIC	Journal articles and documents sent by their authors directly to ERIC. ERIC documents include papers presented at conferences, masters' theses, doctoral dissertations, government reports, curricula, books, chapters in book, and other materials.	Most ERIC documents are available full-text. Journal articles may be available full-text.
PsycINFO	Journal articles and books on topics in psychology and related fields, including education.	Provides bibliographies with article abstract. Allows following of article citations in later publications.
Education Full Text	Journal articles, monographs, and yearbooks related to education.	Substantial overlap with ERIC; however, it does cover 40 journals not indexed in ERIC.

Note: ERIC = Educationai Resources Information Center.

mary of the contents of the article. Most databases allow you to combine several terms to find articles. The advantage of computerized databases is that searching with a specific set of terms is fast. The disadvantage is that computers look only for the words that you input. So you need to think about how to best describe the information that you want. To do this, you will begin with your research question.

As noted above, your research question should begin as a broad statement of a topic that interests you. We suggest that you write out your research question and also describe in a couple of sentences what you would like to find out. You will next need to identify some words or phrases that capture the most important issues or elements of your topic. These may be variables such as a particular instructional approach (e.g., problem-based learning, phonological training), characteristics of a person or group (e.g., learning disability, gender, rural), or a type of setting (e.g., multiage classroom, after-school program, high school). Write down synonyms or related words so you can try out different searches. Once you have a list of terms that capture your topic, select a database and open the search tool. The art of database searching involves learning how to input terms that will connect with the articles most related to your topic. Each database has been organized using a set of "controlled vocabulary," which are terms or key words that the database creators use to categorize the articles in the database. Your next step is to select key words that are most closely related to the terms you have used to describe your topic. ERIC [Educational Resources Information Center] and PsycINFO offer a tool called the *Thesaurus* that describes the key words used and related terms. You can select several key words and enter these into a search box. Finding the right key words may involve trial and error. We suggest that you try out several combinations of key words and see which ones seem to yield the best sources. You can also use an author's name as a search term, a strategy that is often productive because authors frequently conduct multiple studies on a given topic. Also check with your instructor and librarians for new tools or strategies included in the latest versions of the databases to make searching easier.

Terms can be combined in a search using words such as *and, or,* and *not* that are referred to as "Boolean operators." Inserting "and" between the key words instructs the database that you want to find only articles that contain *both* key words. Inserting "or" between the key words instructs the database that you want to find articles that contain *either* of the key words but do not have to contain both key words. Using "and" will narrow your search to fewer articles, and using "or" will broaden it. The operator "not" indicates that articles containing that key word should be eliminated from the search. This may be useful if your first search turns up articles on settings or groups that do not interest you, such as college students or corporate training centers.

ERIC and PsycINFO also provide ways to refine or limit a search to only research reports. PsycINFO also allows you to limit the search to reviews of literature or specific types of research studies such as case studies or experimental studies. Because the database formats change frequently, you should also check with your instructor and librarian for more recent information about how to refine your search. Even if the database does not contain a limiter for the search you wish to do, you can also use words describing what you want as key words. Again, the art of database searching involves learning how to use all of these tools to input terms that will connect with the articles most related to your topic.

Identifying Types of Articles Using a Database Abstract. The initial output from a database search will be a list of citations for the articles that match the terms used in your search organized by date. The citation will include the author(s)'s name(s), title of the article, and place of publication or presentation. In ERIC there will be either an ED or EJ number included with the article. EJ indicates that the article was published in a journal, and ED indicates that it is an ERIC document. ERIC documents include materials that have been submitted to ERIC by educators in a variety of settings. The documents include papers presented at conferences, organizational reports, curricula, manuals, and governmental reports. You will need ED numbers for the reference citations for most ERIC documents, so if you plan to use these articles, jot down the ED numbers. You do not need to include EJ numbers in references. Read through the list of titles and click on the links for the articles that sound most related to your topic. A bibliographic entry and abstract for the article will appear.

Usually the abstract contains the information most useful in deciding if you want to obtain and read the article. Remember that your major goal is to find empirical sources. There is no foolproof way to determine if a source is empirical based on the abstract, so look for descriptions of the research methods and results in the abstract. If you find several articles that are related to your topic, you may want to try out the strategy of following citations described below.

Sources found through databases may include books, journal articles, organizational reports, curricula, conference papers or proceedings, or other materials. Some sources may be available as **full text**, which means that the entire text of the source can be accessed through the computer. In some cases, the source appears as an **html** [hypertext markup language] **file** with sidebar links to sections of the article. At other times, you will need to click a link saying **pdf** [portable delivery format], and a photocopy of the original article will appear. We strongly caution our students against limiting their search to full-text articles only because this will eliminate access to important sources.

Following Citations. Sometimes students find a couple of related studies but not much more on their topics. Following citations is one way of expanding the research base in this case. PsycINFO provides a link to more recent studies that have cited the study that is presented. *Citing* means that the other studies listed this study in their references, and therefore they are likely to be discussing similar issues or problems. Clicking on the link brings up a list of the studies that have cited the one produced by your search. Social Science Citations is another database that allows you to enter any reference and find more recent studies that have cited that reference.

Another strategy for following citations is the one K.H.V. used on her sociology project. Examine the references in the studies you have found and find those that sound most related to your topic. You can enter the author's name and title of the article into a database search to see if the article is available online or simply locate the journal or book in the library.

People as Sources. We often remind our students that people can be sources of information, too, and can even be cited as sources in a proposal. Consider first the people you know who have expertise in the area that you wish to research. These may include persons at your workplace, school, or college and people in the community. Documents, training materials, class handouts, and interviews with people can all serve as sources of information on your topic. One advantage of local people is that they may be able to provide information that is specific to the setting or group that you want to research. One of our students obtained a wealth of information for a paper on home schooling from an interview that she conducted with a professor who was home schooling his own children. Another obtained extensive data on the number of students attending college following an interview with her high school's guidance counselor.

The Internet also provides a way for students to easily contact authors and researchers by e-mail with questions about their research. Our students have found that most researchers are happy to help students with their research as long as they have done their initial homework. You would most likely not get a reply from Howard Gardner if you wrote to simply ask what he knows about multiple intelligence. However, our students have found that researchers graciously respond to their requests for specific data collection tools and answer targeted questions about their methods that were not discussed in their articles. (One of our students received such a response from Gardner after she wrote a carefully thought-out e-mail to him.) It is exciting to find that the people in the databases really exist and like to help out beginning researchers. When communications with people cannot be accessed by others, they are referred to as **personal communications** and are cited in the proposal, along with information on the name of the person and the date when the communication occurred, according to style rules in the *Publication Manual of the American Psychological Association* (APA). For example, if the information in this sentence was based on a conversation with Marguerite G. Lodico on March 7, 2005, you would cite this parenthetically as follows: (M. G. Lodico, personal communication, March 7, 2005).

E-mail discussion groups or "listservs" are another source of information for research proposals. A *listserv* is a group discussion of a topic of common interest that one subscribes to through e-mail. Messages from all members of the listserv are sent to your e-mail address, and you can also send questions or messages to the listserv discussion. Typically, listserv discussions involve threaded conversations where multiple people comment on an issue or on each other's comments by sending messages to the listserv. A list of listservs related to education and instructions on how to subscribe and unsubscribe is available at http://www.edweb project.org/lists.html.

Web Sites: Searching the Internet for Scholarly Sources. As noted earlier, the Internet is an amazingly complex network of information, both good and bad. We advise extreme caution in using any information from a Web site. If you cannot determine the author of information obtained from the Web or the date it was produced, it has no place in a research proposal. However, there are times when much of the research done on a topic is available only through an organization or governmental agency that publishes this information on the Internet. Many researchers also provide additional information on their work on their Web sites. So to use an analogy from skiing, using the Internet as a source is the advanced slope; you need all your skills operating at full capacity to navigate between the reputable and untrustworthy sources available that also change frequently. Table 2.2 discusses the search engines available for searching the Internet.

Below we discuss issues that should be considered in evaluating the quality of information obtained from Web sites.

Authority. It should be clear who produced or is sponsoring the site, and verifiable information about the sponsor should be provided. Look for a link to the information about the author, organization, or sponsor (often called "About Us") and links that allow you to send messages to the Web site creator. A good way to see if an organization is legitimate is to look it up in the *Encyclopedia of Associations*, a book available in many college library reference sections. Sometimes you may need to return to the home page of the Web site by clicking the link to "Home" or truncating the URL back to the domain (the first period in the URL). If you cannot determine who produced the Web site, it should not be used as a source because its authority cannot be established.

Accuracy. Expect few, if any, grammatical or spelling errors. Sources of information should be clearly identified. Factual information such as dates and names

TABLE 2.2 GENERAL AND ACADEMICALLY FOCUSED SEARCH ENGINES AND THEIR WEB SITES.

	Google www.google.com	Yahoo! Search search.yahoo.com	Teoma www.teoma.com	Library Index www.lii.org	Infomine infomine.ucr.edu	Google Scholar scholar.google.com/
Size (Note: estimates of size vary widely)	Estimates up to 8 billion sites. 25% not fully indexed, but can retrieve unindexed sites if search matches title or linked pages.	Over 3 billion pages. Fully indexed.	2 billion with 1 billion fully indexed and 1 billion partially indexed.	Subject directory of over 14,000 sites created by public librarians.	University of California librarians created this directory of 120,000 pages.	Directory of Web sites with scholarly literature such as peer-reviewed papers, theses, books, preprints, abstracts, and technical reports.
Special features or limits	Search limited to 10 words, excluding OR. Indexes only the first 100 KB of page or 120 KB of pdf files.	Shortcut links to dictionary, synonyms, and encyclopedia.	Search results by experts identified separately. Provides links and suggestions for narrowing search.	Links to dictionaries and encyclopedias. Good source for organizations with research resources.	Lets you search within a subject area. General Reference link gives quick access to dictionaries, style guides, maps, news, and organizations.	Search automatically analyzes and extracts citations to other sources and presents them as separate results.
Boolean Logic	AND assumed between words. Capitalize OR. - excludes a word + allows retrieval of stop words (e.g., in, and).	Accepts AND, OR, NOT, or AND NOT. Words must be capitalized to serve as operators.	AND assumed between words. Capitalize OR. - excludes a word. + allows retrieval of stop words (e.g., in, and).	AND implied between words. Accepts AND, OR, NOT, and ( ) for nesting.	AND implied between words. Accepts AND, OR, NOT, and ( ) for nesting.	AND assumed between words. Capitalize OR. - excludes a word + allows retrieval of stop words (e.g., in, and).
Phrase Searching	Put " " around words to search for phrase.	Put " " around words to search for phrase.	Put " " around words to search for phrase.	Put " " around words to search for phrase.	Put " " around words to search for phrase.	Put " " around words to search for phrase.
Advanced Search	Allows you to search for pages that: have all your search terms, contain an exact phrase, have been updated recently.	Allows you to search for pages that: have all your search terms, contain an exact phrase, have been updated recently, or are within a certain domain (e.g., .edu or .org).	Allows you to search for pages that: have all your search terms, contain an exact phrase, have been updated recently, or are within a certain domain (e.g., .edu or .org).	Allows you to search using author, title, subject, publisher, keyword, or sponsor.	Allows you to search using author, title, subject, keyword, research discipline, or Library of Congress subject headings.	Allows you to search for pages that have all your search terms or contain an exact phrase. Also allows search using author, title, subject, publication, or date.

should match those found in almanacs, encyclopedias, or other reference books. If the information in the Web page contradicts information in reputable sources, the author should say so and explain why. If the accuracy of a Web site seems dubious, do not use it as a source.

Objectivity. Look for a statement of the sponsor's point of view, and be sensitive to any expressions of bias. Ask yourself, "Where is the author coming from?" Take the author's point of view into account when you use the material in your paper. An unbiased Web site will also include links to other Web sites or authors providing contrasting points of view. If the Web site provides no balance or never acknowledges other points of view, use the information with extreme caution. If there is advertising on the Web site, it should be separate from the information content. Consider whether the advertising is related to the content of the Web site. An advertisement for a company producing medications for attention-deficit hyperactivity disorder (ADHD) on a Web site discussing treatment of ADHD suggests a strong possible bias.

Currency. The site should say when it was most recently updated, and the update should be reasonable for the type of information being provided. You may need to hunt for the date; the beginning and end of the page are frequently places where updates are noted. If the document is not dated but contains a bibliography, examine the references for currency. According to the APA manual, *n.d.* may be used in the place of a date for a source that is not dated.

Coverage. The site should thoroughly cover its topic within the limits the authors set for themselves. Coverage can be narrow or broad; the important thing is that the site does not claim to provide more information than it does or to be authoritative when it is not.

Summarizing Information from Articles

We encourage students to begin summarizing and abstracting information from articles early in the process of their literature search. There are many different ways to summarize articles, and highlighting parts of the printed article is one way to start. We encourage our students to also begin writing summaries of the studies using one of the templates referred to as an *Article Summary Sheet*, shown in Exhibits 2.2 and 2.3. The article summary sheet for primary, research-based studies asks you to categorize the type of study, identify the research purpose, describe the methods used in the study, summarize the findings and interpretations, and list comments or criticisms that you have or quotes that you might use in your

EXHIBIT 2.2 ARTICLE SUMMARY SHEET
FOR PRIMARY, RESEARCH-BASED SOURCES.

a) Citation of Article for Reference Section (written in APA format)

_____

_____

b) Type of Study

_____ Quantitative

_____ Descriptive/survey; _____ Correlational; _____ Causal-comparative;

_____ Experimental; _____ Meta-analysis; _____ Action research

_____ Qualitative

_____ Ethnographic/case study; _____ Grounded theory;

_____ Phenomenological; _____ Action research

_____ Qualitative and Qualitative Methods Used

_____ Mixed-method: mostly quantitative;

_____ Mixed-method: mostly qualitative;

_____ Mixed-method; equal use of quantitative and qualitative

_____ Action research; _____ Program evaluation

c) Purpose of the Study (less than 70 words)

d) Major Aspects of Methods (description should help you to determine research type)

participants:

data collection tools:

procedures:

e) Key Findings (as they relate to your proposal)

f) Comments: Strengths or Weaknesses, Quotes (include page number(s) on quotes)

_____

EXHIBIT 2.3 ARTICLE SUMMARY SHEET FOR
SECONDARY SOURCES AND NON-RESEARCH-BASED ARTICLES.

a) Citation of Article for Reference Section (written in APA format)

_____

_____

b) Type of Study

_____ Review of literature; _____ Theoretical review; _____ Opinion article;

_____ How-to or experiential report

c) Summary of Major Issues, Arguments, or Theoretical Models in Article

d) Key Authors or Studies Cited

e) Recommendations and Supporting Evidence

f) Comments or Quotes (include page number[s] on quotes)

proposal. The summary does not need to be lengthy, although studies will vary in their complexity. The article summary sheet for secondary sources and non-research-based sources is more general because these sources vary in the information that they contain.

By writing a summary in your own words, you are beginning the process of abstracting information for your review of literature that will be discussed in a later chapter.

As you read and analyze the studies, you can also begin to think about what other information you might need. For example, you might find out that cooperative learning has worked well with fourth graders, but results with students in earlier grades vary, with some groups doing well and others having problems. If the younger students who did well seemed to have better social skills, you might want to look for information on how training students in social skills prepares them for cooperative learning. As you analyze studies, you will also refine your research question in ways that take into account what other researchers have found. Your revised research question might suggest new search key words to try.

When Do I Have Enough?

In every educational research class we have taught, our students want to know how many articles is enough for a research proposal. There is no magic number that automatically translates into an A grade, in part because different topics will have different amounts of research. We have watched several students struggle to find more than eight sound empirical studies on looping or multiage classrooms whereas others find that a search on cooperative learning can turn up several hundred empirical studies. If you are finding hundreds of articles, try to refine your research question so that you can limit your search by including more combinations of variables, group characteristics, or types of settings. If you find only a few related studies, try using different key words. Research on inclusion classrooms might yield different results if you use the word *inclusion* versus *mainstreaming* as your key word. ERIC uses both "mainstreaming" and "inclusive classroom" as key words but not "inclusion." If the research is still limited, think about how your topic might be related to a broader one. One of our students who was studying looping found limited information in her initial searches. However, she learned that teacher-student relationships were an important issue in looping, and so she expanded her literature search to include studies examining how these relationships were built over time in both looped and nonlooped classrooms as part of her literature review.

If you still want to know how many is enough, our general rule of thumb is to keep reading until you feel that the studies are saying the same things. When you feel that you are not learning anything new or that the only new studies are those cited in earlier ones you have already read, you have read enough. This might include 12 studies or 50! The expectations of what is enough may also vary depending on whether you are searching literature for a master's thesis or for a paper that is only one of several requirements for your course. For full-time researchers, the process of reading research continues even after data have been collected as we think about how our study fits into the vast collection of educational research that exists today. If you think about it, this is a good thing because you always have something new to explore.

Chapter Summary

The process of finding and researching a topic is a long journey that requires many decisions and skills. To begin, one must first generate a research topic based on experience, theory, or replication. An initial review of literature yields information on the variables and operational definitions that quantitative research on the topic has examined as well as the themes, processes, and meanings discussed in qualitative studies. Based on this review, the researcher formulates a research question that is further focused and revised as the review of literature continues.

Finding sources for a comprehensive review of literature involves multiple strategies and a wide variety of sources. Literature reviews, theoretical articles, and primary, empirical sources published in peer-reviewed journals are considered the best sources because these provide the most detailed information about research methods. However, secondary sources (e.g., books, monographs), opinion pieces, and experiential reports may also be used in identifying issues or practices that warrant further study.

Strategies for finding sources include locating a review of literature; database searching using ERIC, PsycINFO, or Education Full Text; following citations to locate recent studies citing an earlier study; and using people as sources. Internet Web sites for organizations, governmental agencies, and universities and colleges may also be good sources of research information. However, these sources should be evaluated for authority, accuracy, objectivity, currency, and coverage. A variety of search engines are available for searching for information on the Internet, including some search engines that focus on academic materials.

Information from sources should be summarized with a focus on the methods, results, and conclusions reported in the studies. Article summary sheets provide a useful format for abstracting key pieces of information from articles.

The process of researching a topic may feel endless to beginning graduate students and researchers alike. Although there is no definitive answer to the question, "When do I have enough?" a rough guide is to continue researching until you feel that further studies are not yielding any new information on the variables, themes, processes, or meanings related to your topic. Professional researchers view reading research as an ongoing adventure, although once students have reviewed the major studies on their topics, it is time to begin developing their own ideas for a research study.

Key Concepts

research question

variable

construct

operational definition

outcomes

peer reviewed

primary sources

empirical research

secondary source

review of literature

theoretical articles

opinion pieces or commentaries

"how-to" reports

experiential reports

full text

html file

pdf

personal communications

article summary sheet

Discussion Questions or Activities

1. Identify a topic that could be the focus of a research study, and write two or three different research questions that could be addressed on this topic. Discuss whether quantitative or qualitative methods would provide the best evidence to answer each research question.
2. For the topic you select for your research proposal, locate at least two of the following types of articles: review of literature, opinion article, how-to or experiential report, empirical research study. Compare the articles you found with several other students in the class. Discuss the features that can be used to identify each type of article.
3. Describe the sources and strategies that you have found most useful in researching your topic. Discuss how you revised your original research question based on what you have learned, and identify any further information that you feel is needed to complete your review of literature.

Suggested Reading

Pan, M. L. (2004). *Preparing literature reviews* (2nd ed.). Glendale, CA: Pyrczak Publishing.

CHAPTER THREE

THE RESEARCH PROPOSAL

Chapter Objectives

After reading this chapter, you should be able to

1. Explain the difference between a research proposal and a research study
2. Describe some of the key reasons for writing a research proposal
3. Begin to explain in general terms both the purpose and structure of the major sections of a research proposal (title page; introduction; statement of purpose; review of literature—including hypothesis or foreshadowed questions; method; benefits, limitations, or reflections; references; and appendixes)
4. Outline the key differences between a proposal written for a proposed quantitative study and one written for a qualitative one
5. Begin to conceptualize the organization of a literature review on your topic
6. Describe the difference between a hypothesis and foreshadowed questions

Preparing a Research Proposal

This semester you will likely be involved in reading published research articles and writing a research proposal. Proposals and research articles share certain important characteristics but also have important differences, which is often a source of confusion for students. Proposals and published research articles follow the same general research process. That is, they identify a topic or a research question, review the literature, and develop a hypothesis or a set of foreshadowed questions. For a published article, the researcher carries out the study and reports findings and conclusions. A research proposal is exactly what the term says. It is a proposal to conduct research. It is the basic design of what you would do if you were actually going to conduct a study. A research proposal *does not* involve the collection of data and is written before the study is actually conducted. Research proposals also usually have far more extensive literature reviews and method sections.

The research proposal in this course will be your entry into the exciting world of educational research. Although it may seem like a daunting task at this point, this chapter is designed to help you begin to build the skills you need to develop a proposal that extends our knowledge of educational practices and policies. We enjoy observing how many students who begin this course with little or no research experience are able to obtain high levels of competence. In fact, all the research proposals included at the end of this book were written by our students. This chapter provides a broad overview of the proposal-writing process. Many of the terms used in this chapter that may be unfamiliar to you are discussed in detail in later chapters.

The *Publication Manual of the American Psychological Association* (APA manual) specifies the format for proposals and published studies. Our first piece of advice is to have close at hand a copy of the APA manual or a handout on APA style that may have been developed by your instructor. You will want to use the correct citation format, references format, sequence of topics, and margins. If you have looked at the APA manual, you know that we cannot review all of the specifics in the body of this book. However, in the following section, we will point out some of the key elements of APA style that are required for writing a research proposal.

Writing a research proposal is the first step in conducting and publishing research. At any school or university, anyone conducting research must write a proposal describing his or her plans before the study can be conducted.

Why Write a Research Proposal?

There are several reasons why all researchers, whether they are students in a research course or professional researchers, create a proposal before conducting a study. Proposals describe the process and procedures that will be used by the researcher and allow an opportunity to obtain feedback from colleagues before the implementation of the study. This feedback can be used to improve the proposed study. The sharing of research designs and proposals for research leads to collaboration among colleagues and in many ways is a form of professional development. Each colleague brings to the discussion different expertise, experience, and knowledge that can only enhance the inquiry process. Proposals are also submitted to funding agencies to obtain grant money to pay for the costs of research. Master's and doctoral students may be required to obtain approval of their proposals from a committee of supervising professors. Proposals may also be required from any researcher who is seeking approval from a committee reviewing the ethical issues of the study or who is submitting an article for publication. Figure 3.1 shows how the proposal fits into the process of conducting research.

In addition to providing an introduction to the topic, reviewing the literature and methods, and discussing benefits and limitations (which are described in detail below), a proposal gives the researcher the opportunity to identify and address any ethical issues that are raised by the proposed study.

Anatomy of a Research Proposal

Because at this point in your graduate career you will likely write a proposal before you contemplate writing an article for publication, our focus will be on developing the knowledge and skills necessary for proposal writing. Keep in mind that these skills easily translate to writing for publication. Note that each journal and professional organization has its own particular style; however, the overall process is similar to the process we describe for proposals. The essential difference between a proposal and a published study is that the published article is written after the study has been carried out, and it includes a "results and discussion" section in which the results of the completed study are presented and analyzed. The parts of the research proposal are described below, and samples of quantitative and qualitative research proposals written by our students are included in Appendixes A and B of this book.

Title Page. The *title page* is page number one of your proposal. Several components of the title page require close attention. They include

- The **header:** composed of the first two or three words from the title. It is placed on each page in the upper right-hand corner, five spaces to the left of the page number.
- The **running head:** used in publication (but required in a proposal), the *running head* is also an abbreviation of the title. It should not exceed 50 characters in length. The words "Running Head" (typed as shown in Exhibit 3.1) are flush against the left margin, followed by a colon. The running head is typed in capital letters. The running head can be the same as the header.

FIGURE 3.1 HOW RESEARCH PROPOSALS
AID THE DEVELOPMENT OF RESEARCH.

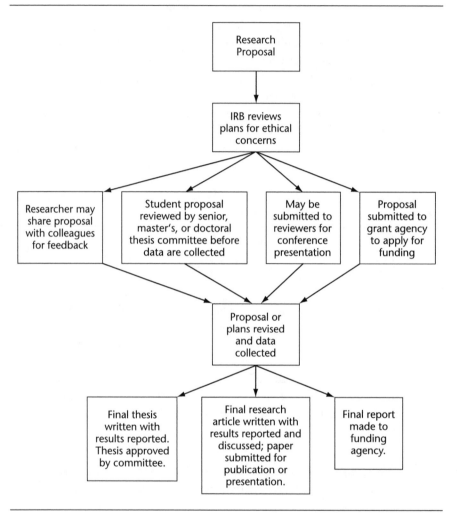

Note: IRB = institutional review board.

• The **title** of the proposal: summarizes the main focus or idea of the proposal as simply as possible. It should be clear, concise, and identify the major variables or theoretical issues to be considered in the study.

• Author's name: your name and that of any coauthor are included here. If coauthors are included, you may choose to alphabetize by last name or prioritize the names in terms of the authors' contributions.

• Affiliation: the name of your institution (if any) is included here.

EXHIBIT 3.1 WRITING TIPS: TITLE PAGE.

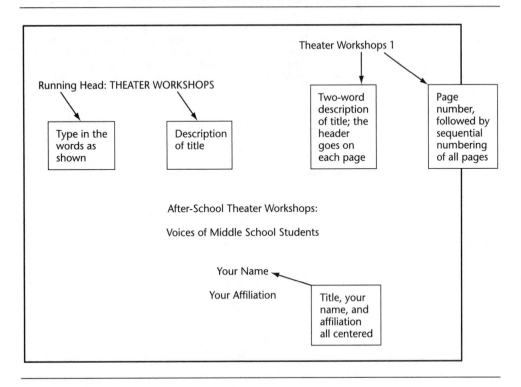

Introduction. Although introductions for proposals tend to vary in length, their purpose is to provide the reader with a broad perspective of the literature and to establish a need or purpose for the particular study being proposed. In essence, the introduction is a miniversion of the much larger review of literature and can be thought of as highlighting certain segments or pieces of it (see Exhibit 3.2). As such, some researchers prefer to write the introduction after they have actually completed much of their literature review. In the event that you write the introduction early in the research process, you should revisit it after you have completed your literature review to be certain that there is consistency between the sections. Specifically, introductions include

- Background information
- Definitions of variables and terms
- Statistics or contextual information that may apply to the topic
- Brief integrated summary of the findings of past research
- A brief rationale for doing the research

EXHIBIT 3.2 WRITING TIPS: INTRODUCTION.

Page 2 begins with the title of the proposal centered in the middle of the page. Then you begin to write the body of the introduction. Remember that the introduction puts the study in context, provides background information and includes a definition of variables or terms. It is basically a miniversion of your review of literature. While you may write a draft of the introduction early in the writing process, you will likely have to go back and modify it to reflect the specifics of your study.

Page 2 looks like this:

Header 2

Title (centered at the top of the page)

Begin writing your introduction!

Even though the introduction is considerably shorter than the review of literature, it too, must have citations supporting the researcher's statements concerning what is being studied. This does not mean that a citation used in the introduction cannot be used again later on in the review of the literature and vice versa. In essence, citations that are mentioned briefly in the introduction can be (and usually are) discussed in detail in the complete review of literature.

Statement of Purpose. The statement of purpose follows the introduction and describes for the reader the main purpose of the study. In an unpublished research proposal, this section is usually labeled *Statement of Purpose* (see Exhibit 3.3); however, published studies often fail to have such a definitive heading highlighting the purpose statement specifically. Whether or not the statement of purpose is clearly labeled, it can be easily identified from its wording, "the purpose of this study was to . . . ." Although there are no universal templates for writing purpose statements, they should be written as clearly and as concisely as possible. Qualitative and quantitative purpose statements are written differently. Quantitative studies clearly describe the variables that will be investigated, whereas studies that are qualitative acknowledge the emerging nature of the questions and topics. Therefore, for qualitative studies, the researcher should explain that as the study progresses, the topics, variables, and questions could be changed or modified.

Review of the Literature. This section of the proposal focuses on describing, summarizing, and critiquing issues, results, and explanations in the literature on the

EXHIBIT 3.3 WRITING TIPS: STATEMENT OF PURPOSE.

You will actually write the phrase "Statement of Purpose" and center it in the middle of the page. A typical statement of purpose uses the following language: The purpose of the proposed study is to (describe the study's purpose here). In addition to describing the purpose of the study, your initial rationale for doing the study will also be included here. Your rationale will be further developed at the end of your review of literature. A typical statement of purpose will look like this:

Statement of Purpose

The purpose of the proposed quantitative study is to describe teachers' attitudes about the effectiveness of inclusion classrooms. Given the popularity of inclusion classrooms and the importance of providing successful learning environments to all students, it is critical to more fully understand these issues from the teachers' perspectives.

topic under investigation. For the purposes of this textbook, the word *literature* is defined as all published articles, records, and documents that are related to the topic of the study. This includes empirical research, reviews of literature, theoretical articles, and even opinion pieces (although a good literature review for a topic with ample empirical research will keep opinion pieces to a minimum). The main purpose of the literature review is to report the state of knowledge on your topic and place your proposed study in a research context by providing an overview of past research studies, published articles, and documents that relate to your topic. The literature reviews in proposals and published studies are held to different standards. You may have noticed that the literature reviews of published studies are often brief, condensed into a few paragraphs or pages, and are sometimes included as part of the introduction; however, in a research proposal, the review of literature is exhaustive and separate from the introduction. From this review of previous research, one is pushed to reflect on their research question and often ask new or modified questions. Reviews of literature are well planned out, typically starting at the broadest part of the topic and gradually refining and narrowing the discussion down to a more focused perspective (Exhibit 3.4).

Statement of the Hypothesis or Foreshadowed Questions. The literature review ends with either a research hypothesis and operational definitions of variables or the refined research question and a set of foreshadowed questions or subquestions (see Exhibit 3.5).

Research Hypothesis and Operational Definitions. For experimental, causal-comparative, and correlational studies, this section of the proposal includes the research hypothesis or prediction of the expected outcome of the study. In the proposal, it is by no means an accident that the hypothesis comes directly after the review of

EXHIBIT 3.4 WRITING TIPS: REVIEW OF THE LITERATURE.

Immediately following the statement of purpose, you will begin your literature review. Type the words "Review of the Literature," and center the phrase. Do not start the literature review on a separate page. It should look like this:

Review of Literature

The literature review begins with a brief introduction (see example below). Here you may want to introduce the literature review by indicating what strands of literature you will be covering and the type of research you found on your topic.

> **Example Introductory Portion of Literature Review:**
> This paper provides a review of the literature on teachers' attitudes toward inclusion and describes many important issues relative to the success of this practice for special and regular education students. Much of the research in this area has been quantitative using a descriptive survey approach.

Although you will not provide detail on all of the articles you have reviewed, you will provide information related to the study findings and methods. If you have followed our suggestions, you have summary sheets (or the equivalent article abstracts) that summarize the articles that are related to your topic. Remember, literature reviews are organized by themes and issues and are challenging to write. Many students want to simply review each article as though they were writing a cookbook listing one ingredient after another. This is exactly what you do not want to do! What follows are the steps you should consider when writing your literature reviews:

Step One: Examine your article summary sheets or article abstracts and highlight or underline the purpose of the study, the methods used, and the findings. Then, as you read over your summary, try to articulate a summary word, topic, or phrase that best applies to the article. Write this on the top of the article summary sheet. For some articles, there may be several summary topics or phrases. You will use these topics or phrases later as means to organize your review.

Step Two: Review the summary words you have generated. It is likely that because the research is all related, there will be overlap in summary words you have generated. Now place each article under the summary word or phrase that best fits. You should now have several piles of articles categorized by their essential focus. Some articles will likely fit in more than one category.

Step Three: Decide how your literature review should be organized. Use the following questions to help guide your organization:
- How can I create a complete picture of what is known about my research focus?
- What studies are most related to my proposed study and least related?
- Which studies support my hypothesis or foreshadowed questions, and which studies conflict with it?
- How can I create a meaningful framework for my study (i.e., lead the reader to the conclusion that my study will answer an unanswered question or provide valuable information to the field, or both)?

Step Four: Begin to write your literature review using the organization you created for your topics. Following your introductory comments, you might want to begin with something like the following example:

> **Example: Transition from introductory comments to body of the literature review:**
>
> One issue that has emerged with frequency in the literature on inclusion is the degree to which teachers believe they have been adequately prepared to work with both special and regular education students. For example, Tomas (2004) found that many regular education teachers believed that they should have taken more courses that deal with special ability children.

EXHIBIT 3.4 WRITING TIPS: REVIEW OF THE LITERATURE, Contd.

Now include in this section of the literature review a discussion of all of the articles that have investigated the same topic (teacher preparation for inclusion). Continuing with the above example, you might transition to the next article by saying something like:

> Similar findings were reported by Johnson (2003). Johnson's study with 25 regular education teachers found that most believed that their special education training was not adequate.

Once you have exhausted the articles on that topic, you can then move on to any other topics you have identified in your articles. Be sure to make clear transitions between the sections such as that noted in bold below. For example:

> **In addition to teachers' attitude toward their preparedness to for inclusion,** researchers who are interested in teachers' attitudes toward inclusion have addressed teachers' perception of the impact of inclusion on the achievement of special and regular education students once they are placed in an inclusion classroom.

You continue this process until you have included all of the articles you believe are critical to your topic. You then conclude the literature review with a brief summary statement that makes connections among the various studies on the topic. Focus on pointing out consistencies or conflicts in methods used or results obtained (or both) among the studies you described. You want to say something like:

> The research in the area of teacher attitudes toward inclusion has demonstrated that many teachers have concerns about the inclusion classroom. Specifically, they are concerned with . . .

literature. Hypotheses are based on and consistent with the findings reported in the literature review. Hypotheses should always be accompanied by operational definitions of variables because these indicate how the variables will be measured or manipulated. Operational definitions may be based on methods used by the studies in the review of literature. However, it is important that the researcher include them at this point to make it clear how the variables will be defined in the study being proposed. If done well, a review of literature will lead the reader to make the same hypothesis—or, at a minimum, to see the logic in your hypothesis.

Research Question and Foreshadowed Questions or Subquestions. In all types of qualitative research and in descriptive-survey research, a research question and a set of foreshadowed questions or subquestions rather than a hypothesis follow the review of literature. Although descriptive-survey research is among the family of quantitative research methods, it tends to be more exploratory and so usually does not include a

EXHIBIT 3.5 WRITING TIPS:
HYPOTHESES OR FORESHADOWED QUESTIONS.

If your proposal includes a hypothesis, it is critical that the hypothesis be written clearly and concisely and be based on the literature review. The types of hypotheses are covered in another chapter, but all hypotheses include the following information:
  • The predicted outcome of the study, including all variables being measured and manipulated
  • A clear identification of all groups in the study
  • A definition of the variables, operationally defined
What follows is an example of a hypothesis written for an experimental design. If you decide to do an experimental study, it should have a similar format. Causal-comparative research would also follow a similar format.

EXPERIMENTAL RESEARCH HYPOTHESES
Research hypotheses for experimental research studies predict how the independent variable(s) will affect the dependent variable(s) in the proposed study. The hypothesis is followed by an operational definition of how these variables will be measured or manipulated. Note that all levels of the independent variable need to be defined.

Sample Research Hypothesis for an Experimental Research Study: It is hypothesized that the science achievement scores of 10th graders will be higher for groups using portfolios than those using separate assignments. For the purpose of this proposed study, the independent variable is the type of assessment, either a showcase portfolio—operationally defined as a portfolio that represents a collection of students' best work; or assignments completed separately—operationally defined as students handing in assignments for separate grades with no final cumulative presentation of their work. For the purpose of this proposed study, the dependent variable is science achievement and is operationally defined as students' scores on an end-of-the-year 10th-grade science curriculum assessment.

QUALITATIVE RESEARCH QUESTIONS OR FORESHADOWED PROBLEMS
In qualitative research, the broad research question is typically broken down into subquestions or foreshadowed questions that can be used to guide observations or interviews. However, one needs to be careful not to limit what the study may find. Questions may be modified throughout the course of the study.

If your proposal includes foreshadowed questions, you must be certain that the questions are specific and will serve as a guide for the method. They should include:
  • The specific questions that will be addressed in the study
  • The way in which the data will be collected
What follows is an example of foreshadowed questions written for a case study or ethnography.

Sample Research Questions or Those Foreshadowed for a Case Study or Ethnography: The broad research question to be explored in this study is, What changes does this student have to make when the focus of his or her instruction changes from a lecture-based teacher-centered approach to a more student-centered alternative assessment method of instruction? Possible foreshadowed questions to be addressed in this study are (1) What does the student decide to include in the portfolio? (2) Are there any changes in the way the student approaches or completes assignments, including both those included in the portfolio and those not included? (3) How does the student view the final portfolio?

hypothesis. Instead the researcher writes a set of subquestions that form the basis for the survey.

Case studies and other types of qualitative approaches use research questions and foreshadowed questions that serve to "guide" the qualitative researcher during the initial investigative process. The research question describes the overall focus of the study, which is then broken down into foreshadowed questions that will be addressed in the study. (They are called *foreshadowed* questions because they are supposed to guide the collection of data without predetermining outcomes.) Both the research question and the foreshadowed questions should be connected with the purpose statement and suggest the types of procedures that will be further explored in the method section. Foreshadowed questions are *not* your actual interview questions, but they do guide interviews or observations.

Method. The first half of the proposal deals with a discussion of past research on the topic and with establishing a need for the proposed study. The second half of the proposal (or the method section) is specifically focused on the proposed study and is essentially describing *how* the researcher plans to carry out the study. Because it is describing what you will do, this section must be written in the future tense. It is broken into subsections as follows.

Participants. A description of the participants, often referred to as the "sample," is the first section found in the method section of the proposal. Methods used to select the participants (otherwise known as sampling techniques) are discussed here, as well as the characteristics of the proposed sample. Keep in mind that for many studies, a more in-depth description of the sample (e.g., age, years teaching, etc.) is developed during the actual data collection efforts through the gathering of demographic information (e.g., by a survey). In such cases, the participant section can be written up with more detail and inserted later, after the study has been completed. However, you should describe the type of demographic data that you plan to collect in this section of the proposal and how you will obtain it. In some cases, participant demographic data can be collected from government agencies, school report cards, or associations that collect and store this kind of information. Many of these organizations provide access to these data through Web pages. Researchers who use quantitative approaches will find that such demographic data may be more available (and applicable) than those who are using a qualitative approach. Qualitative demographic data will be more context-specific and will often require more "undercover" work by the researcher. In qualitative proposals, the participant section describes why this particular setting or these participants qualify as **key informants**. *Key informants* are individuals who have some unique information or knowledge of the phenomena being studied. These descriptions often provide rich detail about the setting and participants and how they (the key informants) will help to answer the research questions. Both quantitative and qualitative proposals must indicate how many participants you expect to have in your study.

Instruments or Methods of Data Collection. For this subsection, quantitative researchers use the term "instruments," and qualitative researchers use the phrase "methods of data collection." The approach you select for your proposal (e.g., quantitative or qualitative) plays a key role in the instruments you will propose to use. Traditionally, quantitative research relies more on standardized instruments to collect data, and qualitative approaches use what are called self-developed interview or observation (or both) protocols. Regardless of the approach, this section should *not* describe *how* the researcher will *use* the instrument but rather should indicate what the instrument or protocol "looks like" *and the reasons or support for selecting it*—in other words, how it will generate the data needed to answer the research question. For those conducting quantitative research using standardized, already established instruments, this section must include critical reliability and validity evidence that supports the use of these instruments. (See Chapter Four for more in-depth information on reliability and validity in measurement.)

For researchers creating their own instruments (e.g., a survey or interview protocol) or conducting qualitative research, this section is called the "Methods of Data Collections" and includes the researcher's description of these surveys, observational checklists, or protocols to guide observations or interviews. For a survey, a description including how many sections the survey has and what type of items are used should be included along with the survey questions in an appendix. For interview or observation protocols, a similar narrative defining the purpose and the broad research questions guiding the observations of behaviors or interviews are included here.

Design. The design section of the proposal is traditionally linked to experimental research. In this section, the researcher discusses the model or design that he or she has chosen and how threats to the study's validity are controlled by the design (these topics are addressed in detail in Chapter Eight on experimental research). Usually, a short narrative accompanied by a table or figure that visually supports the narrative is included. The figure alone should provide a clear sense of the design the research intends to use (see Table 3.1 for an example of an experimental design).

Note that in proposals where a nonexperimental research design is planned, the procedure section immediately follows the instrumentation section, and the type of research proposed (e.g., correlational, case study) is identified at the start of the procedure section.

TABLE 3.1 SAMPLE DESIGN.

Group	Pretest Data	Treatment	Posttest Data
A	Iowa math scores from prior year	A (Use math software program)	Iowa math scores at end of year
B	Iowa math scores from prior year	B (Individual tutoring without computers)	Iowa math scores at end of year

Procedure. This section is often referred to as the "how-to" section. A narrative describes for the reader the process and practices that the researcher plans to use to collect the data using methods that are appropriate for answering the research questions. In this section, the researcher describes how the instrument(s) or data collection tools will be used. Qualitative researchers generally discuss how they anticipate approaching the selected research setting and the tactics or strategies they anticipate using as they begin to ask initial questions and gather preliminary data. Most importantly, the role of the researcher and his or her relationship to the participants are clearly outlined. Quantitative researchers discuss the timeline of the project, when instruments will be given to participants to collect data, and the type of treatments and their duration (if applicable). Keep in mind that not everything always works out as planned, particularly in qualitative studies. Researchers often go back after they have conducted the study and modify their procedure section to accurately reflect the process that actually occurred. Note that although modification in the procedures is often expected in qualitative research, such modifications and deviations from the initial procedures are limited in quantitative research (see Exhibit 3.6).

Benefits, Limitations, Reflections. In this section, the researcher discusses both the benefits and the limitations of the research that he or she is proposing. Benefits typically are twofold, one aimed at the benefits of the research study for advancing knowledge represented by the research literature and the other targeting the benefits for practice. Specifically, the researcher wants to describe how the study will help support and extend understanding of the topic. Typically, this might involve examination of how your research will add to or answer unanswered questions from the last few studies in the literature review (with citations) because these, by their very nature, should be the most closely related pieces of work.

This section also includes a short paragraph summarizing some of the possible implications of the hypothesized findings, focusing on potential benefits to teaching and learning. The final paragraph of this section should focus on limitations of the proposed research. Such limitations tend to focus on methodological

EXHIBIT 3.6 WRITING TIPS: METHOD SECTION.

The method section starts on a separate page, and the heading "Method" must be typed and centered as shown below.

Method

The method section is then subdivided into several sections that are labeled, italicized, and placed flush against the left margin: Note that the proposal should be in paragraph form. Although we use bullets below to identify the type of information included in each subsection, bullets are not used in the proposal. Remember to use the future tense. Do not begin a separate page for each of the subsections.

Participants
Include the following in the participants section:
- Description of the demographic background of the participants (this could include race, ethnicity, age, and gender or other information relevant to the study, such as reading level or classification of disabilities)
- Description of how the participants will be selected for the study
- The number of participants to be included (may change later for qualitative research)
- Discussion of ethical issues and how informed consent will be obtained

Methods of Data Collection or Instruments
When writing your methods of data collection section, you must describe in detail how the data will be collected and what tools and instruments will be used to collect the data. Specifically, for quantitative studies you should
- Describe the measuring instruments (e.g., the survey, test, or behavior checklist or the type of archival data to be collected)
- Provide a rationale for using these instruments (a discussion of how the data obtained from these instruments will provide information to answer the research question)
- Describe how the instruments measure the variables
- Report the reliability and validity of the instruments
- For researcher-developed instruments, describe the construction and validation of the instrument and provide a copy of the instrument in an appendix
If your study is qualitative, this section should
- Describe in detail the data collection tools (e.g., observations or interview protocols or the type of archival data to be collected)
- Describe completely how the data will be collected and by whom
- Describe any triangulation methods you will use to establish credibility of the procedures you have proposed
- Describe methods used to establish dependability of your methods of data collection
- Discuss development of the interview or observation protocol and provide a copy in the appendix

Materials
Not all proposals include a materials section. This section is specifically for studies that include curriculum materials, instructional materials, or any materials, other than measuring tools, that the researcher plans to use as part of the method. Often materials will include things like books, workshop materials, computers, instructional software, and the like

Design
When writing the design section for experimental, be sure to describe the kind of study you are proposing. Specifically, you should
- Describe the approach of the study. Is it quantitative? If so, what kind? Is it qualitative? If so, what kind? Is it a mixed-method or action research study?
- Include a description of the number of groups in the study and if they are treated differently

Procedure
A good procedure section includes the following:
- A description of the role of the researcher (detached observer, interviewer, teacher, etc.)
- Detailed description of the procedures you propose for your study. This description must be sufficiently detailed to allow another person to conduct and replicate the proposed study.
- Use the researcher's point of view to describe how the study will be organized and the participant's point of view to describe the task

limitations. A professional researcher is always aware of the limitations of the methods used in a study and any possible criticisms that might be made of the study by other researchers or practitioners.

References. The references section contains all the references for citations used in the proposal. Unlike a bibliography that lists *all* the references encountered during the research process (but may not have actually cited), the reference page includes *only* those actual references that were used (cited) somewhere in the paper. Most of the citations from the references appear in the review of literature, but citations may be used to support ideas or define variables at any part of the proposal. Reference sections must be in APA style. For further clarification of the APA style, refer to the APA manual, fifth edition.

Appendixes. All researcher-developed tools are included in the appendix section of the proposal (e.g., the final form of any survey, interview protocol, observational protocol, or materials). If multiple instruments are developed, each instrument is to be included in a separate appendix, and each appendix is given a letter label (e.g., Appendix A, Appendix B). These labels are used when referencing the item in the body of the proposal. Note that all appendixes should be referred to in the text.

Chapter Summary

Although the research proposal and published articles have some similar characteristics, unlike the research proposal, the research study goes on to collect, analyze, and report findings and conclusions. A research proposal is necessary for several reasons: for a review of the proposed research and methods by an institutional review board for ethical review, to elicit further feedback and critique from colleagues and peers, and to provide a framework of the study when presenting it to possible participants or administrators of schools or settings where the research will take place. To provide continuity across studies, researchers adhere to a style known as APA. Research proposals should also be written in APA style.

The research proposal is composed of several main sections. The introduction is the first section. It contains a brief overview of the literature on the topic, the statement of purpose, and the study's rationale. This is followed by the review of literature and the statement of the hypothesis or foreshadowed questions or subquestions. Next comes the method section that contains the participants section, instruments or methods of data collection, design, procedures, and finally the benefits and limitations section. References are at the end of the proposal, starting on a separate page. If the researcher has developed an instrument such as a survey or interview protocol, an appendix would contain such material and follow the reference section.

Key Concepts

anatomy of a research proposal

header

running head

title

Discussion Questions or Activities

1. You are writing a research proposal on the charter school movement or a topic of your own choice. Discuss in what ways your proposal would differ if you wrote it from a quantitative and then a qualitative perspective.
2. Discuss why qualitative researchers end their reviews of literature with foreshadowed questions whereas quantitative researchers generate research hypotheses.
3. Some researchers, especially students in an educational research course, might argue that a research proposal is an unnecessary step in the research process. Using the following study as an example, discuss in specific terms why a proposal would be important to the researcher, the institution where the research is being conducted, and to the participants: What is the effect of peer tutoring on the math achievement of at-risk third-grade students?

Suggested Readings

Davitz, J. R., & Leiderman Davitz, L. (1996). *Evaluating research proposals: A guide for the behavioral sciences.* Upper Saddle River, NJ: Prentice Hall.

Pyrczak, F., & Bruce, R. R. (1992) *Writing empirical research reports: A basic guide for students of the social and behavioral sciences.* Los Angeles: Pyrczak Publishing.

CHAPTER FOUR

MEASUREMENT IN EDUCATIONAL RESEARCH AND ASSESSMENT

Preestablished Instruments and Archival Data

Chapter Objectives

After reading this chapter, you should be able to

1. Identify the major types of preestablished, standardized instruments and explain how these are developed and used in educational research and assessment
2. Identify the characteristics of standardized instruments and distinguish between norm-referenced, criterion-referenced, and self-referenced instruments
3. Identify seven broad areas that standardized, preestablished instruments measure and give an example of each
4. Identify the main difference between behavior rating scales and checklists
5. Define archival data and give three examples of archival data found in a typical school setting
6. Describe the appropriate situations when a researcher would use a frequency polygon versus a histogram
7. Describe the purpose of a normal distribution and how the frequency scores are distributed and discuss how frequency scores are clustered for a distribution that is positively skewed, negatively skewed, and bimodal
8. Identify and give examples for the three types of measures of central tendency
9. Identify and give examples of the different types of measures of variability

10. Define what a correlation coefficient is and give an example of a coefficient that shows a strong positive relationship between two variables and one that shows a strong negative relationship
11. Describe the difference between reliability and validity and give several examples for each

Preestablished Instruments and Archival Data

All research studies, regardless whether they are quantitative or qualitative, require the collection of **data** through some type of measurement. *Data* are any type of information collected for use in educational research or assessment. The different types of data include numerical information (e.g., attendance rates, standardized test scores, rank in class), verbal information (e.g., interview transcripts, student writing samples, school board minutes), and graphic information (e.g., photographs or videotapes). Data are collected by instruments such as tests or surveys or by developing protocols (sets of questions and procedures) for observations and interviews. Understanding the design and the development of measuring instruments will help you not only select the appropriate tool for your study but also critically analyze the measures used in your school and in reading research studies. In addition, it is important for practitioners such as teachers, administrators, counselors, or school psychologists to understand the principles of measurement so they can more effectively use data to improve their practice and address accountability requirements.

Although there are many types of instruments, they are often divided into two main categories: preestablished and self-developed. This chapter focuses on quantitative, preestablished measures and **archival data** (data taken from records collected by educators or educational institutions), both of which are types of data used primarily in research and assessment of schools and programs. It will also introduce descriptive statistics used to report data from these instruments and discuss the types of evidence that indicate if these measures are valid and reliable. Chapter Five discusses the processes involved in qualitative measurement and self-developed measures, such as the types used in action research. Issues pertaining to assessment of the quality of self-developed and qualitative measurement processes are also discussed in Chapter Five.

Preestablished Instruments

Preestablished instruments refer to a category of measuring tools that have already been developed and piloted, usually by *someone other than the researcher who is doing the current study.* These instruments may include tests, observational rating scales, questionnaires, or even scoring protocols for interviews. However, an important feature of preestablished instruments is that they are usually standardized measures. A **standardized instrument** is defined as an instrument with the following characteristics:

- It includes a fixed set of questions or stimuli.
- It is given in a fixed time frame under similar conditions with a fixed set of instructions and identified responses.
- It is created to measure specific outcomes and is subjected to extensive research development and review.
- Performance on the instrument can be compared to a referent such as a norm group, a standard or criterion, or an individual's own performance as described below.

> **Norm-referenced tests:** measures in which the scoring indicates how a student's performance compares with that of a **norm group** (i.e., a group of participants who have already taken the instrument and their scores represent the range of possible performance on the measure). The Iowa Test of Basic Skills (ITBS) is an example of a norm-referenced test that is frequently used in educational research and assessment. Test results for individual children or schools may be compared with those of a variety of norm groups. The test includes separate norms for students from high- and low-socioeconomic areas, private religious versus public schools, urban areas, and students for whom English is a second language (Brookhart, n.d.).
>
> **Criterion-referenced tests:** measures in which the scoring involves a comparison against a predetermined standard of performance or a criterion. For example, many states define the range of scores on the state assessment tests that qualify as inadequate, passing, or excellent performance. These tests are often developed using learning standards that serve as the criterion for performance and are often referred to as standards-based tests.
>
> **Self-referenced tests:** tests that measure an individual student's performance over time to see if it improves or declines when compared with past performance. Some standardized instruments provide information that allows both norm-referencing and self-referencing. For example, the Dynamic Indicators of Basic Early Literary Skills is a test designed to allow measurement of individual student progress over time (University of Oregon, 2004).

Typically, standardized tests and measures are designed by researchers at universities or teams with expertise (people called psychometricians) in the area of instrument development who work for test-publishing companies. Once developed, the tests and other measures are used by researchers and practitioners in both conducting research and measuring school outcomes.

Although there is a wide range in what standardized instruments measure, the processes associated with their development are similar across instruments. It is important to understand that much time, energy, and expertise go into establishing a standardized instrument. It is common for these measures to undergo years of work in their creation, plus continuous refinement to ensure their accuracy and reliability. There is also considerable controversy surrounding the use of standardized tests in education, especially those involved in high-stakes testing. Box 4.1 summarizes some of the issues involved in this debate.

Box 4.1 High-Stakes State-Mandated Tests

High-stakes tests are tests that are used to make "high-stakes" decisions. These decisions often include whether a student is promoted to the next grade or permitted to graduate. State-mandated tests are certainly not new. For years, many states used mandated tests to assess student performance in the content areas. However, with the passage of the No Child Left Behind Act (NCLB), states are now mandated to create their own standards for student achievement and must by 2005–2006 demonstrate that students are making adequate progress to meet those standards.

The standards developed by the states form the basis for the tests and also have become part of curricular and instructional decision making. Teachers are *strongly encouraged* to incorporate the standards into their instruction. From a test-construction point of view, most of the tests are multiple choice or essay, and a few states have performance or portfolio assessments. Criterion-referenced scoring is used in most of the states where student performance is compared with some preestablished benchmark that indicates level of performance.

The use of high-stakes state-mandated tests is not without controversy. Many policymakers and government officials believe that these tests will result in positive outcomes related to student performance and quality of education. Generally, advocates of high-stakes state-mandated testing believe that student academic performance will increase; more time will be spent teaching content; and poor-performing schools, teachers, and students will lead to—high expectations for all. Because high-stakes tests report the results for all students, students who have been traditionally underserved (ethnic minorities, the poor, and students with disabilities) will now have their performance monitored more closely (Linn, 2003).

Critics argue that the consequences of these tests will be negative. Among their concerns are that teachers feeling pressured by administrators and the community to improve student performance on these tests will begin to "teach to the test." They will spend more time on test preparation than teaching content. Furthermore, the time that was devoted to further exploration of content in a creative way will be eliminated because of time considerations. Another concern voiced by critics is that the state tests are focused on a narrow set of skills and knowledge rather than higher-level cognitive skills. If this is in fact the case, the curriculum presented to students will be narrowed and focused on lower-level cognitive skills such as memorization and rote knowledge. An equally important concern is that many of the high-stakes state-mandated tests discriminate against low-socioeconomic and ethnic minority children. A frequently asked question is whether test questions measure only content taught in schools or if they measure knowledge acquired outside of school. If tests do include knowledge gained by experiences outside of school, then ethnic minority and poor children are at a disadvantage. Moreover, some research (Darling-Hammond, 2001) has suggested that because of the intense pressure to improve performance, some schools have resorted to pushing low-scoring students into special education, retaining them in their current grade level, or encouraging them to drop out of school.

The actual research on this topic is limited and inconsistent yet vital. However, given the climate of accountability and the regulations of NCLB, further research is essential.

Types of Preestablished Measures

In general, standardized preestablished instruments measure five broad areas: achievement, aptitude, personality, attitudes or interest, and behaviors. **Achievement tests** are generally associated with measuring what a student *has already learned* in school. Achievement instruments tend to measure content knowledge such as facts, concepts, or principles and skills such as computation, problem solving, listening, and writing. Most of the tests used in contemporary high-stakes testing are achievement tests. Many times these tests are developed in what is called a **test battery.** A *test battery* is a collection of several subtests or minitests, each measuring a specific skill such as reading, mathematical literacy, or science. For example, the Iowa Test of Basic Skills (ITBS) includes subtests for vocabulary, comprehension, math computation, and problem solving, just to name a few.

Unlike achievement tests, **aptitude tests** are designed *not* to measure what someone knows, but to *predict what one can do or how one will perform in the future.* Intelligence tests and tests of mental or cognitive abilities are examples of aptitude tests. On an aptitude test, students are asked to demonstrate their ability to solve problems and apply knowledge and skills to solve problems and complete tasks. Tests such as the Wechsler Scales and the Terra Nova are examples of commonly used aptitude tests.

Personality tests or inventories differ from achievement and aptitude tests in that they measure self-perception or personal characteristics. Personality tests usually present the person with a set of questions intended to measure that individual's traits, characteristics, or behaviors. Personality is measured through objective tests such as the Minnesota Multiphasic Personality Inventory or the Myers-Briggs Type Indicator. These inventories require individuals to respond to a set of statements that reflect their personality traits. These types of tests are relatively simple to score in comparison with projective personality tests.

Projective personality tests require individuals to give verbal responses to what they see in unstructured and ambiguous stimuli. The Rorschach Inkblot Technique and the Thematic Apperception Test are examples of projective personality tests. Because these tests involve complex stimuli and responses, the person administering and scoring the tests must be well trained and highly skilled.

Another type of measure commonly used in both research and practice is an **attitude or interest scale.** Like personality tests, these measures typically use self-report questions to assess a person's attitudes toward a topic or interests in areas. For example, career counselors use a variety of interest inventories to help students think about areas of work or study that they might pursue. One such inventory, the Campbell Interest and Skill Survey, allows students to compare their self-reported interests and skills with those of professionals engaged in a wide variety of careers to see if they would be similar to people already in the field. Measures of attitudes toward a wide variety of educational issues have also been created by researchers. An example is the Mathematics Self-Efficacy Scale, a 34-item scale designed to measure one's "beliefs that he or she is capable of performing math-related tasks and behaviors" (Ciechalski, n.d., ¶ 2).

A final category of measures that is useful for both researchers and educators includes **behavior rating scales and checklists.** The rating scales are used to quantify observations of behaviors often to assist in making diagnoses of problems. The rating scales might be completed by a parent, teacher, child, or other school staff. Checklists include lists of behaviors that are simply checked to indicate the occurrence of behaviors. Rating scales present numerical rating scales to assess the frequency or intensity of behaviors. For example, the Achenbach Behavior Rating Scale is often used by school psychologists to assess problem behaviors in children.

Archival Data

Archival data are data that have already been collected, typically by the individual teacher, school, or district rather than by a researcher. There are many types of archival data, but in educational research this typically includes data a school might keep at the individual student level, at grade level, and at building and district levels. Student absenteeism, graduation rates, suspensions, standardized state test scores, and teacher grade-book data are all examples of archival data that might be used in educational research or assessment. It is not uncommon for researchers to combine several different types of archival data in a single study.

With the current emphasis on school accountability, access to archival data has certainly increased. Most states report archival data on the Web sites of school report cards for individual schools and districts. However, there are concerns about the accuracy of these data and the extent to which high-stakes testing may have led some schools to distort their data. (See Box 4.2 for a discussion of this problem in relation to graduation rates.) In addition, the methods used to summarize and present archival data can often result in a distorted picture of a school's performance, a problem that will be illustrated in our next section.

Box 4.2 What Is the Real Graduation Rate for U.S. Students?

With the recent emphasis on educational accountability, graduation rates have come under increasing scrutiny. Under NCLB, state accountability systems are required to include high school graduation rates as one of their accountability indicators. It might seem that graduation rates would be relatively simple to calculate: you divide the number of students graduating by the total number of students. However, questions quickly arise regarding:

• *How do you determine the total number of students*? Is it the total number in the freshman class of a high school? Is it the total number in the junior class? How can you account for students who transfer or move? When and where should students be counted? How do you determine when and if a student has dropped out?

• *Does it matter when and how students graduate?* If a student takes five or six years to graduate, should that student be included in the graduation totals? If students earn a General Equivalent Development certificate, are they included in the graduation totals? If students leave school without graduating and then return to complete their education, should they be counted?

Swanson (2003) examined many of these issues by calculating graduation rates for states and the nation as a whole using three different methods. One method developed by the National Center for Education Statistics (NCES) compared the number of students graduating in a given year with the number of students enrolled for that year plus the number who dropped out in the three previous years. Swanson pointed out that dropout rates are often underreported, and data are not available for some states. The overall dropout rate calculated using the NCES method was 85%, which is the rate frequently reported as representing the national rate. However, the two other methods of calculating graduation rates that did not use dropout rates produced estimates that were at least 10% lower. Both of these estimates used student enrollment or promotion rate in previous years as the basis for their estimates. State graduation rates also differed using the different methods, with some states having graduation rates as low as 48.6%.

NCLB has provided some guidelines for reporting graduation rates. Only students who complete high school within a "standard number of years" (Swanson, 2003, p. 12), which is typically four years, may be counted. However, this method results in wider differences in the graduation rates of different racial and ethnic groups who are more likely to take additional time to complete high school.

Scales of Measurement

It would be nice if measuring educational outcomes was as easy as stepping onto a scale. However, the process is somewhat more complicated than that! Just as you would need to know whether your scale is based on pounds or kilograms, researchers need to know what type of scale was used in creating their educational measures. The scale for an educational measure is categorized based on the range of values or scores produced by the measuring instrument. Specifically, there are four types of variables that can be measured quantitatively, and these are called the levels or scales of measurement: **nominal, ordinal, interval**, and **ratio scales** (Table 4.1).

• *Nominal scales* measure variables that are **categorical**: variables that represent discretely separate groups or categories. This is considered to be the lowest level or scale of measurement. Each person or school would be placed into a single category (e.g., category A, category B) based on its score. For example, let us say that a district reported the number of students who qualified for free or reduced-cost

TABLE 4.1 SCALES OF MEASUREMENT.

Scale of Measurement	Description	Examples
Nominal	Categories	Private versus public school, parenting style
Ordinal	Categories, plus ranking	Olympic medals (gold, silver, bronze)
Interval	Categories, ranking, equal spacing	Reading test scores
Ratio	Categories, ranking, equal spacing, plus true zero	Age, weight, and time

lunch—a measure often used to estimate the number of students from low-income families. Students would be categorized by assigning them to either the Qualifies for Free or Reduced Lunch category or Does Not Qualify for Free or Reduced Lunch category. The data would then be summarized numerically for each category. Other variables that might be measured using a nominal scale would be gender, ethnicity, presence or absence of a disability, or type of leadership style.

• *Ordinal scales*: like nominal scales, ordinal scales categorize persons or things. However, they also place the categories into rank order from highest to lowest or from lowest to highest. Therefore, they allow us to determine who did the best or who did the worst. A commonly used example of ordinal data is high school class rank. Consider the following as four high school ranks and associated GPAs:

Rank	GPA
1	4.0
2	3.8
3	3.6
4	3.2

Students are placed in order based on their GPA, but the data are entered as rank in class. Notice that even though you can now determine the highest to lowest college academic performance, the distance between the scores or the intervals is not equal. The distance between rank 1 and 2 is 0.2, and the distance between rank 3 and 4 is 0.4. This limits the type of statistical tests that can be applied to the data and also limits the conclusions one can draw about differences between persons at different ranks.

• *Interval scales* categorize and rank order the data, thereby including the characteristics of nominal and ordinal data. However, interval data also assume that the distance between the scores is equal. For example, Scott's midterm exam grade in his educational research course is a 65 whereas his roommate Roberto scores a 69. How many points separate Scott and Roberto? No, this is not a trick question! Four points separate the two students. In the same class, Josie scores a 95 and Maria scores a 99. How many points separate these two students? Right, four points. It is assumed that the difference between Scott and Roberto is the same as the difference between Josie and Maria. Although interval data are more sophisticated and precise than either nominal or ordinal data, there are still certain limitations. First, in interval data, there is no true zero point. What does this mean? Let us begin by defining the word *zero*. If you were asked for a definition of zero, you would likely say something like "there is nothing" or "there is an absence of a quality." This is true. However, if poor Harold got a zero on the midterm, does this mean he has no knowledge at all of the topics covered in the class? Probably not! He certainly does not know much about educational research, but he probably has some content knowledge. So in this case, to say that a score of zero means the absence of something is not totally accurate. In addition, interval data have an arbitrary maximum point. Let us say that Helena gets a score of 100 out of 100, and Ramone gets 50 out of 100 points on the midterm. Does this mean that Helena possesses all the possible knowledge of educational research and that Ramone possess 50% of the content? Certainly not! The exam simply went up to 100 points. Receiving a score of 100 does not indicate total mastery of the content, and receiving a score of 50 does not mean mastery of half of the content. Because there is no true zero point, Helena does not have 50% more knowledge about educational research than Ramone.

Most standardized educational measures use interval scales.

• *Ratio scales* are often considered the types of measurement that produce the most precise data. Ratio scales include the properties of nominal, ordinal, and interval variables and also include a true zero point. Consider height: a child who is 3 feet 1 inch tall is 50% of the height of a person who is 6 feet 2 inches. This is true because the variable, height, has a true zero point. A height of zero literally means the absence of height. Also, there is not an arbitrary limit to how tall someone could be. (Professional basketball players get taller each year!) Ratio variables are seen often in the physical sciences but rarely in education. Table 4.1 summarizes the scales of measurement.

Summarizing Data Using Descriptive Statistics

Descriptive statistics are used to summarize data from both preestablished and quantitative self-developed instruments using either graphical or mathematical procedures. Almost every study using a quantitative measure will use descriptive statistics to depict the patterns in the data. Similarly, in educational practice, we often want ways to describe the overall performance of students, teachers, administrators, or schools on some measure. Descriptive statistics are one tool for summarizing this performance for both research purposes and, increasingly, for assessment of educational outcomes at the classroom, school, and district levels.

Frequency Distributions

One of the first questions educators ask when a group has been measured is, "How did we do?" To answer this question, one needs a way to see how the group as a whole did as well as individual students. One way to depict the overall performance of a group is to display the frequency of each score in a **frequency distribution.** The word *distribution* is used to describe the range of scores and their overall frequencies. A frequency distribution displays each score and the frequency with which it occurred in either a table (called a **frequency table**) or in a graph. The scores are ordered from highest to lowest, and the number of persons obtaining each score is listed as the frequency in the second column. For example, in Table 4.2, the number of books that students read (scores) are reported in the first column, and the frequency or number of students who read that many books is reported in the second column. Sometimes possible score values are grouped rather than being listed individually to make the patterns clearer, as in Table 4.3.

Scores may also be displayed in a graph with the scores listed along the *x* or horizontal axis and the frequencies listed along the *y* or vertical axis. If the data represent an ordinal scale of measurement or higher, they are usually connected by a line, as in Figure 4.1, and the graph is referred to as a **frequency polygon.**

TABLE 4.2 FREQUENCY TABLE OF NUMBER OF BOOKS READ BY 30 STUDENTS.

Number of Books	Number of Students
20	1
19	0
18	0
17	0
16	1
15	1
14	0
13	1
12	1
11	1
10	1
9	2
8	1
7	2
6	4
5	5
4	4
3	2
2	2
1	1

TABLE 4.3 SAMPLE GROUPED FREQUENCY TABLE.

Number of Books	Number of Students
17 to 20	1
13 to 16	3
9 to 12	5
5 to 8	11
1 to 4	10

FIGURE 4.1 SAMPLE FREQUENCY POLYGON.

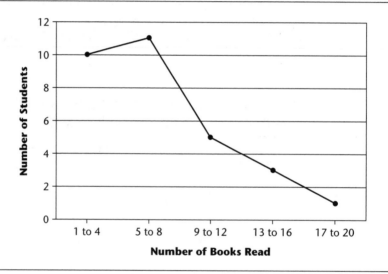

If the data are categorical, each category is represented by a separate bar, as in Figure 4.2, and the graph is called a **histogram.**

So what does a frequency distribution tell us about the scores? At a glance, it shows us how the scores distribute, that is, how closely bunched together or how spread out they are, which scores are most frequent and which scores are least frequent, and whether there are **outlier** scores that are very different from the rest. Distributions of educational measures can take several different forms.

When large groups are randomly sampled and measured (an appropriate procedure for establishing a norm group for a measurement), the distribution often has a shape that is called a **normal distribution.** If the distribution is approx-

FIGURE 4.2 SAMPLE HISTOGRAM.

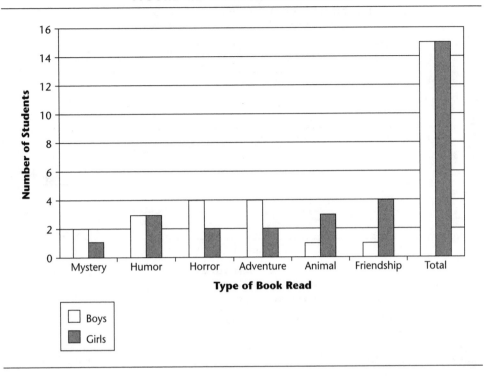

imately "normal," it will look bell-shaped and symmetrical, with the highest point on the curve or most frequent scores clustered in the middle of the distribution. Frequencies of scores will decrease as the distribution moves away from the middle toward either the high or low end of the score values. Most standardized tests present data from a norm group that shows a normal distribution of scores. The symmetrical nature of this distribution allows one to examine a wide range of differences between scores through the full range of the scores. **Skewed distributions** are asymmetrical, meaning the scores are distributed differently at the two ends of the distribution. In a **negatively skewed distribution,** most of the scores are high, but there are a small number of scores that are low. In a **positively skewed distribution,** most of the scores are low, but there are a few high scores. Figure 4.3 shows how test scores for a class in educational research would look under two different conditions.

The outliers in a skewed distribution pull the "tail" of the distribution out in that direction. So a negatively skewed distribution has a low flat tail at the low end

FIGURE 4.3 EXAMPLES OF POSITIVELY SKEWED
AND NEGATIVELY SKEWED DISTRIBUTIONS.

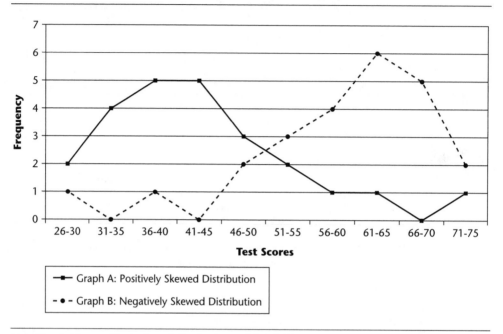

Note: Graph A is a positively skewed distribution and Graph B is a negatively skewed distribution.

of the scores, and a positively skewed distribution has a low flat tail at the high end of the scores.

Some distributions, called **bimodal distributions,** have two clusters of frequent scores seen as the two humps in the distribution, as in Figure 4.4. What does the bimodal distribution show us about the distribution of grades in the distance education class?

What Is a Typical or Average Score? Measures of Central Tendency

Although frequency distributions show the patterns in scores, it is also useful to be able to summarize the performance of a group using a single score for the typical or average performance of a group. These are what researchers call measures of central tendency, and the three most common are the mode, mean, and median.

Mode. The **mode** is the score in a distribution that occurs most frequently. In a frequency polygon, the mode is the score represented by the highest point on the

FIGURE 4.4 GRADES IN DISTANCE EDUCATION CLASSES.

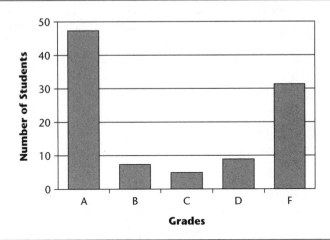

curve. As you just saw in Figure 4.4, some distributions can have more than one mode if two or more scores have similarly high frequencies. (That is why the distribution in Figure 4.4 is called a bimodal distribution.) The mode is a somewhat imprecise measure of central tendency because it simply summarizes the frequency of a single score. If the distribution is asymmetrical, the mode may not be a precise estimate of central tendency.

Mean. The **mean** is the arithmetical average of a set of scores. To find the mean, simply add up the scores and divide by the number of scores. If numbers are in a frequency table, first multiply each score by its frequency. Table 4.4 presents the number of pages printed at campus computer terminals by one class of students during a single semester and illustrates the calculation of the mean.

A college we know recently considered using the mean number of printed pages to set a new policy for the number of free pages students would be allowed. They reasoned that because the mean represented the average number of pages printed, the new policy would allow the average student to do all or most of his or her printing for free. The mean is a widely used measure of central tendency in research and in educational practice. You will often find the mean symbolized as an X with a bar above it, as in $\overline{X}$.

In a skewed distribution, however, the mean can be misleading as a measure of central tendency. The extreme scores in a positively skewed distribution will result in the mean being higher than the central tendency of the group, and the

TABLE 4.4 CALCULATION OF MEAN FROM A FREQUENCY TABLE.

Number of Pages Printed	Number of Students	Number of Pages × Number of Students
300	1	300
280	3	840
260	5	1,300
240	6	1,440
220	4	880
200	2	400
180	2	360
160	1	160
	Total = 24	Total = 5,680

Note: The mean is calculated as: 5,680 ÷ 24 = 236.67.

extreme scores in a negatively skewed distribution will "pull the mean down" toward the low end. Again, using the printing example above, the mean for all of the students at that college was much higher than the average for just the one class because a small number of students printed more than 1,000 pages a semester, and one even printed a million pages! (Of course, the new policy was intended to limit the printing of students like this who were abusing the system.) However, the mean estimated the average number of printed pages per student at a level much higher than was "typical" for most students.

Income is another measure for which the mean is likely to be a poor estimate of central tendency. Income distributions are typically positively skewed. Most of us earn middle to low incomes, but there are a small number of people who earn very high incomes. Imagine what would happen to the mean income of your community if one of the residents was Bill Gates! In a skewed distribution, the best measure of central tendency is the median.

Median. The **median** is the score that divides a distribution exactly in half when scores are arranged from the highest to the lowest. It is the midpoint of distribution or the score in the distribution at which half of the scores are lower and half are higher. To find the median, you would divide the number of scores in a distribution by 2 and round up if there is a decimal. Then count down from the top of the distribution until you have counted that number of scores. See if you can calculate the median for printing for the class in Table 4.4. If a distribution has an even number of scores, the median is the score halfway between the two scores in the middle. If a distribution has an odd number of scores, the median is an actual score.

The median is a stable measure of the central tendency of a set of scores. This means that it is not affected much if there are a few outlier scores in a distribution that are much different from the rest. To return to our example of income distributions, if Bill Gates moved into your community, the distribution of income would not change greatly because the addition of one person would simply move the median up one number in the distribution.

Measures of Variability

So now you know several statistics that can be used to describe the average or typical performance of a group. However, two groups might have the same mean even if they differ considerably in the spread of the scores in their distributions. Consider the two distributions of test scores in Figure 4.5.

Both districts have approximately the same average performance in their students' test scores; the mean for District A is 52.08, and the mean for District B is 52.59. However, District A's scores are much more variable than those for District B. Descriptive statistics can also provide a way to summarize the amount of variability in the scores in a distribution, that is, how widely spread out or scattered the scores are. Two measures of variability frequently used in educational research and assessment are the range and the standard deviation.

Range. The range is the difference between the highest and lowest scores in a distribution. To find the range, you subtract the lowest score from the highest score. This indicates how many points separate these two scores. Although it is easy to calculate, the range is not a precise or stable measure of variability because it can be affected by a change in just one score. For that reason, most educational researchers use the standard deviation as a measure of variability.

Standard Deviation. The standard deviation is the average distance between each of the scores in a distribution and the mean. Now before your eyes glaze over or you begin to wonder how researchers can come up with so many meaningless concepts, let us consider why you would want to calculate such a statistic. Remember that the goal is to summarize the amount of variability in a set of scores. We know that the mean represents the average performance of a group or the center of the group. So one way to describe variability is to consider how far each score is from that center score. It is called the standard *deviation* because it represents the average amount by which the scores deviate from a mean. We will not discuss here how the standard deviation is calculated, but if seeing the numbers helps you understand concepts better, see Appendix C for an example of the calculation of a standard deviation.

FIGURE 4.5 DISTRIBUTIONS OF TEST SCORES FOR TWO SCHOOL DISTRICTS.

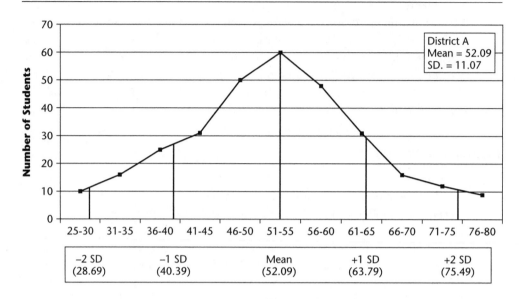

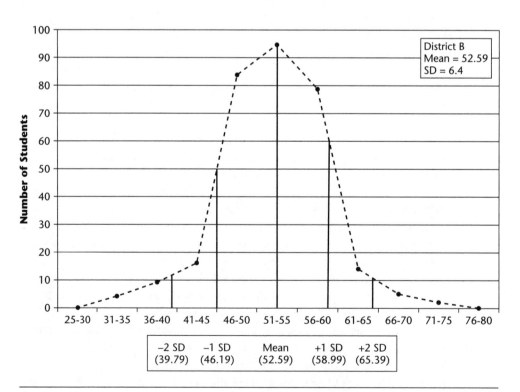

Most research studies and preestablished instruments will report the standard deviations for the data collected. For any distribution of scores, the standard deviation will be a specific number, typically including decimals because its calculation rarely results in a simple number. The larger the number, the more variable are the scores in the distribution. In Figure 4.5 the standard deviation for the scores in District A is 11.07 and is 6.4 for District B. If you examine the scores, you will see that, on average, most of them lie within 2 standard deviations of the mean for both districts. That is, if you subtracted each score from the mean, the resulting number would be a value that was less than two times the standard deviation (22.14 for District A and 12.8 for District B). The standard deviation is widely used in part because of its relationship to the normal distribution, visually represented as the **normal curve** displayed in Figure 4.6, which forms the basis for comparing individual scores with those of a larger group.

Normal Curve. The *normal curve* is a distribution that has some unique and useful mathematical properties. One useful feature of the normal curve is that a certain percentage of scores always falls between the mean and certain distances above and below the mean. These distances are described as how many standard deviations above or below the mean a score falls. Approximately 34% of the scores fall between the mean and one standard deviation above it. Similarly, approximately 34% of the scores fall between the mean and one standard deviation below it. So about two thirds (more precisely, 68%) of the scores will be in the area between one standard deviation above and one standard deviation below the mean. Another 13.5% of the scores will fall in the area that is more than one standard deviation above the mean but less than two standard deviations above the mean. So between the mean and two standard deviations are 47.5% of the scores (34% plus 13.5%). Finally, another 2.5% of the scores are higher than two standard deviations above the mean. Because the curve is symmetrical, 13.4% of the scores will also be in the area that is between one standard deviation below the mean and two standard deviations below the mean. Also, 2.5% of the scores will fall below two standard deviations below the mean. Figure 4.6 illustrates the percentage of scores in each part of the normal curve. These percentages are useful in comparing the performances of persons who have taken an educational measurement. We will describe the types of scores used in educational measurement and then return to this scary but useful figure.

Types of Scores Used to Compare Performance on Educational Measures

Several types of scores are used to compare performances on educational measures.

Raw Scores. **Raw scores** are scores that summarize a person's performance on a measure by showing the number of responses or summing the scores for each

FIGURE 4.6 NORMAL CURVE.

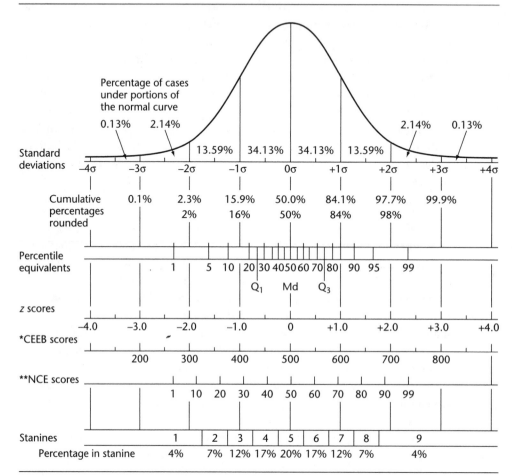

Note: *CEEB refers to College Entrance Exam Board test, for example, SAT; **NCE refers to Normal Curve Equivalent.
Source: Adapted from Seashore (1980).

response. Performance on classroom tests is usually reported as raw scores, but this type of score is not used by most preestablished measures. The reason is that one cannot know what a raw score represents without knowing more about the mean and standard deviation of the distribution of scores.

Percentile Ranks. **Percentile ranks** are scores that indicate the percentage of persons scoring at or below a given score. So a percentile rank of 82% means that 82% of persons scored below that score. Figure 4.6 shows the percentile ranks that correspond to scores based on the number of standard deviations between the score and the mean. For example, reading down from the curve, one can see that a score that is one standard deviation above the mean has a percentile rank of approximately 84. A score that is one half of a standard deviation below the mean has a percentile rank of approximately 31. You can calculate the exact percentile rank of a score if you know how many standard deviations it is above or below the mean. For a computer simulation that calculates the exact percentile rank based on the normal curve, go to the Web site http://www.stat.berkeley.edu/users/stark/Java/NormHiLite.htm.

Standard Scores. **Standard scores** are scores that tell how far a score is from the mean of distribution in terms of standard deviation units. Because standard scores are based on the standard deviation, the normal curve can be used to determine the percentile rank of a person's score based on his or her standard score. Therefore, a standard score shows immediately how well a person did in comparison with the rest of the group taking that measure. Examples of standard scores are z scores and college entrance exams (referred to as CEEB Scores in Figure 4.6) such as the Scholastic Assessment Test (SAT) or Graduate Record Examinations (GRE).

The most basic standard score is the z score, which is calculated in the following manner:

$$z \text{ SCORE} = (\text{SCORE} - \text{MEAN})/\text{STANDARD DEVIATION}$$

Any score can be converted to a z score if the mean of a distribution and the standard deviation are known. If Karyn got a score of 75 on a test with a mean of 65 and a standard deviation of 5, her z score would be as follows:

$$z \text{ SCORE} = (75 - 65)/5 = 10/5 = +2.0$$

As you can see, the z score represents simply the number of standard deviations away from the mean that the score is. Therefore, you can go to Figure 4.6 and determine Karyn's percentile rank, knowing that she is two standard deviations above the mean. Try one more example. Peter got a score of 55 on the same test. What would his z score be? What would his percentile rank be?

Many preestablished measures report student scores as standard scores, allowing a direct comparison of how two students did. Because many people do not like using negative numbers, some measures convert their raw scores into slightly different standard scores. For example, SAT and GRE scores are simply z scores multiplied by 100 + 500. So they have a mean of 500 and a standard deviation of 100. Knowing this, you should be able to use Figure 4.6 to determine the percentage of people who score between 400 and 500 on the SAT. If you need a hint, this would be the area between one and two standard deviations below the mean.

Stanines. **Stanine scores** are a type of standard score that divides a distribution into nine parts, each of which includes about one half of a standard deviation. Students are assigned scores ranging from 1 through 9 based on their performance. All students within a given stanine are considered to be equal in performance. Stanine 5 includes scores 0.25 standard deviations above and below the mean (thus z scores of $+0.25$ to -0.25). Each stanine above or below stanine 5 includes another half of the standard deviation of scores. Again, Figure 4.6 shows the percentage of scores within each stanine.

Percentages. Much of the school accountability data required of schools today is reported as **percentages.** A percentage is calculated by dividing the number of students or schools receiving a given score by the total number of students or schools and multiplying by 100. Although percentages are useful measurements, some types of data may be distorted when percentages are used. When one examines changes over time, the result may change substantially, based on the size of the group being measured. No Child Left Behind requires that schools report the percentage of children from each ethnic group who pass the state test. If a small rural district had a small population of one ethnic group, their results could change substantially if only a few families move into their district. For example, one of the authors of this book worked with two districts with different student populations. District A, a rural district, had only two African American students in grade 4, and District B had over 100 African American students in grade 4. Both of the students in District A failed the state test, resulting in a 100% failure rate. In District B, 50 students failed, resulting in a 50% failure rate. So based on percentage scores, it would seem that District B is doing better even though they have many more students failing. The overall lesson here is that one should always examine both the total number and the percentage of persons when comparing measures.

Grade-Equivalent Scores. A grade-equivalent score is reported in years and months. So 3.4 means third grade, fourth month. A grade-equivalent score reports the grade placement for which that score would be considered average. This means that the average student at the reported grade level could be expected to get a similar score on *this test.* (It does *not* mean that the person is capable of doing work at this grade level.)

Use of Correlation Coefficients in Evaluating Measures

Another type of descriptive statistic used in educational measurement is a correlation. As learned in Chapter One, correlations are measures of the relationship between two variables. Because we visited Chapter One ages ago, let us review some basic ideas related to correlation. (We will discuss correlations in more depth in Chapter Nine.) A correlational relationship is summarized using a descriptive statistic called a correlation coefficient. A positive correlation coefficient means that as one variable increases, the other also increases. A negative correlation coefficient means that as one variable increases, the other decreases. The size of the number (regardless of the sign) indicates how strong the relationship is between the variables. This number can range from a $+1.00$ to a -1.00, both of which represent perfect relationships between two variables. More often, the correlation is a decimal, and the size of the number shows how strongly related two measures are. Correlation coefficients are used extensively to assess the quality of educational measures. Typically, correlations are calculated between scores on two different measures that are thought to be related or between two sets of scores taken on the same measure. High correlations show that the two sets of scores show either high degrees of consistency (reliability) or that they are related in ways that make sense for whatever is being measured (validity). For example, scores on a preestablished instrument that has teachers report on their own teaching practices to measure teaching effectiveness should be positively correlated with principal ratings of teacher effectiveness or with student evaluations. In general, most correlation coefficients used to examine the reliability and validity of educational measures will yield positive correlations, although the size of the correlation will vary depending on what is being assessed. When correlations are computed between two sets of scores on the same measure, one would expect them to be high (0.80 or higher). When correlations are computed between two different measures, one would expect the correlations to be moderately high (0.60 to 0.80) if the instruments are measuring the same construct (such as the example of the teacher self-report of effectiveness and principal evaluations). If the instruments measure related but different constructs, such as a measure of self-esteem and a measure of student achievement, the correlation coefficient would be expected to be lower (0.30 to 0.60).

Evaluating the Quality of Educational Measures: Reliability and Validity

Reliability and validity are the two criteria used to judge the quality of all preestablished quantitative measures. **Reliability** refers to the consistency of scores, that is, an instrument's ability to produce "approximately" the same score for an individual over repeated testing or across different raters. For example, if we were to measure your intelligence (IQ), and you scored a 120, a reliable IQ test would produce a similar score if we measured your IQ again with the same test. **Validity,** on the other hand, focuses on ensuring that what the instrument "claims" to measure is truly what it is measuring. In other words, validity indicates the instrument's accuracy. Take, for example, a fourth-grade state math assessment that requires students to read extensive word problems in answering math questions. Some math teachers might argue that the assessment is not valid because students could know all the mathematical functions to answer the problems correctly but might be unable to answer the questions correctly because of their low reading ability. In other words, the assessment is really more of an assessment of students' reading skills than it is of math ability.

Validity and reliability are typically established by a team of experts as part of the process of developing a preestablished instrument. As part of the development process, the measurement team would work to establish sound reliability and validity for the instrument before it is packaged and sold to researchers and practitioners (see Figure 4.7).

If an instrument does not have sound reliability and validity, the instrument is of no value. Therefore, it is important that beginning researchers and educators in general have at least a basic understanding of issues surrounding reliability and validity to be able to select the most appropriate and accurate instruments to serve as measurement tools for their study.

FIGURE 4.7 OVERVIEW OF THE PROCESS IN DEVELOPING PREESTABLISHED INSTRUMENTS.

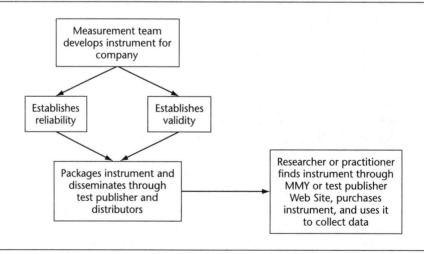

Note: MMY = Mental Measurement Yearbook.

Reliability

Notice that in our initial explanation of reliability, we referred to consistency as meaning obtaining approximately the same score for an individual over repeated testing. Even the most reliable test would not produce the exact same score if given twice to the same individual. This difference is referred to as the **measurement error.** Error in measurement is due to temporary factors that affect a person's score on any given instrument. Factors that influence reliability include

- Test takers' personal characteristics (e.g., motivation, health, mood, fatigue)
- Variations in test setting (e.g., differences in the physical characteristics of the room)
- Variations in the administration and scoring of the test
- Variation in participant responses due to guessing (caused by poorly written items)

Because there is always some error associated with measurement, obtained scores (the actual score the individual received) are made up of two components: the true score plus some error. If a test were perfectly reliable, the true score would be equal to the observed score. Students and researchers alike understand that their score on a given test may not represent their true score (their real knowledge or abilities). In essence, this means that unless an instrument is perfectly reliable, you can never know a person's true score. However, the simple calculation of the **standard error of measurement** (SEM) will allow one to estimate what the true score is likely to be. The SEM takes in account both the reliability coefficient of the test and the variability of the scores of the norm group as calculated by the standard deviation. The formula for SEM is as follows:

$$\text{SEM} = \text{SD}\sqrt{1-r}$$

where SD is the standard deviation of the test scores obtained by the norm group, and r indicates the reliability coefficient of the test calculated from a pilot group.

For example, consider the following situation. Test A has a reliability coefficient of 0.91. This suggests that the test is highly reliable, and therefore, a person's observed score is a relatively good estimate of his or her true score. The scores for test A produce a standard deviation of 9. Let us say that a student's observed score is 70. What would the SEM be for this example? Using our formula, it would be calculated as follows:

$$\text{SEM} = 9\sqrt{1-0.91} = 9\sqrt{0.09} = 9 \times 0.3 = 2.7$$

This means that the student who received a score of 70 might score 2.7 points higher (72.7) or lower (67.3) if she or he retook the test. All preestablished tests should report the SEM. Knowing the SEM is important when a measure is used to make decisions about students (e.g., placement or admission to programs). Decisions about students scoring near a cutoff point should be made cautiously because retesting might result in the student scoring differently with respect to the cutoff. Parents or teachers might consider asking that the student be retested or that additional information be considered.

Essentially, then, reliability is the extent to which the scores produced by a single test correlate. Reliability is a concept that is expressed in terms of correla-

tions that are summarized in a reliability coefficient. The reliability coefficient can assume values from zero to +1.00. The closer to +1.00 the reliability coefficient is, the more highly reliable the instrument. Presented below are several types of reliability. Keep in mind that not all of these types have to be conducted on a single instrument. Typically, at least one is used to establish reliability during an instrument's design and development.

Stability or Test-Retest Reliability (Consistency Across Time). One form of reliability is called stability or test-retest. The purpose of **stability** is to show that an instrument can obtain the same score for an individual if that person takes the instrument more than once. What is the importance of this, you might be asking yourself? Well, imagine an intelligence test that gives a different score for an individual each time it is administered. The first time a student takes it, he receives a score of 140, indicating that he is a genius. However, the second time the instrument is administered, the student receives a score of 104, which equates to about an average intelligence. Which one is the correct score? How would a school psychologist or a researcher who is using this instrument interpret this information? The answer is that they couldn't because the test is unreliable.

Stability of an instrument is also critical when one is trying to infer causality or that a change occurred in a study. Imagine a math assessment that was so unstable that a student received a score of 70 out of a possible 100 the first time the test was taken and a score of 90 out of a possible 100 the second time, even when no type of intervention or independent variable took place between the times of testing! Knowing the instrument's instability, how could you use the measure in a study to determine if changes in student achievement in mathematics were the result of a new math program you planned to implement? You would never really know if the change occurred because of the intervention, the unstable instrument, or both. Therefore, a researcher or a practitioner would want to avoid using an instrument that had poor test-retest reliability.

To establish stability, first a pilot sample of persons is selected. Pilot samples in instrument development are usually large populations, which allow for the greatest degree of generalizability. Once the pilot sample has been established, participants are given the instrument, and scores are obtained for every individual. Next, some time is allowed to pass. The amount of time varies based on the type of instrument that is being developed. The most important thing is that enough time passes so that participants are unable to recall items and perform better on the instrument because of this experience. An average wait time of four to six weeks between instrument administrations is usual. Following the second administration of the same test, the two scores are compared for each individual. Correlations are then calculated on the two sets of scores, which produces a correlation coefficient.

Depending on the instrument's purpose, correlation coefficients ranging from 0.84 or stronger would be considered very strong; however, correlations from 0.35 to 0.64 are more typical and considered to be moderately strong and certainly acceptable. Coefficients of 0.24 to 0.34 are considered to show a slight relationship and may be acceptable levels for instruments that are considered exploratory.

Equivalent-Form Reliability (Consistency Across Different Forms). Another type of reliability the measurement team might decide to establish for the instrument is equivalent-form reliability. This type of reliability is also referred to as *alternative form.* For this type of reliability, two forms of the same tests are given to participants, and the scores for each are later correlated to show consistency across the two forms. Although they contain different questions, these two forms assess the exact same content and knowledge, and the norm groups have the same means and standard deviations.

Internal Consistency Reliability (Consistency Within the Instrument). *Internal consistency* refers to consistency within the instrument. The question addressed is whether the measure is consistently measuring the same trait or ability across all items on the test. The most common method to assess internal consistency is through **split-half reliability**. This is a form of reliability used when two forms of the same test are not available or it would be difficult to administer the same test twice to the sample group. In these cases, a split-half reliability would be conducted on the instrument. To assess split-half reliability, the instrument is given to a pilot sample, and following its administration, the items on the instrument are split in half! Yes, literally split in half—often, all the even- and all the odd-numbered items are grouped together, and a score for each half of the test is calculated. This produces two scores for every individual from the one test, one score for the even-numbered items, and one score for the odd-numbered items. The *Spearman-Brown prophecy formula* is then applied to the data to correct for the fact that the correlations for internal consistency are being calculated on the two halves of the instrument and not the whole original instrument. For the split-half approach to be appropriate, the instrument must be long enough to split in half and should measure a single trait or knowledge domain. In determining the acceptability for coefficients, the research team would use the ranges discussed earlier in test-retest reliability.

Another approach used to establish internal consistency of a measure is to examine the correlations between each item and the overall score on the instrument. The question addressed here is whether a given score consistently measures the same amount of knowledge on the test. For example, consider scores on a 50-item history test taken by high school students. If all items are worth one point, students might get 40 out of 50 points by missing the first 10 items, the last 10 items, or some other mixture of 10 items. Can you say that all of these scores represent the same amount of knowledge? This type of internal consistency is assessed using either the Kuder-Richardson or Cronbach's coefficient alpha formula and is often referred to simply as internal consistency.

Validity

Along with the need to establish reliability for an instrument, the measurement team also has to address the issue of validity by constantly asking themselves the question: Does the instrument measure what it is designed to measure, or is it measuring something entirely different? To add to the confusion, keep in mind that an instrument can be extremely reliable but not valid in that it consistently obtains the same score for an individual but is not measuring what it intends to measure. For example, an educational research professor gives a midterm exam that she believes tests the content of the first half of her course. However, she inadvertently includes items from inferential statistics, which is covered in the second half of the course. This test would lack validity but would likely be reliable. That is, student performance would likely be fairly consistent over time. However, if you have a valid test that measures what it was intended to measure, the instrument will also have reliability. So when constructing a test or using a standardized instrument, validity is the single most important characteristic.

As with establishing reliability, validity is also established during the piloting of an instrument. In most cases, it is done simultaneously with procedures to establish reliability. Validity is usually established through an in-depth review of the instrument, including an examination of the instrument's items to be certain that they are accurately measuring the content or objectives being tested, and by relating scores on the instrument to other measures.

Content Validity. Content validity is composed of two items of validity: **sampling validity** and **item validity.** Both sampling validity and item validity involve having experts examine items that make up the instrument. However, sampling validity is more focused on the breadth of those items, whereas item validity is interested in the depth of the items. Let us say, for example, that the measurement team was working on a math test for fifth grade for the purpose of assessing the knowledge of content at the end of the year. To establish sampling validity, the measurement team might select a sample of fifth-grade teachers who would review the instrument to ensure that there are items on the test representative of the content taught over the entire year of fifth-grade math. This would include items from the first part of the school year, from the middle of the year, and from the end of the school year.

Item validity is concerned about examining each individual item to determine if it measures the content area taught. In other words, do the test items measure the content or objectives for the course or unit being taught? Think about the many times you have taken a test and wondered, "Where did this question come from? I did not read it in the text. I don't remember discussing it in class." Well, it may be that you just forgot, but it could be that the test lacked content validity. Maybe the item just was not covered. To establish content validity, the measurement team would have an expert panel of usually teachers or experts in the field examine the objectives and the items on the test to determine the degree of content validity.

Criterion-Related Validity. Essentially, **criterion-related validity** involves the examination of a test and its relationship with a second measure. It reflects the degree to which two scores on two different measures are correlated. There are two forms of criterion-related validity. **Concurrent validity** examines the degree to which one test correlates with another taken in the same time frame. When might this be done? Let us say that you have developed a new instrument that is quicker and faster for measuring intelligence. To establish its validity, you might administer your new test with an existing, already validated, intelligence test to a pilot group. You would then correlate the two sets of scores from your pilot group, and if you found a high correlation between the two tests, you could then offer your "new fast and easy intelligence test" as a replacement for the existing intelligence test, saying that it has evidence of concurrent validity.

Another type of criterion-related validity is **predictive validity.** Predictive validity uses the score on a test to predict performance in a future situation. In this situation, a test is administered and scored. Let us use the American College Test (ACT) that is taken by many high school juniors and seniors as an example. The ACT (the predictor) is used by colleges and universities around the country as a predictor of college success (the criterion). To determine its predictive validity, one would administer the ACT to a group of high school students and then allow some time to pass before measuring the criterion (college success—in this case, defined as one's freshman grade point average). Once the first-year grade point averages are released, they can be correlated with the ACT scores to determine if it is a successful predictor. If the correlation is high between the ACT and freshman grade point average (and there are some studies that suggest that this is the case), then the ACT is considered to have criterion-related validity in predicting college success.

Construct Validity. **Construct validity** involves a search for evidence that an instrument is accurately measuring an abstract trait or ability. Remember that constructs are traits that are derived from variables and are nonobservable. They include complex traits such as integrity, intelligence, self-esteem, and creativity. In constructing an instrument to measure one of these complex constructs, one must first have well-developed ideas or a comprehensive theory about what the construct is and how people who vary in that construct would differ in their behaviors, abilities, feelings, or attitudes. Consider the construct of self-esteem. The Pictorial Scale of Perceived Competence for Children and Adolescents (Harter & Pike, 1984) grew out of their research on the development of self-esteem. They conceptualized that self-esteem for children comprised four components: cognitive competence, peer acceptance, physical competence, and maternal acceptance. They believed that children have an overall sense of self-esteem that is composed of these separate components. Questions on the instrument reflect this overall theory of what self-esteem is. Examining the construct validity of this instrument means examining whether it really captures the full meaning of the self-esteem construct.

Construct validity is one of the most complex types of validity, in part because it is a composite of multiple validity approaches that are occurring simultaneously. This might include aspects of content, concurrent, and predictive validity. Therefore, many researchers consider construct validity to be a superordinate or overarching type of validity. Fully establishing construct validity also involves a lengthy process of collecting evidence from many studies over time. Below are some of the questions and procedures that might be involved in establishing construct validity.

• Does the measure clearly define the meaning of the construct? Evidence cited as support might include constructing a measure from a well-developed theory or examining whether its questions and parts correspond to research or theories related to the construct.

• Can the measure be analyzed into component parts or processes that are appropriate to the construct? In a test of creativity, the mental processes required by the tasks presented might be analyzed to see if they truly require creative thinking and not memory or reasoning abilities. Factor analysis is a statistical procedure used to see if clusters of questions identified in the statistical analysis match the groupings of questions identified by the test maker as the different parts of the test. So, for Harter and Pike's scale, one would expect the items on Physical Competence to be clustered together by the factor analysis.

• Is the instrument related to other measures of similar constructs, and is it *not* related to instruments measuring things that are different? Researchers want to be certain that the instrument actually measures the construct and not something else. For example, let us consider the construct self-esteem. To validate their measure of self-esteem, Harter and Pike would correlate the self-esteem test with measures of similar constructs as identified in the literature. For example, if the literature says that self-esteem is related to body image and self-awareness, measures of these constructs should correlate with the self-esteem instrument. These correlations would produce confirming or **convergent evidence.** However, they would also want to make sure that the measure did not correlate with measures of constructs that differ from self-esteem. So scores on the self-esteem measure might be correlated with scores on measures thought to be unrelated or only weakly related to self-esteem (e.g., attentiveness, emotionality, or physical activity level) to establish disconfirming evidence (constructs where there was little or no correlation).

    • Can the measure discriminate between (or identify separately) groups that are known to differ? Researchers will sometimes see if the measure yields different scores for two groups who are expected to differ in the construct. Harter and Pike (1984) demonstrated that the self-esteem measure did distinguish between children who had been held back in school and those who were not held back.

Perhaps you can see why it takes a long time to establish construct validity.

Finding Preestablished Measures

Researchers and educators often use preestablished instruments to collect their data. One source that many researchers use is the **Mental Measurement Yearbook** (MMY). University and college libraries and many large public libraries carry this reference book both in their bound collections and through their electronic databases. Essentially, MMY is an overview of a wide variety of measurement instruments. Each instrument described in the MMY includes the following information:

- Complete name of the instrument
- The publisher, date of publication, and most recent edition
- A description of what the test measures
- The population for which the test was designed
- Procedures for administration and scoring
- A critique of the instrument, including its validity and reliability (terms described in detail later in the chapter)

In most cases, the description provided by the MMY is detailed enough to provide the researcher with enough information to know if the instrument might be appropriate for his or her study. The MMY also provides enough information to generate an instrument section for a research proposal. Although this general description of the instrument may suffice initially, it is strongly encouraged that researchers obtain a copy of the instrument and administrative materials for more in-depth review. Preestablished instruments are usually purchased by the researcher and include materials on test administration and scoring, individual testing booklets, and answer sheets. Researchers must purchase original copies of the testing materials from the publisher. Photocopying materials to save costs is tempting but illegal because it is a direct violation of federal copyright law. In some cases, preestablished instruments cannot be hand-scored by the researcher and must be sent back to the publisher for scoring.

Review copies can be obtained by contacting either the publisher or testing company directly. In addition, many institutions may have test libraries that contain a wide variety of tests and other related measurement tools available for review. Special permission may be required by a faculty member for students to check out these materials. A list of Web sites with information about available preestablished measures is included in Box 4.3.

Box 4.3. Web Sites with Information on Preestablished, Standardized Tests

- ETS Test Collection: http://www.ets.org/testcoll/index.html
  The Educational Testing Service (ETS) is the largest private educational testing and measurement organization in the world. This web site includes resources on testing and assessment for educators, parents, students, researchers, and policymakers as well as a searchable directory of over 20,000 tests.
- Buros/ERIC Test Publisher Directory: http://buros.unl.edu/buros/jsp/search.jsp
  This Web directory is part of the Educational Resources Information Center (ERIC) Clearinghouse on Assessment and Evaluation. It includes the names and addresses of more than 900 commercial test publishers, as well as information on over 4,000 tests.
- Association of Test Publishers: http://www.testpublishers.org/memserv.htm
  This is a nonprofit organization whose members are providers of tests and assessment tools for educational assessment, screening for psychological disorders, professional certification and licensing, and other educational or clinical uses.
- Educational and Industrial Testing Service (EDITS): http://www.edits.net
  EDITS specializes in measures for career exploration and counseling and assessments of psychological attitudes and personality traits in children and adults that relate to school and work.
- Psychological Assessment Resources, Inc. (PARI): http://www.parinc.com
  PARI is a commercial publisher of tests and software for assessment of achievement, development, and learning outcomes; intellectual and cognitive abilities; health-related behaviors; personality and psychological problems; and neuropsychological functioning.

- Pro-Ed, Inc.: http://www.proedinc.com
  Pro-Ed, Inc. is a commercial publisher of tests in the areas of speech, language, and hearing; special education, rehabilitation, and gifted education; psychology and counseling; early childhood intervention; and occupational and physical therapy.
- Western Psychological Services: http://www.wpspublish.com
  Western Psychological Services is a commercial publisher of assessment tools in the areas of clinical and school psychology, neuropsychology, special education, family therapy, speech, language, hearing, substance abuse treatment, human resource development, and occupational therapy.

Criteria for Selecting Preestablished Instruments

Just because you find an instrument with a name that sounds like what you are measuring does not necessarily mean that you can use the instrument for your study. Selecting an instrument that is reliable, valid, and appropriate for the population you are studying is not only important but vital to the overall success of the entire study. In other words, a particular instrument may have a high degree of reliability and validity, but for a variety of reasons, it may not be appropriate for the population that the researcher is intending to study. The language used in the instrument may be at a reading level far above the group for your study. Or the test may presume knowledge or experiences that you know your group will not have. If the norm group cited by the instrument differs substantially from the group you intend to study, you should question whether the test will be valid for your study.

As part of the review of the literature, a researcher should examine past studies to see what specific instruments other researchers in similar areas have employed. In addition, the researcher would also want to look for any discussion in past studies or literature reviews that indicate that the instruments are not appropriate or accurate measures and why.

Finally, do not settle for the first measure that you find. Using key search words to search the MMY database should produce several instruments that you can inspect for possible use.

Reliability and Validity in Archival Data

One of the benefits of using archival data is the amount of time it saves. Having the data already collected speeds up a research study considerably, and for this reason, archival data are a favorite of graduate students. However, researchers should proceed with caution when using archival data. Despite their attractiveness, one barrier to archival data is that they have been collected by someone else, and therefore, the researcher cannot have any quality control in their collection.

For example, say that a researcher is investigating the impact of a building-wide behavior program. School Building A adopted a behavior modification program the previous year whereas School Building B (similar to A in all its demographics) did not implement the program. The archival data for this study are both buildings' suspension records. To establish baseline data, the researcher took three years of suspension records from both buildings and determined that both buildings averaged consistently about 300 suspensions each year. Then the researcher used records to examine the number of suspensions during the past academic year when School Building A implemented its program. In this review of the records, the researcher found that School Building A decreased the number of suspensions over the past year by 50%, whereas building B continued to have about 300 suspensions. Sounds like the behavior modification program worked, right? Not necessarily. Inaccuracies in the data from School Building A might be distorting the results. For example, did School Building A, as part of the new program it implemented, revise its criteria for suspension? Let us say that it did and that acts committed by students that were used to get them suspended now are handled by the teacher in the classroom, thus lowering the number of incidents that are reported. In other words, the new criteria simply allowed School Building A to underreport the number of suspensions. It did not mean that the new program worked to prevent them. However, because the researcher was not "on board" with the data collection and only used such data later on to perform the study, the researcher probably would not know that such a change in policy occurred. Other types of archival data are susceptible to inaccuracies such as percentage of student body who receive free or reduced-fee lunch, high-school-dropout rates, and even graduation rates, to name a few.

When working with archival data, it is important to consider possible inaccuracies that the data may contain. If possible, a researcher should validate or double-check the raw data. To do so, the researcher might conduct interviews with the individuals who originally collected the data. The purpose of these interviews would be to gather a better understanding of the methods used in collecting the data. If possible, the researcher would also want to examine the instruments used to collect the data and any information about their piloting and administration. Often such scrutiny of the original data is not possible. If the archival data have so many flaws that they jeopardize the validity of the study's results, then archival data should be avoided altogether, and another method for collecting the data should be employed.

Chapter Summary

All research studies, regardless whether they are quantitative or qualitative, require the collection of data through the use of some type of measurement tool. Preestablished instruments refer to a category of measuring tools that have been developed and piloted by usually someone other than the researcher who is doing the current study. An important feature of preestablished instruments is that they are usually standardized measures. Standardized measures include a fixed set of questions, a framework, and procedures for test administration. They also measure specific outcomes with results compared with a well-defined norm group that has been given the measure at a previous time during the instrument's development. Norm-referenced, criterion-referenced, and self-referenced tests are three types of standardized tests. In general, standardized preestablished instruments measure five broad areas: achievement, aptitude, personality, attitude or interest, and behaviors. Achievement tests measure what students have already learned in school, whereas aptitude tests are designed to measure not what a student knows but to predict what the student can do or how he or she will perform in the future. Personality tests differ from achievement and aptitude tests in that they measure self-perceptions or personal characteristics. Attitude and interest scales are also another type of preestablished measures that assess a person's attitude toward a topic or interest in a certain area. These measures typically gather self-reported information from participants. Although behavior rating scales are used to quantify observable behaviors, checklists only allow the observer to check off the items as they occur.

Archival data are data that have already been collected using standardized instruments. In educational research, these data would be housed at the school building or district level and would include data on student absenteeism, detention or suspension, standardized test scores, and the like.

There are four types of variables that can be measured quantitatively and that make up the levels or scale of measurement. These include nominal, ordinal, interval, and ratio scales. Nominal scales measure categorical variables such as whether a student receives or does not receive free or reduced-cost lunch. Ordinal scales also categorize persons or things, but in addition they place the categories into rank order from highest to lowest or vice versa to indicate who did the best or worst. High school class rank is a common example of ordinal scales. Interval scales categorize and rank order data, but interval data also assume that the distance between the scores is equal. There is also no true zero point for ordinal scales. Ratio scales are considered the type of measurement that produces the most precise data. Ratio scales include the properties of nominal, ordinal, and interval variables and also a true zero point.

Descriptive statistics are used to summarize data from preestablished and quantitative self-developed instruments. Descriptive statistics are used to depict the patterns of the data. One way to depict the overall performance of a group is to display the frequency of each score in a frequency distribution. A frequency polygon is used when working with an ordinal scale of measurement or higher. A line is used to connect the different data points. Categorical data are represented by a separate bar and referred to as a histogram. When large groups are randomly sampled and measured, the distribution often has a shape that is called a normal distribution. Normal distributions will look bell-shaped and symmetrical, with the highest point on the curve or most frequent scores clustered in the middle of the distribution and frequencies of scores decreasing as scores move away from the middle toward either end. Most standardized tests present data from a norm group that show normal distributions of scores. Skewed distributions are asymmetrical, meaning that the scores are distributed differently at the two ends of the distribution. In a negatively skewed distribution, most of the scores are high, with few scores that are low. In a positively skewed distribution, most of the scores are low, with few high scores. Bimodal distributions have two clusters of frequent scores presented in two "humps." Measures of central tendency use a single score that summarizes the typical or average performance of a group. Mode is the score in a distribution that occurs most frequently. The mean is the arithmetical average of a set of scores. The median is the score that divides a distribution exactly in half when the scores are arranged from the highest to the lowest. Another type of measure is the measure of variability, which depicts the distributions of scores for two groups. The range is one measure of variability where the highest and lowest scores in a distribution are given. Standard deviation is another, where the average distance between each of the scores in a distribution and the mean is calculated. The normal curve is used to form the basis for comparing individual scores with those of a larger group. Several types of scores are used to compare performances on educational measures, such a raw scores, percentile ranks, standard scores, stanine scores, percentages, and grade-equivalent scores. For correlational research, correlation coefficients are used to determine the direction and strength of the relationship. A correlation coefficient can fall on a range from $+1.00$ to -1.00. Coefficients that are closest to $+1.00$ or -1.00 are highlight related. Coefficients that fall near zero have no correlation. Coefficients that are positive depict a positive relationship where if one variable increases, the other variable increases, and vice versa. Coefficients that are negative show a relationship where if one variable increases, the other variable decreases. Correlations of 0.80 to 1.00 are highly related, from 0.60 to 0.79 are moderately related, and from 0.30 to 0.59 have little relationship.

Reliability and validity assist researchers in evaluating the quality of educational measures. Reliability refers to an instrument's ability to consistently produce the same results for an individual over time. Validity focuses on ensuring that what the instrument claims to measure is what it truly measures. Several types of reliability may be established for an instrument. These include test-retest reliability, equivalent-form reliability, and internal consistency. The standard error of measure is an estimate of the overall amount of error contained in an individual score. Three broad types of validity that are also established for preestablished measures are content, concurrent, predictive, and construct. When searching for preestablished measures, the MMY is one source that contains a wide variety of measurement instruments and details about their purpose, targeted populations, administration, and reliability and validity. If archival data are used, the researcher should try to ensure that they are valid by examining any template or forms used in the original collection of the data, as well as interviewing anyone who might have had a role in the initial data collection.

Key Concepts

data

archival data

standardized instrument

norm group

achievement tests

test battery

aptitude tests

personality tests

projective personality tests

attitude or interest scale

behavior rating scales and checklists

nominal, ordinal, interval, and ratio scales

descriptive statistics

frequency distribution

frequency table

frequency polygon

histogram

normal distribution

negatively skewed distribution

positively skewed distribution

bimodal distributions

mode

mean

median

normal curve

raw scores

percentile ranks

standard scores

stanine scores

percentages

reliability

validity

standard error of measurement (SEM)

stability

split-half reliability

sampling and item validity

criterion-related validity

concurrent validity

predictive validity

construct validity

convergent evidence

Discussion Questions or Activities

1. Discuss the advantages and disadvantages of using preestablished, standardized instruments. What types of educational constructs do you believe can or cannot be measured accurately through standardized measures? Discuss the reasons for your beliefs.

2. Examine the school report cards for one school or district in your state, and print out examples of descriptive statistics used. Discuss what the graphs and numbers show, and identify some additional ways that descriptive statistics might be used to display the data.

3. Examine the evidence for reliability and validity available for the standardized assessments developed or used (or both) by your state department of education. Discuss whether the evidence for reliability and validity is strong enough to justify the use of these tests as measures of student progress.

Suggested Readings

Holcomb, E. L. (1999). *Getting excited about data: How to combine people, passion, and proof.* Thousand Oaks, CA: Corwin Press.

Kohn, A. (2000). Burnt at the high stakes. *Journal of Teacher Education, 51*(4), 315–327.

Kurpius, S. E., & Stafford, M. E. (2005). *Testing and measurement: A user-friendly guide.* Thousand Oaks, CA: Sage Publications.

Popham, J. (2003). *Test better, teach better. The instructional role of assessment.* Alexandria, VA: Association for Supervision and Curriculum Development

Salkind, N. (2005). *Tests and measurement for people who (think they) hate tests and measurement.* Thousand Oaks, CA: Sage Publications.

CHAPTER FIVE

SELF-DEVELOPED MEASURES AND QUALITATIVE MEASUREMENT

Chapter Objectives

After reading this chapter, you should be able to

1. Identify two different scales used in survey research and describe the unique characteristics of each scale
2. Discuss the purpose of a pilot group in survey development and note two types of reliability that can be established for surveys using a pilot group
3. Identify and describe two types of validity that can be established for surveys using a pilot group
4. Describe the purpose of observational checklists, define interrater and intrarater reliability and describe how a researcher would establish reliability for a checklist
5. Describe three threats to validity that a researcher who is using an observational checklist should consider
6. Describe the key features of observation as a data collection tool and the varying degrees of researcher-participation in this process
7. Discuss the purpose of observational and interview protocols in qualitative research and what should be included in these protocols
8. Distinguish between structured, semistructured and nonstructured interview protocols and outline the general procedures for conducting an interview

9. Describe how documents and artifacts can be used for data collection in qualitative research

10. Discuss six alternative self-developed measures that a teacher can use in conducting action research

Self-Developed Instruments

Although all research approaches can use **self-developed instruments,** descriptive research, single-subject research, and action research are the approaches with which researchers are most likely to develop their own instruments. Self-developed instruments are measures created by the researcher for a specific setting or group of participants. Descriptive-survey researchers design and develop their own surveys to gather the perceptions of their sample participants on current educational issues. Single-subject researchers and action researchers often develop tools to record quantitative data from their observations. Action researchers also develop other instruments or use materials developed for their practice to measure student performance in either quantitative or qualitative ways. Qualitative researchers develop their own interview and observational protocols.

Researchers who use self-developed instruments have to take time during the research process to design and develop them. The point in the research process at which a researcher decides to do this depends on the type of research that is being conducted. Survey researchers develop their instruments following a thorough review of the literature in which they identify key variables and themes and then develop subquestions and survey items. On the other hand, qualitative researchers might develop an initial protocol after they have entered the research setting and have become more familiar with the study's participants. In addition, qualitative researchers would likely modify or refine their protocols as they collect and analyze their data and realign the focus of their study. Even though they develop their own instruments, survey researchers would not think of changing their instruments halfway through their study because they want participants to answer the exact same questions. Action researchers often use a mixture of quantitative and qualitative measures that are developed to fit their setting. Both action researchers and single-subject researchers typically seek measures that fit naturally into the educational setting and are quick and easy to use. In this chapter we discuss the measures used in each type of research and the criteria used to assess the quality of these measures.

Developing Scales for Use in Surveys

Descriptive-survey research has some of the most well-developed procedures for creating instruments of any research area. Much of the process of developing and refining surveys is discussed in Chapter Seven. Here we discuss the process of creating rating scales for the survey items.

Likert Scales

Developed by Rensis Likert for his doctoral thesis, the Likert scale is the most widely used scale in survey research and certainly the one that has found its way into popular culture. Many people actually use the term "Likert scale" without knowing the scale's complexities and uses. The classic use of the Likert scale was to pose questions or items to participants and have them respond using an agreement scale by selecting a number that best represented their response.

Presented in Exhibit 5.1 are some items taken from a survey of preservice teacher candidates. The purpose of this section of the survey was to document candidates' expectations of their field placement experience and the role of technology.

Notice that the Likert scale used in Exhibit 5.1 is what is referred to as a 6-point scale, meaning that there are six possible choices for participants. Depending on the purpose of the study, the researcher may decide to use a 6- or a 5-point scale. The range for a 5-point scale would be strongly disagree, disagree, slightly agree, agree, and strongly agree. Sometimes a researcher chooses to have a neutral response in the middle. In that case, the scale might look something like the one presented below.

Strongly Disagree	*Disagree*	*Neutral*	*Agree*	*Strongly Agree*
1	2	3	4	5

EXHIBIT 5.1 SAMPLE SECTION OF SELF-DEVELOPED SURVEY.

Host Teacher	SD					SA
1. My host teacher will help me find the technology that is available in my school.	1	2	3	4	5	6
2. I expect to spend some of my planning time working with my host teacher to integrate technology into the classroom.	1	2	3	4	5	6
3. I believe that I will learn a lot about integrating technology into instruction from my host teacher.	1	2	3	4	5	6
4. I expect that I will be able to provide expertise to my host teacher in integrating technology.	1	2	3	4	5	6
5. I expect that my host teacher will provide feedback to me regarding my use of technology in my lessons.	1	2	3	4	5	6

Note: 1 = strongly disagree (SD); 2 = disagree; 3 = slightly disagree; 4 = slightly agree; 5 = agree; 6 = strongly agree (SA).

Caution should be taken when including a neutral response in your scale. When the Likert scale was first developed, it did not include a neutral response because Likert did not believe that there were "neutral" people walking around and that even if you were not passionate about an issue, you would at least feel a little something one way or the other. In certain circumstances, using a neutral response is perfectly acceptable and appropriate; however, in cases where a decision may be made based on the data, it is advised not to include the neutral response. For example, if one is constructing a survey to gather teachers' attitudes about an issue in a school building, depending on the situation, many teachers may indicate "neutral" for many reasons (they may fear that their job is on the line, they may not know what is in store for them if the school goes ahead with the project, etc.). However, the administrator has to make a decision based on the information that the survey provides. If results come back with 100% of the staff neutral regarding the project, that is not going to help the administrator. If the neutral response is removed and the staff is "forced" to make a decision one way or another, data showing that 70% of staff are in "slight agreement" with the project helps shed some light on the situation and assists the administrator with the task of making a decision.

Likert scales are often called *agreement scales* because participants are asked whether they agree or disagree with the statements presented. Self-developed measures may include other types of scales in which statements are presented and participants are asked to make different types of judgments, such as the frequency of use, quality, importance, or perceived effectiveness of educational practices or persons in educational settings.

Semantic Differential Scales

Another type of rating scale is the semantic differential scale. Unlike the Likert scale, which uses sentence statements, in a semantic differential scale, participants are asked to make judgments regarding words or phrases describing persons, events, activities, or materials. The ratings are made by checking a point along a line indicating a continuum between two polar opposites. The scale is usually set up so that positive and negative responses occur at each end of the scale with equal frequency. See Exhibit 5.2 for an example of a semantic differential scale that might be used as a quick evaluation of a workshop. One advantage to using semantic differential scales is that responses can be made quickly because little reading is required. However, the information produced is superficial.

Establishing Reliability and Validity for Surveys

After a survey has been developed, it should undergo a **pilot test.** The pilot group would need to be selected and pilot participants instructed as to their re-

EXHIBIT 5.2 SEMANTIC DIFFERENTIAL SCALE.

Workshop Presenters

Knowledgeable	___	___	___	___	___	___	Not knowledgeable
	1	2	3	4	5	6	

Unresponsive	___	___	___	___	___	___	Responsive
	1	2	3	4	5	6	

Helpful	___	___	___	___	___	___	Not helpful
	1	2	3	4	5	6	

Workshop Materials

Useful	___	___	___	___	___	___	Not useful
	1	2	3	4	5	6	

Poorly organized	___	___	___	___	___	___	Well organized
	1	2	3	4	5	6	

Appropriate	___	___	___	___	___	___	Inappropriate
	1	2	3	4	5	6	

sponsibilities. It is through the use of a pilot test that the researcher is able to establish reliability and validity for the self-developed survey.

Stability or Test-Retest Reliability. As discussed in Chapter Four, stability or test-retest reliability consists simply of giving the same measure to the same group of individuals at two different points in time. In other words, a high school science teacher who responds "strongly agree" to an item asking about the use of student portfolios for assessment purposes would hopefully still respond "strongly agree" a few weeks later when filling out the same survey. As part of the piloting process, the researcher would analyze pilot participants' before and after responses to determine the degree of consistency and report such findings using a correlation coefficient.

From time to time, a researcher may find that participants lack consistency on a particular item or series of items. For example, a group of participants might answer "strongly agree" on the first survey administration but answer "strongly disagree" the second time a few weeks later. In cases such as this, the researcher will want to do some further investigating before coming to the conclusion that the item is unstable. To do so, the researcher would contact the individuals and conduct either focus group or one-on-one interviews. For example, let us say that there was inconsistency among a group of teachers regarding the item that asks about technology use in the classroom (item 3 in Exhibit 5.1). On the first round, the group of teachers indicated that they "strongly agree" that they all had positive experiences using technology in their classrooms. However, on the second delivery of the survey, this group indicated that they "strongly disagree." This would certainly constitute an inconsistency for this particular item. However, let us say that in interviewing these teachers, it is discovered that in the time between the two survey administrations, these teachers had a bad experience using technology in their classroom. For example, a computer crashed, and the teachers lost all their work, or a lesson with technology in it did not go as planned. In light of this new information, is this item still considered unstable? The answer is No. The item was perfectly stable for those in the pilot who did not have a bad experience with technology during this period, and it also consistently measured the changes in attitudes for those teachers who unfortunately did have a bad experience during that time period. Items where the researcher is unable to establish a reason for the dramatic shift in participant responses should be refined or deleted from the final survey. Most descriptive-survey researchers who are sending a survey to a sample on a "one-shot" basis typically do not go through the efforts to establish stability for the instrument. However, if the overall purpose of the study is to show a change in participants' attitudes or beliefs, it is necessary to document that the survey has test-retest reliability. By doing so, the researcher is assured that participant responses are indeed changing and that such change in attitude is not merely the result of an inconsistent instrument.

Internal Consistency for Surveys. In Chapter Four, internal consistency was discussed in relation to split-half reliability. Internal consistency can also be established for self-developed surveys, with a slightly different twist. A **reverse item** is a technique or method used by researchers to establish internal consistency by creating two items that are opposite. To be consistent, respondents must select opposite responses when answering the items. For example, if a teacher responds "strongly agree" to the item "Technology provides multiple methods in delivering instruction to all student learners," then the teacher must select "strongly disagree" on the item that appears later in the survey, "Technology does not allow for multiple methods in delivering instruction to all student learners."

Although reverse items are a useful technique, too many of them in a survey may aggravate participants and result in a low response rate. The purpose of reverse items is not to trick participants into making a mistake but to ensure that participants are consistent in their own thinking and that such consistency is being delivered in their responses. So what happens to participants whose reverse items are not consistent? Depending on the sample size and the overall purpose of the study, a researcher may decide to "junk" or remove a participant's survey from the study altogether, especially where multiple reverse items have not been scored consistently.

Developing Surveys from Established Forms. As a result of conducting a review of the literature, a survey researcher might come across a survey that has already been developed and used in a previous study. If the researcher uses the survey without making modifications, the reliability and validity information that has been established can be reported in the new study's instrument section. However, because survey research is interested in current issues, the chances of finding an already-established survey that is addressing the exact same issue from the exact same population is unlikely. Faced with this dilemma, many survey researchers find themselves borrowing both items and scales from already-developed surveys. (A scale is a set of items that are thought to measure some trait, attitude, or behavior. Educational measures often can be broken down into separate scales, each containing items that address different aspects of the construct being measured.) When modifications are made to an already-established instrument, the researcher cannot report its reliability or validity information and must reestablish reliability and validity for the survey. Although it is not uncommon for a researcher to borrow from several established instruments, it is important for the researcher to give credit where credit is due and to cite all authors whose work was adopted in creating the new survey.

Face Validity for Surveys. In addition to establishing reliability, validity also needs to be established during the piloting of a survey. Validity, the ability of an instrument to measure what it intends to measure, applies in much the same way for self-developed instruments as it does for preestablished instruments. However, as in establishing reliability, researchers using self-developed instruments will have to conduct the necessary steps to ensure that their instruments have validity. Presented below are several types of validity that were discussed earlier and how they apply to survey research. These procedures would take place during the piloting process and would occur simultaneously alongside the work to establish sound reliability for the instrument.

Although face validity is often considered a low level of validity and is not emphasized in preestablished measures, it does play an important role in survey design and development. The definition of *face validity* is that the instrument "appears to be measuring" what it intends to measure. This means that on the surface, the questions seem to fit whatever is the described purpose of the survey. Because the researcher is likely to tell participants the exact purpose of the study in descriptive survey studies, high face validity promotes trust and hopefully a better response rate as well. Face validity can be established by having pilot participants ask the following questions as they overview the survey:

- Is the title of the survey aligned with the purpose of the study? For example, if you are gathering high school science teachers' perceptions about curriculum, does the title of the survey reflect that?
- Are the directions clear, and do they accurately relate the intent for which the participants should be answering the questions? For example, if the researcher wants the participants to "reflect back on an experience," is this wordage specifically stated in the directions?
- Does the overall language and reading level of the survey reflect the ability of the group for which the survey will be given?

During the pilot, the researcher would want to make sure that any suggestions made by participants would be incorporated into the final survey to increase its face validity.

Content Validity. The purpose of establishing content validity for a survey is to ensure that the survey is measuring the breadth and depth of the issue that it is intended to measure. As discussed earlier, content validity consists of two parts: sampling validity and item validity. During the piloting process, both of these can be addressed simultaneously. Sampling validity can be established by having participants examine the survey to ensure that there are no additional sections needed to sufficiently address the issue that is under investigation. Because the pilot participants represent the sample that is being surveyed, they are much more aware of the issues of that group than perhaps the researcher, who after all is an outsider. In such cases, the pilot participants might suggest that another section be added to the survey so that the survey covers the issue more completely. Sometimes they may suggest that only additional items be added to the survey.

Where sampling validity examines the breadth of items being asked, item validity focuses on the depth of the items themselves. To ensure item validity, the researcher would also want to instruct pilot participants to review each item carefully and to determine whether the items that make up the sections of the survey in fact belong in those sections. For example, say a researcher is surveying parents about an after-school program and develops a survey, with one of the sections being a checklist of various activities that students might engage in during the program. Among the items such as "chess club" and "in-door soccer," the researcher has accidentally placed a checklist item of "school uniforms." Because school uniforms are obviously not a type of activity, this item would lower the sampling validity of the survey. In this situation, the item should be moved to a more appropriate section on the survey. If no such section exists, the item should be deleted.

In some cases, it may be more appropriate to use a panel of experts to establish content validity because members of the pilot may not have the expertise to critically examine the items. For example, if a researcher is doing a survey of middle-level math teachers regarding high-stakes testing and state math standards, it might be more beneficial to have a panel of math experts examine the survey, in addition to the pilot group.

Developing Observational Checklists

Researchers collecting *quantitative* data use observational checklists when observing participants in a natural setting. Although there are preestablished, standardized observational checklist measures, researchers using observational checklists often prefer to tailor the measure to the exact setting and participants. Researchers, therefore, will either have to adapt preestablished checklists or develop and design their own checklists to gather the kinds of data they need to answer their research questions. These checklists function as a list of criteria or items that the researcher is looking to find. The purpose of such a checklist is to provide a level of rigor to the data collection process and ensure that the data are reliable and valid.

Let us say that a researcher is studying off-task behaviors of fifth-grade students during a math lesson. She decides to observe the class during its 45-minute class period. During the class period, the researcher makes a mark whenever she sees an off-task behavior and reports observing 15 off-task behaviors in all. The measurement questions then become

- Is this number accurate?
- Would someone observing alongside the researcher reach this same number?
- What types of off-task behaviors make up the 15 off-task behaviors?

Without the use of an observational checklist, it would be difficult or impossible to answer these questions. A well-developed checklist would help to standardize the observations. Presented below are guidelines for developing an observational checklist. After reviewing these guidelines, see if you can create a checklist to assist our researcher in studying off-task behavior.

• Identify and define the behaviors to be observed. List the target behaviors separately on the checklist. These might include talking with another student, looking out the window, and the like.

• Organize the checklist so that related behaviors are grouped together. This will make it easier to record your observations.

• Decide how observations will be recorded (e.g., count of frequencies, ratings of intensity, duration of behavior). Provide a space to check off behaviors, record time length, or give a rating scale for the behavior.

• Define the time periods in which observations will occur (e.g., continuous observation for a specified time period, recording for specific time intervals each day or hour, random sampling of time periods).

• Train observers to use the observational measure, or if using it yourself, practice until you can record your observations quickly and accurately.

The researcher would use the checklist while observing the class and simply check off next to the particular behavior every time one of the students in the class performed one of those actions. Exhibit 5.3 presents an example of an observational checklist. A teacher who is conducting an action research study might use this checklist to monitor changes in a student's behavior during the time that an intervention is taking place.

To demonstrate that the newly developed observational checklist is a good measure, one would next need to gather evidence that the checklist is reliable and valid. For an observational measure, the most important type of reliability is consistency or **interrater reliability** between raters or scorers. Interrater reliability is the level of consistency or accuracy when two or more people are observing and recording data on the same observed scenario. For example, researcher A observes the math class and counts 33 off-task behaviors, whereas researcher B observes the exact same class at the exact same time and comes up with only 4 off-task behaviors. The problem with such a wide range of scores is that one cannot determine which one truly reflects what the classroom looks like. For the study to have rigor

EXHIBIT 5.3 OBSERVATIONAL CHECKLIST FOR SELF-ESTEEM.

___ Child is afraid to try new things.

___ Child seems to be hopeful about the future.

___ Child gets discouraged easily.

___ Child is self-directed and initiates activities on own.

___ Child is comfortable making eye contact with others.

___ Child thinks s/he is not important or is unattractive.

or credibility, the checklist must have an acceptable level of interrater reliability. Researchers who create an observational checklist work to establish interrater reliability *before* they go out and collect data for their study. The researcher would recruit persons to serve as observers, train them in the use of the checklist, and then have them observe several classrooms using the checklist. The results from the different observers would be compared after each session. Discrepancies between scorers would be worked out through an in-depth discussion between the scorers following analysis of the piloting scores. Following these discussions, modifications to improve the interrater reliability would be made *before* the checklist is used to collect data from the study's sample.

In some situations, it is necessary for the researcher to show that a checklist is consistent each time the same scorer uses the instrument. This type of reliability is referred to as **intrarater reliability**. To assess this type of reliability, the same rater would use the instrument to score the same set of behaviors more than once. This might be done through the use of a videotape of behaviors, or if the instrument is used to rate written materials, the rater could score the materials twice at different points in time. As in test-retest reliability, you would allow some time to pass between ratings to ensure that the rater is not simply remembering previous ratings. Intrarater reliability is measured by correlating the scores for the two different ratings.

Validity of an observational checklist involves consideration of both its content and its use. The items on an observational checklist might be examined by a group of experts in the areas addressed by the instrument to assess content validity. For example, the experts might examine the items on the observational scale of self-esteem in Exhibit 5.3 to see if these items are consistent with current theories and research on self-esteem. Do all of the items clearly indicate a child's level of self-esteem? Are there other possible interpretations of what a given behavior means? For example, could avoidance of eye contact indicate a cultural practice, such as respect for adults? The validity of a newly developed observational checklist might also be examined in research studies seeking evidence to confirm its validity. Construct validity might be examined by determining if there are correlations between scores obtained using this instrument and other measures thought to be related. The self-esteem scores might be correlated with teacher ratings of the students' confidence or peer ratings of their popularity. (After a series of such studies are published, this self-developed instrument might take on the status of a preestablished instrument!)

All observational measures are susceptible to certain problems that might undermine their validity. Most of these problems occur because the observer who is making a judgment and recording a score might distort the accuracy of what is observed.

Observer bias occurs when the observer's background, expectations, or personal perceptions influence the observation, making it inaccurate. If you are observing students asking questions in a seventh-grade science classroom, your own beliefs about the interests and abilities of males and females in science might influence what you record. You might overlook or categorize questions asked by girls differently from those asked by boys. A similar problem with accuracy in observations is **contamination**, which occurs when the observer's knowledge of the study affects his or her observations. If the observer knows that the researcher expects boys to ask higher order questions, then she or he might be more likely to notice and record this type of question for boys. A well-developed checklist should help avoid errors by clearly describing the different types of questions to be recorded. Other ways to control observer bias are by training observers in the use of the checklist before the study (or by practicing the use of it yourself). Your accuracy in recording could be checked by videotaping the observations and asking a second observer to also rate the behaviors. Contamination is often controlled by keeping observers "blind" (or in the dark) about the expected outcomes of the study.

A final problem that can occur with observational measures is known as the **halo effect**. The halo effect occurs when an initial impression influences all subsequent observations, making them less accurate. If in your first set of observations, Eager Edgar impresses you with his incisive questions and Cautious Caren only makes some simple and tentative comments, your later observations might reflect these first impressions. There might be a tendency to record more high-level questions for Edgar and fewer for Caren, even if Edgar's question asking declines and Caren's increases in sophistication.

Developing Measurement Procedures and Tools for Qualitative Studies

Qualitative measurement is used in professional qualitative studies, program evaluation, and action research. Qualitative research is characterized by flexible, naturalistic methods of data collection and does not use formal instruments to record data. Qualitative data are often gathered in the form of words, pictures, or both. The tools that are used tend to be ones that produce data that allow for rich and thick descriptions of the phenomena being studied. To be scientific and as unbiased as possible, the data collection process must be systematic and the data recorded with accuracy. Qualitative researchers use a variety of research tools, but they often prefer to use observations, conduct interviews, and conduct document analysis (e.g., data from school or public records, documents, pictures, or artifacts).

Use of Observations

Although observation is a large part of how we learn (Bandura, Grusec, & Menlove, 1966), observation as a tool of research requires systematic and careful examination of the phenomena being studied. Specifically, researchers who choose to use observation must conduct their observations in a way that results in accurate, unbiased, and richly detailed information. We casually observe people's fashions, the way they wear their hair, and how they act, but this does not constitute observation as a research tool. Observation as a research tool requires training in both what to observe and how to record the observations.

Degrees of Researcher Participation. When conducting observations, the primary goal is to gather data that are accurate and naturalistic and, to the greatest extent possible, that reflect the reality of the situation as the participants see it. This necessitates that you as the researcher become familiar with the setting and that the participants are comfortable with your presence. Before the start of the observation, you must decide to what degree you will allow yourself to be involved in the setting. There are certainly varying degrees of involvement that you can choose. According to Gold (1958), whose classification of observation is often used to describe the degree of participation of the observer, you could be one of the following:

- *Complete participant.* This means that you are a member of the group, and no one in the group is aware of the fact that you are also an observer. While this might allow a true "insider's" view, it raises ethical concerns because, in essence, you are deceiving the participants.
- *Participant as observer.* In this situation, you are an active member of the group and actively participate in the group's activities and interactions, but each member of the group knows that you are also serving a research role. In essence, a collaborative relationship is developed between the observer and the participants. Although this removes the ethical concerns presented by being a complete observer, you may compromise the natural interaction of the group.
- *Observer as participant.* Choosing to be an observer as participant removes you a bit from group membership. Although you certainly still have a connection to the group, you will not likely participate in the group's activities.
- *Complete observer.* Here you might conduct your observations from behind a one-way mirror or in a public setting. You are not a member of the group and do not participate in the group's activities.

When selecting a role as an observer, you must decide the extent to which you want your activities as a researcher to be overt or covert. This decision may influence how the participants behave, respond, and react. As a qualitative researcher, you need to recognize the influence this might have on the reality of the phenomena being investigated.

Key Features of Careful Observation. According to Goetz and LeCompte (1984) and many other qualitative researchers, careful observation should include at least the following key features:

- *An explanation of the physical setting.* This would include an overall physical description of the space. For example, in a classroom, this description would include the number of desks, the teacher's work station, the number of students, whether or not there were computers and, if so, how many, and any other unique features the researcher feels should be noted.
- *A description of the participants in the setting.* Careful explanation of the participants would include not only who is in the setting but also why they might be there and a description of their roles. In addition, any relevant demographic information should be included.
- *Individual and group activities and group interactions.* The researcher should observe the activities the participants are engaging in. In other words, what is going on in the setting? Are there rules that are being followed? Special note should be made of the particular activities that will help to answer the foreshadowed questions.
- *Participant conversation and nonverbal communication.* Because qualitative data often include direct quotes, conversations should be observed in such a way as to note not only what is being said but also how it is being said.
- *Researcher behavior.* Because the researcher is part of the setting, careful attention must be paid to the influence the observer has on the behavior of the participants. Does the researcher's presence in any way influence what is occurring in the setting?

Observational Protocols

The previous categories are still too broad to be much help in focusing one's observations. Therefore, many qualitative researchers develop an **observational protocol** specific to the topic of the study.

Protocols are generally designed to gather data that cannot be predicted in advance (e.g., conversations, observed natural behaviors, answers to open-ended questions). Even when collecting qualitative data, it is important to have a protocol that will help guide the collection of data in a systematic and focused manner.

Observational protocols may take different forms. In ethnographic or case study research, observational protocols are typically unstructured. Most include brief phrases or questions identifying the types of actions, features of the setting, or interactions to focus on in the observation. In a proposal one might include the foreshadowed questions for the study to identify categories or areas that will be observed although these may change after the researcher enters the field based on the initial observations.

Some observational protocols include a recording sheet to be used in the observation. The recording sheet may simply provide an organized space for recording the details of what happens in a particular setting. Exhibit 5.4 presents an observational protocol and recording sheet for a qualitative program evaluation of an after-school poetry club.

Conducting and Recording Observations. Conducting good observational research takes time and practice. Before beginning, you should carefully prepare for your observations by reviewing the foreshadowed questions of your study to give you a clear idea of what behaviors and activities you will be looking for: they will focus your attention. Using your observational protocol and, if appropriate, a recording sheet, keep the following in mind the following:

- *Keep your observations short.* As your skills improve, you can increase the length of time that you are observing.
- *Be alert to the behavior, conversations, and activities of the participants.* You will want to remember as much from your observations as possible. Making a mental note or jotting down actual notes will be helpful.
- *Concentrate on specifics.* Avoid being global in your observations. Look for examples of specific behaviors.

The observations or "raw data" produced by your observations will form the basis for the results and conclusions you draw in the study. As such, your recording of this information must be detailed, precise, and accurate. Most qualitative researchers write down their observations in the form of **field notes,** which are written descriptions of what the research observes in the field. To control for observer bias, qualitative researchers usually record both **descriptive field notes** and **reflective field** notes. Descriptive field notes include the following information:

- Time, date, location, and length of observations
- List of participants
- Detailed descriptions of persons, interactions, activities, and settings observed
- Verbatim conversations and direct quotes

Reflective field notes include descriptions of the observers' feelings and thoughts about what he or she is observing. These are often recorded as observer

EXHIBIT 5.4 SAMPLE OBSERVATIONAL PROTOCOL AND RECORDING SHEET.

Observational Protocol and Recording Sheet

Foreshadowed Questions:

• What types of topics are addressed in student poems?

• What types of activities do club instructors use to encourage students to write?

• How do instructors provide feedback on student poems?

• How do students in the club interact with each other and with the instructors?

Date of observation:

Time of observation:

Setting:

Participants:

Observer:

Person(s):	Comments	Actions

Observer's Reflections:

comments at the bottom of the recording sheet or as separate entries in a field notes log after the observations. Reflective field notes allow the researcher to reflect on their own feelings, values, and thoughts in order to increase their awareness of how these might be influencing their observations. Exhibit 5.5 presents an example of descriptive field notes with reflective field notes recorded as an observer comment.

Use of Interviews

Most qualitative research includes interviews. The interview might be the major data collection tool of the study (particularly when the behavior of interest cannot be easily observed) or may be used to corroborate or verify observations. An interview is basically a purposive conversation with a person or a group of persons.

Group Versus Individual Interviews. Many qualitative interviews are conducted one-on-one when the interviewer attempts to determine the participant's feelings, interpretation, or reaction to an event (often referred to as a "critical-incident interview") or a set of circumstances or life experiences (also known as "life histories"). In one-on-one interviews, the researcher lets participants express their thoughts in their own words. For example, one-on-one interviews might be conducted with students who lived through the terrorist attacks on September 11, 2001, to capture their individual perspectives. In this same situation, the students could be interviewed as a group, also known as a **focus group interview.** With focus group interviews, the researcher is able to collect data from multiple participants and also to observe and record the interactions and group dynamics that unfold.

Interview Protocols

An important component of conducting a good interview is the construction of the **interview protocol.** An interview protocol should include a brief script for explaining the purpose of the study to the interviewee, places to record the date and background information on the interviewee, and the preliminary questions to be used in the interview. Because the procedures for conducting qualitative interviews are flexible, the questions serve as a starting point. A good interviewer will use the questions to begin the discussion and will then ask additional questions based on the person's responses. The actual interview may look more like a conversation than an interview with set questions and responses. Box 5.1 presents sample questions for students and teachers from the study of playtime by Perkins, Ayala, Fine, and Erwin (n.d., pp. 17–18).

EXHIBIT 5.5 SAMPLE FIELD NOTES.

Setting: 9:00 AM; XXX Preschool; City, State, 2-hour observation conducted by XXX.

Participants: primary focus 4-year-old white male (Max) and 50-year-old lead teacher (Ms. Smith)

Activities Observed: entrance into school, opening activity, structured play time, and playground activities

Observations:

Max entered room at 8:50 AM accompanied by his mom.

After brief goodbye, mom leaves and Max begins to play with toys set out by Ms. Smith.

Ms. Smith welcomes Max. "Hi Max."

Max responds without looking up, "Hi."

Ms. Smith calls all students to opening activity.

Max ignores instruction.

Ms. Smith instructs Max to join activity.

Max joins, after several reminders by Ms. Smith.

Opening song.

All students participate, except for Max. He sits quietly.

Students dismissed to interest center.

Max goes to blocks.

Other children are playing.

Max tries to join and one child says "We don't want you to play. You will just mess things up."

Max growls and continues to try to gain entry into the game.

One child says, "OKAY, you can play but don't knock down our building."

Max cooperates, but sings to himself and does not interact with the children.

Children struggle for the blocks.

Max growls and becomes angry.

Max knocks down the blocks and screams at the children.

They yell back and run to the teacher.

Teacher disciplines Max and puts him into a time-out.

Max growls.

OC: Max clearly has difficulty entering group activity. Even when he does there is almost no interaction with classmates. He does not verbalize his needs, but simply growls indicating his anger and frustration with the situation.

Box 5.1 Sample Interview Questions from Playtime Study

Student Interview Questions

1. Tell me about your science activity today.
2. What would you like to learn more about?
3. Why is it important to know (activity)?
4. What did you learn today that you didn't know already?
5. What observations did you make?
6. What did you enjoy most about the science lesson?
7. Did you learn any new science words today? What were they?
8. If you were teaching a class about this activity, what would you tell the kids?
9. What would you like to tell the people who are running the science program about what did not work, what was hard for you, or what you didn't like (about the activity)?

Teacher Interview Questions

1. What would you say is the level of (name of student)'s engagement in his/her work?
   Can you give an example?
2. How do you accommodate (student)'s individual learning needs?
   What kind of support do you typically provide?
3. What kind of questions does (student) ask you about his/her work?
   Is he/she comfortable asking for help?
   How frequent are his/her questions?
   When does he/she ask questions?
4. Can you describe how (student) learns?
   Can you give an anecdote that illustrates how?
   Does (student) share his/her work with other students?
5. Does (student) observe and learn from what others are doing?
   Can you give an example?
6. Can you give examples of how (student) displays knowledge?
   How does (student) let you know that he/she has understood the lesson?
   What other ways do you know (student) has learned the material?
7. What are (student)'s experiences in science?

Types of Interview Questions. Once you have decided to conduct an interview, you must decide the amount of structure you want in the interview. That is, will you conduct a structured, semistructured, or nonstructured interview? **Structured interview** is one in which the researcher comes to the interview with a set of questions, does not deviate from those questions, and asks the same questions of all the participants. In a **semistructured interview** researchers usually prepare a list of the questions to be asked but allow themselves the opportunity to probe beyond the protocol. **Nonstructured interviews** are more conversation-like and allow for the greatest flexibility. The researchers may simply jot down a list of topics that they want to cover in the interview. Generally, in qualitative research, the researcher will conduct a semistructured or nonstructured interview.

Conducting a Good Interview. As with observational research, conducting interview research requires certain skills and practice with those skills. Often, one of the most critical steps in the process of conducting an interview is determining the right person or people to interview. You will likely need to spend some time in the field observing the group you plan to study to determine which participants can contribute the most to your study.

As noted previously, an important component of conducting a good interview is the construction and use of the interview protocol. Even when collecting semistructured interviews, it is important to have a protocol that will help guide the collection of data in a systematic and focused manner. Box 5.2 provides an example of the questions from an interview protocol. This protocol was developed by Spaulding and Lodico (2004) to study community interest in a nontuition-based alternative school. Imagine the impossible task of trying to collect interview data from thirty community members without such a protocol. How would you remember all the questions? How could you be sure that you asked each person the same question in the same way? Varying a question by changing a few words can sometimes dramatically shift the intent of the question. Notice how the protocol helps to ensure a certain degree of standardization during the data collection process. In qualitative research, the researcher might also ask other questions during the interview to probe unexpected issues that emerge.

Box 5.2 Sample Interview Protocol for Feasibility Study

Community Member Questions

1. If you were to describe your community to someone, how would you describe it?
2. How has the community you just described changed over time? Probe: How has it changed?
     Demographically?
     Economically?
     Religious affiliations?
     School districts or school buildings?

3. Describe the relationship between your community and your local school district or building.
   Strengths
   Barriers
   Areas in need of improvement
   Relationship with parents and parental involvement
4. What kind of response from the community do you think an alternative middle school that is nontuition-based would have? (Describe the program model.)
5. Do you believe an alternative school such as this would serve the community in areas where the public school currently does not? Please explain.

After creating the protocol, you are ready to select and interview participants. However, it is important to note here that when you conduct an interview, there are certain general procedures you should follow.

• *Begin the interview by reintroducing yourself.* Because you are doing qualitative research, you will likely have had some contact with the participant before the interviews. You may also want to introduce the general topic that you will be discussing.

• *Remind the participant of the confidentiality of his or her responses.* At this stage, the participant or guardian will have been told about confidentiality issues and will have agreed to participate in the study. However, it is important to review that information at the beginning of the actual interview.

• *Obtain general descriptive information.* This type of descriptive information could include information about the participant or the issue or phenomenon being studied.

• *Strive for neutrality.* To maximize what participants tell you, it is particularly important that you are a good listener and nonjudgmental in your reactions. Be sensitive, and never act shocked or upset by what you hear. Being judgmental is likely to limit interaction and may cause the participant to question his or her level of trust in you. However, you must recognize that because you are conducting a qualitative interview, your values and personal biases, as well as those of the respondents, are a factor related to the kind of information you gather. As such, anticipate and document these to the best of your ability and consider the possible influence these might have on the data collected.

• *Use effective probes.* If you are conducting a semistructured or nonstructured interview, you will want to follow up on comments made by the participants with **probes.** A probe is a follow-up question that is asked to get clarification about a response. This will help the interviewer get more detailed information and give the respondent a chance to clarify responses. For example, say that you are interviewing a child like Max (discussed in Exhibit 5.5), who has difficulty interacting with his peers. You might ask him the following question: "Tell me some of the things that happened to you in school today." If he responds by simply telling you of an activity he enjoyed and you are trying to solicit some conversation about his interaction with his peers, you might use a probe like "Was there anything that happened today that did not make you happy?" Probes are not questions that you can prepare before the interview because they depend on what the respondent says in answer to your questions. It is important to use probes to gather additional information while recognizing when the respondent does not want to go any further with his or her disclosure. In other words, know when to stop probing!

• *Record the interview data.* There are many ways to record the information given by respondents during an interview. Many qualitative researchers prefer to tape record their conversations to preserve the integrity of the data. This is particularly important because many qualitative studies include verbatim responses as part of the data analysis. In addition, some researchers take field notes or jot down some key responses. If you choose to do the latter, be sure to fill in additional information immediately after the interview.

Use of Documents and Artifacts

Documents and artifacts are another form of qualitative data collection tool. These may include documents or objects that existed before the start of the study or those documents, such as journals, created after the study has begun as requested by the researcher. Documents and artifacts produced before the study by the participants generally include things like public records, personal writings, or instructional materials.

The decision to use documents, artifacts, or both is driven by the research questions you have asked. Again, turning our attention back to Max, say that you are conducting a case study of Max to determine the type of peer interactions he has with his classmates. What possible documents might you want to explore? First, there might be some school records of his attendance or any disciplinary action taken by the school director. Furthermore, you might want to ask Ms. Smith, Max's preschool teacher, whether she has kept a log or diary of the behavior of the children. The records and diary could provide you with further insight into Max and his relationship with his peers. In addition, if a schematic drawing of the classroom is available, you might investigate where Max generally prefers to play. Is it in a solitary play area or one where there is the possibility of group interaction?

Assuming that Ms. Smith did not keep a diary or that the director of the preschool does not keep a disciplinary log, as the researcher, you could ask Max's mother to keep a diary of Max's responses to a set of questions asked of him after school. In this case, the diary would be a document created during, and as part of, the study.

Developing Measurement Tools for Action Research

Action researchers develop and use a wide variety of quantitative and qualitative methods to collect data. All of these methods have as their goal making data collection more systematic. However, because of the intense demands of taking on two roles, a researcher and practitioner, methods of data collection in action research must be simple and must fit into the normal processes of the school or classroom. Most action researchers will not follow the complex procedures involved in formally establishing reliability and validity, although we advise students to consider how they might demonstrate consistency and accuracy in their quantitative measures. Instead, action researchers typically collect data using several brief measures (rating scales, observational checklists, interviews). The data from these different measures are then compared for consistency and accuracy. Below we discuss some of the measures found most frequently in action research studies.

Checklists and Rating Scales

Action researchers frequently use checklists and rating scales as part of their teaching and their research. Teachers might design a checklist or rating scale for the strategies or skills that they hope to see in their students' writing and record information on the skills that they see along with the dates or assignments on which the skills were shown. Exhibit 5.6 presents part of a checklist used at one school to record writing strategies of students.

Checklists might also be designed for students to record their own skills and activities. For example, Exhibit 5.7 displays a checklist that students might use to report on a cooperative learning activity. Students might be asked to report individually on their experiences, or the group might report on all of its members using the checklist

Simple rating scales might be designed to assess student reactions to assignments. For young children, these rating scales might even use nonverbal responses such as the one in Figure 5.1.

Checklists for action research might also be open-ended, with categories identified and space for recording information about student strengths and weaknesses.

Grading Rubrics

As teachers, many of you may be familiar with **grading rubrics.** Rubrics are another type of framework for providing standardization to an observational process. In the case of rubrics, the data that are being collected are often qualitative in nature (e.g., portfolios, papers, drawings, projects), but a quantitative judgment

EXHIBIT 5.6 RATING SCALE FOR ENGLISH OR LITERACY SKILLS.

Raider Open Door Academy English/Literacy Skills Checklist Grades 5 – 8

Grade Level	Writing Competencies	Introduced 0	Progressing 1	Proficient 2	Mastery 3
5,6,7,8	Write to reflect personal ideas				
7,8	Write to reflect multicultural ideas				
7,8	Write to reflect universal ideas				
5,6	Construct simple outlines				
7,8	Use story clusters				
7,8	Use webs				
5,6,7,8	Choose appropriate prewriting strategies				
5,6,7,8	Apply appropriate prewriting strategies				
5,6,7,8	Develop a first draft that focuses on a central idea				
5,6,7,8	Revise writing based on student-teacher collaboration				
5,6,7,8	Edit writing using resources to correct spelling, punctuation, grammar, and usage				
5,6,7,8	Write with developmentally appropriate sentence structure (parts of speech, fragments, run-ons, etc.)				
5,6,7,8	Use a dictionary				
5,6,7,8	Use a thesaurus				
5,6	Write complete simple sentences				
5,6	Write complete compound sentences				
5,6	Write complete complex sentences				

Source: Adapted from Raider Open Door Academy Web site. Retrieved May 12, 2005, from http://nettleton.crsc.k12.ar.us/~ncovey/Literacy%20Skills%20Checklist.htm.

EXHIBIT 5.7 CHECKLIST FOR COOPERATIVE LEARNING ACTIVITY.

Name	Listened to others	Used quiet voice	Cooperated with others	Followed directions	Contributed ideas	Reached consensus

Source: Adapted from On-Line Learning Center (2004). Retrieved May 12, 2005, from http://olc.spsd. sk.ca/DE/PD/instr/strats/coop/lesson.pdf.

FIGURE 5.1 SIMPLE RATING SCALE FOR ACTION RESEARCH STUDY.

How did you feel about the book assignment?

needs to be made regarding the data. This may be a numerical rating or letter grade. The rubric is essentially a set of goals or standardized criteria that are listed along with the various levels of attainment the student or portfolio might achieve: for example, high, medium, or low or achieved, developing, and beginning. Presented in Exhibit 5.8 is an example of a rubric that a faculty member might use to assess a student's final portfolio.

In this case, let us say that the faculty member graded the portfolio using the rubric and gave it a rating of outstanding. Notice that the rubric includes an explanation of the criteria used to obtain the rating. If the instructor was to grade the exact same portfolio again using the rubric a week later and obtain the same rating or close to the same rating a second time, the consistency in obtaining the same score time after time would show that intrarater reliability is present. Keep in mind that an instructor would not keep scoring portfolios over and over again after determining that intrarater reliability existed. If an instructor has not established intrarater reliability for an instrument, the researcher would want to make sure that such reliability has been established before collecting any data. To do this, the researcher would select a random sample of portfolios and score them using the rubric. Then, after some time has passed, the researcher would read and

EXHIBIT 5.8 RUBRIC FOR GRADING A PORTFOLIO.

Evaluation	Criteria	Comments
Outstanding	Evidence of depth and breadth of content is clear.	
	Activities demonstrate confidence and security in knowledge of subject matter.	
	Integration of content knowledge across disciplines is evident.	
	Activities reflect high degree of academic rigor as appropriate to grade or developmental level(s).	
	Content is connected in meaningful ways to student's life experiences.	
	Originality and creativity in assimilation of content are displayed.	
	Content (contents, skills, process, and generalizations) is clearly articulated and meaningful.	
	Knowledge of NYSED Learning Standards is evident.	
	The ability to teach content from multiple perspectives is clear.	
Acceptable	Evidence of content and knowledge of subject are evi-ent but depth and breadth may need further research.	
	Relationships of content tied to other disciplines are logical and adequately communicated.	
	Areas beyond the domain of individual content mastery, clear evidence of processes, and procedures for strengthening mastery are indicated.	
	Knowledge of NYSED Learning Standards is evident.	
	Attempts to include multiple perspectives are evident.	
Needs revisions	Evidence of mastery exists, but it is presented in an unclear manner.	
	Unclear relationship of content mastery to activities and assessment measures is evident.	
	Weak areas of content mastery have been identified, and evidence is provided that these are being addressed.	

EXHIBIT 5.8 RUBRIC FOR GRADING A PORTFOLIO, Cont'd.

Evaluation	Criteria	Comments
	Some facts/content are clearly indicated, but confusion or lack of clarity is evident as activities progress to higher levels of thinking.	
	No evidence there is awareness of NYSED Learning Standards.	
	Content is consistently presented from a single perspective.	
Unacceptable	Weakness in content mastery is evident.	
	Lack of clearly specified learning concepts is evident.	
	Facts or concepts are inappropriate or inaccurate.	
	No evidence is seen of awareness of NYSED Learning Standards.	

Note: NYSED = New York State Education Department. The Learning Standards are state standards or benchmarks for student learning.

score the same portfolios again and compare the two separate scoring for each proposal to determine consistency.

Along with reliability, validity for the rubric should also be established to ensure that what the rubric purports to measure is truly what it is measuring. For example, if the research proposal is made up of eight different sections or components, and the rubric is assessing only five of these, then the rubric's sampling validity may be an issue. To address this, the researcher would include the three outstanding sections. For item validity, the researcher would examine the eight sections of the rubric individually to ensure that each section was specifically measuring what it intended to measure. For example, let us say that the fifth component of the rubric assessed the proposal's sampling section. To establish item validity, the researcher would want to carefully examine how the rubric discriminated between those proposals for which the section scored at the highest level and those that scored at the medium and lower levels for that section. In examination of this, the researcher would also want to ensure that the criteria used to judge a section as exemplary are all criteria that relate to the sampling section and not another section of the proposal, such as procedure or instrument. In some cases, the researcher might use a panel of experts in the content area to examine or validate each section of the rubric to ensure that its criteria are truly those that the experts believe the work should be judged against. As in the example above, a panel of faculty who teach educational researchers would be appropriate to review such a rubric.

Journals

Teachers, researchers, or participants often use journals to record thoughts, feelings, and ideas about the research activities. Journals may be structured by presenting questions for participants to address, or participants may be allowed to enter any thoughts or feelings that they like. Teachers often use journals to reflect on their feelings, perceptions, and interpretations of what they see happening in their classrooms. Journals might also include drawings or diagrams as well as written comments. Some researchers use journals to record notes from their observations. Journals may be actual notebooks or recorded as computer files.

Records and Documents

Educational settings are deluged in paper and computer files! As part of this paper and electronic onslaught, records and documents can reveal much about the inner workings of a school. Minutes of meetings, report cards, attendance records, discipline records, teachers' lesson plans, letters from parents, and written evaluations of teachers are all part of the massive amounts of data available in records and documents. As noted in Chapter Four, much of this archival data is also used by professional researchers. Action researchers are likely to utilize the records and documents produced within their immediate settings. As such, records and documents can be a valuable way to corroborate information from other sources. If a teacher reports in observational notes that student motivation increased as a result of a new instructional strategy, attendance records could be used to back up those claims.

Maps, Photographs, and Artifacts

Maps depicting the layout of classrooms and schools are useful ways to communicate aspects of an action research setting that are hard to capture in words. A map can show at a glance how a classroom is laid out to facilitate discussion or to indicate how certain groups are isolated within a school. Maps may also assist a practitioner in thinking about the interactions, traffic flow, or organization of resources in a school or classroom and might help to visualize alternative arrangements. In addition, maps convey a lot about the context of a classroom, which is important information in this largely qualitative type of research.

Photographs are another type of visual data that can capture rich detail about the people, activities, and context of an educational setting. Researchers might take photographs themselves or might ask participants to take photos using disposable cameras. This provides a useful window into the participants' experiences and perspectives and enables the researcher to share the products of the research—that is, the photos—with collaborating participants. Videotapes and audiotapes are more obtrusive and run the risk of changing participants' behaviors as students "mug for the camera." However, the advantage of videotapes and audiotapes is that they allow the researcher to record actions and interactions more fully and to revisit the events at a later time. This is a major advantage when the practitioner is trying to juggle the roles of researcher and practitioner. In addition, with the current emphasis on outcome-based performance assessment, videotapes and audiotapes allow the researcher-practitioner to document student knowledge, skills, interests, and motivation. For example, Figure 5.2 depicts two youth and an instructor (K.H.V.) admiring a robot constructed by the youth in a technology-based summer camp.

Notice how even in the still photograph, you can see the youth's interest and engagement and the complexity of their mutual creation. Photographs like this allow both the youth and the instructor to reflect on what they have learned.

Schools and classrooms are also full of "stuff" that researchers call **artifacts.** Artifacts are objects used in the process of teaching and learning or products that result from the process of teaching and learning. Artifacts in educational settings might include desks, sample lesson plans, portfolios, textbooks, bulletin boards, a laser pointer, a board used for paddling students, manipulatives, athletic equipment, or anything else found or produced in schools. Artifacts are often examined and described in writing as part of one's observations. Some artifacts might be more systematically analyzed to see if they convey underlying assumptions about the nature of education. For example, textbooks might be examined to see how they portray gender roles, age groups, or ethnic groups. The types of notices posted on bulletin boards might be examined to reveal which groups and events receive the most promotion at a school.

Evaluating the Quality of Measures Used in Action Research

Like archival data, the measures used in action research are not typically subjected to the same level of scrutiny as preestablished measures regarding reliability and validity. However, one can follow the same general principles to provide evidence that the measures are valid and reliable. Grading rubrics provide a way of supporting

FIGURE 5.2 EXAMPLE OF A PHOTOGRAPH
USED IN ACTION RESEARCH STUDY.

the reliability of practitioner-made measures. Content of assignments and tests can also be examined by other teachers or related to a state's learning standards as evidence of validity. In addition, the repeated use of practitioner-made measures and their refinement over time to fit a particular school or classroom provide evidence to support the reliability and validity of measures used in action research.

Videotaping and audiotaping are tools that can also be helpful in establishing reliability for action research measures. If a rubric or observational checklist is being used to gather data from a classroom activity, the situation can be also videotaped. The recordings then can viewed and scored by multiple people at a later date. The data from both the checklist and the videotape can then be compared. Videotaping can also be valuable in training members of a research team who will collect data. Such training is necessary for consistency to be maintained across scorers.

Chapter Summary

In most cases, researchers conducting survey, single-subject, and action research use self-developed instruments to gather data. Survey researchers have the option of using several different methods or scales to collect data from participants. The Likert scale is the most common scale used in survey research. This scale provides a statement and asks participants to respond to a scale composed of a series of quantified responses (e.g., 1 for strongly disagree to 6 for strongly agree). Semantic scales are similar to Likert scales, but for these scales, participants must judge words or phrases describing persons, events, activities, or materials, and these are rated by checking a point along a line that separates two polar opposites (e.g., good and evil).

Like preestablished instruments, reliability and validity must be established for self-developed instruments. Reliability and validity for a survey is established through the use of a pilot test. A pilot test is a "dress rehearsal" when the researcher administers the survey to a representative group from the sample called the pilot group. By administering the survey to the pilot group at two different points in time, stability or test-retest reliability can be established for the survey. Reverse items embedded within the survey will help to establish internal consistency. Reverse items are two items on the survey that, for the participants' responses to be consistent, they must be opposite on these items. Face validity for a survey can also be established by having the pilot group examine the survey for an appropriate title, clear directions, and overall language and reading level. Content validity is established by having pilot group members examine the survey for both sampling and item validity. Sampling validity would be established by having participants examine all the items on the survey to ensure that all the issues that make up the topic are touched on. Item validity is established by making sure that similar items are grouped together. In some cases, a panel of experts other than members from the pilot group needs to be used.

Observational checklists are another type of self-developed instrument that collect quantitative data from observations of participants in natural settings. Checklists function as a list of criteria that the researcher is looking to find. Checklists add to the reliability and validity of the data-collecting process by helping to standardize the observations. Training of multiple observers is also required when using checklists and will increase the consistency or interrater reliability between two raters or intrarater reliability when a judge is rating the same observation (e.g., a teacher's videotaped lesson) or the same materials two or more times. Researchers should be aware of three main threats to validity when using an observational checklist. One is observer bias, which is when the observer's background or perceptions influence the situation. Contamination is another threat and occurs when the observer's knowledge of the study affects his or her observations. The last is called the halo effect, which occurs when the participants that a researcher is observing act in a certain way (usually better than usual), thus distorting the observational data being collected.

Observation is one method used to collect qualitative data. There are several approaches used to collect data through observation: complete participant, participant as observer, observer as participant, and the complete observer. Qualitative researchers are careful to note the characteristics of both the physical setting in which the observation is taking place and the individuals being observed. Interviews are another key method for data collection in qualitative research. Interviews can be conducted in small groups or individually with participants and the researcher. Group interviews are also referred to as focus groups in which the researcher has an opportunity to collect data from multiple participants and to record the interactions and group dynamics as they unfold. A good interviewer should start out by reintroducing himself or herself, restating the purpose of the study, and reminding the participant about confidentiality of responses. Next, general demographic information should be obtained from the participant, and the interviewer should use protocol questions as a starting point and probes to gather more in-depth responses from participants where needed. Documents and other artifacts can also be used as sources for qualitative data.

Action researchers also develop their own instruments. These tools and procedures for their administration are usually less rigorous than most qualitative and quantitative methods used in applied research. Teachers hoping to measure a change in students' skills and competencies frequently use both checklists and rating scales. Checklists might also be designed for students to measure the development of their own skills. Grading rubrics are a common type of framework used by teachers and students to document and measure various aspects of learning. Reliability and validity can also be established for rubrics. Journals, maps, photographs, and artifacts are other alternative forms for collecting data that can be created by students and used to measure outcomes and growth.

Interview protocols are a series of open-ended questions that serve as a framework when conducting an interview. Because most qualitative interviews are typically unstructured, a protocol may serve as a place from which to start the interview. When completed, the actual interview should look more like a conversation than an interview with set questions and responses.

Key Concepts

self-developed instruments

pilot test

reverse item

interrater reliability

intrarater reliability

observer bias

contamination

halo effect

observational protocol

focus group interview

interview protocol

probes

structured interview

semistructured interview

nonstructured interviews

grading rubrics

artifacts

Discussion Questions or Activities

1. A researcher has developed the following research questions: When and how often do teachers infuse technology into the curriculum, and in what ways is technology used? Discuss which of the following techniques would be most useful and why: Likert scale, semantic differential, checklist, rating scale, or open-ended questions. Which would be least useful and why?
2. Discuss how an instrument can be reliable but not valid and why a valid instrument is always reliable.
3. In action research, the researcher and the practitioner assume two roles. Discuss ways to ensure that neither role will be compromised.

Suggested Readings

Denzin, N. K., & Lincoln, Y. S. (2005). *The Sage handbook of qualitative research*. Thousand Oaks, CA: Sage Publications.

DeVellis, R. F. (2003). *Scale development: Theory and applications* (2nd ed.). Thousand Oaks, CA: Sage Publications.

Groves, R. M., Fowler, F. J., Jr., Couper, M. P., Lepkowski, J. M., Singer, E., & Tourangeau, R. (2004). *Survey methodology.* San Francisco: Jossey-Bass.

Krueger, R. A., & Casey, M.A. (2000). *Focus groups: A practical guide for applied research.* Thousand Oaks, CA: Sage Publications.

Seidman, I. (1998). *Interviewing as qualitative research: A guide for researchers in education and the social sciences.* New York: Teachers College Press.

CHAPTER SIX

WORKING WITH RESEARCH PARTICIPANTS

Sampling and Ethics

Chapter Objectives

After reading this chapter, you should be able to

1. Explain purposeful sampling and why it is used in qualitative research
2. Define key informants and why their selection is crucial to qualitative research
3. Know how the type of purposeful sampling can vary depending on the needs of the study
4. Explain the critical features of random sampling, the types of random sampling, and why randomization is important in quantitative research
5. Explain nonrandom sampling techniques and their limitations
6. Understand issues related to sample size and response rate
7. Know the function of an institutional review board committee and what they generally look for in a proposal to conduct research
8. Understand, compare, and contrast the ethical issues involved in qualitative and quantitative research

Selecting Participants

Whichever type of research you decide to conduct, an important consideration involves the selection of the participants for your study. Participants (the politically incorrect term is subjects) are those individuals you will use in your study. They are the adults or children who will receive your treatment, take your surveys, or be under your close observation. The technique you use to select your participants is based on the kind of research you choose to conduct.

Sampling in Qualitative Research

Qualitative researchers select their participants based on their characteristics and knowledge as they relate to the research questions being investigated. As you already know, the researchers' primary concern is to explore individuals in their natural context, and they have little interest in generalizing the results beyond the participants in the study. The sampling procedure most often used in qualitative research is **purposeful sampling.** According to Patton (1990), "The logic and power of purposeful sampling lies in selecting information-rich cases for study in depth. Information-rich cases are those from which one can learn a great deal about issues of central importance to the purpose of the research" (p. 169). So, purposeful sampling is a procedure where the researcher identifies **key informants**: persons who have some specific knowledge about the topic being investigated. For example, let us say that you are interested in discovering how an inner-city after-school program influences the lives of a group of youth of color. To get the insider's perspective, you would select a group of participants who had participated in the particular after-school program under study and who have in-depth knowledge of the program. Qualitative researchers have identified many different types of purposeful sampling procedures. In fact, Miles and Huberman (1994) identify 17 variations, and Patton (1990) identifies 15 strategies for purposeful sampling. Although all of these strategies are useful, Table 6.1 identifies the ones we believe to be most useful to beginning researchers.

If your study is a qualitative one, you will want to carefully consider the types of purposeful sampling discussed and which one will best answer your research questions.

Sampling in Quantitative Research

Unlike their qualitative counterparts, quantitative researchers are interested in generalizing from their group of participants, the *sample,* to the larger **population** from which the sample was drawn. Various decisions regarding the participants must be made by the researcher in order to maximize the generalizability of the study.

A population is the wider group of individuals about which the researcher wants to make statements. Fifth-grade teachers in the United States, high school

TABLE 6.1 SUMMARY OF PURPOSEFUL SAMPLING TECHNIQUES.

Type of Purposeful Sampling	Explanation	Example
Convenience sampling	Least desirable sampling; samples those who are convenient	Students from a graduate class in educational research would be used by the professor as participants
Critical case sampling	Samples those who can "make a point dramatically" (Patton, 1990, p. 174)	Individuals who have had a loved one die in the Iraq War will represent the antiwar position
Extreme case sampling	Individuals selected who represent the extremes	Participants who have the highest number of absences and those who have the lowest will be used for the study
Homogeneous sampling	Individuals with only similar attributes are used in the sample	Participants will be children who have attended preschool and come from similar socioeconomic backgrounds
Intensity sampling	Samples individuals with the strongest feelings about something	Participants who are highly critical of the problems associated with NCLB will be included in the sample
Maximum variation sampling	Sample includes individuals with different views on the issue being studied or who represent the widest possible range of the characteristics being studied	Participants who hold opinions ranging from pro-stem cell research to anti-stem cell research will be used in the study
Purposeful random sampling	One of the other purposeful sampling procedures is used, followed by a randomization procedure	Use intensity sampling to identify persons who are anti-NCLB. Then a random sample of 15% will be selected from this group
Snowball or network sampling	Participants who possess certain characteristics are selected and asked to refer others with similar characteristics	Teachers who infuse technology in the classroom will be asked to nominate colleagues who do the same; these colleagues will be included in the study
Typical case sampling	Individuals selected because they represent the norm and are in no way atypical	Teenage participants who enjoy music will be included in the study

TABLE 6.1 SUMMARY OF PURPOSEFUL SAMPLING TECHNIQUES, Cont'd.

Type of Purposeful Sampling	Explanation	Example
Theory-based sampling	Participants are selected in an ongoing way, e.g., the researcher identifies participants, analyzes data, and then decides who to collect data from next as the theoretical framework emerges	Sufficient preoperational children are selected to test Piaget's theory; researcher next selects formal operational thinkers to test other parts of the theory

Note: NCLB = No Child Left Behind Act.

principals on the East Coast, or parents who have children in day care in Chicago are all examples of populations. Let us say that a researcher was interested in conducting a survey study. Ideally, the survey researcher would want to send surveys to every member or individual within these populations. Although these large populations are referred to as **ideal populations,** sampling every person in these populations is not realistic or doable. Time, money, and other resources such as staffing typically make it impossible for the average survey researcher to reach all members of an ideal population. Therefore, the researcher has to forgo these grand expectations and select a smaller or **realistic population.** Presented below are samples of ideal populations, followed by those of realistic populations.

- Ideal population: Fifth-grade teachers in the United States
  Realistic population: Fifth-grade teachers in New York City
- Ideal population: High-school principals on the East Coast
  Realistic population: High school principals in Pennsylvania
- Ideal population: Parents who have children in day care in Chicago
  Realistic population: Parents who have children in day care in three neighborhoods on the west side of Chicago.

In some situations, even these realistic populations may not be so realistic. For example, surveying all the fifth-grade teachers in New York City or high school principals in Pennsylvania might exceed the study's resources. In addition, the researcher must be able to obtain a complete list of persons in the realistic population. Some researchers refer to this as the **sampling frame.** For teachers, administrators, and school districts, researchers can consult their state education department and state educational organizations to obtain these lists. For other populations, local, state, and national organizations may help identify possible participants. For some studies, such lists do not exist. For example, a college counseling center might want to identify participants for a study of students who are depressed but have not previously sought services. In this case, they might run an advertisement in the student newspaper asking for participants for their study.

After you have identified a list of possible participants, the next step is to select a **sample.** A sample is a smaller group selected from a larger population (in this case, a realistic population) that is representative of the larger population. Samples allow researchers to work with a smaller, more manageable subgroup of the realistic population.

Types of Random Sampling

The most important aspect of sampling is that the sample must represent the larger population from which it is drawn. **Random sampling** is a technique or tool that produces essentially a miniversion of the initial population. Random sampling is conducted in such a way that every person in the population has an equal and independent chance of being selected. This means that when a person is selected, it does not affect the chances of anyone else being selected. Take, for example, a technique often used in grade school spelling lessons. Remember your elementary teacher asking everyone in your class to form a line and to count off by ones and twos to establish teams of spellers? Is this an example of random sampling? No, the moment you got in line with your classmates and the teacher said, "Okay, count off by ones and twos," your group membership was decided. If your best friend, immediately to your left, was a one, then you had to be a two—and there was no chance that the two of you would be on the same spelling team. This scenario violates the requirement that the selection of one person cannot have an effect on whether another person is chosen or not.

Simple Random Sampling. Simple random sampling involves the random selection of individuals from the realistic population as a whole. First, the researcher must obtain a complete list of names for all individuals who make up the realistic population. To select a simple random sample, each person on the list of the realistic population is assigned a number. For example, if the list contains the names of 20 individuals, then the number 01 is assigned to the first person on the list, and number 02 to the second person on the list, and so on, until all 20 people on the list have been assigned a number. Next, a random sampling table (usually generated by computer) is used, similar to the one in the third column in Table 6.2.

Random number tables present clusters of number strings that have been randomly generated. To use the table, simply begin anywhere you want and select

TABLE 6.2 SIMPLE RANDOM SELECTION.

	Possible Participants	Random Numbers
01	Steve	22
02	Tonya	05
03	Ramone	18
04	Juan	04
05	Derrick	07
06	Tony	24
07	Liz	16
08	Jean	14
09	Dean	48
10	Margie	41
11	Kate	17
12	Maria	12
13	Ismael	12
14	Jim	10
15	Donna	19
16	Heta	45
17	Aviva	27
18	Richard	32
19	Ron	08
20	Travis	18

a number. If number 05 is selected, person 05, Derrick, is then selected for your sample. At this point, you can move up or down or in any direction on the table that you wish to select your next number because, after all, the table is random. For example, if you move down the column of random numbers, the next number is 18, so Richard would be added to the sample. If a number is selected that is not on your list of individuals in the population (such as 48 in our example), simply move to the next line of the random numbers. Continue this process until you have your entire sample.

Stratified Random Sampling. There may be times that a simple random selection will not generate the type of participants needed in a sample. For example, if a researcher conducting exit polling during an election uses a simple random sampling procedure to choose individuals to survey as they leave the polls, just by chance he or she would not get a representative sample of Democrats, Republicans, and Independents. For such a poll, a researcher would want to obtain a sample that was proportional to the number of Democrats, Republicans, and Independents in the geographic area being studied. A **stratified random selection procedure** would allow the researcher to stratify along the variable of party affiliation—that is, to select a sample that was more representative of the population. If possible, the researcher would obtain a list of eligible voters according to political party and then randomly select the appropriate proportional number of participants from each group. So whenever subgroups are critical to creating a sample that represents the entire population, stratified random sampling is the most precise sampling technique. Variables that are used to stratify a sample in educational research might include, race, ethnicity, socioeconomic status, years of teaching experience, grade level, or school location: urban, suburban, and rural.

Cluster Random Selection. In the field of education, simple random selection is often not possible. For example, if you are surveying teachers in a particular state, you might not be able to obtain a list of individual teacher names, but you can get a list of school buildings for the state. In this case, **cluster random selection** may be useful. Instead of assigning numbers to individuals, in cluster random selection, numbers are assigned to the cluster or subgroup within the realistic population. In the example above, each school building would include a subgroup (or cluster) of teachers. The building would be assigned a number, and buildings would be randomly selected using the random number table described previously. By selecting clusters, you reduce the number of schools you need to visit or the number of contact persons you need to identify. The important thing to remember is that cluster random selection is a procedure where entire groups and not individuals are randomly selected. This procedure allows the researcher to select clusters randomly and is actually a simpler technique than selecting individuals randomly. However, to be certain that the sample accurately reflects the population, a researcher would likely have to select multiple clusters. The number of clusters you select would be determined by the number of clusters in the population.

Nonrandom Samples

Random selection of the sample allows a researcher to generalize the results of the study back to the entire population from which the sample was drawn. Because of limited time, resources, or purpose (or all of these), a researcher may conduct a study where teachers or students in one school building or one district are included in the study. This type of nonrandom sampling is referred to as **convenience sampling.** Although a sample of convenience requires fewer resources, it severely limits a study's generalizability. In this case, the study's results are only "good for" or generalizable back to the teachers in the school building or district, whichever the case may be. Depending on the overall purpose of the study and how the results of the study will be used and disseminated, lack of generalizability might not be an issue. If the purpose of the study is to use the results to make decisions at either the school building or district level, then such sampling methods are adequate. However, if the intent of the study is to add to the academic or professional knowledge base on a subject by publishing on a national level, such sampling techniques would be considered a major flaw in the study design. **Census sampling** is another nonrandom sampling technique used in quantitative research. In census sampling, the researcher surveys the entire realistic population without drawing a random sample from the population. This technique may be used when the study has unlimited resources or the realistic population is not too large. Census sampling is frequently used by educators who are only trying to obtain data on their own school or district. Such data can be useful in learning about that particular school or district; however, remember that the results cannot be generalized to other schools or districts because the sample was not chosen randomly.

Sample Size and Survey Response Rates

Although random selection certainly plays a pivotal role in a study's credibility, the size of the sample that one selects from the realistic population is also important. If the sample is too small, it may not fully represent the population from which it was drawn, and therefore, the findings from the study cannot be generalized back to the wider audience, even though random sampling practices were used.

Even though there are no "hard or fast" rules for determining sample sizes, there are some general guidelines to consider when planning a study. For survey research, if the population is fewer than 200 individuals, the entire population should be sampled. This would be considered census sampling. At around a population of 400, approximately 50% of the population should make up the sample, and populations over 1,000 require about 20% for an appropriate sample. For large populations of 5,000 or more, samples of 350 to 500 persons are often adequate. For correlational studies, a minimum of 30 participants should be tested. Experimental research studies generally require at least 30 participants per group. These generalizations are based on the work of Krejcie and Morgan (1970), and their article should be consulted for more precise information about sample size.

Ethical Issues and Participants

In addition to considering how the participants will be selected, researchers have many ethical responsibilities to the participants and to the profession they represent. Regardless of the type of study you choose to conduct, research ethics is an important consideration. Most professional organizations have their own codes of ethics (see the American Psychological Association and the American Sociological Association for examples). In addition, colleges, universities, and other institutions that conduct research have **institutional review boards** (IRBs) whose members review proposals for research to determine if ethical issues have been considered. If you are conducting research in a noncollege setting, either an elementary or secondary school or a community organization, there may not be a committee called an "IRB." In this case, you will need to find out who will review your proposal and the procedures you will need to follow to obtain approval. For the most part, issues of ethics focus on establishing safeguards that will protect the rights of the participants. The traditional and often dominant issues that emerge when considering research ethics involve obtaining **informed consent** from participants, **protecting them from harm,** and **ensuring confidentiality.** Informed consent means that participants have been given information about procedures and risks involved in the study and have been informed that their participation is voluntary and they have the right to withdraw from the study without repercussions. IRB committees typically scrutinize research proposals for these issues and will weigh any potential risk to the participants against any possible gains for science. Keep in mind that the process for addressing ethical issues might change the participants in your study. This may happen because some of the people that you have selected will not agree to be in the study or the IRB may not give you permission to use those participants. Even if you use a random sampling procedure, the final participants in your study are volunteers. All quantitative researchers should consider how this might change the representativeness of the sample or exclude key informants.

The members of the IRB review proposals and will examine the methods described in the proposal to ensure that all ethical considerations have been addressed and that sufficient detail of the actions to be taken by the researcher are provided. As was already mentioned, most institutions whose students, professors, and staff conduct research have their own IRB committees with specific guidelines for study approval. IRB committees are mandated by national legislation (National Research Act, Public Law 93–438). To be well versed in specific requirements and procedures, you should contact your own university or college's IRB committee. IRB committees typically require that the researcher prepare a document that includes the following:

• A cover page where the researcher introduces the principal investigator and his or her qualifications and contact information, the project title, and the type of research that is being proposed.
• A detailed description of the study. This would include a summary of the literature, the research method, the significance of the research, and particulars

about the location and duration of the study. The committee will want the specifics on any treatment (for experimental research) and any instruments or protocols that might be used.

• A description of the participants. The researcher would need to include background information on the individuals in the sample and the sampling procedures to be used. If the participants are to be selected from a specific institution (school, hospital, club, etc.), then written permission is needed from the director or principal.

• Discussion of inducements, benefits, or compensation to be offered to the participants. If the participants are provided any incentives to encourage their participation in the study, the specifics should be explained.

• Analysis of the risks and benefits. If there are any potential risks to the participants, the researcher would want to clearly indicate how the benefits would outweigh any risks.

• Informed consent, confidentiality, voluntary nature of the project, and debriefing activities. A description of the procedures for obtaining informed consent must be described in order to obtain IRB approval. This is particularly important when children younger than 18 years are being used as participants. In this case, parental consent must be obtained. Most IRB committees require that the researcher submit copies of the informed consent forms. This consent form must include at least the following information:

Detailed description of the project

Description of any potential risks involved

The voluntary nature of the study

A confidentiality statement

Some educational studies might be considered IRB exempt. These are studies that involve commonly accepted educational practices and those that report the results of educational tests (such as those published on Web sites). For example, new instructional practices or program evaluations commissioned by the school to refine ongoing practice would be exempt. You must consult your IRB committee if you believe that your study falls under this category. Some IRB committees also have expedited forms that can be used under specific circumstances. Once again, to determine the type of IRB form that is necessary for your study, you should contact your IRB committee. Most important, the IRB must be submitted and approved before any data are collected. So be sure to start this process early.

Keep in mind that the procedures outlined in one's IRB proposal are not cast in stone, meaning that they can be modified to meet the ever-changing needs of the researcher and the overall study and its purpose. This, in fact, is common. In many situations when researchers enter the field and start conducting their study, they find that the real-world situations vary considerably from what they had envisioned when creating their proposal on paper. Minor changes to a proposal method typically do not require one to go back and be "reapproved" by the committee or board that initially reviewed and approved the study. Some examples of these modifications might include increasing the study's sample size or modifying items on the survey following its pilot. Because of its exploratory nature, modifications are expected in qualitative research. When conducting a case study or ethnographic study, it may be necessary to submit a series of small research proposals to the committee, instead of one large proposal. This will allow the qualitative researcher to start out with broad procedures when entering the research field and to maintain the ability to refine the process as the study progresses.

Ethics in Qualitative Research

Although all research studies must be approved by your institution's IRB committee, there are some unique ethical considerations surrounding qualitative research studies because of their emergent designs. That is, by its nature, much of what occurs in qualitative research is unknown by the researcher at the beginning of the study. Although the study does have a framework that includes likely questions and observations, unanticipated issues might arise as the study proceeds.

Informed Consent. The emergent nature of qualitative research makes the task of obtaining informed consent a difficult one. Informed consent is based on the scientific realism framework where researchers know before a study begins what measures will be used and what treatments will be given to participants. According to Eisner (1998), "the notion of informed consent implies that researchers are able to anticipate the events that will emerge in the field about which those to be observed are to be informed" (p. 215). This type of consent is inconsistent with most qualitative research. For example, a researcher decides to conduct a study where the interactions of middle school girls are observed and documented during their study hall periods. The participants and their parents are told that a researcher will observe the interactions that occur and will conduct a focus group interview that centers on middle school girls' involvement in cliques. All girls and their parents consent to participate. During the focus group interview, the girls decide that they are going to tell Mary (one of the middle schoolers) that they do not like her and do not want her to be part of the group. Mary is devastated and embarrassed by what has occurred in the focus group interview. You might say, she, her parents, or both signed an informed consent, and that is certainly true. But what parent or child would agree to be part of such a study if they knew that it might result in a hurtful and uncomfortable situation? Probably, not too many! In addition, during the focus group, the interviewer might change or add questions (probes) to those planned in the protocol based on the responses of the group or issues raised by the participants that the researcher did not anticipate. Because of the emergent nature of the study, it may not be possible to provide full information about the methods that will be used in the study.

Protection from Harm. Protection from harm is one of the most basic of ethical concerns. It applies to both physical and emotional harm. Several issues need to be considered here. First, a qualitative research study by its nature does not impose a treatment and occurs in a naturalistic setting. As such, the researcher does not have to be concerned about whether or not he or she is doing something harmful to the participants or placing them in a harmful situation. However, in a qualitative research study, the researcher, to varying degrees, becomes involved with the participants. The fact that the researcher becomes part of the group or asks certain questions could potentially influence behavior in a way that produces unwanted or adverse consequences. For example, you are conducting a phenomenological study that includes interviewing high school students of color about their perceptions of institutionalized racism at their school. Because of your questions, many hurtful experiences suffered by the participants are brought to the surface. The emotional distress experienced during the interview by itself might present a source of potential harm that the researcher must consider. This might be handled by making sure students have a person with whom they can discuss their feelings. What if, however, as a result of their discussion, the students decide to mobilize and demand changes from the administration of the school? Researchers who believe strongly in the advocacy paradigm would take pride in such an outcome. Taking the scenario one step further, say that as part of the mobilization, the students get into a violent encounter with individuals who are part of the institutional structure (an administrator or a teacher). In this situation, the qualitative investigation resulted in unanticipated harm (a violent encounter) to the participants of the study. The lesson here is that researchers must consider carefully the actions they take with the participants and, wherever possible, provide for ways to deal with unanticipated outcomes.

Confidentiality. In general, most researchers promise confidentiality to the participants of their studies. However, can this promise always be kept? Are there situations where a qualitative researcher must, or at least should, consider breaching confidentiality? Consider the following. You are a qualitative researcher who is observing an after-school program at an inner-city elementary school. One of the staff members is unduly harsh, negative, and unfair to the young children. This staff member, along with others, has signed a consent form allowing you to conduct observations as long as his or her confidentiality is protected. Should you inform the principal of the school about the behavior of the after-school staff member? Is your primary responsibility to your study or your participants? Where do our loyalties lie? Obviously, this is a decision that needs to be made by the researcher. However, according to Lincoln and Guba (1985), the relationship that develops between the researcher and the participant should be of primary importance. A good qualitative study also provides substantial information on the context of the study and provides a detailed description of the group or setting studied. The extensive detail may make it difficult to keep confidential the persons or school being studied.

Ethical Issues in Quantitative Research

As is the case for qualitative studies, quantitative studies are also faced with unique ethical challenges. These challenges will come under scrutiny from the IRB committee because in experimental and single-subject designs, researchers are attempting to change or influence the behavior of the participants.

Protection from Harm. The ethical obligation to protect participants from harm applies to both the treatment and control groups. Clearly, no researcher would set up a treatment that will change behavior for the worse, right? We certainly hope not. Researchers usually expect experimental treatments to improve the performance of participants, and as such, they must carefully consider the nature of the treatment. However, consider this scenario. What if a treatment is likely to produce substantial benefits for the experimental group? Would it be ethical to deprive the control group of the treatment? For example, if you have developed a teenage pregnancy prevention program that you expect will truly help prevent early sexual activity by teens, can you in good conscience deny giving this program to the control group? Many experimental studies now simply deliver the treatment to the control group after the study is completed. In these cases, the control group might be referred to as **waiting-list control group.** However, if the study lasts six months to a year, it may be too late for some youth! Another approach is to deliver different amounts of the treatment to the different groups so that no group is completely deprived. For example, one group might get the prevention program one day a week and another get it two days a week.

Informed Consent. Informed consent can also be tricky in quantitative research. Telling participants the purpose of the study in advance might change how they respond to the treatment or how they act during the study. If you want to see if a new video decreases teachers' gender bias, you cannot just tell participants that your study is examining how to reduce gender bias. As soon as they hear this, they are likely to begin to change or hide any of their assumptions about gender. They also might interpret the video differently if they realize that you are trying to change their behavior. Although most researchers avoid outright deception of participants, they may give their participants general descriptions of the purpose and procedures for their study: "I am studying how teachers interact with their students," rather than "I am studying if teachers give preferential treatment to boys or girls." If participants are not given full information about the study, however, it is necessary to **debrief** them afterward by explaining the full purpose of the study. Many researchers use this as an opportunity to share the results of the study with the participants and provide information about the study's findings.

Confidentiality.   Finally, some quantitative studies, especially experimental and quasi-experimental designs, require pretesting and posttesting participants. Typically, you want to be able to see if your treatment has changed the scores from the pretest to the posttest. Some of the statistical tests require you to pair up pretest and posttest scores for the participants, which presents a possible problem for confidentiality. In this case, you might want to assign each participant a number or code that will allow you to later link the pretest and posttest scores.

Chapter Summary

A sample is a group or individuals that a researcher uses in a study. Samples are composed of what are referred to as "participants." Depending on the type or approach of the study, a sample would be selected from a larger population in different ways. Qualitative researchers focus on selecting participants based on a certain characteristic that they wish to investigate and are not interested in generalizing their findings beyond the settings they are studying. Purposeful sampling is a common procedure used in qualitative research that identifies key informants or persons who have specific knowledge about the topic being studied. The type of purposeful sampling that a researcher may decide to use depends on the purpose of the study.

In quantitative research, samples are selected in such a way that they can be generalized back to the larger population from which they were originally drawn. Although the researcher would like to generalize to the ideal population or widest population possible, most researchers have to settle for working with a smaller realistic population. Researchers use a sampling frame or list to select participants from the realistic population. Random sampling is a technique used by quantitative researchers to ensure that the sample represents or "looks like" the realistic population from which it was selected. Simple random sampling is the basic method used by quantitative researchers when individuals are randomly selected. Other methods include stratified random sampling (to ensure the representation of subgroups) and cluster random sampling (the random selection of entire groups instead of individuals). Nonrandom techniques include convenience and census sampling. In convenience sampling, a single setting such as a school district or teacher's classroom may be selected for the quantitative study. A major limitation of convenience sampling is the lack of generalizability beyond the initial sample. Census sampling is when the survey researcher uses the entire realistic population without randomly selecting a sample. Sample size is another important aspect of sampling. Survey research requires a sample size of approximately 50% for populations around 400; for larger populations of 5,000 or more, a sample of 350 to 500 individuals is appropriate. Correlational studies require a sample of at least 30 individuals total. For experimental studies, a sample of 60 individuals total, 30 in the treatment group and 30 in the control group, is required. Researchers have to submit their proposals to an institutional review board for review to ensure that ethical considerations are being met and that no harm could possibly come to participants. Informed consent, protection from harm, and confidentiality are three main areas that make up the review process.

Key Concepts

purposeful sampling

key informants

sample

population

ideal population

realistic population

sampling frame

random sampling

cluster random selection

convenience sampling

census sampling

institutional review board

informed consent

waiting-list control group

Discussion Questions or Activities

1. You are conducting a qualitative research study that is investigating the lives of inner-city children in a small urban area. Discuss how you would go about collecting your sample and who your key informants might be.
2. A researcher has been asked to study the views of citizens on public education in New York City. She has come to you for your expert opinion on sampling in quantitative research. Discuss the possible options for her study and recommend which sampling procedure you believe would be the best technique for her study and why.
3. You are a member of your institution's IRB committee. You are considering a proposal that would be investigating the effects of social skill training on autistic children. Discuss all of the important elements that should be included in this proposal for it to receive your approval.

Suggested Readings

Mauthner, M., Birch, M., Jessop, J., & Miller, T. (2002). *Ethics in qualitative research*. Thousand Oaks, CA: Sage Publications.

Newman, D. L., & Brown, R. D. (1996). *Applied ethics for program evaluation*. Thousand Oaks, CA: Sage Publications.

CHAPTER SEVEN

DESCRIPTIVE-SURVEY RESEARCH

Chapter Objectives

After reading this chapter, you should be able to

1. Define the purpose of survey research and describe the various types of survey research
2. Distinguish among research questions, survey subquestions, and individual survey items
3. Outline the first four steps in carrying out descriptive-survey research
4. Name the different components of a survey (cover letter, demographics, survey body, and instructions) and describe the essential elements of each, along with why the element is important and the function(s) the element serves
5. Explain the meaning and importance of confidentiality in survey research and distinguish confidentiality from anonymity
6. Outline the criteria for writing good survey questions
7. Distinguish between the different types of survey research

Research Vignette

As an administration intern at a local high school, Alysia has been asked by the school principal to determine the students' perceptions of the new dress code that will be implemented in the school beginning with the new school year. Alysia is also taking an educational research course as part of her educational administration certificate program. She consults with her professor and decides that the best way to study perceptions is to conduct a descriptive-survey research study. The high school is made up of grades 9 through 12, and the total school population is 2,500. She decides to randomly select 50% of the students. She constructs a survey with 20 response items where students have to circle a number on a scale of one through five indicating the degree to which they agree with the statement (a Likert scale). She also includes three open-ended questions to allow the students an opportunity to express any further feelings or opinions. Before she sends out the survey, she gives it to a group of students in their study hall and asks them to critique it. Based on the feedback she receives, she constructs the final survey and mails copies to the random sample with a self-addressed stamped envelope. In her cover letter, she asks that the surveys be returned to her within three weeks. Her initial return rate is 20%.

Characteristics of Descriptive-Survey Research

There are many misperceptions about what research *is*, what research *does*, and the various research approaches that can be *used* to answer a research question. Descriptive-survey research is by no means excluded from these misperceptions. Many people believe that descriptive-survey research is not valid or rigorous in its approach; in fact, nothing could be further from the truth. Overexposure to survey research may be what drives these common misperceptions.

Survey research is everywhere. Take, for example, the last time you sat down to enjoy a meal with your family or friends after a long week of graduate school, and the phone rang right as the meal was set on the table. You answered it to find a telemarketer on the other end explaining that she was conducting a brief survey and would like to ask you some questions about the radio station you listen to on your way to work each morning. And as you are about to hang up, she adds, ". . . and it will only take a second of your time." Famous last words, right?

Whether someone comes up to you in the shopping mall with a clipboard full of questions, calls you on the phone, or sends you a paper survey in the mail (or by e-mail), all of these are examples of descriptive-survey research, and they share the following common characteristics:

- A preestablished instrument has most likely been developed by the researcher.
- Most responses to the questions on the survey are quantitative (e.g., ratings) or will be summarized in a quantitative way.

- The sample is selected from a larger population or group to allow the study's findings to be generalized back to the larger group.

The various approaches to survey research have the same purpose: gathering opinions, beliefs, or perceptions about a current issue from a large group of people. In educational research, these issues can be wide ranging and may include, but are certainly not limited to, high-stakes testing, parental involvement, school improvement, classroom instructional practices, behavior management techniques, and after-school or summer enrichment programming.

Writing a Research Question

Although descriptive-survey research is a type of quantitative research, it begins with a **research question** and a set of **subquestions** as in qualitative research. Presented below are some examples of research questions:

1. What do elementary and middle-level teachers believe are the main benefits, barriers, or both, of integrating technology into their instruction?
2. What do high school administrators perceive to be the issues surrounding school safety?
3. What do parents of elementary school students believe are ways to become more involved in school and school-related activities?

Notice how these research questions illustrate the characteristics of descriptive-survey research. First, in each example, *who* is being surveyed (the sample) is clearly specified: elementary and middle-level teachers, high school administrators, and parents of elementary school students. Second, all questions include verbs or "action" words that inquire about people's *perceptions* or *beliefs* of their thoughts, feelings, and actions. Third, the current issue being investigated is clearly defined: technology integration, school safety, and parental involvement in school activities.

As you examine the vignette, what do you think Alysia's research question was for her study? It is likely that her question was something like the following: "What are student perceptions of the new uniform policy?"

Writing Subquestions

After generating a research question (like the ones above), students are often perplexed by how they can "fill up" an entire survey with the one research question they have created. The answer is, they cannot. The research question should be thought of as a broad research question, and although it is certainly important and every survey study needs to begin with one, the researcher must also work to develop more specific subquestions. Consider as an example the above research question, "What do elementary and middle-level teachers believe are the main benefits and barriers to integrating technology into their instruction?" To follow are some examples of subquestions that would support this research question:

1. Do elementary and middle-level teachers believe that they have made changes to their pedagogy in integrating technology, and if so, what were they?
2. In what types of professional development activities have these teachers participated? What other professional development do they believe is necessary to assist them further?
3. Do elementary and middle-level teachers believe that using such technology has had an impact on student learning and achievement, and if so, what are some examples and evidence?

Although these subquestions are specific, they are still aligned with the research question. Each subquestion is chipping away at some aspect of technology integration, trying to get at an understanding of it from a different perspective. In a descriptive-survey research proposal, like the one you will likely write for this course, these subquestions would be listed at the end of the review of literature on the topic of technology and teacher instructional practices and will serve as a guide for writing specific survey questions. In other words, subquestions make up the main sections or *categories* of the survey. Note that the subquestions are *not* quantitative in nature. It is in the detailed survey questions (which we will discuss later in this chapter) that the researcher provides the structure that allows participants to provide quantitative responses. Generally, subquestions emerge as the researcher is conducting the extensive review of the literature on the topic. Creating subquestions is an ongoing process; the more you read and learn, the more you will want to go back and refine your subquestions. In fact, researchers commonly go back and make revisions to these subquestions while developing their actual surveys.

Like any other descriptive-survey researcher, Alysia would have to write subquestions for her initial question. Following a literature review into school uniforms, the subquestions for her student survey might include the following:

1. How do you believe that school uniforms will affect the sense of community at the school?
2. How do you believe that school uniforms will affect academic performance?
3. What effect, if any, do you believe that school uniforms will have on the safety of your school?

Steps for Doing Descriptive-Survey Research

The process of descriptive-survey research includes the following steps:

- Designing and developing the survey
- Selecting the sample
- Piloting the survey
- Administering final survey and collecting data
- Analyzing data

In this chapter, designing and developing the survey, selecting the sample that will pilot the survey, and administering the survey will be discussed. Data analysis was discussed earlier in Chapter Four.

Step 1: Designing and Developing a Survey or Questionnaire

A **survey** or **questionnaire** is the main tool or instrument used to collect data in a descriptive-survey research study. Because survey researchers typically study issues and behaviors that change over time, they usually develop new instruments or refine existing ones. A common misperception about survey development is that it is easy: just put some questions down on a piece of paper, and *voila!* You have a survey ready to mail out to the participants. This could not be further from the truth. Although they may appear to be easy, survey design and development require a significant amount of knowledge, planning, and skill to execute correctly.

Presented below is an overview of the different elements of a survey. Keep in mind that not all surveys are the same, but in general, most surveys should have all or almost all of these components.

Cover Letter. Instructions or directions that the researcher provides to help guide the participant are some of the most important (and difficult) aspects of survey development. Because the researcher wants to make sure that the surveys are answered accurately and returned, directions and a statement of the purpose of the study need to be the first things a participant sees. A cover letter is one method that researchers commonly use to relay such important information to participants. Cover letters tend to work best for surveys that are being sent to participants through the mail. For situations where the researcher is collecting data from a site—for example, from a large group of teachers attending professional development training in technology literacy—cover letters are unnecessary. In those situations, it is appropriate for the researcher to read aloud to the group the directions and other information that would appear on such a cover letter as part of an introductory statement. If a cover letter is not used, a paragraph that appears at the top of the survey can contain the essential information needed. Box 7.1 is a sample of what Alysia might write for her directions.

Box 7.1 Student Perception Survey

Note: Please Return by July 30

You have received this survey as part of a research study. The purpose of this study is to investigate student perception of school uniforms. This survey was designed to gather your beliefs about uniforms and how you believe uniforms will influence your school. Your responses are confidential and will not be shared with anyone in any way that identifies you as an individual. Only aggregated data will be presented in the final report. Your participation in this survey is completely voluntary and will not affect your grades. Your time and cooperation are greatly appreciated. If you have any questions regarding this survey or the study in general, please contact: Alysia Johnson, Administration Intern, Baker High School, 123 Main Street, Los Angeles California.

Whether you use a cover letter or an introductory statement, the following information must be present in both:

• *Purpose.* You must provide the participants with information about the purpose of both the survey and the research project as a whole. If your survey is asking participants about prior experiences, such as a professional development training or a new intervention-strategy program, you must clearly indicate that the purpose of the study is to collect information, opinions, or both, related to those specific prior experience(s). As the researcher, you must help to place the participants in the proper context for answering the questions. Do not assume that participants will make connections to those specific past experiences without being specifically instructed to do so. Such assumptions may result in invalid data that do not reflect the participants' true beliefs or understandings about the experience or phenomena you are studying.

• *Confidentiality statement.* As you likely remember from our ethics discussion, one of the most important duties of a researcher is maintaining **confidentiality.** To do this, the researcher must ensure that what a participant says or reports will not be shared with anyone in any way (this also includes the write-up of the study) that would result in an individual being identified. Although this sounds simple enough, survey researchers are often faced with the dilemma of not being able to report certain findings because individuals could be identified and what they said directly attributed to them. This can be a considerable problem when surveying in a small school district or other setting where there may be only one or two individuals in a particular position. Take, for example, a one-building K–12 school district in a rural community (yes, they do exist). In these districts, typically there is only one teacher per grade level. What if the findings indicated that the gym teacher, the English teacher, or the first-grade elementary teacher was disappointed with the administration for its inability to address issues surrounding students with special needs? The researcher would not be able to reveal this specific information for fear of directly violating confidentiality. In larger settings, such concerns pose less of a problem. Take, for example, a large urban school district with many buildings at the elementary, middle, and secondary levels. A researcher could comfortably report that 50% of the first-grade teachers in the district believed that the administration is not meeting the needs of all students. With a large number of teachers in the district, it would be virtually impossible to trace this finding back to the specific teachers with such concerns. Researchers should always carefully consider the issues that surround confidentiality. See Box 7.2 for a research example.

Box 7.2 Ethical Issue in Descriptive-Survey Research

Surveys in educational settings are often used to assess the incidence of self-reported problems in youth. For example, the Youth Risk Behavior Survey (YRBS), which is administered in hundreds of high schools each year, asks youth to report on how frequently they use drugs, engage in sexual activities, smoke, feel depressed, or engage in binge eating or vomiting to control their weight. The YRBS was designed by researchers at the University of Michigan to monitor changes over time in these risky behaviors. Surveys are also used in more local studies to determine the extent of problem behaviors in a school or community or to monitor changes in problems when a prevention program is introduced. These surveys have the potential to reveal problems that were previously unknown. However, one ethical dilemma that confronts survey researchers is that students revealing the problems cannot be helped unless confidentiality is violated. Remember that confidentiality means that student responses cannot be shared with anyone, including parents. If a survey revealed that several students at a school were seriously depressed to the point of thinking about suicide, what might the researcher's ethical responsibility be?

Legally, researchers are not required to report this type of problem. However, there are a variety of ways in which they might address the ethical concerns about doing nothing to help a student who might hurt himself or herself. Some researchers might provide a general report to the school indicating that problems exist in certain areas and recommending that the school promote specific counseling services to address these. In fact, some researchers might work with the school in advance to make sure services are available in case the survey reveals problems. If the students' answers indicated a need for more immediate attention, the researcher might arrange to talk with the students in private, expressing concern and making services available to them individually.

Often graduate students confuse confidentiality and *anonymity*. Unlike confidentiality, anonymity means that the survey does not require the participants or **respondents** to provide their name or any information that identifies them in any way (e.g., grade level currently teaching, number of years in current teaching position, name of school building). An anonymous survey is one that contains no demographic information that could be used to identify an individual. Survey development theory would support the use of an anonymous survey to increase the number of completed surveys that the researcher receives back. Participants are more likely to provide valid information if they believe there is no way that what they report will be traced back to them. Although these two benefits are certainly good reasons for using anonymous surveys, they make it impossible for a researcher to follow up with participants to collect any further in-depth information or validate what they have said.

• *Statement of voluntary nature of study.* In the introductory statement or cover letter, the researcher must inform participants that participation in the study is entirely voluntary. Participants must be informed that their lack of participation will not result in negative consequences. As you can see, Alysia made this clear to the students in her study. She told them that failing to participate would not influence their grades. For survey studies where the participant has no real "buy in" (a stake in the issues being explored by the survey), the decision to participate or not in the study would likely have little if any consequence. However, if a researcher was surveying people receiving social services or mental health services, respondents might fear that participation or nonparticipation could result in loss of their services. In this type of situation, a researcher must include a sentence that clearly states that participation or lack of it will not affect receipt of services. In addition, the researcher must inform participants that they have the right at any time to withdraw from the study or may choose not to answer any question.

• *Contact information.* The cover letter or introductory statement must provide contact information for use by participants in the event that they have a question or need further clarification on an item. The name of the **principal investigator** (also called the "P.I.") should be listed somewhere, along with the name of the institution, group, or agency sponsoring the study (if there is one), a physical mailing address, phone number, and e-mail address (if available).

The cover letter or introductory statement must also include instructions on how to return the survey (e.g., there is a self-addressed-stamped envelope [SASE] enclosed) and a deadline date for the return of the survey (on average, two weeks following the receipt of a survey is adequate; anything shorter or longer can lower response rates). Finally, the researcher can include any additional information specific to the study that he or she believes to be important and should thank the participants for their time and cooperation.

Demographics. The next major section of a survey is the demographics section. **Demographics** are descriptors that provide detailed information about participants in the study. The specific demographics you gather depend on the study you are conducting. If your participants are teachers, you might want to know what grade levels they teach, how long they have been teaching, their area of expertise, and so forth. These are the typical demographics of interest to educational researchers. Presented in Exhibit 7.1 is an example of demographics that Alysia might gather for her study on students.

When deciding on the type of demographics you are going to include in your study, you might want to consider the following guidelines:

• *Demographics should be derived from the literature review.* When reviewing past studies on your topic, be sure to note what demographics have been used in the past, as well as demographics that "emerge" from the literature. For example, you are interested in the topic technology integration and teacher pedagogy. On examination of the literature, you discover that there is a consensus in the education field that the use of technology by teachers is somehow related to the length of time one has been a teacher. In other words, teachers who have been teaching more years are less likely to integrate technology into their teaching than new teachers. In creating demographics for the survey, you would certainly want to

EXHIBIT 7.1 SAMPLE DEMOGRAPHICS SECTION.

Sex: ____ male ____ female Age: ____ 12–13 ____ 14–15 ____ 16–17 ____ 18–19 ____ other

Grade level: ____ 9th ____ 10th ____ 11th ____ 12th

Years in public school (fill in): ____ years

Any prior experience wearing uniforms? ____ yes ____ no

make sure that you have items gathering information on the number of years one has been teaching. Otherwise, you will have hundreds of surveys from teachers but no way to determine whether there was a difference between those teachers who have been teaching longer and those new to the field.

• *Demographics should be used for specific purposes and not as a "shotgun" approach to gathering all possible information on participants.* Many researchers pack as many demographics into a survey as they possibly can. Caution should be taken when selecting demographics. Too many demographic items may frustrate participants and negatively affect their desire to fill out the survey. Some participants may have concerns about how demographic information will be used, especially information on race and ethnicity.

• *Demographics can go at the beginning or end of the survey, depending on their purpose.* Although demographics traditionally appear at the beginning of a survey, in some situations it may be more appropriate to end the survey with demographic items. The decision to put the demographics later rather than sooner depends on how important these are to the researcher and to the study. If demographics are imperative to the study, then they should go at the beginning of the survey when the participants are fresh and ready. If demographics are not imperative, they should go last, allowing the participants to exert most of their energies (and brain power) on answering the survey items.

Body of the Survey. The development of individual survey items is often confusing to those who have not created a survey. Students often mistakenly think that the subquestions *are* the survey questions. As we noted in the section on writing subquestions, the subquestions are written at the end of the literature and represent the main sections or categories of the survey. The researcher then uses these categories to generate survey items.

For example, in Alysia's study on student perceptions of school uniforms, one of her subquestions involved determining how students believed school uniforms would influence their school community. As in the example provided in Exhibit 7.2, the theme of "School Community" becomes the main header for that section of the survey. Notice how all the questions under that section pertain to school community and solicit a *quantitative* response. The number of individual survey items in each section depends on the topic and can vary among the different categories or themes of the survey. There is no "definitive" number of items that make up a survey. In general, for the purposes of the research proposal in this course, you should aim for 8 to 12 items for each category. In examining the five items presented, can you think of any other possible items that could be included for this section as they relate to outcomes?

EXHIBIT 7.2 STUDENT PERCEPTIONS OF THE IMPACT OF SCHOOL UNIFORMS ON THE SCHOOL COMMUNITY.

Read each question below and respond by circling the number that represents how you feel.

1 = strongly disagree; 2 = disagree; 3 = slightly disagree;
4 = slightly agree; 5 = agree; 6 = strongly agree

I think we will see positive changes in the behavior of students in school cafeteria	1 2 3 4 5 6
I believe there will be less competition among students.	1 2 3 4 5 6
I feel that students will get along better.	1 2 3 4 5 6
I am very positive about how school uniforms will influence my school.	1 2 3 4 5 6
I believe my school will be a better place.	1 2 3 4 5 6

Directions for Each Section. To ensure accuracy of the data, it is essential that, as the researcher, you provide instructions that clearly tell participants what to do (and think about) when answering each item of the survey. Although directions are touched on in a general sense in either the cover letter or in the beginning of the survey, each section or "theme" of the survey should include specific directions immediately preceding the detailed survey items. (Note the italicized directions in Exhibit 7.2). This is important because in some situations, each section of the survey may be intended to gather different types of information, and although the questions all look to be the same (let us say that they all refer in some way to school community), in fact, the researcher may want the participants to reflect and think about the sections quite differently. Putting certain parts of the directions in ALL CAPS, italics, *underlined,* or **bold (OR ALL FOUR)** are effective ways of getting the participants' attention.

Last, when writing directions for each survey section, clearly define any potentially ambiguous terms. This will help to increase the accuracy of the data. For example, if you are surveying elementary teachers regarding their technology use, using the word *technology* in the directions could mean different things to different people. You, the researcher, might be operating under the definition that "technology" means computers—and nothing else. However, some of the teachers filling out the survey might have a broader definition of the term, which includes overhead projectors, VCRs, cable in the classroom, and the like, in addition to computers. (One of us actually encountered a group of teachers that believed, and reported, that Scotch tape is technology.) In these examples, participants' broader definitions of the term "technology" would lead the researcher to over-report the use of technology in the study.

Criteria for Writing Good Survey Items. As discussed earlier, descriptive-survey researchers usually develop their own instruments. Sometimes they may borrow or modify items from surveys developed by other researchers. One should always ask for permission to use or adapt items from other researchers. Regardless of whether items are developed by the researcher or borrowed, all items should meet certain criteria for good survey items.

• *Be clear and concise in the language used.* Define all terms that could be interpreted differently from what you intend. For example, if you are interested in studying teachers' use of *constructivist* instructional approaches, it would be better to reword this term or define it. If you are ultimately interested in learning about teachers' use of hands-on instruction, then you should modify the wording so that it is more specific and clear and use the words "hands-on learning."

• *Make sure that each survey item gathers data on one central idea or question.* Although it is tempting to ask participants two questions in one item to save time and space, this will result in confusion, and it will be impossible to interpret responses. For example, consider an item asking participants to respond on a scale of "strongly agree" to "strongly disagree" to the following statement: "I believe that school uniforms will make the cafeteria and the halls more friendly." If a participant agrees strongly with this statement with regard to the cafeteria but disagrees with regard to the halls, how should the participant respond to this item? Strongly agree? Strongly disagree? Not applicable? To fix these problems, the researcher must break this question down into two separate questions, each containing one of the essential ideas.

• *Avoid using double negatives.* For example: "It is not good practice for teachers to not meet the needs of all their students." As you read this item, you probably felt yourself stop and think about it for a second before answering it, right? It is difficult to determine what a response of "strongly agree" or "strongly disagree" would mean in this case.

• *Make sure that items (particularly demographic items) have response sets that do not overlap.* This is a common mistake, even in professional surveys. Consider a survey item that asks participants to indicate annual income levels. If you have selections that overlap, as in the example below, it will be virtually impossible for you to decipher who has selected the correct response for their income level.

Indicate your income level by checking one of the categories below.

__ $0–$10,000

__ $10,000–$30,000

__ $30,000–$50,000

__ $50,000–$80,000

__ $80,000–$100,000

__ $100,000 or more

If you were trying to fill out this demographic item and you made $50,000 annually, which one would you select, $30,000-$50,000 or $50,000-$80,000? What if, like you, 99% of the sample made $50,000, and they all selected the first choice but you selected the second? The finding that 99% of the sample made $30,000-$50,000 and that only 1% made $50,000-$80,000 would be incorrect. In fact, in this example, the entire sample made $50,000 that year.

• *Include all possible responses.* For example, if you are asking participants how many times that week they used technology in their classrooms and you provide a frequency checklist like the one below, it is important that you provide a "zero" or "none" category.

How many times did you integrate
technology into your lessons last week?

__ 0   __ 1–3   __ 4–6   __ 7–9   __ 10–12   __13 or more

If you did not provide a zero as a possible answer, many of your participants may not be able to provide an accurate answer (assuming someone never used technology), and the data will overestimate the degree of technology integration. If the zero response is not provided, and 100% of teachers filling out the survey had not used technology in their teaching the week before, they either leave the question blank or might select the next item that most closely represents their situation: 1–3 times. If 60% chose "1–3," the researcher would report that 60% of respondents used technology one to three times in the week before being surveyed when really none had.

Including all possible responses also includes the use of the category "Other." The benefit of a researcher providing this category is that it opens the response setup so that the participant can provide the most accurate response possible. If you use the category "Other," be sure to provide a place for the participant to actually write in the detailed response. However, if an overwhelming number of respondents select the "Other" category on many different items, this could mean that the researcher has not properly identified the sample of participants or has not included viable responses for all participants. Remember, it is from a thorough review of literature that you will determine what viable responses to your questions are.

• *Write items that do not assume information about the participants.* In today's diverse society, it is easy for researchers to make assumptions about the background of participants. For example, questions that are related to family should not assume that every family has two parents, working parents, siblings, and so forth.

• *Write items that allow participants to express what they really believe rather than suggesting a particular answer.* Researchers may inadvertently use a survey to obtain data to support their preexisting beliefs, writing items in such a way as to suggest that certain responses are "better" than others are. Items that are written in a way that lead participants to the response that the researcher wants them to give (even though the researcher is not aware of this) are referred to as **leading questions.** For example:

> Educational research, one of the most important classes in
> graduate school, should be how many credits?   __ 1   __ 2   __ 3   __ 4

This would be a leading question because you are making an assumption that Educational Research is one of the most important classes in graduate school (because this may be true for you).

Step 2: Selecting the Sample

Out of all the quantitative approaches, survey research tries to use the largest sample possible. In many cases, survey research is conducted with either a census population, meaning the sampling of the entire population (e.g., all the teachers in a school district or building), or a randomly selected sample for a larger population (like in Alysia's study). One thing to keep in mind when selecting your sample for survey research is that not everyone who is selected for your sample and sent a survey will participate in the study by filling it out and mailing it back. This becomes a major barrier to the generalizability of the findings. Even though a survey researcher randomly selects a sample to represent the larger population, those who in fact end up returning the survey may become a "subsample" that is unlike the original sample who received the survey.

Step 3: Piloting the Survey

Any survey should be pilot-tested with a small group of persons similar to those who will be in the final sample. Think of piloting as a kind of dress rehearsal for a survey. Participants who make up a pilot sample are usually chosen at random and are given the survey to complete but are also asked to examine the survey on many different fronts: clarity of language and terms, basic spelling and grammar, depth and breadth of subquestions and items, and overall psychometric properties of the instrument (e.g., scales are correct, etc.). Hopefully the survey will be sound enough for the members of the pilot group to complete it. When piloting your study, provide an additional sheet to the survey for pilot participants to write any comments, suggestions, or questions they have about the survey. Like Alysia, you should use this feedback to make corrections or refinements to the final survey.

Step 4: Administering the Survey

Many practical steps need to be considered in administering the survey.

Mailing. The paper-pencil, mail-out, mail-back survey has been the traditional method for survey administration. This method has many benefits, especially from a measurement perspective. First, it helps to ensure that the confidentiality of the participants' responses will be maintained. The researcher mails surveys directly to a group of teachers, who fill them out and mail them back using an enclosed SASE. This helps to ensure that no one except the researcher will have access to the information on the survey.

This method of administration also has disadvantages. The cost of postage may be a factor with large samples. Also, to use this method, the researcher must have mailing addresses for participants. When surveying teachers, obtaining a home mailing address is unlikely. However, it may be possible to send surveys to each teacher at their school building.

Other Methods. As discussed earlier, using the telephone to assist in the delivery of a survey is one alternative method for survey administration. The benefit of this approach is that the researcher can collect data within a relatively short time as opposed to the mailing method, which may take three to four weeks for responses to come back. Phone surveys also allow the survey administrator to encourage participation and increase response rates by personally explaining the purpose of the survey, answering questions about the study, and establishing rapport. A problem with using the telephone, however, is that the researcher must have phone numbers of the participants. Unless participant phone numbers are readily available, this method should be avoided. Looking up phone numbers, unless they are grouped somehow in a directory, is time-consuming and not worth the effort. Marketing firms sometimes generate phone number samples randomly, but this approach is not likely to produce a sample representative of any meaningful educational population. Timing is another problem with using the telephone for educational research surveys. If contacting teachers, do not expect to call them during the day at school, even though most schools have phones in class-rooms, and teachers have voice mail. Leaving messages either on voice mail or with the main office typically results in low response numbers. In this situation, it would be better to try to contact the teachers at home.

Although they are not ideal, sometimes researchers have to use other, less "controlled" approaches to administer and collect surveys. If, for example, a re-searcher is surveying teachers in a school district or building and does not know the names of the teachers (or how many teachers are in the school), identifying a key person within the school to assist in coordinating such efforts is imperative. In this case, the researcher would send a package of surveys to the key contact per-son at the school, and this "insider" would coordinate the efforts: giving the sur-veys to the individual teachers. Once the teachers have filled out the surveys, the contact person would collect and mail them back to the researcher. With this method, the researcher has to spend little effort in the actual administration of the survey; however, the **validity** of the data can be severely compromised, depend-ing on the selection of the key contact person and that person's relationship to the participants. Imagine that a researcher has selected the school principal as the key contact person. Now, try imagining that you are a teacher dissatisfied with work-ing at the school. Would you be willing to give your boss a survey where you have indicated your dissatisfaction? Having the principal give out the surveys, then col-lecting completed surveys in a secure drop box within the school building might provide a solution to such a problem.

An increasingly popular method of obtaining survey data is through the use of the Internet. Surveys can be e-mailed to groups and responses returned elec-tronically, or a group can be invited to visit a Web site to complete a survey. One advantage of online surveys is that the survey can be set up so that data are au-tomatically entered and tabulated.

Internet surveys are most valid and effective when the researcher can obtain a list of e-mail addresses for the realistic population. Another approach is to send a message to a listserv or electronic discussion group focused on the issues ad-dressed by the survey. For example, Kennedy and Voegtle (2000) surveyed ally groups at junior and senior high schools by posting their cover letter on the list-serv of an organization that had set up over 600 ally groups for gays and lesbians. The cover letter invited members of the listserv to participate in the study and provided a password for accessing the survey (an important caution so that the sample could be controlled).

Response Rate. After a survey has been developed and administered, the final concern of a survey researcher is the **response rate.** The response rate is the percentage of persons in the sample who complete and send surveys back to the researcher. One never gets back 100% of the surveys sent out. Research shows that response rates vary considerably depending on the purpose of the study, the relationship between the participants and the researcher, and the subject of the survey. Even after several reminders, response rates of 30% to 50% are typical. Response rates will be higher in situations where the people being surveyed have a greater interest or stake in the topic or results: for example, perhaps they attended a three-week symposium on the topic the summer before, or the survey results may lead to changes in the curriculum that they are teaching. In these situations, response rates may be 80% or higher. Some methods of survey administration, such as Internet surveys, have particularly low response rates. In the study of ally groups mentioned previously, Kennedy and Voegtle (2000) had a response rate of less than 5% despite repeated reminders to participants to complete the study survey. Although the survey data were unusable, they did collect archival data from ally group Web sites, which were analyzed to complete the study.

Lower response rates can have serious implications for the generalizability of the results of a survey study. Even when the sample to which the survey was distributed was randomly selected, a 50% response rate may result in a final sample that is not representative of the population. Often people who have extreme opinions about an issue (either in favor of or against it) take the time to respond to a survey, and those in the middle (not really caring one way or another) may be less likely to take the time to fill the survey out and return it. If most of the randomly selected sample for a survey does not respond, the findings reported may be misleading because if everyone who had been part of the sample had actually responded, the findings might be different.

Types of Survey Studies

If you have been involved in a survey study, it was probably the most common design known as the **one-shot survey design.** This approach is pretty much what it sounds like: surveys are mailed to participants at one particular point in time to gather their perceptions about a current issue. However, by altering the pattern of survey administration and sampling, different types of studies can be conducted, allowing a wider array of research questions to be answered. In other words, by changing *when* and *to whom* the surveys are administered, different kinds of research questions can be asked and answered. Presented below are several commonly used survey designs, along with examples of research questions that would help guide their development.

Designs That Follow the Same Sample Over Time

In some cases, based on the type of question being asked, a survey researcher might draw a sample from a defined population and then continue to survey the participants from the sample over a period of time. Keep in mind that this particular approach will only allow the researcher to ask questions of the same group of participants. With this design, the researcher can determine how the participants changed over time and keep track of the different experiences they may have had over time. Only individual changes could be monitored. Presented below are different designs where the researcher is doing this and is using the same sample over time.

Annual Panel Survey Study. In an annual panel survey study, the researcher selects a sample of participants, surveys them, and repeats the survey with the same group for several years. As an example, consider a study designed to examine the perceptions of new teachers as they graduate in May from their teacher preparation programs and enter the teaching field the following fall. A random sample of 3,000 newly graduated teachers could be selected from across the country and the entire sample surveyed *annually* for the next five years, each May, to find out their perceptions of how well they were trained and how satisfied they are with their career as a teacher.

Follow-up Survey Study. Let us say that the researcher was also interested in knowing whether these new teachers stayed in the teaching field or found employment in other areas. In a follow-up study, these new teachers might be surveyed initially on graduation, again the following year, and maybe for a couple of years after that (an annual panel survey). Some time would lapse (maybe four or five years), and then the same teachers would receive a survey to "follow up" to find out how they are doing. Keep in mind that some of these teachers may have left the field during the time when no survey was administered. A follow-up study would help the researcher document the rate at which teachers are leaving the field.

Longitudinal Survey Study. A longitudinal survey study is similar to a follow-up study in that a sample is selected and the entire sample is sampled periodically, but unlike a follow-up survey, the main function of the **longitudinal study** is to track participants over an extended amount of time. It would not be unusual for a longitudinal study to stretch out 10, 20, or 30 years. The purpose for collecting data over this long of a period is to investigate how participant perceptions or attitudes about an issue change (sometimes dramatically) over many years and to follow participants as their lives progress and their interests and philosophies change.

Designs That Select Different Samples Over Time

As discussed earlier, the point at which data are collected from a sample using a survey defines the approach and the types of questions such a study can answer. Researchers who are interested in documenting **trends** employ data collection designs that typically select different samples from the same or different populations over time. Presented below are some examples of those various designs.

Trend Survey Study. Trend studies are typically used to examine the perceptions of groups that are having or have had a shared experience at a particular time. For example, a researcher may want to ask new teachers fresh out of their pre-service teacher education programs about their perceptions of their preparedness to be a teacher. In this situation, the researcher is *only* interested in what *each group* of *new teachers thinks* (maybe capturing some of their unrealistic expectations or naiveté). The researcher is *not* interested in documenting initial perceptions and then showing how that same group's perceptions changed over time; rather, the researcher wants to describe the perceptions of each new group of teachers as they graduate and document any trends that emerge. For example, would new teachers graduating in different years have different perceptions as to the value of courses that focused on content versus pedagogy?

Cohort Survey Study. For this design, the researcher uses the same population each year but selects different samples from that group over time. For example, a sample of new teachers entering the field would be surveyed the first year. The next year, the same group of teachers selected the prior year (and now completing their first year of teaching) would be used, but another sample would be drawn from the original group who entered the profession that first year. This process would repeat itself again and again for a number of years. Keep in mind that one of the barriers to this design is that a large sample must be available initially for the researcher to be able to draw repeatedly from the group and not survey the same person more than once.

Other Types of Descriptive Research

In addition to surveys, descriptive researchers use other quantitative instruments to describe behaviors or to compare groups. In some studies, researchers may use either self-reports or observational measures to describe individuals at a particular point in time. However, remember that the goal of these studies is to simply describe behavior and not to infer relationship or causality. For example, Brady

(1989) used observational measures to describe the types of questions that teachers used in class discussions. As a descriptive study, Brady simply identified the patterns of questions used by teachers. This type of descriptive study typically uses observational checklists or rating scales to describe behaviors of interest.

Self-reports are another type of measure used in descriptive studies. For example, Larson (1989) examined the activities of adolescents by having them self-report on what they were doing at randomly selected times during the day. Larson used an experience sampling procedure where adolescents completed a written report on their activities when their provided beepers went off. The results were summarized in a pie chart that showed the percentage of time engaged in each activity. The researchers did not try to change the activities of the adolescents but simply described what the adolescents were doing. Larson examined age and gender differences in the reported activities. This type of study is sometimes referred to as **descriptive comparative** because it describes differences between groups but does not to try to explain why these differences occur. The types of group differences that are explored in descriptive-comparative studies often involve demographic variables such as age, ethnic group, sex, grade level, or job position.

Chapter Summary

Descriptive-survey research is one of the most common types of quantitative research in education. Researchers use cover letters to accompany their surveys. The cover letter defines the purpose of the study, discusses confidentiality of data, and provides the researcher's contact information. The survey itself is composed of different sections that gather different types of data. The first section of the survey is called the demographic section and collects personal information about the participants. The body of the survey is made up of similar items grouped together. These groupings are aligned with the research subquestions the researcher is asking. When writing survey items, the researcher should adhere to some basic criteria. Survey items should be written in clear, concise language. Items should gather data on one central idea or question and should avoid leading statements and should watch for double negatives. In selecting the sample for a survey study, researchers often use the census population or select random samples out of the realistic population to have the widest generalizability possible. Before surveys are administered to the sample, a pilot study is typically conducted. The pilot study selects fewer individuals from the sample and conducts a test run with the survey to fine-tune it. The researcher will use feedback from participants in the pilot study to make modifications to the survey before administering it to the remaining sample. Surveys can be administered to participants using several methods. Whereas alternative methods for survey administration such as e-mail, phone, or in person are used, the traditional mail-out, mail-back method continues to be the most widely used procedure. Survey researchers also need to be concerned about the response rate or number of surveys that participants fill out and return. A study that has less than a 50% response rate may be reporting findings that are distorted and do not accurately reflect the beliefs or attitudes of the total sample who received the survey.

There are different types or designs of survey studies. The most common design is the one-shot design where the researcher, after piloting the survey, administers it once to the sample. Annual panel survey studies, follow-up studies, and longitudinal survey studies are designs that follow the same sample over time. Designs that select different samples over time include trend and cohort surveys. Designs that follow the same or different samples over time both require surveys to be administered multiple times. In addition, some descriptive studies use observational measures or self-reports to describe groups at one point in time or to describe differences between groups that differ in demographic variables.

Key Concepts

> research question
>
> subquestions
>
> survey
>
> questionnaire
>
> confidentiality
>
> demographics
>
> leading questions
>
> response rate
>
> one-shot survey design
>
> longitudinal study
>
> descriptive comparative

Discussion Questions or Activities

1. A researcher is conducting a study that examines the perceptions of patients receiving mental health services. The overall purpose of this study is to describe the types of services these patients are receiving and whether they believe these

services are affecting their quality of life. The researcher is planning on administering the surveys through the help of the patients' counselors. Discuss any benefits or limitations that you see in this researcher's approach, and what, if any, alternative methods could you suggest to help improve the study's methods.

2. A researcher is interested in surveying fourth graders for the purposes of describing how they feel about high-stakes testing and how, if at all, they prepare for these tests. From a developmental perspective, discuss some possible challenges this researcher might encounter in designing such a survey for students at this age.

3. A researcher is surveying teachers in an urban school district as to whether they believe a new elementary math program is effective. The math program is a controversial subject among many of the school staff. In all, the district has six elementary buildings. The researcher has decided to use anonymous surveys. From a measurement perspective, discuss some of the benefits of using this approach and limitations in reporting findings.

Suggested Readings

Abrams, L. M., Pedulla, J. J., & Madaus, G. F. (2003). Views from the classroom: Teachers' opinions of statewide testing programs. *Theory into Practice, 42*(1). Retrieved Dec. 20, 2004, from Academic Search Premier.

Brown, M., & Bergen, D. (2002). Play and social interaction of children with disabilities at learning/activity centers in an inclusive preschool. *Journal of Research in Childhood Education, 17*(1), 26–37.

D'Andrea, M. (1994). Concerns of Native American youth. *Journal of Multicultural Counseling & Development, 22*(3). Retrieved June 16, 2004 from Academic Search Elite database.

Groves, R. M., Fowler, F. J., Jr., Couper, M. P., Lepkowski, J. M., Singer, E., & Tourangeau, R. (2004). *Survey methodology.* San Francisco: Jossey-Bass.

CHAPTER EIGHT

EXPERIMENTAL RESEARCH

Chapter Objectives

After reading this chapter, you should be able to

1. Identify the distinctive characteristics of experimental research.
2. Explain the difference between directional, nondirectional, and null hypotheses
3. Explain the operational definition of a variable using examples of such definitions for both a dependent and an independent variable
4. Define extraneous variables and describe the main techniques and designs used by experimental researchers to control them
5. Define seven threats to both internal and external validity and explain ways to control for each threat
6. Explain the different types of experimental designs
7. Explain methods used by researchers in single-subject designs

Research Vignette

Johanna is a graduate student in secondary education who is interested in math achievement and computers. Her literature search has shown that there is relationship between math achievement and the number of computerized tutoring sessions that a student receives. Much of the research she has found suggested that further study should use methods that will allow researchers to conclude that computerized tutoring sessions cause *increased* math achievement. Recognizing the strongest way to demonstrate a cause-and-effect relationship, Johanna decides to conduct an experimental study. She realizes the difficulty of conducting research in schools, but her part-time professor is the superintendent of a local school district. Her professor, after reviewing her institutional review board proposal, agrees to allow her to conduct the experiment. Johanna randomly selects 60 seventh graders from a pool of 175 students enrolled in an after-school tutoring program. After Johanna randomly selects her 60 seventh graders, she randomly assigns 30 to the computerized tutoring group and 30 to a noncomputerized tutoring group that receives tutoring from a teacher (note that the number of computers available is limited so that only 30 students can have access to computers). She selects a teacher identified by the principal as an excellent math teacher to run the noncomputerized group. Students in the computerized tutoring group are supervised by but receive no instruction from the teacher. In the computerized tutoring session, the teacher answers questions related to working with the computer. In the traditional tutoring session, she provides materials with math problems and works individually or in small groups with students. Participants in both groups are **pretested** using a math achievement test, and then both groups attend 30-minute after-school sessions for 30 weeks. (A pretest is a test given before the experimental treatment.) The groups are then **posttested** with an alternate form of the same test. (A posttest is a test given after the experimental treatment.) The results indicate that the computerized tutoring group outperformed the noncomputerized tutoring group on the posttest.

Understanding Experimental Research

Experimental research, which comes out of the scientific realism framework, is thought by many to be the only type of research that can result in findings that suggest causal relationships. What makes experimental research distinctive from other forms of quantitative research is that the researcher controls or manipulates how groups of participants are treated and then measures how the treatment affects each group. In technical terms, the researcher controls or manipulates one or more independent variables and examines the effect that the experimental manipulation has on the dependent variable or the outcome of the study (Table 8.1).

The independent variable is the variable that refers to how participants are treated. Participants are usually assigned to different groups that receive different treatments. In the field of education, the independent variable might be curricu-

TABLE 8.1 EXPERIMENTAL RESEARCH.

Group Assignment	Independent Variable	Dependent Variable
Experimental or treatment group	Computer-assisted tutoring sessions	Math achievement as measured by math test XXX
Control or comparison group	Noncomputerized tutoring sessions	Math achievement as measured by math test XXX

lum materials (e.g., skill-based readers versus literature), instructional styles (e.g., group learning versus individual) or specialized training (e.g., receiving training or not), to name just a few. The outcome of the study is the dependent variable, which is typically measured by some test or a measuring instrument that produces quantitative data.

Consider as an example Johanna's study on math achievement and a computerized tutoring program. In such a study, the independent variable would be the type of tutoring. The researcher would decide (or manipulate) the individuals who would receive the computerized tutoring and those who would receive tutoring from a teacher. In other words, the researcher would expose one group of participants (the experimental or treatment group) to computerized tutoring and the other group (the control or comparison group) to noncomputerized teacher-led tutoring. Math achievement, the study outcome, would be the dependent variable and is used to determine if any difference resulted from the manipulation of the independent variable (type of tutoring).

Simultaneous to the consideration of the independent and dependent variables, researchers must consider any potential variables that could influence the groups' performance on the dependent variable. Remember that at the end of a study, the researcher wants to conclude that the treatment caused any differences found between the experimental and control groups. To legitimately do this, the researcher has to be certain that no other variables could cause the differences. Technically, the researcher wants to control for **extraneous variables.** An extraneous variable is a variable that could influence the participants in the study and ultimately influence the dependent variable. Returning to our example of seventh graders and math achievement, if a difference were found at the end of the study, we would want to conclude that the reason or cause of the difference was computerized tutoring. For us to have confidence in this conclusion, our two groups must be as similar as possible with the exception of the treatment, in this case, computerized tutoring. Johanna did this by pretesting her participants. Ways to control for extraneous variables are discussed later in this chapter.

Steps in Planning and Conducting Experimental Research

Experimental studies closely follow a prescribed set of procedures that are detailed in the research proposal. Once an experimental study begins, there is little deviation from these procedures. The researcher takes an active role in setting up the study but, unlike a qualitative researcher, does not play an interactive role with the participants. As we noted earlier, setting up an experimental study is useful in determining cause-and-effect relationships. For example, the following research questions might lead to studies attempting to establish cause-and-effect relationships: Does computer use *cause* an increase in math achievement? and Does social skill training *have* an *effect* on the communication skills of preschoolers?

Either one of these studies would use the following steps for conducting experimental research:

- Select a topic
- Review the relevant literature and define a research question
- Develop a research hypothesis
- Select and assign participants to groups
- Select measurement instruments
- Define and administer experimental treatments
- Collect and analyze data
- Make a decision about the hypothesis
- Formulate conclusions

Remember that in preparing a proposal, you will proceed through all but the last three of these steps. In a proposal, these final steps may be replaced by the benefits-and-limitations reflections section of the proposal (see Chapter Three). Note, however, that in the method section of a proposal, you will need to discuss how you plan to collect and analyze the data.

Selecting a Topic. As with other research methods, the experimental researcher bases the topic selection on personal interest, experience, and an initial review of the literature. Typically in experimental research, the researcher is interested in determining if some treatment causes a significant change in behavior.

Reviewing the Relevant Literature. The researcher does an exhaustive literature review to determine the findings of current research on the topic of interest. This means that the researcher examines past literature to determine how others have researched the same topic, what variables or issues were studied, discussed, or both, and what the findings of those studies indicated. With this knowledge, the researcher generates a research question and designs the procedures to be used in the study, often borrowing methods used in prior research for his or her own study. An exhaustive literature review is necessary to allow the researcher to make an educated and informed prediction (a research hypothesis) about the expected outcome of the study.

Developing a Research Hypothesis. A **research hypothesis** is an educated guess that states the expected outcome of the study. The researcher is "educated" through the literature review. Based on the findings of the literature review, the researcher develops and states a hypothesis that indicates the expected causal relationship between the variables. For example, in our study on type of tutoring sessions and math achievement, a research hypothesis might be as follows:

> It is hypothesized that students who receive computerized tutoring sessions will demonstrate a higher level of math achievement than students who receive noncomputerized tutoring sessions.

The variables math achievement and type of tutoring sessions must then each be operationally defined. With an **operational definition,** a variable is defined in terms of how that variable will be measured, manipulated, or both. In this case, the researcher would define math achievement (the dependent variable) as a score on the math test selected to measure achievement (here you would actually name the test). Independent variables are operationally defined by explaining the procedures used to deliver the different treatments to the experimental and control groups. In our example, computerized tutoring sessions might be defined as using computer programs (identifying the specific software) to review math concepts for students during the after-school tutoring sessions. Noncomputerized tutoring sessions would be defined as having the teacher present the same math concepts and problems using noncomputerized methods, such as work sheets, during the after-school tutoring sessions.

There are three types of hypotheses in experimental research, which are described in detail below and summarized in Table 8.2.

Directional Hypothesis. A **directional hypothesis** states the direction or the expected outcome. That is, the researcher feels confident enough to suggest which group would outperform the other group(s), as in the above vignette:

> It is expected that the computerized tutoring group will perform **significantly better than** the group receiving noncomputerized tutoring instruction.

TABLE 8.2 HYPOTHESES IN EDUCATIONAL RESEARCH.

Type of Hypothesis	Definition
Directional[a]	States that a difference between the variables is expected and predicts the direction of that difference
Nondirectional[a]	States that a difference between the variables is expected but does not predict the direction of the difference
Null	States that no difference between the variables is expected

[a]Often referred to as the research hypothesis.

Researchers state a directional hypothesis if the literature suggests that there is sufficient evidence to predict the direction of the difference between the groups.

Nondirectional Hypothesis. A **nondirectional hypothesis** simply states that there will be some difference between the variables, but the direction of that difference is not being predicted. Let us say that as you review the literature on computer-assisted instruction and math achievement, you find that the evidence is not strong enough to suggest that the computer group will outperform the noncomputerized classroom instruction group. In fact, it is possible that teacher-led tutoring might lead to higher scores. In that case, you might suggest the following hypothesis:

> It is hypothesized that **there will be a significant difference** between the computerized tutoring group and the noncomputerized group in math achievement.

Null Hypothesis. The **null hypothesis** states that no significant difference between the variables is expected after the treatment is applied. The null hypothesis is implicit in all experimental research. That is, inferential statistics (discussed in greater detail in Chapter Ten) always test the null hypothesis, and in most cases, the researcher hopes to disprove the null hypothesis in favor of the research hypothesis. In our example, the null hypothesis would be

> It is hypothesized that there will be no difference in math achievement between the computer using tutoring group and the non-computer-using group.

Selecting and Assigning Participants to Groups. Most experimental studies have at least two groups, often referred to as the experimental and control groups. In an experimental study, the researcher *randomly selects* and *randomly assigns* participants to groups. Remember that from our earlier discussion of sampling, random selection allows the researcher to take the findings based on the sample and generalize those findings back to the entire population. For example, let us say that you are interested in conducting a research study on fourth graders in a particular inner-city school district. A list of all the fourth graders in the district would be your defined population. From that population, you would randomly select the desired number of participants to obtain the sample for your study. Although the study would be conducted on the sample of fourth graders, ultimately, you would want to make statements about the population. The type of randomization procedure used can vary from study to study, but the ultimate goal is still generalization. In reality, for practical reasons, many experimental researchers do not randomly *select* subjects. The lack of random selection limits the generalizability of results. However, random *assignment* of individuals or groups to treatments is an important feature of experimental research.

Selecting Instruments. Instruments or measurement tools for an experimental study are selected with the same care and attention as in other types of research. First, you want to be certain that the instrument you select is an appropriate measure for your dependent variable. Let us say that in Johanna's study, her research hypothesis is

> It is hypothesized that the seventh-grade students who receive computerized tutoring will have higher math achievement scores than seventh graders who received noncomputerized teacher-led tutoring.

The dependent variable in this study is math achievement. An appropriate instrument would be a math test that would be valid and reliable for seventh-grade students receiving either method of tutoring.

Selecting Controls for Extraneous Variables. There are several techniques for controlling for extraneous variables presented below. Most of these techniques describe what researchers call the **design** of a study. Design refers to the number of groups in a study, how they are treated, how the individuals are assigned to groups, the number of independent variables, and when the dependent variable is measured.

Control Groups. One of the most important features of experimental designs is the inclusion of a control group. In some designs, the control group is a separate group that receives no treatment or a different treatment than the experimental group but is equal to the experimental group in every other way. The study is set up so that extraneous variables will affect both groups in the same way. A variation on the use of control groups is having participants serve as their own controls by measuring them at least once before and after the treatment. This is common in single-subject research, which is discussed in more detail later in this chapter.

Random Assignment of Individuals to Treatments. Random assignment of individuals to treatments is a technique used in experimental research to control for possible differences between participants. By randomly assigning persons to treatments, the researcher assumes that many differences in the backgrounds and experiences of the participants will be equally distributed among the groups. However, often in educational research, it is not possible to randomly assign individuals to groups because persons are already in intact groups, such as classrooms. Therefore, other techniques such as those described below are used.

Matching. Matching is a control technique in which the researcher takes steps to ensure that extraneous variables are equally represented in the experimental and control groups. If Johanna believed that gender might influence her dependent variable, math achievement, she could use a pairwise matching of participants where for every male in the experimental group, she would match that male with a male in the control group (and do likewise for females). Although this would work effectively for an either/or variable like gender, it would become more complicated if she were concerned about more than two possible values for a variable: for example, a variable like intelligence or achievement that can have a wide range of values. If Johanna were trying to control the extraneous variable of intelligence, she would have to obtain IQ scores on each participant and then do a pairwise matching procedure for IQ. When she assigns a person with an IQ of 120 to the experimental group, she would have to assign a person with an IQ of 120 to the control group. Matching to control multiple extraneous variables or to control for extraneous variables with a wide range of possible values can be a complicated process. This process might eliminate potential participants because there is no individual match for them. This inability to match is especially likely for participants who are high or low in the characteristic that is being matched.

Comparing Homogeneous Subgroups. To make the selection process a bit easier while still controlling for extraneous variables, researchers often set up a study where they are comparing homogeneous subgroups. For example, in a study where IQ was the extraneous variable, a researcher could propose setting up several IQ groups, each with a range of IQ scores. The use of the Wechsler Intelligence Scale for Children-Revised (WISC-R; a well-known intelligence test) could be proposed to establish a high-IQ group (a score of 115 and above), an average-IQ group (a score of 85 to 114), and a low-IQ group (a score of 60 to 84). Note that these cutoff scores are arbitrary and are based on an average IQ of 100. Although this procedure would facilitate the selection of participants for the study, the generalizability of the findings would be limited to the IQ ranges used for the study, and such limited generalizability would have to be noted as a potential concern by the researcher.

Pretesting of Participants. A common type of experimental study, called **quasi-experimental study,** involves random assignment of whole groups to treatments. To ensure that the groups are similar, researchers often administer a **pretest** to both groups. A pretest basically measures whether the experimental and control groups are starting out equal. Essentially, it is a check of whether there are preexisting differences between the groups in abilities or other characteristics. If there are preexisting differences, then one would not be able to conclude that differences at the end of the study are due to the treatment. For example, you decide to conduct a study in Elementary School West that is investigating a new reading program. You obtain permission from the building administrator to conduct your study, but the administrator tells you that only Ms. Johnson and Mr. Garcia's classes can be used. To conduct an experimental study in such a situation, the researcher would randomly assign the classes to treatment and control. How? You might flip a coin. If it lands with the head up, Ms. Johnson's class members receive the treatment, and if the "tail" is up, Mr. Garcia's class is assigned to the treatment group. A pretest would help the researcher to determine if the two groups were equal at the start of the study.

Holding Extraneous Variables Constant. Some extraneous variables can be controlled by holding them constant between experimental and control groups. In experimental research, the types of variables that are held constant often pertain to the setting or the teachers. If you were comparing two different methods of instruction, you might control for the time of day, the classroom temperature, or the concepts covered by keeping these the same for the treatment and control groups. If two different teachers taught the two methods, you could attempt to control for the quality of the teaching as an extraneous variable by requiring both teachers to have the same number of years of teaching experience (of course, the limitation to this control is the fact that quality of teaching is not solely a matter of years of experience). The lack of control over quality of teaching would be a criticism of the study and should be discussed as a limitation of the study.

Factorial Designs. A factorial design is one that includes multiple independent variables. Based on the review of the literature, a researcher might identify a potential extraneous variable and decide to build it into the study as an additional independent variable. This means that the final data will be analyzed for possible differences due to each independent variable. These might include variables that can be manipulated by the researcher or characteristics of the participants. For example, instead of matching for gender, Johanna might decide to build it into her study as an independent variable. This would allow her to see if different types of tutoring work better for boys or girls. To further explore the potential effects of both gender and type of tutoring, the researcher could combine these variables into one design with two independent variables, type of tutoring and gender. Figure 8.1 shows the groups that would be included in this design.

Statistical Control of Extraneous Variables. A common way to deal with extraneous variables is to measure and statistically control them. There are a variety of statistical tests used for this purpose, most of which are discussed in Chapter Ten. One statistical procedure used as a mechanism of control is **analysis of covariance** (ANCOVA). ANCOVA is defined as a procedure where participants' **posttest scores** (scores on the dependent variables obtained after the experimental treatment is given) are statistically adjusted for differences in **pretest** scores (pretest scores are obtained on the dependent variable before the experimental treatment is given). Sounds like real "massaging of the data," doesn't it? Well, in some sense, that is what ANCOVA is. Assume that you have decided to conduct a research study that examines the effect of a literature-based reading program compared with a program that uses the skills-based method of instruction. You go to a school district and get permission to use Holly Elementary School. Principal Wonderful tells you that you can use Ms. Excited and Mr. Boring's first-grade classes. No random selection of participants is allowed, so you randomly assign one class to the literature-based instruction and the other to the skills-based method of instruction. However, being the smart researcher that you are, you are concerned that there might be some initial differences in the students' reading abilities. If the participants are different in reading ability at the beginning of the study, then any

FIGURE 8.1 FACTORIAL DESIGN.

	Computerized Tutoring	Noncomputerized Tutoring
Male	Group 1: Computerized tutoring for males	Group 2: Noncomputerized tutoring for males
Female	Group 3: Computerized tutoring for females	Group 4: Noncomputerized tutoring for females

difference you might find at the end of the study could not be attributed to your experimental treatment. You decide to test each group before the start of the study, and indeed, you find that Ms. Excited's class has some students reading at the second-grade level whereas Mr. Boring has a class that is reading pretty much at the first-grade level. Rather than abandon your study because of the differences in the groups, you would use an ANCOVA! The ANCOVA procedure would statistically remove any advantage held by Ms. Excited's class so that the two classes could be compared fairly.

Defining the Experimental Treatments. A major part of creating a research proposal is defining the treatments to be administered to the participants, also known as the *research plan*. This plan should describe all procedures to be used in the study. Specifically, what happens to the participants in each group? How does the treatment for the experimental group differ from that of the control group? The procedures for an experimental study are described in detail before the beginning of the experiment, and typically, there is little or no deviation from the plan once the study begins. The key to the plan is the differentiation between the experimental and control groups. This is essential because often the goal of an experimental study is to prove that the experimental treatment has made a difference.

Analyzing the Data

The data produced by experimental studies are quantitative, and as such, the researcher who actually conducts a study examines the data using statistical procedures. The type of statistical analysis depends on the type of data you collected. As you recall from Chapter Four, there are several levels of measurement involved in the collection of data: nominal, ordinal, interval, and ratio. The researcher must select a statistical test that is appropriate for the level of measurement used in the study. The following table presents some common statistical tests that are used to analyze data at different levels of measurement. Note that ANOVA refers to *analysis of variance*.

Variable	*Statistical Test*
Nominal	Chi square
Ordinal	Mann-Whitney *U* test
Interval	*t* test, ANOVA, multiple regression
Ratio	*t* test, ANOVA, multiple regression

Although the names of these statistical tests might be meaningless to you now, they are presented so that you can begin to recognize them when they are described in the research that you are reading. Many of these tests are explained in greater depth later in this book.

Making a Decision About the Hypothesis

The data collected and analyzed will provide either support for your research hypothesis or evidence to the contrary. Remember that, in general, the researcher wants to reject the null hypothesis, which states that there is no real difference between the treatment groups—in other words, that any difference found was due to chance and not to the experimental treatment. Decisions about the null hypothesis are based on probability, which is covered in depth in Chapter Ten.

Formulating Conclusions

The decision made about the hypothesis in an experimental study is based on statistical analysis of a study's data and forms the basis for the conclusions of a study. Confirming a research hypothesis can add to the body of knowledge on a topic and have practical implications. If a researcher finds in a controlled experimental study that one-to-one mentoring decreases student dropout rates, this would be an important finding and might support a conclusion or recommendation that schools invest in mentoring programs. Think about how many potential dropouts would stay in school if they received one-to-one mentoring. However, when a research hypothesis is found to be false (i.e., the experimental treatment did not make a difference), the conclusion can be equally important. Using the same example, if the null hypothesis about a mentoring program is *not* rejected (meaning there is no difference between the treatment groups), consider the money a school district might save if mentoring programs did not work—money that could be used to investigate other programs to keep students in school. Whatever the result of a study, the conclusions must be consistent with the data. Regardless of whether a study produces a supported research hypothesis, the conclusions can still be important to the field of education.

Threats to Experimental Validity

Validity in experimental research is generally divided into two concepts: **internal validity** and **external validity**. *Internal validity* is the degree or extent to which the differences in the dependent variable are due to the experimental manipulation and not some extraneous variable. In other words, at the conclusion of the study, if the two groups are different, are they different because of the treatment? If Ms. Excited's and Mr. Boring's classes are different, what caused the differences? As a researcher, you would want the differences to be due to the manipulated variable, in this case, reading instruction. *External validity* is the degree to which the results are generalizable beyond the sample used for a study. If a difference is found between Ms. Excited's and Mr. Boring's classes (the sample), would the findings be generalizable to other first graders in the district or other first graders generally? See Box 8.1 for an example of how these concepts were dealt with in an actual study.

Box 8.1 Internal and External Validity in Action!

What Works in the Lab Might Not Work in the Classroom

In an attempt to fulfill the requirements proposed by NCLB [No Child Left Behind Act], a researcher worked to establish a proven practice by conducting a true experimental study. The purpose of this study was to show the effect of a computer-based curriculum on elementary school students' statewide scores in an English Language Arts Test(ELA). To do so, the researcher randomly selected fourth graders from a population of five large urban school districts. Parents of the students all agreed to have their child participate in the study. Once students were selected for the study, they were then randomly assigned to a treatment group and a control group. Students in the treatment group were exposed to the computer-based lessons. These lessons had been carefully developed to address areas in reading where students in the districts had shown weaknesses on their state ELA assessments. Students participated in these lessons for 30 minutes per day in a computer lab setting where activities were carefully monitored and timed. Students in the control group received instruction on ELA through classroom course work that their teachers provided. To control for the extraneous variable of time engaging in instruction, the researcher interviewed teachers in the control groups and determined that they, too, spent about 30 minutes per day on ELA. Students were pretested using a reading-literacy instrument. This instrument was analyzed by experts and determined to be aligned with the state assessment. The study took place over the last 12 weeks before the ELA assessment. Students in both groups were given a posttest: the same form that they had taken as the pretest measure. Students in the treatment group, who received the computer lessons, had significantly higher gains on the posttest measure than students who had received the classroom lessons. In addition, students who received the computer-based lessons also outperformed those in the control group on that year's ELA assessment. The researcher continued to replicate the study, working with other school districts across the state whose students had similar gaps in reaching the state benchmarks on the ELA. During replication, the researcher had consistent results with the earlier study. Under NCLB, the computer-based lessons were designated "a proven practice" because experimental research had been used to show the effects of this method. As a result of this, the computer-based lessons were "packaged" and given to middle elementary teachers throughout the state, "guaranteed" to increase student outcomes on the ELA assessment. Although teachers were eager to adopt and use the computer-based lessons, they found that, for the most part, student scores did not increase. In fact, it appeared that the computer modules had little impact. But wait a minute! How could that be? After all, was not this a proven practice? The answer is yes, under the laboratory-like conditions in which it was being studied. However, what the researcher failed to consider was the external validity of the study's findings. The moment that the computer-based modules were no longer administered in a lab where everything was conducted in a controlled and organized way and implemented into the classroom—a setting that we know does not always go as planned—the study's results were no longer valid or true. For example, we know from the literature and research on teaching and pedagogy that teachers generally do not adopt new curriculum and lessons without modifying them to meet the needs of their students. No matter how good a prescribed curriculum might be, teachers tweak it a little here and there to make it work for their classrooms. So, one thing that happened to this proven practice is that teachers took it and implemented it in different ways. Many could not spend the entire 30 minutes of class time using the computer-based module, and so they began to "fit it in" a few minutes here and a few minutes there. This did not give students enough exposure to the computer modules to make any difference. In addition, and perhaps the most important aspect, was that most of the school districts did not have a lot of technology. Some of the classrooms had only one computer, and for those that did, many did not have a compact-disk player or the necessary memory to run the program. Therefore, a method that was shown to be effective in an experimental study, where the conditions were controlled to address threats to the study's internal validity, limited the external validity of the study to the point that it was no longer applicable to the very settings for which it was intended.

Most of our understanding of these principles is based on the work of Bracht and Glass (1968), Campbell and Stanley (1971), and Cook, Campbell, and Peracchio (1979), who identify the specific threats to external and internal validity. There are seven threats each to internal and external validity.

Sounds overwhelming? Rest assured that you are not alone. Most students as well as professors of educational research moan and groan when it comes to learning and teaching about threats to experimental validity. This dismay is due in part to the fact that the concepts are often presented in an abstract form that lacks sufficient relevance to students. Faculty look for ways to make this section interesting and relevant. In our collective 35 years of teaching this course, we still struggle with ways to make these threats meaningful to our students. We have embedded these threats in actual research examples in an attempt to make the concepts more relevant. Refer to Tables 8.3 and 8.4 when reviewing these examples. Note that each of these threats can be controlled through one of the control techniques listed above. See if you can anticipate how to control each threat as you read the examples.

TABLE 8.3 THREATS TO INTERNAL VALIDITY.

Threat	Definition	How to Control
History	Event that occurs outside of the study and affects the dependent variable	Include an appropriate control group
Maturation	A personal change as the result of growth or maturation that can occur in physical, mental, or emotional functioning	Include an appropriate control group
Testing	Pretest of participants on what is being measured on the posttest results in improved scores	Include an appropriate control group
Instrumentation	Instruments used in the study lack reliability, validity, or both	Use reliable or valid instrument(s); train observers and use short observation periods
Statistical regression	The tendency of scores to regress toward the average score, bringing higher scores down and lower scores up	Include a control group selected using same criteria
Differential selection of subjects	Use of already-formed groups that might be different	Use random assignment to groups; pretest participants to see if groups are similar
Mortality	Subject attrition or dropping out	Pretest to obtain information for examining who dropped out of one group and eliminate a similar participant from the other group to maintain equivalent groups; maintain contact with both treatment and control groups

TABLE 8.4 THREATS TO EXTERNAL VALIDITY.

Threat	Definition	How to Control
Pretest-treatment interaction	Pretest sensitizes participants to the treatment, and outcome would be different if the participants had not been pretested	Include appropriate control groups who also receive pretests and a treatment group that receives no pretest
Multiple-treatment interaction	Participants are exposed to multiple treatments that are part of some overarching treatment or simply exposed to more than one treatment; when this occurs, it might be difficult to determine which treatment resulted in any difference that is found, limiting generalizability	Limit the number of treatments delivered, or deliver different treatments at different times; if one treatment has many components, establish comparison groups receiving different components
Selection-treatment interaction	Differences between groups due to lack of random assignment or use of already-formed groups interact with the treatment variable, limiting generalizability to the general population	Pretest groups to see if they differ in any way that might affect treatment effectiveness, or randomly select a representative sample of the population for whom the treatment is intended
Specificity of variables	The more specific the conditions (time, place, participants, tests) are, the more limited the generalizability of the study	Replicate studies with different samples, measures, and settings
Treatment diffusion	Experimental group communicates with control group, providing the latter with information about the experimental treatment; this kind or level of communication might not occur in other studies, thereby limiting the generalizability of the results	Limit communication by conducting the study at different sites or by asking participants not to discuss what occurs until the study is over
Experimenter effects	Researcher may exert unintentional influence on the outcome of the study; if the study was conducted by another researcher, results might be different	Use researchers who are "blind" or "double blind"; increase researcher self-awareness
Reactive arrangements	Simply being part of a study can affect one's feelings, behavior, and attitudes	Provide information to keep participants from trying to guess the study's purpose; extend study until reactive effects wear off

Threats to Internal Validity

Researchers should be aware of the following threats to internal validity.

History. As part of your safe-school plans, you are conducting a series of training sessions for teachers that are designed to improve their sense of well-being and safety. The training session lasts for three months, and as a part of the study, you administer a pretest and a posttest that measure one's overall sense of well-being. So far, so good. Let us say that your study was being conducted during the shootings that occurred at Columbine (Colorado) High School where two students went on a shooting rampage that resulted in the deaths of many. Has your study been influenced by this event? Certainly! Scores on your posttest will likely be lower than they might have if this tragic event had not occurred. *History is an event that occurs outside of the procedures planned for the study and affects the dependent variable.* Obviously, the longer your study is, the more that history is a potential threat. History does *not* mean the personal history of your participants. History is especially a problem when studies do not include a control group. Notice that our example refers to only one group getting a pretest and then a posttest. If the study included a control group that did not receive the workshops but did hear about the Columbine tragedy, we could still see if our workshop helped the teachers who received it because the threat of history was controlled for by keeping it constant between the experimental and control groups.

Maturation. As a preschool teacher, you notice that many of your students have difficulty holding a crayon correctly. You decide to work on ways that promote more efficient ways to hold a crayon, a fine-motor skill, so that students will be better able to use a pencil when they get to kindergarten. You set up a miniexperiment where you evaluate each student's fine-motor skills and then take five minutes each morning to "train proper crayon holding." At the end of three months, you evaluate the students' fine-motor skills again and find that your treatment worked. Before you give yourself a pat on the back, think about this. Was it your fine-motor "treatment" that made the difference, or was it simply a function of natural change in your students? Perhaps maturation or time improved their performance! *Maturation, then, is a personal change as the result of growth, which can occur in physical, mental, or emotional functioning.* How could you control for maturation? Again, using a control group is one solution because the control group would also be maturing. Because both the treatment and control groups are maturing simultaneously any differences between groups after the treatment can be attributed to the independent variable.

Testing. Many experimental studies involve giving participants a pretest. Let us say that a researcher conducts a study of the effectiveness of a lesson designed to improve students' knowledge about the Vietnam War. The researcher gives students a pretest that assesses their knowledge at the start of the study and proceeds to give them a two-hour lesson on the war (the treatment). Two days later, students are given the same test, and performance improves. Was it the lesson that improved their performance, or was it simply the short time between test-taking sessions? Did they simply recall the information from the first test on the second test? *Testing threat refers to changes in participants' posttest scores that occur because of what they remember from a pretest.* Researchers can control for a testing threat by using a control group; however, a simpler approach might be to simply increase the amount of time between the pretest and posttest to make it less likely that participants will remember the pretest questions.

Instrumentation. Not all tests are created equal. Some tests are harder or easier than others. Some are more reliable and valid than others. If your assessments do not accurately measure the variables, the result is an inaccurate assessment of performance. So, even if at the end of your study you demonstrate a difference between groups, it might not be due to the manipulation of the independent variable but simply a function of poor assessments. Instrumentation is a threat to internal validity *if instruments that lack good reliability and validity are used.* Unlike the examples we have given thus far, the validity threat posed by instrumentation is *not* controlled for by using a control group. To control for instrumentation, make sure you use instruments with good reliability and validity (instruments that have been tested and documented in the literature as valid and reliable measures of your variables of interest). In studies using observers who are recording behaviors, make sure that the observers are unbiased, well trained, and not fatigued by long observation sessions to ensure reliability and validity of observations.

Statistical Regression. Assume that you are conducting a study where you decide to use only students who score in the top and bottom 10% of a class on an algebra pretest. As a result of using extreme scores, you could expect statistical regression (in more common terms, *movement of scores*) to the mean on an algebra posttest, even if the groups received different treatments. This means that students who scored at the top 10% would regress downward toward the mean, and those who scored in the lower 10% would regress up toward the mean. (If the word "regress" throws you, think of this as a bounce-back effect, bouncing up or down somewhat after the pretest.) At the end of the study, you would not know if the difference between the groups was due to your treatment or to statistical regression. *Statistical regression, then, is the tendency of scores to move toward the average score, bring-*

ing the higher scores down and the lower scores up. How do you control for statistical regression? Yes, control groups to the rescue! If you select participants for both the treatment and control groups in the same way, regression will happen in both groups and so will be controlled.

Differential Selection of Participants. Experimental researchers who randomly assign participants to groups assume that this process controls for possible differences in preexisting abilities. However, random assignment is not always possible due to ethical or practical considerations. When random assignment is not possible differential selection of participants may be a problem because the researcher is forced to using already preexisting groups. Suppose you are conducting a study in which you must use either a convenience sample or cluster random sample because you have to work with established classrooms. In either case, you will be using groups that have been formed before the start of the study. You have no idea how the groups were formed, and in fact, they might be different from each other. Suppose that one class ends up being an honors class and the other class selected is a more heterogeneous mix of students. This would result in the groups being different before they are exposed to the treatment condition. If the honor students outperform the heterogenous students, what would be the cause of the difference: the treatment or individual differences between the groups (differential selection)? To eliminate the threat of *differential selection of participants or using already-formed groups that might be different,* most researchers give participants a pretest whenever they are forced to use intact groups. Issues with differential selection occur frequently in educational research.

Mortality or Attrition. No, this does not mean that your treatment is so severe that some of your subjects die; it means they *drop out of your study.* The problem with mortality is that you have no control over who drops out. Imagine two groups of students who are mostly equivalent at the start of a study. Then, for some reason, some of the brightest students drop out of the experimental group but not the control group. The groups would no longer be equivalent. Once again, if there is a difference at the end of the study, is it due to the treatment, or to the fact that the groups are no longer equal due to mortality? Researchers who are planning or conducting long-term studies are particularly concerned about this threat. One way to effectively deal with the risk of participants dropping out and changing the nature of the groups is to use a pretest. If a participant with a particular score drops out of the experimental group, a control group member with a comparable score on the pretest can be eliminated, thereby *controlling for mortality or subject attrition.* Mortality may also be a problem in studies using control groups compared with a treatment group receiving an intervention program. If persons in the control group are not receiving any communication or attention from the researcher while the treatment group is in frequent contact due to the intervention, it is likely that mortality will be greater in the control group. It is also likely that highly motivated control group members are the ones most likely to seek help elsewhere and so drop out, making this an important threat to internal validity. Communication with control group members during long-term studies may be a way to maintain their participation, thereby managing this threat to validity.

Threats to External Validity

Recall that external validity is the degree to which the results of a study are generalizable to populations outside the sample used in the study. The seven threats to external validity are listed in Table 8.4.

Pretest-Treatment Interaction. First, pretest-treatment interaction is a problem only when a pretest is used in a study. In some circumstances, *the treatment interacts with or sensitizes the participants to the treatment, and the outcome would be different if the participants had not been pretested.* When might this occur? Consider the following. You are conducting a study where the experimental treatment is a workshop designed to improve students' sensitivity toward diversity. Your pretest is a measure of student awareness of their personal attitudes toward diversity. The pretest itself may make them more aware of the issues of diversity and its importance in their lives. If at the end of the study the experimental group is more sensitive to issues of diversity, could your results be generalizable to all other groups receiving the training, or would the findings be generalizable only to groups that received the pretest on attitudes toward diversity? One way to control for pretest treatment interaction is to use a pretest that does not increase participants' awareness of what behaviors you are trying to change. Professional researchers often use complex designs that include treatment groups that are not pretested to control for pretest-treatment interaction.

Multiple-Treatment Interaction. Some studies *expose participants to multiple treatments that are part of some overarching treatment or simply expose them to more than one treatment. When this occurs, it might be difficult to determine which treatment resulted in any difference that might be found.* For example, a researcher conducts a study that hopes to determine the effect that attending a charter school has on achievement. In reality, a charter school might include many different treatment components, all of which could affect achievement. For example, a charter school might have more smaller class sizes and school uniforms. At the end of the study, the charter school students seem to be outperforming their counterparts in regular public school classes.

Could the results be generalizable to all charter schools or just charter schools with the same treatment components as the one under investigation? Multiple treatment interactions can be controlled by limiting the number of treatments delivered or delivering different treatments at different times. If one treatment has many components, seek out comparison groups receiving different components. For example, one might compare charter schools that have smaller class sizes with those that have school uniforms.

Selection-Treatment Interaction. As we discussed earlier in the section on internal validity, the threat of differential selection of subjects occurs when already-formed groups are used in a study, and the groups are different at the start of the study. Any time already-formed groups are used or participants are not randomly assigned individually, the generalizability of the study is greatly compromised. In the following example, *already-formed groups potentially could interact with the treatment variable.* You are thrilled to learn that Principal Johnson has just given you permission to conduct a research study designed to determine if cooperative learning improves the math achievement of first graders. However, she tells you that you can use Mr. McDuff and Ms. White's first-grade classes and cannot randomly form your groups. You have had no control over how Mr. McDuff and Ms. White's classes were formed, so to attempt to manage internal validity, you decide to randomly assign the two classes to treatment and control. Ms. White's class gets the treatment (cooperative learning), and Mr. McDuff's becomes the control group (whole class instruction). Unbeknown to you, Ms. White's class contains students who are socially skilled, and they work extremely well on the cooperative learning task. Mr. McDuff's class has students who are not as socially skilled. At the end of the study, the cooperative learning group outperforms the control group. Does this mean that you can generalize your findings to all first graders, including Mr. McDuff's class? Certainly not! If cooperative learning requires a certain level of social skills to work well, it may be effective only for students who have these skills or when their teachers work with them to develop skills as they use the cooperative learning strategy. In this example, an initial difference between the two groups interacted with the treatment to make it more effective, but it is not clear if the treatment will be effective with groups that do not have good social skills.

Specificity of Variables. All experimental research is conducted in a specific location, at a specific time, with a specific population, with variables measured with a certain instrument and under a specific set of circumstances. *The more specific the conditions are, the more limited the generalizability of the study.* A study that is conducted with fourth graders in an inner-city school district, using a specific instructional approach, during the first hour of school, with a specific teacher, and with reading achievement measured with the ABC achievement test may be applicable only to a similar setting. This is one reason why often the purpose of research studies is to replicate previous studies with different groups in different settings using different measures. Any single study has limited generalizability, so it is often useful to replicate studies. However, the criticism of specificity of variables can be avoided by randomly selecting persons and schools that are diverse, using measures that are widely regarded as reliable and valid, and using treatments that can be easily replicated in other settings without specialized resources or circumstances.

Treatment Diffusion. Anytime you conduct a study with an experimental and a control group, you run the risk of the two groups communicating with each other, thereby "diffusing" or making the treatment less distinct. One of us (M.G.L.) ran into this problem with the second graders she used in her dissertation research on strategy use, memory, and metacognition (knowledge about one's own cognitive strategies and skills). The treatment group received metacognition training in the form of playing a game, and the control group learned to use a simple repetition strategy. Each participant was trained individually, but when some of the control group participated in the posttest memory task, they used the metacognition strategy (game) that the experimental group was taught. When the author asked them how they knew to use this strategy, the second graders indicated that their friends (in the treatment group) told them about the game! An interesting outcome, yet not one anticipated by the researcher! Be aware of the *possibility that your experimental group might communicate with your control group, providing the control group with information about the experimental treatment,* and consider how you might design your study to limit or prevent this communication.

Experimenter Effects. Good experimental researchers are careful about their own influence on the research they are conducting. Remember that in quantitative research, the researcher maintains an independent and separate role. However, there are times when the *researcher may exert unintentional influence on the outcome of the study.* These influences can be the result of the personal attributes of the researcher or may occur because the researcher's expectations affect his or her behavior and the performance of the participants. Personal attributes include gender, race, age, or emotional disposition. Researcher influence due to expectations that affect the behavior of research participants (also known as experimenter bias) can occur if the researcher, hoping to obtain a difference between the experimental and control groups, gives the experimental group any unintended advantage (more testing time, slower instructions, more attention, positive feedback for correct responses, etc.). Note that bias can occur unintentionally and even unconsciously, especially if researchers have strong expectations regarding which group will do better. When bias is present, generalizability is limited because other researchers may not obtain similar results. To control for experimenter effects, researchers who are in contact with participants are kept **"blind"** as to the expected outcome of the study or regarding which group is the treatment or control group. The term **"double blind"** means that the researcher knows neither who is in which group nor what the expected (hypothesized) outcome is. This means that someone must be hired to carry out the study, which may be impractical! It is far more practical to be on guard against researcher effects.

Reactive Effects. Have you ever been part of a research study? If so, you know that *simply being part of a study can affect your feelings, behavior, and attitudes.* One way that reactive arrangement is manifested is through the **Hawthorne effect**. The Hawthorne effect occurs when participants' behavior is affected by their mere participation in the research study and not directly attributable to the treatment. This finding is based on a well-known study conducted at the Hawthorne (and thus the name) Plant of the Western Electric Company in Chicago. The researchers in this study investigated ways to improve the productivity of workers. The independent variable in the study was the amount of light intensity, and the dependent variable was worker productivity. As the amount of light intensity increased, the worker productivity increased. The researchers decided to see what would happen if the light intensity was decreased. Well, guess what? Productivity went up even under conditions of lower light intensity. The workers, aware that they were participating in a research study, increased their productivity regardless of the treatment because they thought the changes indicated that the company cared about them.

Another common reactive-effect threat to external validity is called **novelty effect.** Often a new treatment is more effective than an older approach simply because it is new and different. After a while, the novelty wears off, and the new treatment is no better than the older treatment. For example, say that a high school teacher decided to put on a hat each time she was introducing a new concept in class. She uses this treatment in two of her classes (the treatment group) for two weeks but not in two other classes randomly assigned to be her control group. She finds that the treatment group shows better understanding of the concepts than the control group. However, the effect may simply show that students pay attention when something new is happening in class. If she continues the hat routine for two months, she may find that it is no longer effective. *The novelty effect means that a treatment is effective only when it is new or novel and that the treatment's effectiveness will not generalize beyond this initial period of time.* In a research study, reactive effects due to novelty are controlled for by extending the period of the study long enough so that any novelty effect will have worn off.

Single-Subject Research Designs

Single-subject research designs are a type of true experimental design with a unique twist: the sample size is limited to one participant or a few participants who are treated as one group. In single-subject designs, the participant serves as both the treatment and the control group. You might be asking, how does a participant serve in both groups? Good question! The researcher measures participant behavior repeatedly during at *least* two different points in time, when a treatment is not present and again when a treatment is present. The periods during which the treatment is not present are called **baseline periods,** and the periods during which the treatment is given are called **treatment periods.** Consider the following study. You are a special educator who is conducting a study to determine if a reward system using praise as a reward (the independent variable or treatment) would increase the time on a task (dependent variable) for a student with attention-deficit hyperactivity disorder (ADHD). The participant's behavior would be measured in phases, before the treatment (baseline phase), during the treatment, and after the treatment (discussed below as an "A-B-A design"). The data for the baseline phase would serve as the control group data and would be the point of comparison with the behavior exhibited during the treatment and posttreatment phases of the study.

Types of Single-Subject Research Designs

The most commonly used single-subject research designs are A-B-A designs and multiple-baseline designs. In all single-subject designs, the A phase of the study represents a series of baseline measurements. The B phase of the study involves the measurements that occur during treatment. In addition, all single-subject designs include continuous measurement of behavior throughout all of the phases.

A-B-A and A-B-A-B-A Research Designs.
The simplest single-subject research design is the A-B-A design. In this design, the researcher obtains baseline data, delivers the treatment, and then after withdrawing the treatment, measures baseline data again. Using the example of time on task and rewards as an example, the researcher would collect data on the number of minutes the participant spends on the task to determine a baseline. The treatment phase or rewards would then be given as the child is engaged in a task. The time on task would be measured again through the treatment phase and when the treatment was withdrawn. See Figure 8.2 for an example of how data from an A-B-A design would be graphed. Some

FIGURE 8.2 SAMPLE A-B-A DESIGN.

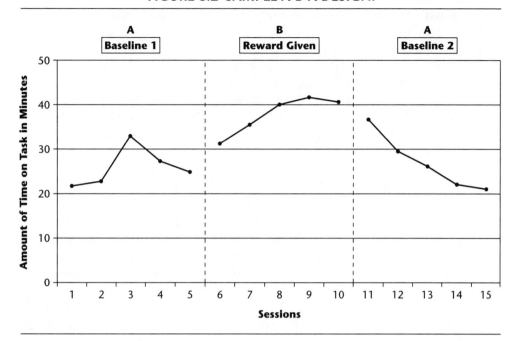

researchers, especially in this example, would choose to use an A-B-A-B design. In this case, the study would end with the reintroduction of the intervention or treatment. If, in fact, the treatment was effective, it would not be good practice to withdraw it!

Multiple-Baseline Designs. In cases with potential ethical issues, such as the one described above, the researcher might choose a multiple-baseline design. Multiple-baseline designs are used when the behavior learned during the treatment phase cannot be unlearned (learning to discriminate between the letters O and Q, for example) or when it would be unethical to even attempt to reverse the behavior (a reduction in self-stimulatory behavior of an autistic child). The basic difference between multiple-baseline designs and A-B-A-B designs is that the withdrawal of the treatment phase is eliminated. In multiple-baseline designs, the intervention is examined by collecting baseline data on more than one behavior (or person or setting) and applying the treatment sequentially on a time-lagged basis. This means that we begin to apply the treatment to different behaviors (or persons or settings) during different phases of the study. The goal of multiple-baseline designs is to determine if the treatment is effective across different people, settings, or behaviors. For the sake of developing an in-depth understanding of single-subject research, we have decided to focus our discussion entirely on multiple baselines across behaviors (remember, they can be conducted across people or settings). This is how a multiple-baseline study works. First, the researcher identifies at least two behaviors that he or she wants to see changed in a participant. The two behaviors must be different but be similar enough so that a single treatment would be effective. Let us say that a teacher wanted to help a child with severe ADHD learn how to control some disruptive behaviors through the use of a cueing response such as touching her cheek (rather than a spoken reprimand). Our teacher might identify three inappropriate behaviors: getting up out of one's seat, speaking out of turn, and talking to oneself. In this design, you would first take baseline measures of all three behaviors four times during the first week. During week 2, the teacher would cue the student for out-of-seat behavior but not for speaking out of turn or talking to oneself. All behaviors would be measured four times again. During week 3, the teacher would cue the student for out-of-seat behavior and for speaking out of turn but not for talking to oneself. All behaviors would be measured four times again. During week 4, the teacher would cue the student for out-of-seat behavior, speaking out of turn, and talking to oneself. All behaviors would be measured four times again. If the treatment of cueing is effective, each disruptive behavior should change in frequency only when the cueing response is applied to it. Figure 8.3 shows a graph of how the data from this study might look if this treatment was effective.

Whichever type of single-subject design you choose, there are certain rules that any good researcher should follow. Box 8.2 lists these rules.

Box 8.2 The Four Rules of Single-Subject Research

"Thou shall"

- Use *reliable, nonobtrusive measures.* This helps to avoid both a testing effect and pretest sensitization. Observational measures are frequently used.
- *Clearly describe how the treatment is administered and what happens* during all time periods.
- Keep conditions for the *baseline and treatment periods as similar* as possible to avoid a history effect.
- *Follow the single-variable rule.* Only one variable should be changed from baseline to treatment conditions.

FIGURE 8.3 SAMPLE MULTIPLE-BASELINE DESIGN.

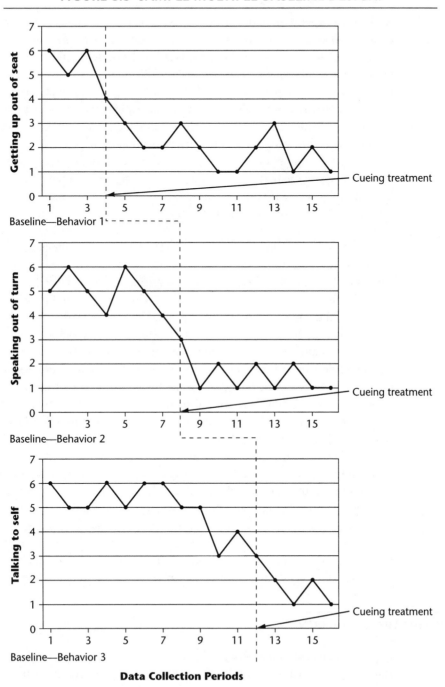

External and Internal Validity

As with the experimental designs discussed earlier, single-subject designs are concerned with issues of external and internal validity. In fact, single-subject research is subject to rather low external validity. Why? If the study is conducted on only one person or a small group of persons, realistically the participants will not likely be representative of the population, and therefore, the generalizability of the findings will be low. For single-subject research, then, replicability is the way that a researcher can in fact generalize the findings. If the treatment used in a single-subject study is conducted in other settings with other participants and still produces the same findings, in essence, the findings can be generalized. Internal validity (the degree to which changes in the participant occur as a result of the treatment) can be ensured in single-subject research if the researcher carefully obtains baseline data: measurements of behavior over a period of time and before the implementation of the treatment. In our example above, a researcher decides to determine if rewards will increase time on task for a child with ADHD. Before the implementation of the treatment, rewards, the researcher would measure the participant's time on task behaviors multiple times. It is critical that the baseline data be collected for a sufficient period of time so that the researcher can see either some stability or some trend emerge from the data. In the case of the child with ADHD, the researcher would want to get a sense of how often the child is on task. Observing the child two or three times would not give an accurate measurement of this behavior. Whereas the amount of time on task is likely to vary some from day to day, if a sufficient amount of time is spent observing behavior during the baseline phase of the study, a trend can be determined. How long is a sufficient amount of time? There is no hard and fast rule for this. The researcher must determine, based on his or her observations, when to begin the treatment phase. A word of caution is warranted here. If the participant's behavior becomes detrimental to his or her well-being, it is better to start the treatment as soon as possible and to forgo the stable baseline phase (even if doing so will threaten the internal validity of the study). In addition, with respect to internal validity, remember that only one variable can be manipulated at a time in a single-subject design. If in the study the researcher was to manipulate not only the reward (one independent variable) but also the lighting in the room (another independent variable) while we were recording the change in time on task behavior, we would not know which independent variable contributed to the change.

Chapter Summary

Experimental research is thought by many to be the only type of research that can suggest true causal relationships. Experimental research is distinctive from other forms of quantitative research because the researcher controls for or manipulates how groups of participants are treated and then measures how the treatment affects each group. The researcher controls for or manipulates one or more independent variables and examines the effect that the experimental manipulation has on the dependent variable or outcome. The independent variable refers to how participants are treated. In education, the independent variable might be curriculum materials, instructional styles, or specialized trainings, to name a few. The outcome of the study is the dependent variable, which is measured by a test or measuring instrument that produces quantitative data. Aside from these variables, experimental researchers must consider any potential variables that could influence the groups' performance on the dependent variable. These are called extraneous variables. True experimental research includes studies in which participants are randomly selected and randomly assigned to treatment conditions. Quasi-experimental research involves random assignment of whole groups rather than individuals to treatments. Although not all experimental studies follow the exact same procedure, most do follow a standard pattern of practices: selecting a topic, reviewing the literature, defining a research question, developing a research hypothesis, selecting and assigning participants to groups, selecting measurement instruments, analyzing data, and forming conclusions. There are three types of hypotheses used in experimental research. The directional hypothesis states the direction or the expected outcome of the study, whereas the nondirectional hypothesis simply states that there will be some difference between the variables, but the direction of that difference is not being predicted. The null hypothesis states that there will be no significant differences between the variables after the treatment is applied. The design of the experimental study is used to control extraneous variables. Design refers to the number of groups in the study, if the participants are pretested, how they are treated, how the individuals are assigned to groups, the number of independent variables, and when the dependent variables are being measured. After data are collected in an experimental study, they are analyzed to determine whether they support or do not support the hypothesis. Notice that we did not say that the data prove or do not prove the hypothesis. To say so would imply a certain bias on behalf of the researcher. Another important aspect of an experimental study involves consideration of threats to internal and external validity. Internal validity is the degree to which the difference in the dependent variable is due to the experimental manipulation and that something other than the independent variable is not causing the dependent variable to change. External validity is the degree the results are generalizable beyond the sample of the study. Single-subject designs are a type of experimental design; however, just like the name says, the study is conducted with only one participant or a small number of participants. Single-subject studies typically gather baseline data on the individual before the treatment is administered and continue the collection of data after the treatment is introduced.

Key Concepts

independent variable

dependent variable

extraneous variables

research hypothesis

operational definition

directional hypothesis

nondirectional hypothesis

significant difference

null hypothesis

research design

quasi-experimental study

pretest

analysis of covariance

analysis of variance

posttest scores

internal validity

external validity

blind and double-blind

Hawthorne effect

novelty effect

baseline periods

treatment periods

ABA, ABAB, and multiple baseline designs

Discussion Questions or Activities

1. An experimental study has been designed to determine the effectiveness of a new reading program on the reading comprehension of first-grade students. As the researcher, discuss the following:

   likely sampling technique

   possible research hypotheses (both nondirectional and directional) extraneous variables that should be considered and ways to control for those variables

      ways you might operationally define your dependent variable

      what you would need to know about the treatment or independent variable

2. In the above study, the researcher sets up the procedure so that one group receives the new reading method and the other group receives the existing method. He decides to pretest both groups to be certain that both groups score about the same on the dependent variable. Each group is then measured with the same posttest. Discuss one threat to internal validity and one threat to external validity. How might the researcher design a study to deal with both of the threats you have described?

3. Design a single-subject research study on a research topic of your choice using each of the following: A-B-A, A-B-A-B, and multiple-baseline designs. Describe the type of baseline you would collect and how often you would collect it before beginning your treatment. Select and justify which design you believe is the best to research your topic.

Suggested Readings

Sandoval, W. A., & Bell, P. (2004). Design-based research methods for studying learning in context [Special issue]. *Educational Psychologist, 39*(4).

Sample Experimental Studies

Keeling, K., Smith Myles, B., Gagnon, E., & Simpson, R. L. (2003). Using the power card strategy to teach sportsmanship skills to a children with autism. *Focus on Autism and Other Developmental Disabilities, 18*(2), 103–109.

McKinney, C. W., & Jones, H. J. (1993). Effects of a children's book and a traditional textbook on fifth grade students' achievement and attitudes toward social studies. *Journal of Research and Development in Education, 27*(1), 56–62.

CHAPTER NINE

NONEXPERIMENTAL APPROACHES

Causal-Comparative and Correlational Research

Chapter Objectives

After reading this chapter, you should be able to

1. Define causal-comparative research and differentiate it from experimental research in terms of procedures and its ability to provide evidence of causation
2. Explain the steps involved in conducting causal-comparative research
3. Define the elements of a scatterplot and be able to interpret the strength and direction of correlational relationships displayed by scatterplots
4. Explain the essential differences between and provide examples of

   a negative and a positive correlation

   a linear relationship and a curvilinear relationship

   correlation and causation

5. Outline the purpose and characteristics of relationship studies
6. Outline the purpose and characteristics of prediction studies and

   differentiate between predictor and criterion variables

   describe key differences between prediction studies and relationship studies

7. Summarize the steps for conducting a correlational study

8. Define the term statistical significance and the difference between statistical and practical significance
9. Explain its ability to provide evidence of causation relative to relationship and prediction studies and in relationship

Research Vignette

Rose is a counselor at an urban high school. She frequently talks with students who are working while they attend high school. Although Rose knows that students value their spending money, she is concerned that working might interfere with their studies. She wonders if there is a difference in grades between students who work and those who do not. She decides to collect some data to examine her hypothesis that students who work will have lower grade point averages than students who do not work. When she meets with students, she asks them if they are employed and how many hours a week they work. After a couple of months, she soon has records on the employment status of over 100 students. Some students work only 5 hours a week or less, but many work 15 hours a week or more. Rose decides to compare students who work five hours or less with those who work more than 15 hours a week. Knowing that students might differ in more than just their employment status, she decides to select two groups of juniors whose grade point averages for their freshman year were all 3.0 or better. (She assumes that they were not working during their freshman year because few jobs are available to young adolescents.) Rose finds that the students who worked 15 hours or more during their junior or senior year had grade point averages that were on average 0.5 points below those who worked five hours or less. She concludes that her hypothesis was supported and begins to discuss her concerns about work and school with her students.

Causal-Comparative Research

Like experimental research, causal-comparative research involves comparing groups to see if some independent variable has caused a change in a dependent variable. Causal-comparative research also sets up studies so that possible extraneous variables are controlled. However, the types of research questions addressed in causal-comparative research involve variables that are difficult or impossible to manipulate experimentally, often because they are experiences that have already occurred. Rose's study is one example of a causal-comparative study. Following are some questions that might be addressed using causal-comparative research.

- Do children with a history of abuse have lower levels of academic achievement than children with no history of abuse?
- Do students who are retained a grade have high school graduation rates different from those who are not retained?
- Are women who attend a same-sex college more likely to attain leadership positions after graduation than women who attend coed colleges?

Note that in these questions, we are attempting to see if one variable (abuse, retention, working, or type of college) causes a change in another variable (academic achievement, graduation rates, or leadership). However, we cannot ethically or practically manipulate the variables that are thought to cause change. Causal-comparative research designs permit the study of the effects of variables that have already occurred or are difficult to manipulate experimentally with human research participants. In many causal-comparative studies, the independent variable has already occurred, e.g., child abuse. This is why the researcher cannot control or manipulate the independent variable; it has already happened.

In other studies, it might be possible to manipulate such variables, but it would be unethical to do so. For example, researchers could not ethically retain one group of research participants for a grade to study the effect of retention on academic performance. Sometimes it may simply be impractical to manipulate the independent variable. If students are already in classrooms with teachers who have established instructional practices, it may not be feasible to randomly assign classes to treatments or individual students to treatments. In this case, a causal-comparative study might be required.

Steps in Causal-Comparative Research

Causal-comparative research often looks deceptively simple. One identifies two groups that had different experiences and then measures how this affected them. However, high-quality causal-comparative research requires careful thinking at each stage. The steps involved in doing causal-comparative research are summarized below.

- Select a topic
- Review literature to identify important variables
- Develop a research hypothesis
- Clearly define the independent variable
- Select participants using procedures to control extraneous variables
- Select reliable and valid measuring instruments
- Collect data

- Analyze data to see if the groups differ
- Interpret the results

Each of these steps will be described in more depth below.

Selecting a Topic. In causal-comparative research, the topic is likely to be based on past experiences that are thought to have a strong effect on persons' later behaviors.

Reviewing Literature to Identify Important Variables. The researcher reviews literature to identify what research has revealed about the impact of the past experience on later behavior. Potential extraneous variables might also be identified through the review of literature. For example, if one was examining the leadership positions of women who attended same-sex versus coed colleges, one might find that students at single-sex colleges tend to come from families with higher levels of income and education. Also, the researcher might find useful information about the methods used to select samples in past studies or measure possible dependent variables. If one wanted to compare children with a history of abuse and those with no history of abuse, studies might reveal how these researchers were able to identify possible participants. Based on a review of the literature, one would identify an independent variable (prior experience or group difference that cannot or should not be manipulated) and a dependent variable that might be affected by this independent variable.

Developing a Research Hypothesis. Research hypotheses for causal-comparative research take a form that is similar to experimental research hypotheses because both types of research include an independent and dependent variable. The research hypothesis would state the expected causal relationship between the independent and dependent variables. For example, the research hypothesis for the study of working part-time and high school achievement might be

> It is hypothesized that students who are employed 15 hours or more a week will have lower achievement than students who are employed five hours or less a week.

In this hypothesis, being employed or not employed is the independent variable. The dependent variable would be achievement as measured by high school grade point average.

Clearly Defining the Independent Variable. In causal-comparative research, the independent variable describes the different past experiences of the participants.

It is important to be clear about the exact differences in the experiences of the two groups being compared. In our opening example, employment was defined as working 15 hours or more per week. In studying single-sex versus coed schools, one might want to indicate what male-to-female ratios are included in the coed schools. In the study of children with and without a history of abuse, one would discuss how the information documenting the abuse was obtained. The definition of the independent variable identifies the two populations from which participants will be selected.

Selecting Participants Using Procedures to Control Extraneous Variables. Unlike experimental research, the participants in causal-comparative research already belong to groups based on their past experiences, and so the researcher selects participants from these preexisting groups. An important consideration in designing causal-comparative studies is whether the two groups are similar (comparable) except for the independent variable on which they are being compared. If two groups are formed because they differ on the independent variable, but they also happen to differ on other extraneous variables, the researchers will not know whether group differences on the dependent variable are caused by the independent or extraneous variables. If the employed students were found to have lower scores on a measure of scholastic aptitude, we would have to ask whether their lower academic achievement (the dependent variable) is the result of their employment (independent variable) or their lower academic aptitude (extraneous variable). To rule out the influence of the extraneous variable, the counselor selected groups of students with different levels of employment but with similar aptitudes (based on their freshman grade point averages). Ideally, the two groups should be selected randomly, which Rose did not do. Therefore, she cannot generalize the results of her sample to the whole population of students at her school.

Typically, researchers will try to select participants who differ on the independent variable but are comparable in other ways. Causal-comparative researchers use the same controls for extraneous variables as those used in experimental research (except for random assignment). These include matching, holding a variable constant, comparing homogeneous subgroups, pretesting (when a researcher is comparing intact groups who are about to receive a treatment that cannot be randomly assigned, such as a new curriculum), use of factorial designs, and statistical controls such as the use of **analysis of covariance** (ANCOVA) or **multiple regression.** Although these were described in Chapter Eight, we should point out that matching and ANCOVA are especially common in causal-comparative designs because random assignment cannot be used to make sure that participants are similar. To use these controls, the researcher must obtain measures of the extraneous variables. If a researcher wants to use matching to make sure that the group of participants who have been abused are similar in family income to the group of participants who have not been abused, then information on family income must also be obtained. The most common way that researchers today control extraneous variables in causal-comparative studies is by statistically estimating the effect of the extraneous variable on the dependent variable. Some statistical tests, such as *multiple regression,* use correlation coefficients to compare the size of effects of the independent variable and extraneous variable on the dependent variable. Another statistical procedure, *analysis of covariance,* or ANCOVA, compares the mean scores of the two groups after the effect of the extraneous variable has been removed. This test estimates how much the extraneous variable affects the dependent variable, and it statistically adjusts the group means to take into account the initial differences between the groups. However, again, to use these statistical controls, there must be a reliable and valid measure of the extraneous variable. Much of the work in designing a high-quality causal-comparative study is focused on measuring and controlling possible extraneous variables.

Note that the random selection of students by itself does *not* control for extraneous variables that might differ between the two groups. If students working fewer than five hours a week generally have parents with higher levels of education than students working 15 hours or more a week, randomly selecting students may result in samples that still differ in parental education level. The random selection would ensure that each group is representative of its population. However, if the two populations differ in parental education, so will the two samples randomly selected.

Selecting Reliable and Valid Measuring Instruments. Selecting appropriate instruments is an important issue in all types of quantitative research. A researcher interested in the question of same-sex versus coed colleges and leadership positions would certainly need to find or develop a measure that accurately measured the dependent variable or types of leadership positions participants had held.

Collecting Data. In causal-comparative research, there is no treatment to administer. So once the sample and measures have been selected, carrying out the study simply involves obtaining data from the selected participants on the measures. If the measures are archival data, then this may involve obtaining permission to access the records. If a measure involves completion of a questionnaire, procedures must be established to distribute these to the participants and have them returned or the researcher could administer them in a group setting. Note that obtaining permission or lack of return of the measures might change the sample and open the possibility that extraneous variables have not been controlled.

Analyzing Data to See If the Groups Differ. Data are usually reported as frequencies or means for each group. Inferential statistical tests are used to determine whether the frequencies or means reported for the groups are significantly different from each other. These are the same statistical tests used in experimental research (listed in Chapter Eight). Based on the results of these tests, the researcher would either accept or reject the null hypothesis.

Interpreting the Results. If the results of the statistical test are significant and extraneous variables have been well controlled for, the researcher can conclude that the study provides support for the research hypothesis. However, one should always be cautious about stating that a causal-comparative study has "proved" that a causal relationship exists. Causal-comparative research is valuable in identifying *possible* causes or effects, but it usually cannot provide definitive support for the hypothesis that one of the variables studied *caused* the observed differences in the other variable. Evidence from causal-comparative studies is considered to be weaker evidence of causality than experimental studies, which show that a dependent variable changes *only after* the researcher has manipulated the independent variable. When many causal-comparative studies have been conducted by different researchers working with different samples in different settings and consistent results emerge from these studies, the combined evidence from these studies provides stronger evidence of causality. This has been the case with research on smoking and lung cancer. The probability that these results could occur by chance if smoking does not cause lung cancer is so slight that most scientists who have worked in the area have accepted the combined results as compelling evidence of a causal relationship.

Correlational Research

Is there a relationship between the number of hours that children watch television and their weight? Is there a relationship between the number of teacher absences and student test scores? How can we predict which high school students are most likely to do well in college? What is the relationship between adolescent drug use and alienation from school, having delinquent peers, school failure, and parental use of drugs?

These are examples of research questions that can be explored using correlational research. The purpose of correlational research is to measure two or more variables and examine whether there are relationships among the variables.

First, a cautionary note about what researchers mean when they use the word *relationship* or *correlation*. In research, two variables are said to be "related" when there is an association between the variables such that different amounts or levels of one variable tend to go with different amounts or levels of the other variable in a systematic way. For example, consider how the following picture (Figure 9.1) suggests that there is a relationship between watching television and body weight.

The drawings suggest that there might be a relationship between the number of hours that people watch television and their weight. The more hours one spends watching television, the higher one's weight is likely to be. In fact, Andersen, Crespo, Bartlett, Cheskin, and Pratt (1998) carried out a study examining just this relationship. They collected data from children between the ages of 8 and 16 years that included the number of hours they watched television and their body mass index (a measure of the amount of body fat).

Note that Andersen et al. (1998) did not claim that watching television directly causes weight gain. One does not absorb calories directly from the television set! However, there is a relationship between watching television and weight, *possibly* because either persons who watch a lot of television eat more food while

FIGURE 9.1 TELEVISION WATCHING AND BODY WEIGHT.

6 hours a day   4 hours a day   2 hours a day

they view TV or they are less physically active than persons who watch less television. In this study, the authors also collected information about the children's participation in physical exercise to see if this variable was related to television watching, weight gain, or both. Many correlational studies do just this, measuring multiple variables and examining the relationships between them. Remember that in saying the variables are related, researchers simply mean that there are patterns in the data that show an association between the variables. Leaping to the conclusion that one variable *causes* another variable to differ is an inference that is only weakly supported by correlational research. In correlational research, it is best to be tentative when explaining the relationship between two variables, especially if there may be other, related variables that have not been measured (such as exercising or eating habits, as in our earlier example).

Differences Between Causal-Comparative Research and Correlational Research

Like causal-comparative research, correlational research involves quantifying the relationship between two or more variables. However, causal-comparative research is more often used to examine variables that involve dichotomies (such as having a history of abuse or not) or categories (such as single-sex versus coed school). Correlational research is more likely to explore relationships among variables that are continuous.

In addition, causal-comparative research typically involves comparing two groups on one dependent variable. Correlational research often measures many different variables. Although good causal-comparative studies certainly attempt to control many different extraneous variables, the major focus of the study is on whether the two groups differ with respect to the dependent variable. This difference is usually reported in terms of differences between group means rather than by using correlation coefficients.

Displaying Correlational Relationships

To examine relationships between variables using correlational research, first, one must obtain a measure of each variable identified in the research question for every person in the study. We might enter this data in a table such as Table 9.1. These data show the performance of Olympic gold medal winners in the high jump and the long jump. Note that each athlete has two scores, one for the long jump and one for the high jump. Looking at these data, can you see any relationship between the two scores?

TABLE 9.1 SAMPLE TABLE SHOWING RELATIONSHIP BETWEEN TWO VARIABLES.

Athlete No.	Long Jump, inches	High Jump, inches
1	249.75	71.25
2	282.87	74.80
3	289.00	71.00
4	294.50	75.00
5	299.25	76.00
6	281.50	76.25
7	293.12	78.00
8	304.75	76.38
9	300.75	77.63
10	317.31	79.94
11	308.00	78.00
12	298.00	80.32
13	308.25	83.25
14	319.75	85.00
15	317.75	85.75
16	350.50	88.25
17	324.50	87.75
18	328.50	88.50
19	336.25	92.75
20	336.25	92.50
21	343.25	93.50
22	342.50	92.00

Source: Adapted from Boggs, R. (n.d.) Retrieved March 16, 2005, from http://exploringdata.cqu.edu.au/datasets/oly_gold.xls

It does seem that longer long jumps go along with higher high jumps because both sets of numbers increase as we go from athlete 1 to athlete 22. However, a better way to see the relationship between two variables is through a graph known as a **scatterplot.** In a scatterplot, each person in the study is represented by one point on the graph. Values of one of the variables are plotted using the vertical or *y* axis of the graph, and values of the second variable are plotted using the horizontal or *x* axis of the graph. Each point represents the score for one person on both variables 1 and 2. Figure 9.2 displays the data from Table 9.1 in a scatterplot.

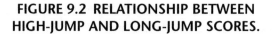

**FIGURE 9.2 RELATIONSHIP BETWEEN
HIGH-JUMP AND LONG-JUMP SCORES.**

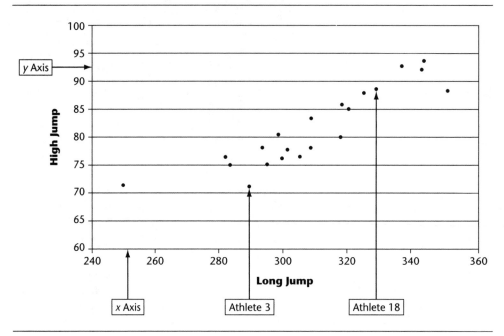

In this case, the scores for the high jump are plotted on the y axis, and the scores for the long jump are plotted on the x axis. Note that each point in the graph represents one of the athletes. The data points representing athletes 3 and 18 are indicated.

With the use of the scatterplot, we can examine the patterns within the overall group to determine both the direction and the strength of the relationship or "correlation." Remember that each data point represents *two scores* for each person, so as we move from left to right, we see how both variables are changing. If the data points tend to cluster in an upward pattern as we go from the left to the right side of the graph, this suggests that as high-jump scores go up, long-jump scores also go up. We call this a positive correlation. On the other hand, if the data points tend to go down as we move from the left to the right, this suggests a negative relationship. If we plotted data on physical exercise and weight for children aged 10 years, we might expect there to be a negative relationship or a negative correlation (as one variable goes up, the other goes down). This is shown in Figure 9.3.

FIGURE 9.3 SCATTERPLOT OF CHILDREN'S
WEIGHT AND AMOUNT OF PHYSICAL EXERCISE.

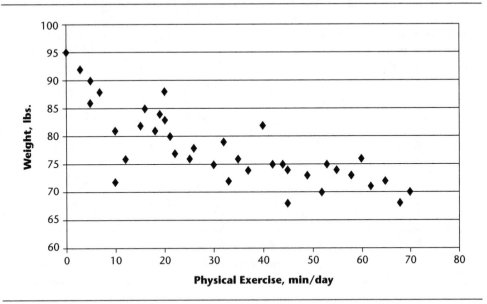

So far, we have discussed how a scatterplot shows us the *direction* of the relationship between two variables. However, it also depicts the *strength* of the relationship. If the data points are scattered in an inconsistent way, the relationship is said to be weak. If the data points tend to be grouped in a narrower pattern along a line, the relationship is said to be moderately strong. This is because the association is more systematic; as one variable changes, the other changes in a way that is visually predictable. In other words, if you were asked to predict the weight of any 10-year-old child who engaged in physical exercise 40 minutes a day, you could make a rough estimate based on the graph in Figure 9.3. Researchers make these predictions by plotting a prediction line that is calculated using a statistical formula that plots the line so that it is as close as possible to all of the points in the scatterplot. Predictions for individuals are made by locating the value of one variable (in this case, exercise) on the prediction line and reading the corresponding value of the other predicted variable (in this case, body weight). See Figure 9.4 for an example of a prediction line and how it would be used to predict the body weight of a child who exercised 40 minutes per day.

The direction and strength of a correlation can also be summarized numerically using a correlation coefficient. A correlation coefficient is a number that can

FIGURE 9.4 SCATTERPLOT WITH PREDICTION LINE.

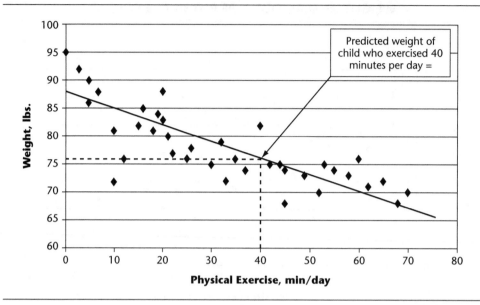

be as large as +1.00 or as low as –1.00, but usually it is a decimal somewhere between these two numbers (e.g., +0.65 or –0.48). The size of the number indicates how strong the correlation is, and the plus or minus sign indicates the direction (if the relationship is positive or negative). As noted in the introductory discussion of correlational research in Chapter One, a large number shows a strong relationship regardless of whether the coefficient is positive or negative. A positive correlation is not "better" or "stronger" than a negative correlation; it simply indicates that the variables move in the same direction (as one goes up, the other also goes up) whereas, in a negative relationship, variables move in *opposite* directions (an increase in one variable is accompanied by a decrease in the other variable).

Although the direction, positive or negative, usually makes sense, for students who have not taken a statistics course, the concept of a correlation coefficient (the numerical portion) may be mysterious. Note that the coefficient does *not* represent the percentage of times the scores are related—a common misconception! The coefficient indicates the degree, or extent, to which the variables covary or go together. The best way to see this is in a scatterplot. Figure 9.5 shows the scatterplots for correlations of different strengths.

Note that the scatterplots in which data points are closer together along a line tend to have higher correlation coefficients regardless of whether they are posi-

FIGURE 9.5 SCATTERPLOT REPRESENTATIONS
OF CORRELATION COEFFICIENTS OF DIFFERENT SIZES.

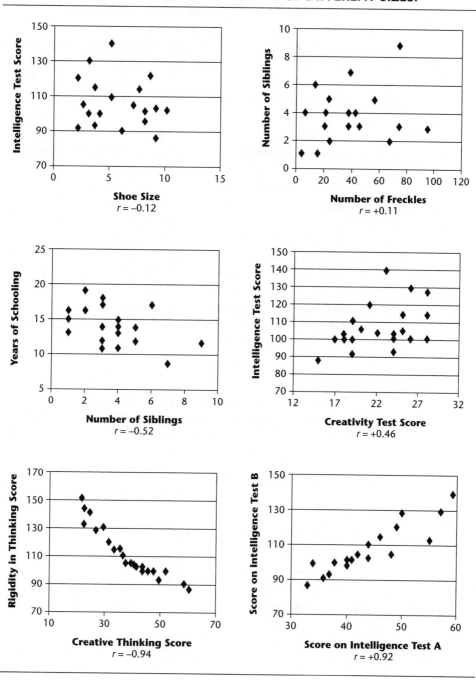

tive or negative. Scatterplots in which scores do not fall closely along a line show weak relationships and have lower numerical coefficients (again, regardless whether they are positive or negative). A weak correlation means that there is some tendency for the variables to go together, but there is also a lot of variability in the extent to which this occurs. Using our earlier example, if television watching and weight are weakly correlated, there will be a few children who watch little television but are overweight and others who watch a lot of television and are slender. This shows up in the scatterplot as widely scattered data points and in the correlation coefficient as a smaller numerical value. So, the size of the correlation coefficient gives us an overall estimate of the extent to which scores on two variables will be related in a way that is consistent across one large group of people.

Correlational relationships can also differ in whether they are linear or curvilinear. A linear relationship means that as one variable changes, the other variable changes by an amount that is predictable using a straight line as the prediction line. In a curvilinear relationship, the direction of the relationship may be different at different levels of the variables. For example, the relationship between test anxiety and test scores is often curvilinear. A little anxiety is good because it gets one to study, but high levels of anxiety may interfere with learning or test taking, as depicted in the scatterplot in Figure 9.6.

Let us now turn to looking at how correlational research is conducted using two different types of designs: a relationship study and a prediction study.

**FIGURE 9.6 SCATTERPLOT OF RELATIONSHIP
BETWEEN ACHIEVEMENT TEST SCORES AND TEST ANXIETY.**

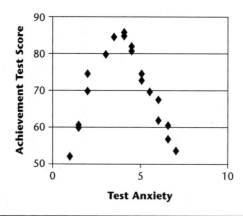

Relationship Studies

One of our graduate students, a teacher in New York City, posed the following research question, "Is the number of days teachers are absent related to student test scores?" He had observed great variability in the number of days teachers were absent both in his own high school and in data for the city as a whole as reported on the State Department of Education Web site. Because scores on the New York State tests also varied greatly across the schools, he wondered if there was a relationship between the two variables, teacher absences and student test scores. His proposal outlined a plan for examining this research question through what is called a relationship study.

Relationship studies usually include the following characteristics:

- *Measurement of at least two (but usually more) variables thought to be related.* Typically, relationship studies include many variables because there are few educational or psychological phenomena that are so simple that they can be explained using only two variables. The measured value of variables can vary continuously in small increments (such as the number of days absent) or can be divided into discrete categories such as high, medium, or low (such as number of students receiving free lunches at a school). Variables should be carefully selected based on a review of previous research, with explanations offered for why each variable is included in the study.
- *Data are collected from* one *randomly selected sample of participants.* The sample may consist of individuals, classes, schools, or other groupings (e.g., school districts, states, families), as long as a score for each variable can be determined for each person or group being studied. Persons or groups will also differ in certain characteristics that the researcher is studying. However, the separate units are all considered to be members of one group. So male and female students compose one group of high school students who vary in gender. Tenured teachers are a group that varies in their years of teaching experience.
- *Data are collected at one point in time.* Relationship studies appear simple because there are no interventions or programs to set up and no need to observe participants over time. Data are collected "all at once," often by combining the measurement of several variables into long questionnaires that are broken into separate groups of questions to measure the different variables during the data analysis. For example, a questionnaire might measure an adolescent's communication with parents through questions 1 to 10, the extent of their agreement with parental values on questions 11 to 20, and the degree to which their decisions are influenced by discussion with parents on questions 21 to 25. Although the questions are presented altogether, the questionnaire actually includes subscales (groups

of questions) that measure different variables. Alternatively, data may be collected using measures from existing records (such as attendance rates, test scores) or from separate questionnaires. However the data are collected, all measures are taken at a single point in time or represent measurements of variables at a single point in time.

• *Scores on each variable are obtained for each individual.* The researcher must obtain a score for each member of the group on each of the variables being examined. Much of the method section in a correlational study will discuss how these scores were obtained for all participants in the study.

• *Correlations are computed between the scores for each pair of variables using statistical tests.* The results of correlational tests are used to explain how the variables are related.

Relationship studies often look complex because researchers frequently measure many different variables. Some studies may look at 10 or more variables at once! As the number of variables increases, so does the number of relationships that must be examined. Consider how our student's proposal developed.

He decided to use data from the State Department of Education; therefore, he proposed gathering data about the number of teacher absences for each school and the number of students passing the state test of English-language skills at that school from the State Department of Education Web site. (Note that he could have proposed obtaining data on the number of days absent for each individual teacher and the number of students who passed the state tests for each teacher, but he knew these data would be difficult to obtain.) To avoid being overly simplistic, he proposed examining several other variables that were also available on the State Department of Education Web site as well. He included the number of students receiving free or reduced-cost school lunches as a measure of the number of low-income families. He also included a measure of the number of students for whom English was a second language. So his proposal included four variables: teacher absences, students passing the state test, number of students receiving free lunches, and number of second-language learners. Figure 9.7 shows all the possible combinations of these four variables. Noted in *italics* are the student's predictions that were made as part of the student's research proposal and are based on his review of literature.

In a published study (versus the proposal done for this course), the *actual* correlation coefficients between each pair of variables would be presented in a table referred to as a **correlational matrix.**

What can one conclude from a relationship study? The safest conclusion is that variables that show large correlations are related. In this case, that would mean that as teacher absences increase, the number of students with free lunches also in-

FIGURE 9.7 PREDICTED CORRELATIONS BETWEEN TEACHER ABSENCE, NUMBER OF STUDENTS RECEIVING FREE LUNCHES, NUMBER OF SECOND-LANGUAGE LEARNERS, AND NUMBER OF STUDENTS PASSING STATE TEST.

	No. of students receiving free lunch	No. of second-language learners	No. of students passing state test
1. Teacher absence	Correlation between 1 and 2. *Moderately high positive correlation*	Correlation between 1 and 3. *Low or no correlation*	Correlation between 1 and 4. *High negative correlation*
2. No. of students receiving free lunch	—	Correlation between 2 and 3. *Low or no correlation*	Correlation between 2 and 4. *Moderate to high negative correlation*
3. No. of second-language learners	—	—	Correlation between 3 and 4. *Low or no correlation*

creases (positive correlation). As teacher absences increase, the number of students who pass the state test decreases (negative correlation). As the number of students with free lunches increases, the number of students who pass the state test decreases, although to a lesser extent than for teacher absences. Although it may be tempting to conclude that teacher absence or low family income are *causes* of low test scores, the evidence to support this is weak because there are so many other variables that have not been measured or controlled that might also contribute to low test scores. Perhaps teachers who are absent frequently are poor teachers. (Their absence may indicate a lack of commitment to teaching.) It may be the poor teaching not teacher absence by itself that causes low test scores. Relationship studies are often referred to as "exploratory" because they suggest relationships between variables that need additional study before claims of cause-and-effect relationships can be made.

Prediction Studies

A prediction study is another design used in correlational research. Like relationship studies, prediction studies examine correlations between variables, but the goal is to identify one or more variables that can *predict* changes in another variable measured at a later point in time. For example, Proctor, Moore, and Gao

(2003) used a prediction study to examine the relationship between television viewing and weight by looking at correlations between daily hours of television viewing during childhood and body fat during adolescence. In this case, television viewing during childhood predicted the amount of body fat during adolescence. In a prediction study, the variable that is measured at the earlier point in time is called the **predictor variable** because it is used to predict something occurring later. The variable that is being predicted is called the **criterion variable.** In Proctor et al.'s study, the hours of television viewing in childhood was the predictor variable and body fat during adolescence was the criterion variable.

The characteristics of prediction studies are listed below, and in many respects, they are similar to those of relationship studies. The major difference is that the behavior or experience measured by predictor variables occurs *before* the behaviors or experiences represented by criterion variables.

• *Identification of one or more predictor variables and one or more criterion variables.* Based on a review of literature on the topic, the researcher specifies in advance which variables are considered predictor variables and which are considered to be criterion variables.

• *Data are collected from* one *group of participants to measure variables representing two different points in time.* The behaviors or experiences represented by the predictor variables must precede the behaviors or experiences represented by the criterion variables. In many studies, the collection of data on the predictor variables precedes collection of data on the criterion variables. However, predictor variables may be measured using records or self-reports of behaviors that happened earlier. In this case, data could be collected for both the predictor and criterion variables at the same time, but the data represent behaviors or experiences that occurred at different points. For example, student grades in high school might be collected from existing records to see if these predict grade point averages in college. Both the high school and college grades would be collected at the same time.

• *Data are collected from* one *group of participants.* As in relationship studies, prediction studies collect measures of all variables on a single group of randomly selected participants.

• *Scores on each variable are obtained for each individual.* Because variables in prediction studies are often measured at two points in time, prediction studies may involve data collection procedures and methods for staying in touch with participants over time.

• *Correlations are computed between the predictor variables and the criterion variables.* The results of correlational tests are used to examine whether there is a significant relationship between the predictor and criterion variables. If a strong relationship exists between a predictor variable and a criterion variable, the predictor variable can be used to make predictions regarding the criterion variable. This is done by statistically generating a prediction line similar to that shown in Figure 9.4. Correlational tests may also examine whether several predictor variables can be combined to yield a more accurate prediction of the criterion variable. In the example discussed earlier, in addition to high school grades, colleges might use Scholastic Assessment Test (SAT) scores and other achievement test scores to predict student grade point averages.

Steps in Conducting a Correlational Study

The steps for conducting either a relationship or prediction study are as follows:

- *Based on a review of literature, identify two or more variables that you predict might be related.* Often correlational research seeks to expand the understanding of complex phenomena by selecting new variables or new combinations of variables and examining the relationships among them. Assume that a review of literature yielded one study that found that underaged drinking was negatively correlated with parental monitoring and a separate study showing that underaged drinking was positively correlated with peer acceptance of drinking. A proposed new study might examine all three of these variables within one group to see whether peer attitudes or parental monitoring was more strongly related to youth drinking.
- *Select a sample of individuals for whom data for the variables can be collected and who represent the larger population to which the study results will apply.* Ideally, individuals should be selected randomly from a larger population. The sample should contain at least 30 individuals (or separate entities, such as schools in our example of teacher absenteeism and student test scores). Larger samples will increase the generalizability of the results.
- *Identify a measure for each variable.* The most complex part of doing a correlational study is finding or developing measures for the variables. For example, if you are interested in self-esteem as a variable, how is that translated into a number? Care must be taken to ensure that the measures are reliable and valid.
- *Collect the data.* Data for each variable must be obtained for each person in the study. Because pairs of scores will be correlated, it is important to have a way to link data from different measures so that scores belonging to the same person can be grouped together. This may be particularly difficult in prediction studies in which data are collected at different points in time. To preserve confidentiality, scores for each person on the predictor variable are usually identified with a number code that is linked to a list of names kept in a locked cabinet. This list is used only to code data collected later on the criterion variable so that scores can be grouped. See Box 9.1 for an example of a researcher maintaining confidentiality.

Box 9.1 Ethical Issues in Correlational Prediction Studies

Correlational prediction studies examine whether a measure taken at one time can predict a later behavior. To do this, researchers must be able to link the two measures taken by each participant. To protect confidentiality, however, no identifying information may be kept with the measures. How can one preserve confidentiality over a long period of time and still manage to connect each person's earlier score to their later score? For example, if a researcher administers a questionnaire on career aspirations to children in eighth grade and later collects information about their final high school grade point averages, how can she or he know which career questionnaire should be paired with which high school grade point average?

One way that researchers do this is by numbering the questionnaire measures often used in correlational research and attaching a removable sheet that includes the person's name and the number on his or her questionnaire. The sheets with identifying information are removed either before the person completes the questionnaire or shortly thereafter. A list is constructed of the persons' names and numbers. This list is kept in a locked file, and no one except the head researcher is allowed to access it. All data are tabulated anonymously, usually by persons who cannot access the list. When the second measure is taken later, the list is used to pair up each person's two measures. After the data have been paired and entered into the computer, the list is destroyed.

• *Analyze the data using statistical tests.* The test used will depend on whether the data consist of variables that are **continuous** (changing in small increments, such as for test scores) or **dichotomous** (separated into distinct categories, such as gender or tenured and nontenured). Table 9.2 lists the most commonly used statistical tests for examining relationships between pairs of variables.

• *Interpret the results.* Both the size and strength of correlation coefficients are considered in interpreting results. Issues relating to statistical versus practical significance of correlations are discussed in the next section.

Evaluating Correlational Studies

Several issues must be taken into consideration when evaluating correlational studies, such as the sampling techniques, the reliability and validity of the measurements, whether the results are of statistical or practical importance, and how carefully the variables are selected.

TABLE 9.2 COMMON STATISTICAL TESTS
FOR EXAMINING RELATIONSHIPS BETWEEN VARIABLES.

Statistical Test	Symbol Used for Correlation Coefficient	Type of Variables and Remarks
Pearson product moment correlation	r	Two continuous variables and samples of 30 or more; most stable test with smallest amount of error
Spearman rho correlation	ρ	Data reported as ranks or continuous variables in studies with samples smaller than 30
Point-biserial correlation	r_{pbis}	Used when one variable is continuous and the other is dichotomous
Phi coefficient	Φ	Used when both variables are dichotomous
Eta or correlation ratio	η	Used when relationship is expected to be nonlinear

Sampling Issues

In Chapter Seven, we discussed how survey research frequently uses random sampling techniques to select a sample. Like other types of quantitative research, the goal of correlational studies is to generalize their results to a larger population. To make valid generalizations, random sampling techniques must be used in selecting a sample. For example, to determine if SAT scores accurately predict freshman grade point averages, one would need to select a representative sample of students applying to colleges. If studies do not use random samples, caution must be exercised in generalizing the results and conclusions of the study.

The size and heterogeneity of a sample may also affect the results of a correlational study. In general, wide variability in scores is helpful in a correlational study because it allows one to see the patterns between the variables for high, middle, and low scores. If scores on a variable for a particular sample are too homogeneous, it is said to have **restriction of range,** meaning that the full range of possible scores is not represented. Restriction of range may mask the true relationships between variables in a correlational study. Consider the scatterplot that we examined earlier showing the relationship between weight in pounds and physical exercise (Figure 9.3). What would happen if our sample was restricted to only children who exercised 30 or more minutes a day? Figure 9.8 shows this scatterplot with the restricted range on level of exercise.

The scatterplot shows that when we restrict the range of children to those who do exercise 30 minutes or more a day, the correlation between weight and

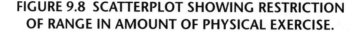

FIGURE 9.8 SCATTERPLOT SHOWING RESTRICTION OF RANGE IN AMOUNT OF PHYSICAL EXERCISE.

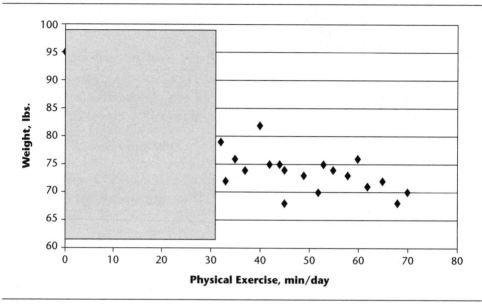

exercise appears to be much weaker than it did in Figure 9.3. In a correlational study, the best way to see the true relationship among the variables is to have samples that are heterogeneous with a wide range of scores on the variables of interest.

Reliability and Validity of Measurement

Because correlational research involves the measurement of many different variables, the quality of the measures used is a major consideration. As discussed in Chapter Four, reliability and validity are two concepts that are used to judge the quality of educational measures. Reliability refers to the consistency of measurement. Validity refers to whether the measure accurately and appropriately measures whatever it is supposed to measure. Correlational studies should always discuss evidence for the reliability and validity of their measures. If no evidence of reliability or validity is provided or available, the results of the study may be suspect. For example, if the children exaggerated the amount of time that they exercised, the data would not accurately represent the true relationship between weight and exercise.

Statistical and Practical Importance

As noted earlier, correlational studies often report relationships among many different variables. For example, Figure 9.9 shows results from a study on bullying that included seven variables examining types of bullying and victimization (being bullied) and perceptions of school safety. In the correlation matrix, each variable is numbered, and each cell in the table shows the correlation between two variables.

The double asterisks (**) indicate which of the correlations are **statistically significant.** A correlation is considered statistically significant if the probability that the correlation was obtained due to chance is less than .05. This probability is usually noted on a correlational matrix using the notation, $p < .05$. In the example, above "$**p < .01$" at the bottom of the matrix indicates that the probability of correlations labeled with a double asterisk being due to chance is less than .01 and therefore, statistically significant. If a correlation is not statistically significant, it means that any relationship observed between the variables could have occurred due to chance. Researchers would assume that a nonsignificant correlation coefficient indicates that the variables are not truly related.

FIGURE 9.9 CORRELATION MATRIX FOR STUDY OF BULLYING.

	2	3	4	5	6	7
1. Been in a physical fight	+0.35**	+0.33**	+0.23**	+0.33**	+0.32**	−0.16**
2. Used a weapon	—	+0.54**	+0.19**	+0.50**	+0.32**	−0.19**
3. Been arrested	—	—	+0.13**	+0.41**	+0.22**	−0.12**
4. Been teased because of race or gender	—	—	—	+0.33**	+0.38**	0
5. Been threatened with a weapon	—	—	—	—	+0.42**	−0.22**
6. Had property stolen or damaged	—	—	—	—	—	−0.22**
7. Perceived school safety	—	—	—	—	—	—

Note: N = 3,542; **p < .01.

Go & Murdock (2003).

The p values listed at the bottom of a correlational matrix or following a correlation coefficient are referred to as the **significance level** of a correlation. A small p value (e.g., $p < .01$ is smaller than $p < .05$) means that it is unlikely that the correlation could have been due to chance. Researchers assume that a smaller p value means that they can have greater confidence that there is a true relationship between the variables. However, a small p value does *not* mean that the correlation is *practically* important. Even very small correlations can be statistically significant if a large sample is used. Consider that in the bullying example, even a small correlation of -0.12 (between "Been arrested" and "Perceived school safety") was significant at $p < .01$. In fact, all 21 correlations in this study were reported as statistically significant at $p < .01$. One reason that this occurred here is this study used a large sample of more than 3,000 persons. With large samples, even very small correlations are likely to be statistically significant. However, is there any *practical* importance to knowing that two variables have a weak relationship?

The practical importance of a correlation depends on the size of the correlation coefficient and the way in which it is going to be used. Slight to low-moderate correlations may be useful to researchers who are trying to build models of how many different variables are related. However, they would not be accurate in making predictions about the performance of a group. So a college looking for a test that can predict the overall performance of their freshman class would want one that research had revealed to have a moderately strong or strong relationship with freshman grade point average. For individual predictions, such as those made by a college admissions committee, strong or very strong correlations would be required. Table 9.3 summarizes the interpretations and practical uses of correlation coefficients of different sizes in educational research, based on work by Cohen and Manion (1994).

Careful Selection of Variables

As noted earlier, both relationship and prediction studies may include a large number of variables. The variables in a study should be carefully selected based on previous research. Researchers should avoid what is sometimes called a "shotgun approach" in which any and all variables that the researcher can think of are included in the study. The shotgun approach is a poor research practice because correlational tests examine relationships between each pair of variables. Therefore, including a large number of variables means that many different correlation coefficients must be computed to examine the relationship between each pair of variables. It is likely that some of these correlation coefficients will be significant due to chance. If a significance level of .05 is used, then 5 times out of 100, one

TABLE 9.3 PRACTICAL USES AND
INTERPRETATIONS OF CORRELATION COEFFICIENTS.

Size of Correlation	Strength of Relationship	Possible Uses or Interpretations
0 to 0.19	No relationship or weak relationship likely to be statistically significant only in large samples of 1,000 or more	If statistically significant, may show weak relationship between variables, but no practical use in either relationship or prediction studies
0.20 to 0.34	Slight relationship detectable in samples of 100 or more	Useful in examining relationships among variables, but not accurate for group or individual predictions
0.35 to 0.64	Moderately strong relationship	Typical range of correlation coefficients for relationship studies; may be useful for group predictions
0.65 to 0.84	Strong relationship	In relationship study, shows a strong association; accurate prediction for groups possible; at the high end of this range, accurate individual prediction possible
0.84 or greater	Very strong relationship	Correlations this high are rarely seen in relationship studies and would indicate that the 2 measures are measuring the same variable; accurate individual prediction is possible; studies of reliability or validity would also seek relationships this strong

may get a significant correlation due to chance. If all combinations of 7 variables are tested, 21 correlation coefficients will be computed (as in the bullying study discussed above). It is likely that at least one of these correlations was significant due to chance. However, there is no way to tell which of the correlations were due to chance and which represent true relationships between variables. In addition, including a large number of variables involves a lot of extra work for both the researcher and, possibly, the participants. The researcher must find additional reliable and valid measures for each of variables, and the participants may then have additional questions to complete on the measures. However, including multiple variables *is* a good research practice if one has reason based on previous research to expect that the variables will be related.

Correlation and Causation

Traditionally, researchers have been hesitant to infer that a correlation between two variables indicates a causal relationship. Traditional research wisdom admonishes, "correlation does not mean correlation." Many older educational research books insist that it is never appropriate to infer causation from a correlation, and indeed, there is good reason to exercise caution when thinking about whether a correlation indicates that one variable causes another to change. Consider the following correlation:

> *There is a positive correlation between average outside temperature and the number of children with broken bones seen at hospitals.*

Does this finding mean that warm weather causes broken bones? Of course not! During warm weather, children are more likely to play outside in active pursuits and fall down, and this is what causes the broken bones. In correlational research, playing outside would be considered an **intervening variable:** the variable coming between air temperature and broken bones that is the true causal variable (Figure 9.10).

Now consider the following finding:

> *There is a positive correlation between the amount of disciplinary control parents use and a child's behavior problems.*

Does the amount of disciplinary control cause the child's behavior problems? Here it is more tempting to infer that there is a causal relationship because other

FIGURE 9.10 EXAMPLE OF INTERVENING VARIABLE.

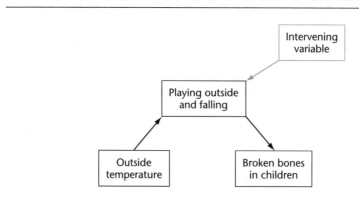

research shows that parenting that involves discussion and reasoning with children is correlated with fewer behavior problems. However, we know that parents also modify their parenting based on their child's behavior and personality. In other words, the child's behavior problems may cause the parents to use more or less control in their parenting. In reality, the direction of causation works in two ways: parenting may partly cause behavior problems, but children's behavior problems also cause parents to change their parenting. If the above examples have not convinced you that correlation is not sufficient to prove causation, consider a study found by one of our graduate students. This study reported that parental involvement in homework was negatively correlated with student achievement! Does this mean that parental involvement in homework causes students to do more poorly in school? What other explanations might you give for the correlation? The study explained that parents of students who had difficulty in school spent more time helping their children. If students were doing well, the parents did not need to provide help. Again, the direction of the causation was not clear based on just the existence of a correlation.

As we noted earlier, many older educational research books insist that it is never appropriate to infer causation from a correlation. However, whether a correlation can be used as evidence of a causal relationship depends on both the design of the study and the type of statistical test used to analyze the results. Box 9.2 discusses the types of evidence required to show that one variable causes another to change in relation to correlational, causal-comparative, and experimental research.

Box 9.2 Inferences About Causation

What does it mean to say that one thing causes another to change? Common sense suggests that it is easy to tell if one thing causes a change in another. Take, for example, the observation that during the summer, temperatures are hotter. Many people assume that the earth must be closer to the sun during the summer because usually the closer a hot object, such as the sun, is to you, the warmer it makes you feel. However, in the northern hemisphere, the sun is actually farther away from the earth during the summer than during the winter. It is the angle of the sun's rays (which are more direct during summer) that causes hotter days. So, in this case, common sense is not sufficient. One must be careful about the type of evidence presented to support inferences of causality.

Researchers have identified several levels of evidence that can be used to support inferences about whether one variable truly causes a change in another variable. The types of evidence are listed below in order of increasing strength. Note that each higher level also assumes that the lower levels are true.

• *Correlation: one variable occurs in association with another variable.* If two variables occur together frequently and covary in systematic ways (e.g., are correlated), it is possible that one is causing the other to change. However, this type of evidence is considered weak for reasons discussed in the text.

• *Timing: one variable precedes another.* Because change happens over time, a cause must precede the effect that it controls. Therefore, if experiences represented by a variable occur *before* behaviors measured by another variable, evidence that the experience caused the change in the behavior can be inferred. However, it is possible that other variables were also changing at that time. Unless these other variables are controlled (see below) one cannot be certain which variable produced the change in behavior.

• *Control of other possible variables.* If other possible variables can be controlled, evidence of causation is strengthened. However, it is usually not possible to know if all other possible causal variables have been controlled. Correlational research attempts to control other possible variables through measurement of multiple variables and the use of statistical controls. (See discussion of multiple regression below.) In causal-comparative and experimental research, such variables are called **extraneous variables** and are controlled through a variety of statistical and procedural methods.

• *Direct manipulation of one variable followed by a change in another variable.* The strongest evidence of causation occurs when one directly manipulates or changes one variable while controlling as many other variables as possible. This is the method used in experimental studies.

Applying the information in Box 9.2, prediction studies offer stronger evidence of causation than relationship studies, although this evidence is not as strong as the evidence provided in experimental studies. The next section will discuss one sophisticated statistical test, multiple regression, used in correlational studies to examine correlations while controlling for other variables. Many researchers now consider this technique as a viable way to provide evidence of causation in correlational studies.

Multiple Regression

The statistical tests discussed earlier were designed to examine relationships between pairs of variables. However, as understanding of the issues in education has progressed, researchers have looked for ways to examine relationships among multiple variables. Multivariate correlational statistics provide a way to examine multiple variables at once and to separate the contributions of different variables.

Multiple regression is used for two purposes: first, it allows examination of relationships between two variables after the influence of other variables has been removed. Second, it allows examination of how accurately a combination of several variables can predict a criterion variable. For example, say you wanted to predict first-grade students' performance in learning to read. You hypothesize that several variables might predict later reading achievement: the number of hours per week that parents read to their child, the child's phonemic awareness of the sounds, the number of children's books in the home (a measure of the literacy environment), and the child's interest in reading. Assume that you have reliable and valid measures of each of these predictor variables for a group of first graders and can obtain a measure of their reading scores at the end of first grade (the criterion variable). However, you know that parents who read to their child are also likely to have books at home for the child. So these predictors will overlap in their contributions to final reading scores, although not completely because some parents may be able to afford more books than others or may make up for lack of time to read with their child by buying books. So it is helpful to be able to separate the contribution of reading to a child from having books at home. Multiple regression provides a way to do this by calculating correlation coefficients, referred to as **beta weights** for each predictor variable. The beta weight indicates the relationship between the predictor variable and the criterion after the effects of all other predictor variables have been statistically removed. Beta weights are similar to simple correlation coefficients in that they measure the association between two variables; however, they also isolate the contribution made by each predictor variable by statistically controlling the overlap of that variable with other predictor variables. The beta weight allows you to see the relationship of reading to the child to the criterion variable (reading scores) *separate* from that of the number of books at home. A multiple regression also allows you to see how several predictor variables together might improve a prediction. **Coefficients of multiple regression,** symbolized as R, are calculated to show how much the correlation increases as each predictor variable is added to the analysis. Results of a possible multiple regression analysis for the study of reading are presented in Table 9.4.

In the table, the largest beta weight is 0.20, and it indicates that phonemic awareness by itself is the best predictor of reading performance. The next most accurate predictor is parent reads to child. Of these four predictors listed, the child's interest in reading is the least powerful predictor, as shown by the lowest beta weight of 0.11. In the third column, 0.20 again shows the correlation of phonemic awareness and reading performance. The next coefficient, 0.30, shows the correlation between phonemic awareness combined with parent reads to child and reading performance. Similarly, the coefficient of 0.35 shows the correlation

TABLE 9.4 MULTIPLE REGRESSION ANALYSIS FOR STUDY OF READING.

Predictor Variable	Beta Weights	R Coefficient of Multiple Regression
Phonemic awareness	0.20	0.20*
Parent reads to child	0.18	0.30*
No. of books at home	0.16	0.35*
Child's interest in reading	0.11	0.38

*p < .05.

between reading performance and the three combined predictors: phonemic awareness, parent reads to child, and number of books at home. Finally, the co-efficient of 0.38 indicates the correlation of the combination of all four predictor variables with reading performance. Note that the accuracy of the prediction goes up (shown by the increasing value of the R) as predictor variables are added. The coefficient of multiple regression, R, indicates if the addition of each predictor variable significantly improves the accuracy of the prediction. In this case, all predictors except the child's interest show a statistically significant improvement in reading performance.

Multiple regression is becoming the most popular statistical test used in correlational research and is used in causal-comparative and experimental research as well because it allows a more realistic picture of the many different variables that comprise complex educational phenomena.

Chapter Summary

Like experimental research, causal-comparative research involves comparing two groups to see if some independent variable has caused a change in a dependent variable. Unlike experimental research, however, causal-comparative research is able to investigate research questions where the independent variable cannot be manipulated because of ethical concerns or because the variable has already occurred. Socioeconomic status, preschool attendance, and number of siblings are examples of variables that cannot be manipulated. Although it may appear simple, there are a series of steps a researcher must adhere to conduct a quality causal-comparative study. As in other types of cause-effect studies, the researcher would select a topic, conduct a thorough review of the literature, identify an independent variable, and carefully define it. Next, the researcher would select two pre-established groups to study: one group for implementing the treatment or independent variable of interest to the researcher, and the other group using the other method. The researcher would also attempt to control for extraneous variables. At the end of the two treatments, the researcher would collect data from the participants using a reliable and valid measurement tool and compare the results of both groups on the measure to determine whether a significant difference was found. If such a difference between the two groups is found, then the difference is attributed back to the independent variable. Unlike causal-comparative research, correlational research examines relationships and looks to see if there is an association between the variables such that different amounts or levels of one variable tend to go with different amounts or levels of the other variable in a systematic way. Causal-comparative research is often used to examine variables that involve dichotomies (such as having a history of abuse or not) or categories (such as single-sex versus coed school). Correlational research is more likely to explore relationships among variables that are continuous. In addition, causal-comparative research typically involves comparing two groups on one dependent variable. Correlational research often measures many different variables. To conduct a correlational study, the researcher must have two variables (or scores) for each participant. A scatterplot is a graphic representation used in correlational research. In a scatterplot, each person is represented by one point on the graph where values for one variable are plotted on the vertical or y axis and values of the second variable are plotted on the horizontal or x axis of the graph. A positive correlation is represented if the data points cluster in an upward pattern, from the left to the right side of the graph. A negative correlation is shown when data points move downward from the left to right side of the graph. The strength of the relationship can be determined by the "scattering" of the data points. Weak relationships are depicted when data points are scattered inconsistently. Moderately strong relationships are shown when points are grouped in a narrower pattern along a line. Researchers use prediction lines to better understand the prediction of one variable to the other. The results of correlational studies are shown using a correlation coefficient. Results closest to $+1.00$ or -1.00 are considered strongly related. Coefficients near zero are said to represent no relationship between variables. A positive or negative relationship is determined by whether the results are in plus or minus values. In published studies, the *actual* correlation coefficients between each pair of variables are presented in a table referred to as a correlational matrix. There are two types of correlational studies: relationship and predictive studies. Relationship studies seek to determine if a relationship exists between two or more variables, whereas the purpose of predictive studies is to identify one or more variables that predict the results of participants on another variable. In analyzing their data, correlational researchers need to identify the type of data and select the appropriate statistical analysis. Like other types of quantitative research, the goal of correlational studies is to generalize their results to a larger population. To make valid generalizations, random sampling techniques must be used in selecting a sample. A minimum of 30 participants is required for a correlational study. The size and heterogeneity of a sample may also affect the results of a correlational study. Measurement tools used to collect data for the variables in a correlational study must be reliable and valid. Ultimately, the researcher wants to conclude that there is a statistically significant relationship between the variables that is not due to chance. A correlation is considered statistically significant if the probability that the correlation was obtained due to chance is less than .05. This probability is usually noted on a correlational matrix using the notation, $p < .05$. Multiple regression is another approach to correlational research that moves our understanding from one that is a relationship between variables to that of an inference of causality.

Key Concepts

scatterplot

positive correlation

negative correlation

prediction line

linear and curvilinear relationships

correlational matrix

predictor variable

criterion variable

continuous and dichotomous variables

extraneous variables

restriction of range

significance level

beta weights

multiple regression

intervening variable

analysis of covariance

Discussion Questions or Activities

1. A researcher wants to know if children of parents who are teachers are more likely to become teachers themselves than children whose parents are not teachers. Discuss how you might conduct this study using a causal-comparative approach. In your discussion, consider how you would define the independent and dependent variables, how you would select the sample, and how you would control for possible extraneous variables.

2. Your school is attempting to develop procedures for predicting which applicants will be the most effective teachers during their first two years of teaching. Based on your study of educational research, you recognize that a correlational prediction study would be one way to examine this issue. Identify possible predictor variables that could be measured for each of the applicants for teaching positions in your school. Also discuss how you might measure their teaching effectiveness. Finally, indicate which predictor variables you believe would have the highest correlation with the criterion variable of teaching effectiveness.

3. Compile a list of variables or events that seem to be correlated but that are unlikely to be causally related (such as the broken bones and weather example in the chapter). If possible, identify variables or events common in educational settings. Discuss reasons why people are likely to falsely believe that correlated events are causally connected.

Suggested Readings

Dimopoooulos, D. I., & Pantis, J. D. (2003). Knowledge and attitudes regarding sea turtles in elementary students on Zakynthos, Greece. *Journal of Environmental Education, 34*(3), 30–38.

Fisher, J. L. (1995). Relationship of intelligence quotients to academic achievement in the elementary grades. ERIC Document Reproduction Service No. ED 388 428. Retrieved Apr. 14, 2005, from ERIC database.

Johnson, B. (2000 Apr.). *It's beyond time to drop the terms* causal-comparative *and* correlational *research in educational research methods textbooks.* Paper presented at the annual meeting of the American Educational Research Association, New Orleans. ERIC Document Reproduction Service No. ED 445 010. Retrieved Oct. 10, 2004, from ERIC database.

Sample Causal-Comparative Study

Beier, S. R., Rosenfeld, S. D., Spitalney, K. C., Zansky, S. M., & Bontempo, A. N. (2000). The potential role of an adult mentor in influencing high-risk behaviors in adolescents. *Archives of Pediatric and Adolescent Medicine, 154*(4), 327–331.

CHAPTER TEN

ANALYZING QUANTITATIVE DATA

Chapter Objectives

After reading this chapter, you should be able to

1. Distinguish between pie charts, frequency graphs, and "box-and-whisker" graphs and interpret data presented in each
2. Define what sampling error is, what implications it has for a study, and the generalizability of its findings
3. Define what standard error of the mean is and how it is calculated
4. Define what a test of significance is and how this test is used by researchers in testing the null hypothesis
5. Describe the different choices a researcher has regarding the null hypothesis and the implications of type I and type II errors
6. Describe the four steps in analyzing data using inferential tests and identify the requirements for selecting parametric and nonparametric tests
7. Identify commonly used inferential statistical tests and explain how these tests are used, interpreted, and selected based on the type of data and the number and type of variables in a study

Initial Examination of Quantitative Data

At the conclusion of any quantitative study, there will be data in the form of numbers. To make sense of the data, the researcher generally begins to summarize them in the form of descriptive statistics. As you learned earlier in this book, these descriptive techniques include the following: graphing the data in the form of frequency polygons, bar graphs, or histograms; measuring central tendency and variability; and measuring relationships. Although many of you are not collecting real data for your proposals, you will be reading quantitative research and should be able to interpret these statistics to fully understand the findings of the studies you are reading.

Interpreting Graphs

As educational professionals, you will be asked to interpret data that have been graphed in a variety of ways. Although we discussed graphing earlier in the book, here we will focus the discussion on the interpretation of graphs associated with the results sections found in quantitative studies. All results sections include a narrative interpretation of the data, but graphs often help to further explain the results in a visual way. The displays of data may take different forms. The following describes graphs taken from different research studies that illustrate the different ways that results can be represented.

Figure 10.1 displays a **pie chart** of the distribution of AIDS cases in U.S. young women aged 13 to 19 years through June 1996. Pie charts are typically used for variables that have been measured and the responses separated into categories. The percentages of responses that fall into each category are displayed in a pie chart. As Figure 10.1 shows, most young women contract AIDS through heterosexual contact.

Earlier we examined the concept of frequency distributions. In a results section, frequency graphs typically present the dependent variable on the y axis and the independent variable on the x axis. If there is more than one independent variable, these may be represented in different bars or lines. Figure 10.2 shows the annual attrition rate for teachers in Indiana between 1965 and 1987. This is broken down by both teacher age and the year in which the attrition rate was measured. The graph shows that attrition rate is high when teachers are young and drops to almost zero between ages 35 and 55. It begins to rise again as teachers age. At a glance, the graph shows when teachers are most likely to leave the teaching profession.

FIGURE 10.1 DISTRIBUTION OF AIDS CASES AMONG U.S. WOMEN AGED 13 TO 19 YEARS THROUGH JUNE 1996.

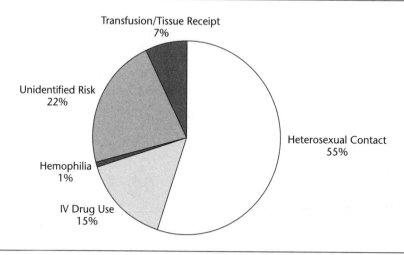

Transfusion/Tissue Receipt
7%

Unidentified Risk
22%

Heterosexual Contact
55%

Hemophilia
1%

IV Drug Use
15%

Note: IV = intravenous.

Source: From the Centers for Disease Control and Prevention (1996).

An unusual graph is the "box-and-whisker" graph represented in Figure 10.3. This figure shows the mean number of correct answers on three mathematics tests in schools in Japan, Taiwan, and the United States for first and fifth grades. Each country's scores are displayed in a box with a vertical line at each end (the whiskers). The means are represented by the lines in the middle of the boxes. The whiskers show the full distribution of scores. The box shows the scores that fall between the 25th and 75th percentiles.

The results in Figure 10.3 suggest that U.S. students have much greater variability in their scores than children in Japan and Taiwan and also have a lower average score in each area tested. Although there are many possible reasons for these differences, the figure conveys a lot of information quickly about the performance in each country and how it changes from first to fifth grade.

Interpreting Measures of Central Tendency and Variability

As part of researchers' initial examination of the data, they often calculate measures of central tendency and variability (concepts we discussed earlier in this book). In articles, means and standard deviations (a measure of variability) are typically presented in tables. These tables summarize the performance of the

FIGURE 10.2 ANNUAL ATTRITION BY TEACHER AGE, SELECTED YEARS.

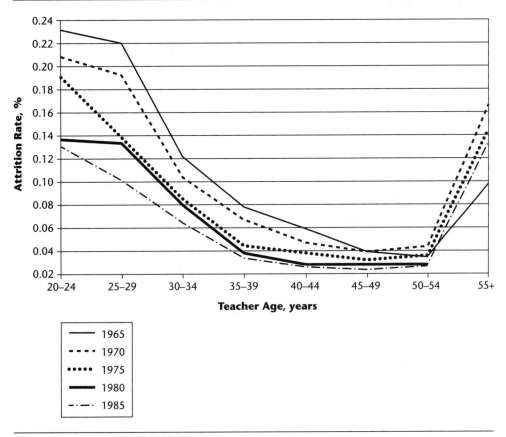

Source: From Grissmer, Kirby, Rand, & Santa (1991).

groups. Although we know that our students do not like to look at numbers, these tables provide a quick way to get an overall picture of the performance of the groups. Table 10.1 shows the means and standard deviations for a study examining the effectiveness of teaching self-regulated learning strategies to students with learning disabilities. The researchers calculated the mean number of words written by students during three baseline periods and during three treatment periods in which self-regulated strategies were taught. They also calculated the standard deviations during each period. The table shows how the mean number of words written increased from baseline to treatment conditions although the variability in number of words written (the standard deviations) remained similar throughout baseline and treatment conditions.

FIGURE 10.3 "BOX-AND-WHISKER" GRAPHS SHOWING
THE DISTRIBUTION AND MEAN NUMBER OF CORRECT ANSWERS
ON THREE MATHEMATICS-RELATED TESTS IN SCHOOLS
IN SENDAI, JAPAN; TAIPEI, TAIWAN; AND CHICAGO.

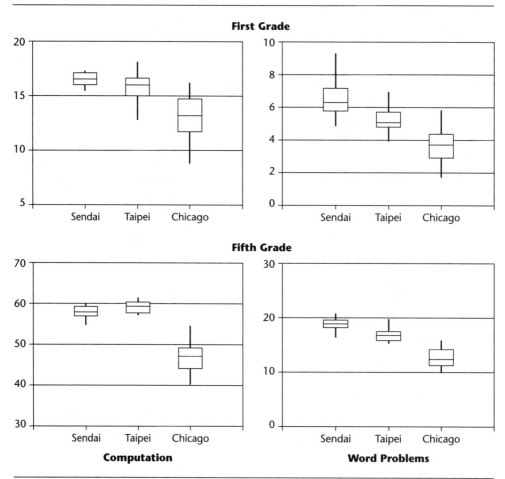

Source: Adapted from Stigler & Perry (1990).

TABLE 10.1 MEANS AND STANDARD DEVIATIONS FOR THE NUMBER OF WORDS WRITTEN.

	Baseline	Baseline	Baseline	Treatment	Treatment	Treatment	Treatment
Mean	95	95	97	106	115	142
Standard deviation	8	11	8	10	9	13

Source: Adapted from Chalk, Hagan-Burke & Burke (2005).

Beyond Descriptive Statistics: Inferential Statistics

Although researchers use descriptive statistics to summarize sample data, in certain types of studies they also want to draw conclusions about the population from which the sample was drawn. In this case, numbers that they obtain from the sample (e.g., the mean and standard deviation) are called statistics, and the corresponding values in the population are called **parameters.** In inferential statistics, the sample values are our best estimate of what the population parameters are likely to be. Correlational studies, causal-comparative studies, and experimental studies may use inferential statistics to draw conclusions about population parameters. As professors of educational research whose classes almost entirely comprise practitioners, we often struggle with how much information we should present to our students about inferential techniques. How much is too much information and not particularly relevant to the professional lives of practitioners? How much information is needed for the practitioners to understand some of the research they might read and allow them to become critical consumers of research? We have tried to achieve a balance by presenting the underlying concepts critical to the understanding of inferential statistics as they relate specifically to correlational, causal–comparative, and experimental studies. These concepts are similarly applied across all quantitative studies that use inferential techniques, with slight variation depending on the type of study, the type of data, and the type of statistical tool used. We also present a sample of commonly used inferential statistical tests in educational research.

Underlying Concepts

Quantitative studies, such as experimental studies, generally want to know if the results obtained on the sample would also be true if the entire population was included in the study. In other words, are the results generalizable to the population from which the sample was selected? Remember that when experimental researchers do a study, they have two overall goals. First, the researcher wants to determine if an experimental treatment causes a difference between two groups. Second, using randomization procedures, the researcher hopes to generalize or draw similar conclusions about the population. Therefore, drawing conclusions about the population based on the sample results is an important component of experimental research.

Consider the following example presented earlier in Chapter Eight: A researcher conducts a study on the effectiveness of computerized tutoring on the scores of seventh graders on a standardized achievement test. The researcher for the school district randomly selects 60 seventh graders from a population of 175 seventh graders enrolled in an after-school tutoring program. Next 30 students are randomly assigned to the experimental group (computerized tutoring) and 30 students to the control group (no computerized tutoring). The study proceeds for six months, and the researcher administers the standardized test. The sample statistics indicate that the mean performance of the experimental group exceeds the mean performance of the control group. Although the researcher is happy with the results (e.g., the sample data indicate that the treatment made a difference), another goal of experimental research is to generalize the findings back to the population. The researcher would ask the following question: How likely is it that the difference between the sample means would also be true of the population means, or how confident can I be that the difference I found between the sample means represents similar differences in the population parameters? The only way to answer this question with 100% certainty would be to conduct the experiment with the entire population. Because the researcher is not likely to conduct the study with the entire population, he or she uses inferential statistics and probability to determine the answer.

So, in the case of our computerized tutoring example, the researcher would want to know if similar results would be obtained if the entire population was used in the study. In other words, does the difference found between the computerized tutoring and noncomputerized tutoring group reflect a true difference, or is the difference due to chance? The word "true" has technical meaning. A true difference would indicate that the results collected on the sample, in fact, would reflect the population parameters and that the difference found between the groups is due to treatment and not merely to chance. Experimental researchers hope that the differences do in fact reflect a true difference because their goals are twofold: to generalize the results of the sample back to the population, and to attribute any differences found between the groups to the treatment. This is one of the main reasons why they use some random technique in their study, either random selection or random assignment. However, although randomization is the best way to increase the likelihood that the sample is representative of the population, it does not guarantee that the sample represents the population.

Sampling Error

What are the chances that even when using a randomization technique, the researcher in the above study would end up with a sample that was identical to the entire population of seventh-grade students? If your answer was almost zero, you are right! There is always going to be variation between the sample and the population. This variation that you would expect in any experimental study is called **sampling error.** Sampling error is the expected variation due to chance that exists between the sample and the population. Keep in mind that as your sample size increases, the sample will be a more accurate representation of the population and the less sampling error you will have.

However, as a researcher, you will always have sampling error unless you do not select a sample and you use the entire population! So how can you end up with a sample that represents the population as accurately as possible? In other words, how can you get a sample mean to be an accurate reflection of the population mean? One complicated and impractical way would be for the researcher to draw multiple samples from the population and calculate the mean of the means. Sounds confusing, right? Well, consider this. The mean of the means will likely be a good estimate of the population mean. You would expect each sample mean to be somewhat different just by chance. But taken together, calculating the mean of the means would probably get you close to the population mean. The best way to explain this is by giving you actual data. Figure 10.4 shows a distribution of 100 scores, or our population.

Let us say that I randomly select a sample of 15 scores and calculate the mean. Sample 1 includes the following numbers: 87, 56, 99, 76, 67, 89, 56, 34, 97, 67, 71, 66, 89, 99, and 98. If I calculate the mean, there is likely going to be some sampling error, right? Right. Every sample will have some sampling error or variation due to chance. In fact, the mean of sample 1 is 76.74, and the population mean is 68.56; the difference between these two numbers is due to sampling error. Now let us take two more random samples of 15 scores. Sample 2 is made up of the following: 76, 78, 90, 55, 78, 18, 90, 23, 87, 29, 34, 45, 67, 99, and 88, and the mean is 58.4. The scores for sample 3 include: 98, 35, 75, 93, 67, 98, 56, 99, 12, 88, 76, 74, 93, 52, and 87. The mean for sample 3 is 73.53. As you can easily see, there is error associated with each of the random samples. None of them is exactly equal to the population mean. Now let us take the mean of the samples 1, 2, and 3, or the mean of the means. This mean is approximately 69.82 and is a closer estimate of the population mean.

FIGURE 10.4 A DISTRIBUTION OF 100 SCORES.

76	23	45	67	89	90	98	87	76	78
34	46	78	90	34	78	23	56	87	98
80	67	98	99	55	67	69	34	67	98
76	56	78	89	23	35	76	87	98	60
45	67	87	98	90	76	56	45	43	65
76	88	99	88	98	87	65	54	78	55
45	76	89	12	34	56	87	89	90	87
67	86	45	45	66	88	99	87	66	55
34	23	67	87	79	75	57	67	54	23
97	29	18	71	73	91	74	93	52	87

Now, what is the chance that a busy researcher is going to want to select multiple samples and conduct the study several times? You are right if you said *never*! So what is a researcher to do? Well, there are some interesting characteristics of sample means. First, sample means are thought to be normally distributed. Just what does that mean? Well, if a large number of sample means is selected from a population, the means will form a normal distribution. The distribution of sample means is like any other normal distribution in that it has a mean and a standard deviation. Only in this circumstance, the standard deviation has a special name, the **standard error of the mean** (SEM). Using the characteristics of the normal curve, the sample mean, sample standard deviation, and the SEM (calculated with a relatively simple formula shown below) helps the researcher to estimate where the population mean is likely to fall. N equals the number of subjects in the sample.

$$\text{Standard Error of Mean} = \frac{\text{Standard Deviation}}{\sqrt{N-1}}$$

Estimating the population mean requires that the researcher use probability and the characteristics of the normal curve (Figure 10.5). Before you throw your hands up in total confusion, let us use some actual data. Let us say that you randomly select a sample from a population, and the sample mean is equal to 100 and the standard deviation is equal to 12. Based on our earlier discussion, what do you know about this mean? You know that there is some sampling error associated with this mean. So all we can do is estimate where the population mean is likely to fall because we are going to use only one sample. The way we can estimate the population mean is to calculate the SEM. In our example, let us say that we calculate the SEM using the above formula and find that it is equal to 2. We can then build **confidence intervals** around the sample mean and predict with probability where the population mean is likely to fall. A confidence interval uses the principles of the normal curve and probability to estimate the range of values that the mean might assume.

FIGURE 10.5 NORMAL CURVE.

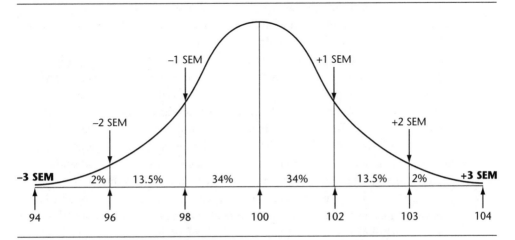

So, in this situation, based on a sample mean of 100 and an SEM of 2, we can predict the following:

- With 68% confidence, the population mean will fall between 98 and 102
- With 95% confidence, the population mean will fall between 96 and 104
- With 99% confidence, the population mean will fall between 94 and 106

Note that as a researcher, you would want your SEM to be as small as possible. Why? A small SEM would mean that your confidence intervals would be small, and you would be more likely to know where the mean of the population falls. The key to a small SEM is sample size. Thus, as the size of the sample increases, the size of the SEM decreases. This is perfectly logical! Finally, you might say. If the sample size is large, then it must be more representative of the population, and therefore, your sampling error and SEM will be smaller.

Critical Concepts: The Null Hypothesis, Statistical Significance, and Error

All statistical procedures test the null hypothesis. That is, in experimental studies, they test that there is no true difference between the sample means and that any difference that was found was due to chance and not treatment. The chance explanation is the null hypothesis. The goal of the researcher generally is to reject (not support) the null hypothesis and to accept (support) the research hypothesis. So in our example, the null hypothesis would be that there would be no difference in achievement between the computerized tutoring group and the noncomputerized tutoring group and that any difference found was due to chance. The researcher wants to reject this null hypothesis and conclude two things: one, that the treatment made a difference and, two, that the difference also exists in the population (remember the generalizability of the study).

What allows the researcher to make a decision about the null hypothesis? In other words, how does the researcher know if the null hypothesis is true (the difference was due to chance) or false (the difference was due to treatment)? To make these conclusions, the researcher applies a **test of significance** to the data collected in the study. Tests of significance (to be discussed more at the end of this chapter) are statistical tools that allow the researcher to make decisions about the null hypothesis. Consider the following. At the end of an experimental study, there is likely to be at least some difference between the experimental and control groups. How does the researcher know if the difference is large enough to conclude that the difference was due to treatment and not simply to chance? To make such a conclusion, the researcher applies a test of significance to the data. Given that the researcher's conclusions will be based on data from the sample, any conclusions drawn must be based on probability. Remember that we did not test the entire population but only the sample. The researcher sets the acceptable probability level at the start of the study before the data are even collected. In fact, it is written into the research proposal in studies that actually collect data, or at least it should be! In education, the generally acceptable probability level (p value) is less than .05, or 5 out of 100. What does this mean? It means that the researcher will not conclude that there is a true difference (rejecting the null hypothesis) unless the probability of obtaining the differences by chance is less than 5% out of 100%, or .05. This is translated into statistical significance. In other words, the researcher is 95% confident that the difference reflects a true difference, is due to treatment, and therefore represents a statistical significance. At times, the researcher will set the probability level at .01, or the researcher is willing to tolerate only a 1% out of 100% risk that the difference is due to chance and not treatment. In these cases, the differences between the means must be large. When reading research, how will you know if the study has found statistical significance? Simple. The researcher will indicate in the narrative of the findings section that statistical differences were found and will also report in a table of findings the type of test and its numerical outcome. The numerical outcome will have an asterisk (*) next to it or a p value ($p < .05$) indicating statistical significance.

Because these decisions are always based on probability, there is always a chance that an error will be made. To examine these errors, let us look at the choices the researcher has relative to the null hypothesis:

- *Choice 1*: The researcher concludes that the null hypothesis is true. If the researcher concludes that the null hypothesis is true, he or she is saying that any difference between the sample means is due to chance and not the treatment. This means that the researcher is concluding that the difference between the sample means is too small to conclude that the population means differ. Let us say that in the population, the null hypothesis is in fact true. The researcher has made a correct decision and fails to reject the null hypothesis. Yeah!
- *Choice 2*: The researcher concludes that the null hypothesis is false. By concluding that the null is false, the researcher is saying that the difference found is due to treatment and not to chance. Great news for the researcher! The researcher is saying that the difference found between the sample means is large enough to draw the conclusion that a similar difference also exists in the population. In reality, the finding from the sample is also true of the population. The researcher has once again made the correct decision, only this time, he or she will reject the null hypothesis. Right again!
- *Choice 3*: The researcher concludes that the null hypothesis is false, but in reality (i.e., in the population), it is true. Sorry, the researcher has now made a

mistake. The researcher incorrectly concludes at the end of the study that the treatment made a difference and therefore rejects a null hypothesis that is actually true.

• *Choice 4*: The researcher concludes that the null hypothesis is true. So, what is being said here? The difference found was due to chance and not treatment. But in this case, the true state of the population suggests that the difference was in fact due to treatment. Once again, a mistake has been made. The researcher fails to reject the null hypothesis and draws the wrong conclusion.

These mistakes have names. In choice 3, the researcher has made a type I error: rejecting a null hypothesis that is really true. In choice 4, the researcher has made a type II error: failing to reject a null that is false. The probability level or significance level ($p < .05$ [or .01]) determines the chance of making a type I error. So, if the selected probability level is .05, the researcher has a 5% chance of making a mistake or a type I error. Obviously, if the researcher sets the probability level at .01, there is only a 1% chance of making a type I error. The less chance of being wrong you are willing to tolerate, the greater the difference between the sample means is needed to reject the null hypothesis and say that the difference was due to treatment. What if the researcher was not willing to chance making a type I error and sets the probability level at $p < .0001$? Well, in this case, the researcher would have a very small chance of making a type I error but would increase his or her risk of making a type II error. The researcher would hardly ever reject a null hypothesis and may miss an actual significant difference. See Exhibit 10.1 for an illustration of the difference between type I and type II errors.

EXHIBIT 10.1 TYPE I AND TYPE II ERRORS.

		True Status of Null Hypothesis	
		True	False
Researcher's Conclusion	True	The researcher is right!	Type II error
	False	Type 1 error	Right again!

Source: Adapted from Gay & Arasian (2003).

Understanding the basic conceptual framework of inferential statistics should help you to read and understand some of what is written in the results sections of research studies. However, you should know that we have simply provided you with an overview of the concepts that are critical to a basic understanding of inferential statistics. There are many more complicated concepts that you will learn about if you continue your studies beyond the master's degree level.

Analyzing Data Using Inferential Tests

With a basic understanding of hypothesis testing, let us turn our attention to the process used by researchers who conduct quantitative studies in which they use inferential techniques. As is hopefully clear, a basic component of the inferential process is to test the null hypothesis and make a decision about its veracity. There are systematic steps that a researcher takes to engage in this investigation. In fact, many of these steps actually are taken before the analysis stage of the research. They are as follows:

Step One: Review the Null Hypothesis

Having stated the research hypothesis (or alternate hypothesis) at the conclusion of the review of the literature, the researcher reviews the null hypothesis. Remember that the null hypothesis states that there is no real difference or relationship between the groups or variables and that any difference found was due to chance. For example, the research or alternate hypothesis is as follows:

> The computerized tutoring group will perform better on a standardized achievement test than the noncomputerized tutoring group.

The corresponding null hypothesis would be that

> There is no difference in the performance on a standardized test between the computerized tutoring and the noncomputerized tutoring group.

Step Two: Decide on Probability Level

Before the data collection and after the researcher clearly states the null hypothesis, the researcher sets the significance level or the probability level (p value). That is, what criteria will you use to reject the null hypothesis and conclude that the difference you found was due to treatment and not to chance? The researcher usually decides to set the probability level at either .01 or .05. Remember what this means? If you set the probability level at .01, 1 out of 100 times, the difference is due to chance, and if you set it at .05, the risk is 5 out of 100 times that the difference will be due to chance. Most educational researchers set the probability at .05, preferring not to miss a true difference that might exist.

Step Three: Select the Statistical Tool

Although we are defining the selection of the statistical tool as step 3, in reality, many researchers know what test they are going to use even before they begin their research. Many researchers simply prefer one statistical tool over another. However, if they have not made a decision, here is where they must select the statistical test. Many statistical tests are used in educational research, and some of the most commonly used ones are listed in Table 10.2.

The researcher decides on the statistical test to use in part based on the type of data, type of hypothesis, and the number and type of variables in the study. One of the first decisions related to choosing the statistical technique is to decide whether to select a **parametric** or a **nonparametric** test. Parametric tests are generally preferred because they are believed to be more powerful tests. A powerful test is one that is more likely to allow the researcher to reject a false null hypothesis. However, to use a parametric test, the following assumptions about the data must exist:

- The data must be interval or ratio
- The subjects must be independent of one another (i.e., randomly selected)
- The variable being measured must be normally distributed in the population, or at least the type of distribution must be known
- The variability of the dependent variable in the two population groups must be the same. This is a statistic called the **variance** (which is the standard deviation squared).

Some violation of these assumptions is acceptable, with the exception of independence. This means that even if all of these assumptions are not met, parametric tests may still be used. Nonparametric tests are used primarily when the data are nominal or ordinal or whenever the assumptions for parametric tests are gravely violated.

Step Four: Calculate the Results of the Statistical Test and Make Decision About Rejecting the Null Hypothesis

Following the collection of the data, the researcher then calculates, typically with computer software programs, the selected statistical test. The statistical test will produce a value. For example, let us say that our researcher who is examining the

TABLE 10.2 COMMONLY USED INFERENTIAL STATISTICAL TESTS.

Statistical Test	Type of Data	Number and Type of Variables	How Used and Interpretation
t Test	Interval	1 independent; 1 dependent	Used to test the difference between two group means; a significant t value shows that a true difference exists between the group means
Analysis of variance	Interval	1 or more independent; 1 dependent	Used to test the difference between the means of two or more groups; a significant F ratio shows that a true difference exists between the group means
Analysis of covariance	Interval	1 or more independent; 1 dependent	Used to test the difference between the means of two or more groups after the influence of an extraneous variable (covariate) has been statistically removed; a significant F ratio shows that a true difference exists between the group means
Chi-square	Nominal (frequency counts or percentages)	2 or more frequency counts or percentages	Used to test whether the observed frequencies (the frequency counts or percentages from the data) show a true difference from the frequencies expected if all categories were equal
Pearson product-moment correlation	Interval	2 variables that are both measured	Used to test whether the relationship between two variables is greater than would be expected due to chance; a significant r shows that a true relationship exists
Multiple regression analysis	Interval	2 or more independent; 2 or more dependent	Used to see if the independent variable predicts changes in the dependent variable when other variables are held constant; a significant R value means that the independent variable can predict differences in the dependent variable

difference between computerized and noncomputerized tutoring decides to compute a *t* test at the .05 level of significance on the achievement data. The *t* test will be used to determine if the researcher should reject the null hypothesis. The *t* test will produce a *t* value, and the researcher will compare that value with those of a table of *t* values (or a computer printout of these values).

Each statistical test has associated with it degrees of freedom (df). The concept of degrees of freedom is beyond the scope of this book, but typically they are equal to the number of groups minus one. All practitioners really need to know is that to compare the obtained value with the tabled value, you must know the degrees of freedom. Even though this will likely be done for you by the computer program, here is how it was done in the days before we used computers to analyze data. Let us say that the calculated *t* value in our study is 8.4. At the .05 level of significance and with 1 df, the table value is equal to 12.71 (trust us, we looked this up). Because our value is 8.4, it is less than the table value. Therefore, our *t* value is not large enough for us to reject the null hypothesis. What does this mean? It means that the difference between the means was not large enough for us to reject the null hypothesis. The difference we found was due to chance and not to the treatment, in this case, the computerized tutoring.

Designs with More Than One Independent or Dependent Variable

As is evident from Table 10.2, there are research designs that can include more than one independent or dependent variable. Under those circumstances, the analyses becomes a bit more complicated. Although we will not discuss all of these designs, we will illustrate one design with more than one independent variable, referred to as a *factorial design.*

There are times when researchers want to examine more than one independent variable (as was the case with the example of computer use and class size) or at least one independent variable and a **control variable.** A control variable is a variable that the researcher has identified as one that could confound the outcome of the research study. A good example of a control variable can be seen in the study on computer use and gender. As a good researcher, you conduct a literature review investigating the existing research on computer use as an instructional tool to improve the math performance of elementary school children. You discover that a recurring theme in the literature is that boys and girls react differently to computer use and that this reaction can influence math achievement, the dependent variable in the study. So, perhaps either boys or girls will do better when exposed to computer use (the experimental treatment). To investigate not only computer use but the potential **interaction** of computer use and gender, the researcher could set up a 2 × 2 factorial design. A 2 × 2 factorial design has two factors (or independent variables) and two levels. The method of instruction is one factor, and the two levels are computer use versus no computer use. Gender is the other factor, with boys and girls representing the two levels. Thus, a 2 × 2 design would include four cells, as depicted in Exhibit 10.2.

To explain further the concept of interaction, Exhibit 10.3 includes hypothetical outcomes for the dependent variable math achievement. Our hypothetical math achievement test consisted of a 100-point exam. We have reported the **cell means** for each group. Researchers might examine the **main effects (the primary or main variables or factors in the study).** The primary variables in the study were method of instruction and gender. To examine these main effects, the researcher would collapse the cells and obtain an overall mean. So, for the no-computer-use group, the mean or average performance was 77.5 (cell 1 plus cell 2 divided by 2). The mean performance for the computer-use group was 87.0 (cell 3 plus cell 4 divided by 2). Based on these means, the computer-use group outperformed the no-computer-use group. In addition, when examining gender, the mean performance for the boys was 74.0 (cell 1 plus cell 3 divided by 2) and 90.5 (cell 2 plus cell 4 divided by 2) for the girls. This suggests that the girls outperformed the boys. However, was there an interaction between gender and method of instruction? The main effect of computer use suggests that computer use was better than no computer use, but was this true for both boys and girls? Examine the cells. In reality, the boys did better under the computer-use condition, and the girls did equally well under both conditions. Such a result might suggest that computer use is an effective way to improve math achievement in boys, but it has little effect on the math achievement of girls. Many researchers choose to diagram interaction effects using a graph. Interaction effects are depicted as nonparallel lines, as shown in the graph in Figure 10.6.

EXHIBIT 10.2 A 2 × 2 FACTORIAL DESIGN.

	Boys	Girls
No computer use	Cell 1; boys who get no computer use	Cell 2; girls who get no computer use
Computer use	Cell 3; boys who get computer use	Cell 4; girls who get computer use

EXHIBIT 10.3 A 2 × 2 DESIGN SHOWING MEAN SCORES OF BOYS AND GIRLS ON A MATH ACHIEVEMENT TEST.

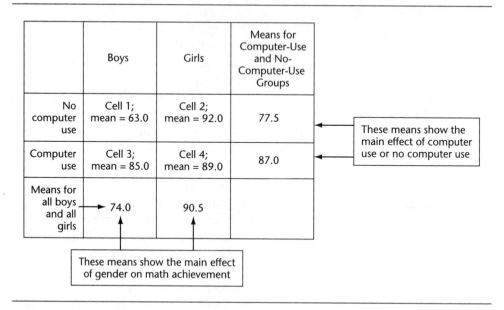

	Boys	Girls	Means for Computer-Use and No-Computer-Use Groups
No computer use	Cell 1; mean = 63.0	Cell 2; mean = 92.0	77.5
Computer use	Cell 3; mean = 85.0	Cell 4; mean = 89.0	87.0
Means for all boys and all girls	74.0	90.5	

These means show the main effect of computer use or no computer use

These means show the main effect of gender on math achievement

FIGURE 10.6 GRAPH SHOWING INTERACTION OF GENDER AND COMPUTER USE.

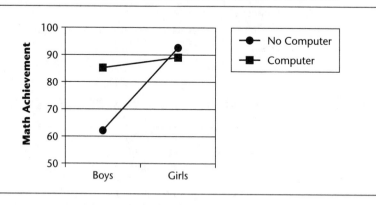

Although it can be difficult to understand all the numbers involved in complex inferential tests, such as a factorial design, remember that complex analyses allow us to examine multiple variables. By examining multiple variables, we get closer to accurately describing the complexities of real life. No one thinks you can accurately describe a classroom using only one or two variables! So inferential statistics are simply another tool for increasing our understanding of the many factors that influence educational processes and outcomes.

Chapter Summary

Although researchers use descriptive statistics to analyze data, studies that want to make inferences about the population from which the sample was drawn require a higher level of analysis to be conducted. Tests used to make inferences about a population based on a sample are referred to as inferential statistics. Correlational studies, causal-comparative studies, and experimental studies employ the use of inferential statistics to draw conclusions. In experimental research, the researcher wants to know if the experimental treatment caused a difference between the two groups and hopes to make generalizations of the findings back to a wider population by using randomization procedures. Even though an experimental researcher goes to the trouble of using randomized procedures to ensure that the sample is representative of the larger population from which it was drawn, sampling error can occur. Sampling error is not the fault of the researcher but is merely a reality of randomization. When testing a hypothesis, the researcher's goal is to reject the null hypothesis and accept the research hypothesis. In making these conclusions, a researcher applies a test of significance. This test uses statistical tools that allow the researcher to make decisions about the null hypothesis. Commonly used inferential statistical tests include t test, analysis of variance, analysis of covariance, chi-square, Pearson product moment correlation, and multiple regression analysis.

Key Concepts

parameters

true difference

sampling error

standard error of the mean

test of significance

parametric or nonparametric

variance

control variable

interaction

cell means

main effects

Discussion Questions or Activities

1. Search your state's education department or other related Web pages and examine the different ways data are presented. Find an example of a pie chart, a frequency graph, and a box-and-whisker graph and have a discussion as to the meaning of such data and whether the way in which it is displayed made any bearing on your interpretation.
2. In quantitative research, statistical tests are often the most complicated parts of a research study. Discuss why these tests are needed and how they relate to the concepts of sampling error and generalizability.

Suggested Readings

Almer, E. C. (2000). *Statistical tricks and traps: An illustrated guide to the misuses of statistics.* Los Angeles: Pyrczak Publishing.

Best, J. (2001). *Damned lies and statistics: Untangling numbers from the media, politicians, and activists.* Berkeley: University of California Press.

Creighton, T. B. (2001). *Schools and data: The educator's guide for using data to improve decision making.* Thousand Oaks, CA: Corwin Press.

CHAPTER ELEVEN

QUALITATIVE RESEARCH

Chapter Objectives

After reading this chapter, you should be able to

1. Summarize the key characteristics of qualitative research
2. Outline the basic steps to conducting a qualitative research study
3. Define foreshadowed questions and create several examples
4. Compare and contrast ethnographic, case study, phenomenological and grounded-theory research.
5. Understand the criteria used to evaluate qualitative research.

Research Vignette

Rayna, a graduate student in special education, is observing a newly integrated preschool that was set up at her university. As she observes the classroom through a one-way mirror, she watches the anxious faces of the students in special and regular education, and the parents and teachers. Although today her observations are from the "outside looking in," she knows that, beginning tomorrow, she will have an opportunity to become immersed in this classroom of learners. Her field experience will require that she spend 20 hours a week observing and helping the students and teachers. She reflects on all the research and theoretical principles that suggest that inclusion will have a positive impact on the social, emotional, and cognitive development of all of the children. Rayna wonders, "How will this new learning community influence the students and their parents and teachers?" As a graduate student who is also enrolled in a research class that requires original research, Rayna decides that she will conduct a study on this classroom. Recognizing the richness of data that will be available, she decides that her study would be best conducted using a qualitative approach.

Understanding Qualitative Research

Qualitative research, also called interpretive research or field research, is a methodology that has been borrowed from disciplines like sociology and anthropology and adapted to educational settings. Qualitative researchers, as you already have learned, use the inductive method of reasoning and strongly believe that there are multiple perspectives to be uncovered.

Qualitative researchers focus on the study of social phenomena and on giving voice to the feelings and perceptions of the participants under study. This is based on the belief that knowledge is derived from the social setting and that understanding social knowledge is a legitimate scientific process.

The following are the key characteristics of qualitative research:

- Studies are carried out in a naturalistic setting.
- Researchers ask broad research questions designed to explore, interpret, or understand the social context.
- Participants are selected through nonrandom methods based on whether the individuals have information vital to the questions being asked.
- Data collection techniques involve observation and interviewing that bring the researcher in close contact with the participants.
- The researcher is likely to take an interactive role where she or he gets to know the participants and the social context in which they live.
- Hypotheses are formed *after* the researcher begins data collection and are modified throughout the study as new data are collected and analyzed.
- The study reports data in narrative form.

How does Rayna's study fit into the description provided for qualitative research? At this point, you might want to reflect on why Rayna would want to choose a qualitative study to examine her questions.

Steps in Conducting Qualitative Research

Qualitative researchers use scientific methods to answer their research questions, although the steps they take are much more flexible and fluid than those in quantitative research. In general, these steps include the following:

- *Identifying a research topic or focus.* The topics are typically identified by the researcher based on experience, observation in the research settings, and readings on the topic. Although topics are set at the beginning of the study, the focus of the study may be rewritten during the data collection phase.
- *Conducting review of literature.* The researcher reviews the literature to identify important information relevant to the study and to write a research question. This literature review often continues while data are being collected and allows the researcher to refine the research question. There is some disagreement among qualitative researchers about the extent of literature review that should be done before the start of a research study. Those who argue for a limited review typically fear that if too much literature is reviewed, the researcher will enter the setting with preconceived notions about what she or he is investigating. Although it is important to have some knowledge about the issue being investigated, too much knowledge may reduce the researcher's openness to all possible realities.
- *Defining the role of researcher.* The researcher must decide to what degree she or he will become involved with the participants. In general, because of the nature of qualitative research, the researcher has close contact with the participants. To get a true sense of reality, as it is perceived by the participants, the researcher must to some degree become part of the culture that is being investigated. To portray the participants' perspectives, the researcher needs to develop an "insiders" point of view.
- *Managing entry into the field and maintaining good field relations.* Once the researcher has clearly defined the research topic or focus, a field of study (e.g., a place to conduct the research) must be identified. The selected field must be consistent with the research topic. If the topic or focus is charter schools, the researcher must decide what constitutes a charter school and which charter school would best help to answer the research questions. Once the researcher has identified the field of study, he must then prepare to introduce himself and the nature of the study to the school administrators. This must be done with care and consideration because the school is likely to want to know exactly what the study is designed to do and how both the study and the researcher's presence will influence the day-to-day functioning of the school. Remember, in qualitative research, as the researcher, you must come to know the participants in the study well enough to understand

their perspectives and, therefore, will likely want to become part of the field in some way. (As part of his ethnographic doctoral thesis, one of our colleagues enrolled as a student in a high school mathematics class to better understand what students wanted to get out of school. To enroll in the class, he had to obtain permission from the instructor and the principal of the school.) Once institutional permission is granted, you must obtain all the necessary permissions from those who will be participating in the study (and from guardians or parents if the participants are younger than 18 years). After gaining entry into the field, good field relations must be established and maintained. The establishment and maintenance of good field relations requires that trust and credibility are established. Sensitivity, honest communication, and nonjudgmental interactions are critical characteristics of a good researcher and a necessary part of field relations.

• *Selecting participants.* Recall that the participants for qualitative research are selected through **purposeful sampling.** The researcher will need to examine his or her foreshadowed questions and use them as a basis for the selection of participants. Depending on the types of questions asked, the researcher will want to select the participants so that they will be able to provide the key information essential for the study. For example, if you are conducting a study to explore the value that single mothers place on a Head Start afterschool program their children attend, you would want to select single mothers who have firsthand knowledge of the program. See Table 6.1 for a summary of purposeful sampling techniques.

• *Writing foreshadowed questions.* **Foreshadowed questions** are designed by the researcher and are based on the topics or research questions identified both at the start of the study and as the study progresses. Foreshadowed questions help the researcher to focus data collection and allow the data collection to proceed in a systematic way. For example, let us say that the topics for a study are the social and academic environment of an entire language classroom. Based on initial observations in the field and the review of literature, foreshadowed questions might include:

How does the teacher organize the language arts lesson?

What are the students doing during the language arts lessons?

How do the teacher and students feel about their language arts instruction?

How does the teacher introduce and promote student writing?

As you can see, these questions are designed to guide the researcher as she or he proceeds with data collection procedures.

• *Collecting the data.* The researcher next moves on to collecting data. Data collection in qualitative research generally includes observations, interviews, and document analyses. Researchers will typically include more than one data collection technique to validate findings. These different data sources are later compared with one another in a process called **triangulation.**

   • *Analyzing the data.* Data in qualitative research are analyzed through the reading and review of data (observation notes, interview transcripts) to detect themes and patterns that emerge.

   • *Interpreting and disseminating results.* The researcher summarizes and explains the themes and patterns (results) in narrative form. Interpretation may also involve discussion of how the findings from this study relate to findings from past studies in this area. Furthermore, qualitative researchers attempt to share their findings with other professionals through journals, reports, Web sites, and formal and informal meetings.

Types of Qualitative Research

Although there are many types of qualitative research, we have decided to focus on the methods that are most commonly read and utilized by our students, most of whom are school practitioners. These include ethnography, case study, phenomenology, and grounded-theory research. Each of these research approaches incorporates the key characteristics of qualitative research.

Ethnography

The word *ethnography* is derived from the Greek words *ethos* ("tribe") and *graphos* ("something that is written"). Literally, then, ethnography is the science of writing about tribes or, to use more contemporary language, writing about cultural groups. Ethnographic researchers hope to provide rich narratives or descriptions of the communities or cultures under investigation (Miles & Huberman, 1994).

   The overarching purpose of ethnographic research is to discover the essence of a culture and its unique complexities in order to "paint a portrait" of the group, its interactions, and its setting. According to LeCompte and Schensul (1999), ethnography is a research method useful in the discovery of knowledge that is embedded within a culture or community. There is no consensus about exactly what culture means, but most sociologists and anthropologists believe that culture refers to attitudes, knowledge, values, and beliefs that influence the behavior of a particular group of people. Embedded in this definition is the recognition that shared experiences and interactions shape the individuals within the group. Ethnographers hope to explore these shared experiences by understanding what people do, say, and believe. This, of course, necessitates that the researcher develop a close relationship with the participants in the study. This relationship is enhanced by data collection procedures that bring the researcher and participants into close communication. Often, ethnographers (and also case study researchers) rely on **key informants** or persons who are knowledgeable and who can provide the richest insights into the culture of the group and the issues addressed in the study. Qualitative researchers typically talk with key informants informally many times throughout the study, checking on how they perceive and interpret events or activities. Key informants may help the researcher learn the unwritten rules guiding interactions and communication in a group and may give advice on how to approach particular situations. For example, our colleague who enrolled in a high school mathematics class had one key informant who told him where students hung out after school. He found that conversations at the hang-out provided some of his best data on student feelings about school. Ethnographic research reports are usually lengthy, often taking the form of books. A major goal for ethnographers is to provide a "richly detailed description" (what anthropologists call a **thick description**) of the situation, capturing the full complexity of the nuances in interactions, cultural practices, and beliefs of the group. Good ethnographic studies should help readers feel that they are actually living the experiences of the groups studied and see the world through their eyes.

A good example of an ethnographic researcher is Jonathan Kozol who has written many books about the lives of inner-city youth and families. In one study he wanted to portray the struggles and dreams of families living in poverty in Mott Haven, a community in the Bronx, New York. To accomplish this, he immersed himself in ethnographic research, living in the community of Mott Haven for several months at a time. Kozol's investigation brought him close to the children, families, and religious and educational leaders in the community. Through his work in the community, participants came to trust Kozol and to share with him their innermost feelings and perspectives on being poor and of color. Some of his key informants included the director of an after-school program and her assistant. By using primarily observations, interviews, and the language of his participants, he provided an insightful view of life in an urban community (see *Amazing Grace* and *Ordinary Resurrections*).

Ethnography requires a tremendous amount of time and personal commitment on the part of the researcher. It is a research method chosen when questions or topics are embedded in cultural complexities and the researcher wants to come to understand cultural reality from the perspectives of the participants. The following are examples of studies that might be explored through ethnographic research:

- A study that explores the value of education and its influence on family life in a poor rural community

- A study designed to illuminate the out-of-school curriculum (those issues faced by students outside of the classroom) experienced by adolescent males of color growing up in an urban community
- A study designed to discover the social and academic culture of charter schools

Case Study Research

Case study research is a form of qualitative research that endeavors to discover meaning, to investigate processes, and to gain insight into and in-depth understanding of an individual, group, or situation. According to Smith, as cited in Merriam (1998), case studies can be differentiated from other forms of qualitative research by the fact that these studies focus on a "single unit" or a **bounded system.** What, you might ask, constitutes a bounded system? According to Merriam, boundedness can be determined by asking "whether there is a limit to the number of people involved who could be interviewed or a finite amount of time [for observation]. If there is no end (actually or theoretically) to the number of people who could be interviewed or to observations that could be conducted, then the phenomenon is not bounded enough to be a case" (pp. 27–28).

To begin a case study, researchers first identify the problem or question to be investigated and develop a rationale for why a case study is an appropriate approach to be used in the study. The problem or question is framed through experience, observation, and review of related research. Once the questions are clear, the researcher must decide which type of purposeful sampling procedures can be used to identify persons who will be observed or interviewed.

In our opening vignette, for example, one way for Rayna to conduct her study would be to propose a case study. Using her on-site observations, she would begin to generate some initial questions. She might ask a question about the nature of the interactions that occur between the children in special education and regular education. Or she might ask a question about the parents' feelings about how the children are relating to each other. Depending on the specific questions asked, she might want to use intensity sampling (parents with the strongest attitudes) or maximum variation (parents representing a wide range of opinions). Once the participants have been identified, Rayna could use a variety of data collection tools to gather data. In case studies, no one qualitative method is used. Instead, multiple techniques including interviews, observations, and at times, the examination of documents and artifacts are employed.

One likely beginning data collection point Rayna might want to consider is to interview parents either individually or collectively. Once again, her on-site observations will help her determine which parents she might like to interview. The selection of the participants would be based on their ability to contribute to an understanding of the phenomenon being studied, in this case, the perception of interactions between students in regular and special education. Rayna's interviews would likely continue by talking with the teachers and the administrators.

In addition, because case studies often use multiple data collection activities, Rayna would likely observe the children in class, at lunch, or on the playground. These observations would focus on the nature of the interactions that occurred in each of the settings. Notice that the settings are naturalistic and would allow Rayna to observe the children in their routine behaviors. These observations would produce the findings that could be triangulated with the interview data, increasing the validity of Rayna's data, findings, and conclusions. However, no matter where Rayna observes she should carefully record the data collected from the field.

A case study could be proposed if you are conducting a study that gets you close to a particular individual, group, school, classroom, program, or event. As in ethnographic research, your goal would be to provide a richly detailed description (a thick description) of the situation, to capture the full complexity and uniqueness of the case information. Some examples, in addition to Rayna's study would include

- A study exploring the classroom management techniques of an "Urban Teacher of the Year"
- A study that explores the way a home-schooled child relates to his or her parent-teacher
- A study designed to document the process of grieving for a class of second graders who are dealing with the recent death of a classmate

Phenomenological Research

Phenomenological research looks closely at an individual's interpretation of his or her experiences. Phenomenologists attempt to understand the meaning of an experience from the perspective of the participant. They recognize that there are many different ways to interpret the same experience and never assume that they (the researchers) know what things mean to the people they study. Because phenomenologists appreciate that experience is varied and complex, they usually collect extensive amounts of data over time from their participants. To begin a study, phenomenologists spend time observing and interacting with several potential participants to learn the language and modes of interaction most appropriate to their lives. Several initial interviews might be conducted to identify aspects of a person's experience that can guide the creation of questions for more in-depth interviews. During this initial data collection phase, the phenomenologists spend time reflecting on what they have observed and what their participants tell them.

It is through this silent reflection that a phenomenologist begins to construct the reality of the participant(s) and begins to make interpretations. During this re- flection stage, the researcher must suspend, or at least put on hold, any precon- ceived notions of the reality of the participants' experiences. It is only after the researcher gains some insight that in-depth data collection can begin. The data collection typically involves several group or one-on-one interviews with partici- pants discussed earlier in Chapter Five. These multiple interviews allow participants to reflect on their experiences and to add to what they said in earlier interviews. Whereas to a certain degree all qualitative research engages in this kind of process, the phenomenologist focuses more on the essence of the human experiences and relies heavily on interviews as the most unbiased way to understand what the ex- periences mean to participants. According to Patton (1990), "The assumption of essence, like the ethnographer's assumption that culture exists and is important, becomes the defining characteristic of a purely phenomenological study" (p. 70).

Wanting to understand the human experience and how experiences are in- terpreted differently by different people would certainly be an appropriate reason to conduct a phenomenological study. Some example studies might include

- A study that attempts to capture the feelings and emotional reactions of chil- dren who attended school in the area directly around the World Trade Center after the terrorist attacks
- A study designed to explore the reactions of families to the birth of a special needs child
- A study that illuminates the life stresses experienced by single parents

Grounded Theory

Consistent with the key features of qualitative research, grounded-theory research uses the inductive approach and collects data using multiple techniques over a long period of time. However, in grounded-theory research, the data collected are continually reviewed to build a theory that is "grounded" in the data. This method is based on the work of Glaser and Strauss (1967), who are generally responsible for the introduction of this approach. Do not confuse this type of theory with the "grand" theories you are probably used to studying. These kinds of studies do not result in a theory such as Piaget's theory of cognitive development or Freud's psy- chosexual theory. Grounded theories are practical theories that are designed to be used in the context of the field studied, as well as in other similar settings. Grounded theorists differ from other qualitative researchers in that they hope that their findings can be generalized to other settings. Grounded-theory researchers have refined the process of analyzing qualitative data and use the term **constant**

comparison to describe this sophisticated method of data analysis. Constant comparison is a procedure where the researcher compares one component of the data with other components of the data to determine similarities and differences. Unlike triangulation where a researcher compares data from different sources (observations and interviews, for example) to validate responses, components in constant comparison may come from the same data source. For example, a study by Bell and Bromnick (2003) collected data to further examine the concept of an "imaginary audience" that David Elkind (1967) had proposed to describe the self-consciousness of adolescents who were constantly trying to anticipate what others thought of them. Bell and Bromnick interviewed youth to identify areas about which they worried. Initially, they compiled a comprehensive list of all the reasons given by the youth for worrying. The categories on the list were then compared with each other and analyzed for similar patterns or links. Categories that were similar or linked were combined, resulting in 11 different areas of worry, such as what other people think, image or appearance, the future, family, friendship, and fitting in. Further analysis of the interviews with the youth regarding these categories revealed that their worries had a basis in reality. They reported that their worries came out of pressures from other people or reflected comments in which they were judged by others. Based on several waves of data collection and analysis, Bell and Bromnick concluded that a new theory of adolescent egocentrism was needed that recognized the "social reality" of adolescent worries and the existence of real, not imaginary, audiences who judged the actions of these youth.

Remember that the goal of all of these examples is to develop a theory. Thus, the end result of each of these studies would be an analysis of the data to produce a theory:

- A study that investigates the grieving processes of parents who have lost a child to death
- A study designed to explore strategies used by inner-city teachers whose students perform at the state benchmarks for achievement in language arts
- A study that investigates why a particular magnet school with a diverse and poor population has students who perform at or above grade level.

Evaluating Qualitative Research

Although qualitative research studies make for good reading, students often are uncertain about how to evaluate whether the studies are "good research." Because many qualitative studies focus on in-depth description instead of providing evidence that certain outcomes have been achieved, students often ask, "What's the point of this study?" One common error is using criteria that are appropriate for *quantitative* research to judge the goodness of qualitative studies. For example, the study of Max referred to in Exhibit 5.5 might be criticized because the sample of one child is not representative and the results could not be generalized to other children. However, this argument ignores the major goal of qualitative research, which is to provide an in-depth understanding of a limited setting, group, or person. This in-depth understanding may be cultivated through detailed descriptions, but it also involves deep analysis of *how* educational processes occur and *how* certain outcomes are achieved. Criteria for evaluating qualitative research differ from those used in quantitative research in that they focus on how well the researchers have provided evidence that their descriptions and analysis represent the reality of the situations and persons studied. Many different criteria have been proposed for evaluating qualitative studies, and Lincoln and Guba (1985) provide extensive discussion of these criteria. Here we will focus on four major areas and the types of evidence that researchers might present.

Credibility

Credibility refers to whether the participants' perceptions of the setting or events match up with the researcher's portrayal of them in the research report. In other words, has the researcher accurately represented what the participants think, feel, and do and the processes that influence their thoughts, feelings, and actions? Credibility parallels the criteria of validity (including both validity of measures and internal validity) in quantitative research, although qualitative researchers do not discuss extraneous variables in the assessment of credibility. Rather, they look at whether the researcher's methods are likely to yield accurate and deep pictures of the research setting and participants.

Evidence in support of credibility can take several different forms. First, a good qualitative study should discuss how the researcher engaged in repeated, prolonged, and substantial involvement in the field. Did the researcher spend enough time in the setting and take part in meaningful interactions with the participants? Is it likely that the effects of an observer being present have abated and a strong level of trust and rapport has been established with participants? The amount of time that is sufficient will depend on the nature of the study, but all qualitative studies should indicate how much time was spent in the field and how the researcher established relationships with the participants.

A second aspect of credibility involves checking on whether the researcher's interpretation of the processes and interactions in the setting is valid. All qualitative researchers collect multiple sources of data to ensure that they have a broad representation of the places and persons studied. The information provided by these different sources should be compared through triangulation to corroborate the researcher's conclusions. If the sources provide conflicting information, the researcher should discuss possible reasons for the conflict. Another way to provide evidence supporting the hypotheses that emerge during qualitative research is **negative case analysis.** Negative case analysis involves examining the data for examples that contradict or disconfirm the hypothesis. When negative instances are identified, the researcher should revise the hypothesis or provide an explanation of why the case does not fit.

Because qualitative researchers often take a social constructivist or emancipatory-liberatory framework, they may not expect that all participants will share the same perspectives. So it is essential to seek out and present a balanced view of all possible perspectives. To ensure that the researcher's own biases do not influence how the perspectives are portrayed, many researchers use **member checks** in which the transcribed interviews or summaries of the researcher's conclusions are sent to participants for review. In addition, researchers continually monitor their own subjective perspectives and biases by recording reflective field notes or keeping a journal of their thoughts. Another strategy is to have a **peer debriefer,** a colleague who examines the field notes and meets with the researcher on a regular basis, asking questions to help him or her reexamine assumptions and consider alternative ways of looking at the data. In many action research studies, collaboration and regular meetings with other practitioners may serve the function of peer debriefing.

Researchers taking an emancipatory-liberatory framework may also insist that evaluation of a study include **attention to voice** (Lincoln, 1995). The question is, who is speaking for whom? Does the researcher seek out and engage persons who are least empowered in the society? Are these voices given detailed coverage and a prominent place in the analysis? Studies taking a emancipatory or liberatory approach may also insist that data be examined from a theoretical framework, such as feminist theory.

A final and demanding strategy used by some qualitative researchers is an **external audit.** In an external audit, an independent researcher examines all of the data collected in a study with the following questions in mind:

- Are the findings grounded in data? Is there a clear connection between each finding and some part of the data?
- Are the themes appropriate to the data? Are all interpretations and conclusions supported by the data?
- Have researcher biases been well controlled?

Dependability

Dependability is a criterion for qualitative research that parallels reliability, although it is not assessed through statistical procedures. Dependability refers to whether one can track the procedures and processes used to collect and interpret the data. Good qualitative studies will provide detailed explanations of how the data are collected and analyzed. Dependability is often the difference between an experiential report that simply summarizes a researcher's conclusions and an empirical, research-based qualitative study that includes a thorough explanation of methods. Although it is not possible for qualitative studies to include all of their data in their results, many qualitative researchers make their data available for review by other researchers.

Transferability

Although qualitative researchers do not expect their findings to be generalizable to all other settings, it is likely that the lessons learned in one setting might be useful to others. However, qualitative researchers insist that readers must make this judgment because the appropriateness of the lessons depends on the contextual similarities and differences of the sites. **Transferability** refers to the degree of similarity between the research site and other sites as judged by the reader. Transferability is assessed by looking at the richness of the descriptions included in the study as well as the amount of detail provided regarding the context within which the study occurred. Because the reader is the person who must judge transferability, richly detailed or thick descriptions enable the reader to make judgments about the similarity of the participants, schools, resources, policies, culture, and other characteristics of the research site and the reader's own site. So transferability is not whether the study includes a representative sample; it is how well the study has made it possible for readers to decide whether similar processes will be at work in their own communities by understanding in depth how they occur at the research site.

Promoting Action and Collaboration

Action researchers and qualitative researchers taking an emancipatory-liberatory framework often evaluate research based on whether it has stimulated action that will improve education or enhance the lives of persons with little power. Lincoln and Guba (1985) refer to this as **catalytic authenticity,** asking whether the research has stimulated change for the better in ways that are truly desired by the study participants. Evidence that this has occurred should include descriptions of how participants collaborated with researchers in determining what changes needed to occur and in planning any actions. Many researchers also emphasize that the benefits and privileges of doing research should be shared with participants. This may take the form of sharing royalties from the publication of a book or obtaining funding to make it possible for research participants to take part in presentations at conferences. Educational conferences are increasingly enriched by the participation of teachers, students, and community members in presentations. If the ultimate goal of educational research is to improve education, the criterion of promoting action and collaboration is one way to evaluate if the research was worth doing! Table 11.1 summarizes the criteria for evaluating qualitative studies and the types of methods for meeting these criteria.

TABLE 11.1 CRITERIA FOR EVALUATING QUALITATIVE STUDIES.

Criteria	Methods to Meet Criteria
Credibility and control of researcher bias	Prolonged and meaningful participation in setting
	Triangulation of multiple data sources
	Negative case analysis
	Participant review of interview transcripts
	Member checks
	Peer debriefer
	Attention to voice
	External audit
Dependability	Detailed description of data collection and analysis procedures
	Use of videotape and audiotape
	Data made available for review
Transferability	Rich descriptions of setting, participants, interactions, culture, policies, etc.
	Detailed information on context and background
Promoting action and collaboration (catalytic authenticity)	Description of collaboration with participants
	Description of ways in which research changed the lives of participants
	Coauthorship of publications
	Sharing royalties and other benefits of publication

Chapter Summary

Qualitative research is a methodology that has been borrowed from disciplines like sociology and anthropology and adapted to educational settings. Qualitative researchers use inductive methods of reasoning and believe that there are multiple perspectives to be uncovered. Qualitative researchers focus on the study of social phenomena and give voice to the feelings and perceptions of the participants under study. Qualitative studies are carried out in naturalistic settings, where researchers ask broad research questions designed to explore, interpret, or understand the social context and where participants are selected through nonrandom methods based on whether the individuals have information vital to the questions being asked. As part of the process, the qualitative researcher is likely to take an interactive role in which she or he gets to know the participants and the social context in which they live. Quantitative research is driven by a hypothesis, but in qualitative research, the hypotheses are formed *after* the researcher begins data collection and are modified through the study as new data are collected and analyzed. Triangulation is a process used by qualitative researchers for data analysis when different data sources are compared with one another. In qualitative research, results from the study are reported in a narrative form. There are several types of qualitative research. Ethnography is one type of qualitative research where the researcher tries to provide a rich narrative or description of the communities or cultures under investigation. The overarching purpose of ethnographic research is to discover the essence of a culture and its unique complexities to paint a portrait of the group, its interactions, and its setting. Case study research is a common form of qualitative research that endeavors to discover meaning, to investigate process, and to gain insight into and in-depth understanding of individuals, groups, or situations. Case studies are differentiated from other forms of qualitative research by the fact that they employ a bounded system or, in other words, have a limit to the number of people involved who could be interviewed. Phenomenological research is another type of qualitative research that looks closely at individuals' interpretation of their experience and attempts to understand the meaning of an experience from the perspective of the participants. Multiple one-to-one interviews with an individual are typically used with phenomenological research. The last type of qualitative approach is grounded theory in which an inductive approach is used to collect data; however, the data are constantly compared to review them and to build a theory that is grounded in the data. One should not critique qualitative research on the basis of quantitative methods. Instead, qualitative research should be evaluated based on four major areas: credibility, dependability, transferability, and promoting action and collaboration.

Key Concepts

purposeful sampling

foreshadowed questions

triangulation

key informants

thick description

bounded system

constant comparison

negative case analysis

member checks

peer debriefer

external audit

transferability

catalytic authenticity

credibility

dependability

Discussion Questions or Activities

1. Gaining entry into a school to conduct qualitative research is often a complex process. Consider what specific issues you would review with the director of a private all-girls middle school where you are conducting research on peer relationships.
2. Select a topic that you could research with qualitative techniques. Write a statement of purpose and several foreshadowed questions for that topic. Select one of the following: ethnography, case, phenomenology, or grounded theory and

   • Justify your selection
   • Discuss your primary method of data collection
   • Describe how you would triangulate the data

Suggested Readings

Anderson, E. A., Kohler, J. K., & Letiecq, B. L. (2002). Low-income fathers and "Responsible Fatherhood" Programs: A qualitative investigation of participants' experiences. *Family Relations, 51*(2). Retrieved Dec. 12, 2004, from Academic Search Premier.

Deering, R. D. (2001). An ethnographic study of norms of inclusion and cooperation in a multiethnic middle school. *Urban Review, 28,* 21–39.

Denzin, N. K., & Lincoln, Y. S. (2005). *The Sage handbook of qualitative research.* Thousand Oaks, CA: Sage Publications.

Glesne, C. (2006). *Becoming qualitative researchers: An introduction.* Boston: Pearson Education.

Mills, L. J., & Daniluk, J. C. (2002). Her body speaks: The experience of dance therapy for women survivors of child sexual abuse. *Journal of Counseling & Development, 80,* 77–85.

CHAPTER TWELVE

MIXED-METHODS AND ACTION RESEARCH

Chapter Objectives

After reading this chapter, you should be able to

1. Discuss the purpose of mixed-methods research and describe the strengths and weaknesses of this approach
2. Identify three types of mixed-methods design and describe each one
3. Overview the six steps in conducting mixed-methods research
4. Define action research and list its key characteristics
5. Discuss the different types of action research and those individuals who have played a major role in the development of this area of research

Research Vignette

Dale is a middle school counselor who is concerned about the stresses experienced by young adolescent students at his school. Dale wants to convince his principal and school board to provide funding to support new after-school programs. He decides to gather data on the problems that youth at the school are experiencing to find out what types of programs are most needed. Knowing that the board will want to know how frequently the problems occur, he initially decides to gather information through a quantitative questionnaire that measures the number of stressful events youth have experienced. The questionnaire that Dale selects lists many different stressful events, such as getting a bad grade, parents fighting, getting into fights with friends, moving, or losing someone you loved through a death. Youth completing the survey are asked to check off all the events that they have experienced in the past year and to indicate which event was most stressful. Dale will then calculate the percentage of youth selecting each response and report which types of events are most frequent and how many youth are experiencing them. However, Dale decides that he also wants to collect some qualitative data to provide greater depth and meaning to his report. To accomplish this, he adds a question asking the students why the event they identified as most stressful was so difficult. Dale plans to select several youth based on their answers to this open-ended question and interview them in depth to find out how they coped with the event. He obtains permission from the school and most of the students' parents to conduct his research study. As he analyzes the questionnaire results, he notices that one boy has checked that both his dog and his father died in the past year. The boy picked his dog dying as the most stressful event because they were so close. Dale decides to interview him because his answer is unusual. In his interview, the boy explains that the dog had been a present from his father on his seventh birthday. He and his father often took walks with his dog. "When my father died, my dog comforted me. I always talked with him about my father. So when my dog died, it was like losing my dad all over again and also my best friend."

In his board presentation, Dale presents data from his questionnaire showing that numerous youth reported stressful events involving the loss of a loved one. He illustrates the difficulties experienced by the youth using several stories from his interviews. (Note: He obtains permission to use the stories and also carefully protects confidentiality of the youth by omitting any identifying details.) He then makes a request for funding to support programs on grief and loss for the students.

Mixed-Methods Research

Quantitative and qualitative research methods may seem so different that you might wonder why anyone would think of combining both approaches in one study. Dale's story illustrates the value of mixing these two types of data. If only quantitative data had been collected, the board might not have understood the depth of the emotions that were represented by the events checked on the list. The boy's choice of his dog's death as the most difficult event in the past year might have seemed bizarre or suggested that he was having problems with his father. However, the qualitative data provided a context for understanding the boy's grief and his sensitivity to the importance of his dog in dealing with the death of his father. It was also a moving story that showed how difficult and lengthy the grieving and coping process can be for youth. On the other hand, stories by themselves might not be convincing. The quantitative data (percentage of youth reporting each type of stressful event from the questionnaire) provided a broad picture of the types of stressful events reported by several hundred youth. Together, the combination of qualitative and quantitative data conveyed both the scope of the problems that many youth were experiencing and how they were struggling to cope with difficult emotions.

Educational researchers are increasingly recognizing the value of collecting both quantitative and qualitative data. One of the major advantages is that it combines the strengths of both qualitative and quantitative research, providing both an in-depth look at context, processes, and interactions and precise measurement of attitudes and outcomes. In mixed-methods research, the researcher has flexibility in choosing methods of data collection, and the presentation of results can be convincing and powerful when both summary numbers and in-depth portraits of a setting are included.

However, mixed-methods research also has some disadvantages. Perhaps most relevant to students beginning to study research is that it requires knowledge and skills in both qualitative and quantitative methods. In addition, a mixed-methods study usually requires more time and resources to complete than a study using only one type of data. The researcher must spend time developing quantitative measures and also in the field collecting qualitative data (or pay graduate assistants to do this). Data analysis also entails both the use of statistical calculations and analysis of themes and patterns. The complexity of mixed-methods research occurs partly because these designs use both qualitative and quantitative methods of data collection extensively. Just adding a couple of open-ended questions to a quantitative measure does not constitute a true mixed-methods study.

In this chapter, we examine several approaches to research that combine quantitative and qualitative research methods. First, we examine **mixed-methods research designs:** approaches involving well-developed procedures for collecting and analyzing both quantitative and qualitative data that are used primarily by professional researchers and program evaluators. Second, we examine **action research:** research conducted by practitioners in their own school settings to identify and take actions to remedy problems that occur in their practice. Because of its practical orientation, action research generally uses both quantitative and qualitative data as well.

Barriers to Mixed-Methods Research

Until recently, quantitative and qualitative researchers were largely isolated from each other because they reported their studies in separate conferences and journals. There were some exceptions to this isolation, particularly among researchers working in the field of evaluation where qualitative methods were frequently combined with descriptive survey methods (Reichardt & Rallis, 1994). Studies of institutions and organizations also frequently used a combination of surveys, interviews, and archival data. Creswell (2003) notes that a study by Jicks in 1979 stimulated much interest in how *triangulation* of quantitative and qualitative data might improve the accuracy of understanding complex social situations. However, these procedural advances were limited by debates about the underlying assumptions of researchers using mixed methods.

As noted in Chapter One, quantitative and qualitative researchers tend to adopt different theoretical frameworks. Quantitative researchers are more likely to be scientific realists who emphasize objectivity, and qualitative researchers are more likely to be social constructivists who emphasize subjective realities. Because these two approaches include some contradictory assumptions about the nature of the real world, questions about the validity of combining these approaches were raised. Would not one framework dominate, thereby undermining the integrity of data collected under the less dominant approach? However, some researchers pointed out that one could use both frameworks by recognizing that some aspects of educational settings have an objective reality (e.g., classroom arrangement) whereas others might be more subjective (e.g., student experiences with teachers). Many mixed-methods researchers also adopted a pragmatic framework that emphasized using any method that helped address current problems. As a resolution, Greene and Caracelli (cited in Creswell, 2003) proposed that mixed-methods researchers acknowledge their philosophical assumptions by reporting their theoretical frameworks as they collect both quantitative and qualitative data.

As researchers began to appreciate how quantitative and qualitative data might complement each other in understanding educational problems, debates about theoretical frameworks gradually subsided. Focus shifted to the discussion of procedural methods for acknowledging the priority and sequence of quantitative and qualitative data in mixed-method designs.

Characteristics of Mixed-Methods Research

Although there are different ways of conducting mixed-methods research, Creswell (2003), a prominent mixed-methods researcher, has identified the following as characteristics shared by all these designs:

• *There is a strong rationale for using mixed methods.* As noted above, because mixed-method designs are still not the norm, researchers usually explain their reasons for collecting both quantitative and qualitative data.

• *Both quantitative and qualitative data are collected.* The researcher may decide to emphasize quantitative data more than qualitative data, may emphasize qualitative data over quantitative data, or may emphasize both equally. However, in all studies substantial amounts of both quantitative and qualitative data are collected.

• *The researcher decides whether to prioritize the quantitative or qualitative data or to consider these as equal in importance.* Although all mixed-methods research studies collect both quantitative and qualitative data, some designs emphasize one type of data over another. In Dale's study, the questionnaire results were his major focus because he wanted to determine the types of problems that his program needed to address. The interviews were considered to be a way to add depth to the youth's reports of stress so that Dale could convince administrators or funders that the problems experienced by the students were not trivial.

• *A sequence for collecting the quantitative and qualitative data is set.* Both types of data may be collected simultaneously, or one type of data might be collected first, as in Dale's study.

• *A design is chosen to determine how and when each type of data will be collected and analyzed.* Several types of designs have been identified based on the sequence of data collection analysis.

• *Visual aids are used to portray the research design.* Given the complexity of mixed-methods research, diagrams or other visual aids are often used to summarize the steps in conducting the research. Samples of these diagrams are presented in the next section discussing three common mixed-method designs.

Mixed-Method Designs

In mixed-methods research, the word *design* refers to the decisions about which type of data is given priority and when each type of data is collected and analyzed. The most common designs sequence the use of qualitative and quantitative methods. In the **explanatory design,** data are collected in two phases, with quantitative data collected first and qualitative data collected at a later time. Often the quantitative data are emphasized and the qualitative data are used to illustrate or further explain the quantitative findings. Dale's study would be considered an example of an explanatory design. Other reasons why one might use an explanatory design would include

• To examine outlier scores or extreme cases in more depth. The qualitative data would help to create a deeper understanding of the persons who seem to stand apart from the rest of those in the study. For example, Newman and Spaulding (1997) conducted a survey of schools taking part in a National Science Foundation program regarding what teachers saw as the most important outcomes for their students. Several schools that had an extremely high number of students receiving awards at science contests were selected, and teachers at these schools were interviewed to gain a better understanding of how they were using the program.

• To examine one level of a multilevel system more completely. For example, one might survey an entire school about high-stakes testing and then interview teachers in the grade levels where testing occurs.

Another type of mixed-method design is the **exploratory design,** which also includes two phases. In exploratory designs, the qualitative data are collected during the first phase of research, and quantitative data are collected during the second phase of research. This design has been widely used by program evaluators to develop surveys for use in studies in which not enough is known at the start about a topic or program to create an accurate quantitative survey. A small number of persons are first interviewed, and the qualitative data are analyzed to identify the major themes, questions, ideas, issues, or perspectives that should be included in the survey. The survey would then be sent to a larger group and the results summarized numerically. A strength of this design is that the qualitative data can be used to design an instrument that uses the language of the groups for whom it will be used. An example occurred in a study that one of us (D.T.S.) conducted in which fifth-grade students were interviewed about a new writing curriculum that required students to write rough drafts. In interviews with the students, the researchers found that the students did not know the phrase "rough draft." Instead, they referred to their initial drafts as "sloppy copies." The researcher used the students' phrases in the final survey question to make sure that they understood the questions.

Another use of an exploratory design would be to first conduct case studies of several sites to identify key characteristics that might be used to develop a quantitative instrument that could be used to conduct a correlational analysis of a larger number of sites. For example, Shablak, Cavino, and Spaulding (2005) used an exploratory design to study schools classified under No Child Left Behind standards as in need of improvement. They first selected 10 schools and conducted case studies in which they used observations, interviews, and document review to describe the procedures and activities that the schools were using to address their problems. They also interviewed teachers and administrators about the outcomes that they were seeing at their schools. Following analysis of the qualitative data from the case studies, they developed a survey with questions yielding quantitative data that they sent to 100 schools classified as in need of improvement. The surveys produced extensive high-quality data from this larger group, as shown by the fact that few participants needed to use the "other" category for any of the questions.

The most complex mixed-method design is a **triangulation design** in which quantitative and qualitative data are collected simultaneously. The goal is to combine the strengths of both types of methods by applying them to the same situation at the same time. It is called a *triangulation design* because the data from the quantitative and qualitative methods are compared (or triangulated) to see if they produce similar findings. Thus, the design provides both a more complete picture of the topic studied and enhanced credibility because of the use of multiple methods. Figure 12.1 summarizes processes involved in the three types of mixed methods designs.

FIGURE 12.1 EXPLORATORY, EXPLANATORY, AND TRIANGULATION DESIGNS.

Exploratory Design

| Qualitative data are collected and analyzed.

Major emphasis is placed on qualitative data. | | Quantitative measure is developed or refined based on qualitative data.

Quantitative data are collected and analyzed with goal of building on or explaining the qualitative data. |

Explanatory Design

| Quantitative data are collected and analyzed.

Major emphasis is placed on quantitative data. | | Qualitative data are collected to follow up or refine results from quantitative data. |

Triangulation Design

| Quantitative and qualitative data are collected at the same time.

Both types of data are given equal emphasis. | | Qualitative and quantitative data are analyzed together.

Results from qualitative and quantitative are triangulated or compared to see if findings are similar. |

Steps in Conducting Mixed-Methods Studies

Carrying out a mixed-methods study is somewhat more complex than using either a quantitative or qualitative approach alone because one must consider both types of data at each step. The exact processes depend on the type of design that is chosen, however, Creswell (2003) identifies the following steps as a general guide to conducting a mixed-methods study:

1. *Determine the feasibility of using mixed methods.* Ask yourself if you have the time, knowledge, and resources required to use a mixed-method design.
2. *Identify a clear rationale for using mixed methods.* Assuming that it is feasible to use a mixed-method design, what are the reasons why both quantitative and qualitative data are needed to investigate your research topic?
3. *Determine strategies for collecting data and select a research design.* Consider how and when you will collect both types of data. What methods will you use to collect the different types of data? Which type of data will be given priority, or will you emphasize both equally? In what order will you collect the data, or will it be collected at the same time?
4. *Develop research questions for both the quantitative and qualitative data.* The format of your questions will depend on the type of design you choose. However, the research question should be linked to your rationale for collecting each type of data. If you are planning an exploratory or explanatory (two-stage) design, you may not be able to identify your second research question until the first phase of your study has been completed. As in qualitative research, the research question or hypothesis might emerge as you conduct the study.
5. *Collect both the qualitative and quantitative data.* The order in which you collect the data will depend on the type of design selected. This step will typically involve a lengthy period of time because there will be either two separate phases of data collection or one phase involving collection of two different sets of data.
6. *Analyze the data either separately or concurrently.* For explanatory and exploratory designs, the data will be analyzed sequentially. For triangulation designs, the data will be analyzed at the same time.
7. *Write the report in a manner consistent with the type of design.* In the write-up of the study, methods of data collection and analysis are usually integrated for triangulation designs and separated for explanatory and exploratory designs.

Evaluating Mixed-Methods Research Studies

Because mixed-methods research always includes two different types of data and may involve two different phases of data collection, it should not surprise you that criteria for evaluating these studies are often complex. Studies should be examined to see if they were designed and carried out in a manner consistent with the characteristics and steps described earlier. In addition, criteria appropriate for specific quantitative and qualitative research approaches must be considered, depending on the type of mixed-method design used. For example, if a survey is being administered, one might ask whether the survey was pilot-tested and what the response rate was. If case studies are being used, one might ask if the researcher spent an adequate amount of time in the field and collected data from multiple sources. Following are some general questions that Creswell (2003) suggests asking to evaluate a mixed-methods study:

- Is there a clear rationale for using each type of data?
- Is the type of design clearly described or clearly presented in a visual manner?
- Are the sequence of data collection and the priority given to each type of data clear?
- Are there research questions for each type of data, and are these appropriate given the sequence and priority of data collection and analysis?
- Are the data collection procedures clearly described? Is evidence of the quality of the methods of data collection presented, as appropriate, for both quantitative (reliability and validity) and qualitative (credibility and dependability) measures?
- Are the procedures for data analysis consistent with the type of design chosen and appropriate to the research questions asked?
- Does the written report have a structure that is appropriate to the type of mixed-method design being used?

Action Research

Action research, as its name implies, is a type of research oriented to enacting immediate changes in an educational setting. It has the potential to produce change quickly because the research is carried out by educators in their own work settings. Common alternative terms used to describe this type of research include *teacher research* (Cochran-Smith & Lytle, 1993), *practitioner research* (Anderson, Herr, & Nihlen, 1994), and *emancipatory praxis* (Lewin, 1948). Mills (2000) defines action research as "any systematic inquiry conducted by teacher researchers, principals, school counselors or other stakeholders in the teaching/learning environment, to gather information about the ways that their particular schools operate, how they teach, and how well students learn" (p. 6).

The idea for contemporary action research grew out of writings by Kurt Lewin (1948), who advocated "research leading to social action" as a way to challenge established educational practices. Both Lewin and Lawrence Stenhouse, the founder of the Center for Applied Research in Education, believed that traditional research (e.g., approaches discussed in Chapters Seven, Eight, Nine, and Eleven) was too slow and disconnected from the everyday world of education to really improve practice. They encouraged educators to become involved in research as a way to improve their own practice. Stenhouse argued that research would liberate teachers from the dictates of professional researchers and said that "researchers [should] justify themselves to practitioners, not practitioners to researchers" (cited in Cochran-Smith & Lytle, 1993, p. 8). Not all action researchers are out to change the system, but all share a belief that they have the knowledge, power, and skills to study and improve their own practices and the lives of those with whom they work. Underlying all action research is the assumption that practitioners are capable of independent action and systematic inquiry into their own educational practices. Furthermore, action research is based on the assumption that as insiders, practitioners have valuable knowledge that needs to form the basis for making decisions about schools.

As you can probably tell, action research takes either the emancipatory-liberatory framework or the pragmatic framework as its philosophical basis. Its major goal is to find ways to change the lives of everyone involved in education for the better. In fact, action researchers often claim that educators have a professional responsibility to reflect on their own practice. The information they gather through action research should empower them to change educational institutions and question established practices. Action researchers who take an emancipatory-liberatory framework are often actively involved in seeking new policies, programs, or resources to assist groups who are denied power within educational systems. These researchers might study the problems of groups, such as students who are retained, students with disabilities, parents who speak English as a second language, or nontenured teachers. In all cases the researcher would work collaboratively with persons in the groups to identify possible solutions. This type of action research is often referred to as **critical action research** or **critical pedagogy.**

Action research based on a pragmatic framework involves looking at issues or problems in one's own classroom, school, or educational setting to see how practice can be improved. If Dale in our opening example continues his research by collaborating with students, parents, teachers, and others at the school to set up the grief-and-loss program and assess its effectiveness, his research would be a type of action research using a pragmatic framework. This type of action research is often referred to as **practical action research.** Examples of both critical action research and practical action research are presented later in this chapter.

Characteristics of Action Research

Characteristics that are common to all types of action research include

- *It is conducted in the practitioner-researcher's own educational setting and the practitioner takes an active part in the research.* The setting can be a classroom, school, district, or community program; the situated nature of the research is what enables the research to draw on insider perspectives. It also ensures that the research is based in the reality of everyday educational practices.
- *It involves collaboration with other educators and persons involved in the educational process.* Practitioners involved in action research often work with others at the school, including other teachers, school psychologists, speech therapists, counselors, staff, or the school principal. Students, parents, and community members are also frequently involved in action research to assure that all perspectives are heard. Because many of the measures used in action research are qualitative, this representation of multiple perspectives enhances the credibility of the research. It also makes the job of balancing the roles of being both a practitioner and a researcher more manageable. Although action research emphasizes that action researchers can work independently, they do also collaborate with professional researchers at times. Researchers at colleges might assist in developing measurement instruments or in collecting and analyzing data. However, the research is characterized by a mutual respect for the expertise that each person brings to the process.
- *It focuses on taking action to change and improve educational practices.* At some point, all action research involves action. This action might be as simple as changing an assignment for the next school year, or it might involve a rethinking of how students are graded. At the school or district level, changes in policies for retaining students or assigning students to special education might result from an action research project. One of our students used her action research project to find out what students thought about parental involvement. Based on her findings she changed some of her roles for parents within the classroom.
- *It is ongoing and includes several waves of data collection, reflection, and action.* Because action researchers are educators who deal with problems in their everyday practices, research continues beyond the initial data collection. All good research builds knowledge incrementally. In action research, lessons learned in the initial wave of data collection may lead to new questions, refinements in practice, or identification of new problems. Action researchers are uniquely positioned to con-

tinue to collect data and extend their research into these new areas. Therefore, action research typically includes several waves of data collection, reflection on the data, and trying out actions to improve one's practice.

Steps in Conducting Action Research

Action research is fluid and flexible, so it is inappropriate to prescribe a set sequence of steps to follow. However, the following steps, which describe a common sequence for action research, will hopefully provide some guidance for students setting up their first action research project.

1. *Reflect on your practice and identify a problem or something you want to improve.* This can be something unusual that you have observed in your classroom that piques your interest or mystifies you or something you want to understand in more depth. It is important, however, that you have access to the setting to collect data and have an ongoing role within it.

2. *Set the problem in a theoretical and research context by reading published literature on the topic.* This usually means reading research (both traditional and action research), theoretical writings, and reflections (including experiential reports) by other educators on your topic or problem. Although action research acknowledges that each setting is unique, researchers seek out information to help them understand what might be going on in their setting. Because of the cyclic nature of action research, the review of literature is often ongoing throughout the process of collecting data and reflecting on it.

3. *Reflect on your own experiences with the problem.* Action researchers spend a good deal of time reflecting and thinking about their own practice. This is certainly a characteristic of all good educators. However, in action research, these reflections are recorded often in journals or are shared with a collaborative group. The researcher reviews notes or meets with collaborators on a regular basis to plan and think about what actions are needed. In addition, action researchers frequently reflect on how to use published theories, research, and experiences of other educators to create possible explanations for what is happening in their own settings.

4. *Identify persons with whom you can collaborate.* Collaborators should include persons who can help you in your reflections and data collection and analysis. This might be colleagues at your school or site or persons who share similar interests at other schools or colleges. Action researchers, especially those involved in critical action research, also frequently collaborate with students, parents, community members, or other persons with an interest in the educational outcomes of their practices. This reflects the more democratic nature of action

researchers who avoid hierarchical distinctions between researchers, educators, and persons being educated.

5. *Make a plan for systematic data collection (not just armchair impressions!).* Like qualitative research, action research is flexible. Research questions may be modified as data are collected and hypotheses emerge after the study begins. However, to qualify as research, action research must include a plan for systematically collecting and analyzing data. Decisions need to be made regarding what types of data will be collected. How will the data be collected? Will measures need to be developed? What measures will best fit into the setting and not intrude on the usual practices? Most action researchers collect at least two different types of data, often including both quantitative and qualitative data. The measures should be appropriate to the setting, including some types of archival data that are already being collected, such as attendance records or report card grades. Data collection must also involve simple and short procedures that will not interfere with the normal activities in the setting. A classroom teacher who wants to conduct interviews might schedule these as part of parent-teacher conferences or conduct brief interviews with individual students while others are working in groups. The research plan should also include consideration of the length of time for data collection, determination of times when data will be collected, the frequency and places where collaboration will occur, and identification of methods to check on the quality of the data. Someone simply sitting down at a computer and reconstructing what happened in his or her classroom over the past month is *not* doing action research. Planning and systematic collection of data are essential to maintain the integrity of action research.

6. *Collect and analyze your data, reflecting on what you are learning throughout the process of data collection.* Like qualitative researchers, action researchers analyze the data as they go. The types of data collected may be changed based on what you learn. In part, this reflects the fact that action research is embedded in an ongoing set of educational activities and is being conducted by a practitioner who modifies practices to fit the needs of learners. Action researchers do, however, review all of their data at some point to see what it suggests about their practices. Both qualitative data analysis techniques (e.g., identification of themes and patterns) and descriptive statistics (e.g., graphs, means, and measures of variability) might be used to summarize the data.

7. *Create a plan of action based on the results.* Based on what they have learned in the analysis of the data, action researchers then decide what they need to do to improve their practices. This might include modifications or refinements of lesson plans, new outreach to parents, development of new programs, or changes to existing school policies. This step distinguishes action research from other types of research and is an essential part of the process.

8. *Plan the next cycle of research to carry out your action plan and assess whether it improves practice.* After action is initiated, action researchers begin the next cycle of research by carrying out the action plan and continuing to collect data to monitor the changes in student learning or school-based practices. If the action plans include major changes in routines, there may be substantial changes or additions to the research plans. These might include new methods of collecting data or new collaborations. However, true action researchers are committed to continuing the action research cycle to make sure that what they do is effective.

9. *Analyze all of the data collected and reflect on its meaning for practice.* One of the hardest aspects of action research is making time to complete the analysis of the research. Often data collection seems effortless because the data collected may involve procedures that a practitioner is doing anyway as a normal part of practice. However, reviewing the notes, numbers, journals, papers, and other types of data can be time-consuming. It is often useful to review the data with collaborators who can help to interpret what the data show about the problem and analyze any changes that resulted from the action plan. Descriptive statistics may be used to analyze numerical data and themes or patterns analyzed for qualitative data. Ultimately, however, the practitioner must decide what the meaning of the data is for practice. If students report that they are embarrassed when their parents come to class, should a teacher find roles for parent volunteers outside the classroom? Or should the teacher examine what parents have done in the classroom that could be changed to make it less embarrassing?

10. *Form tentative conclusions and determine what questions remain to be answered.* As in all good research, the results of one study usually suggest ideas for new ones. Action research is an ongoing process of continuing to reflect on practice, identify problems, and formulate new research questions and action plans to remedy the problems. So it never ends, at least as long as the practitioner feels there are still ways to improve practice. Once an action researcher has built a network of collaborators, it is also easier to keep the process going.

The steps involved in action research are summarized in Figure 12.2.

Types of Action Research

As noted earlier, there are two major types of action research: critical action research and practical action research. The goal of critical action research, is liberation through knowledge gathering. Critical action researchers believe that all research should be socially responsible, aimed at enhancing the lives of all persons but especially those who are marginalized or who lack the power to improve their own lives. Critical action researchers often address issues such as sexism in schools, racism or prejudice embedded in an educational system, physical and

FIGURE 12.2 PROCESSES INVOLVED IN ACTION RESEARCH.

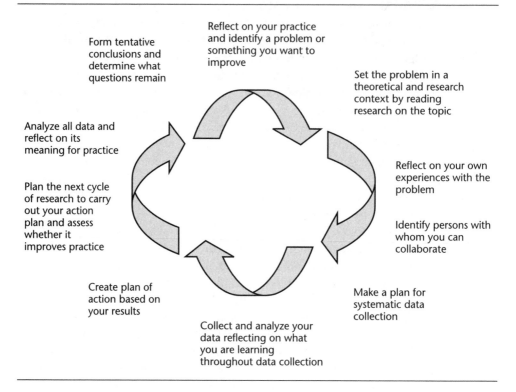

Form tentative
conclusions and
determine what
questions remain

Reflect on your practice
and identify a problem or
something you want to
improve

Set the problem in a
theoretical and research
context by reading
research on the topic

Analyze all data and
reflect on its
meaning for practice

Reflect on your own
experiences with the
problem

Plan the next cycle
of research to carry
out your action
plan and assess
whether it
improves practice

Identify persons with
whom you can
collaborate

Create plan of
action based on
your results

Make a plan for
systematic data
collection

Collect and analyze your
data reflecting on what
you are learning
throughout data collection

emotional barriers to persons with disabilities, or the isolation experienced by persons who are gay or lesbian.

Critical action researchers also believe that just as education requires a respectful dialogue between teacher and student, research must also be democratic and equitable. All persons involved in the research have valuable knowledge and skills that should be used and valued. Research should involve extensive collaboration with members of the community, who are the only persons who have the right to specify what changes would enhance their lives. Finally, critical action researchers believe that action should be informed and linked to values held by the persons whose lives the research examines.

Paulo Freire (1970), a Brazilian educator, developed many of the earliest ideas about critical action research based on his work on literacy with indigenous peoples in Brazil. He proposed that researchers work collaboratively with persons in a community to identify problems that arose from real-life situations and seek solutions to these problems by questioning and reflecting together. Freire's work is profiled in the final chapter of our book. Here we present an example of critical action research.

Bruce King (1990) was a biology teacher whose students raised questions about a toxic dump that was less than two miles from their school. The dump was labeled hazardous by the Environmental Protection Agency but was not scheduled for cleanup. King encouraged his students to ask questions and pursue research about the issue. In the process, they learned about how societal and political considerations might conflict with ethical decision making and identified strategies that could be used to address the problems posed by the dump. In the process, the students and teacher created a curriculum together for exploring issues relevant to science and society.

Practical action research also aims to improve the lives of people involved in education, but the research typically has a more practical orientation. It is based in everyday practice and typically focuses on making small changes at a local level. Although practical action researchers often are not as advocacy oriented as critical action researchers when they begin their research, they may become more politicized as they investigate the problem in their educational setting. For example, a practical action researcher might begin to explore the problems experienced by students who are receiving special education services. If the research reveals that students of Latino origin are unfairly classified as needing special education services at the school, the practical action researcher might decide to take a critical action stance by investigating how these decisions are made. It is important to realize that both types of action research involve action, and sometimes it is unpredictable where those actions will lead. Both practical and critical action researchers share a commitment to involving participants in the research as equal partners, as can be seen in the following example of practical action research.

Jordan and Hendricks (2002) conducted an action research study aimed at increasing student engagement in literacy learning in their classroom. Their initial research question was, "How does student choice in learning activities and assessment affect student engagement?" In class discussions, they solicited student input on assignments and set up student contracts allowing them to choose their own learning tools from activities based on seven of Howard Gardner's multiple intelligences. For example, students could write a book report, present oral discussions of the book, or do dramatic reenactments of the book. Cooperative learning groups were formed based on students' preferred learning styles. Groups completed in-class assignments on vocabulary building, did peer-to-peer reading, and discussed the book. Their methods of data collection included student journals, interviews with students, work samples, and an attitude survey of the students. Their data showed that the students liked having input but were uncomfortable with "too much freedom." Their grades improved, but some did not understand the contracts. Jordan and Hendricks were unsure how much the specific book used in the assignments might have contributed to the increase in engagement. They concluded that student engagement had improved but that they needed to continue the research with a new book and refine their assignments and contracts.

Evaluating Action Research

Action researchers do not typically use the complex statistical procedures involved in quantitative research to evaluate results obtained through quantitative data, although they do offer other evidence that their measures are reliable and valid, as discussed in Chapter Five. As Dale did, they might also use descriptive statistics to summarize and present their quantitative data. Similarly, practical action researchers do not engage in lengthy analysis of the conceptual and theoretical meanings behind their qualitative data to the extent that most qualitative researchers would (although critical action researchers do frequently engage in analysis of the larger social and cultural issues involved in their research). However, action researchers often use similar procedures as qualitative researchers to ensure that their results are dependable and credible. Therefore, one can evaluate action research using some of the criteria discussed in Chapters Seven, Eight, Nine, and Eleven, always taking into account whether the criteria are appropriate given the nature of the setting. For example, if an action researcher developed a survey, it might be pilot-tested and response rates considered. However, the questions might be simpler and procedures in developing them might be more streamlined than would be the case in traditional survey research. If an action research study includes case study methods, the practitioner's previous knowledge of the participant might be incorporated into the research, resulting in a shorter length of study. Considering whether action research meets some of the criteria for other types of research helps to build confidence in the scientific nature of its results. However, simply applying these criteria without considering the unique nature of action research would undermine its purpose. In addition, because action research often employs several different approaches in the cycles of data collection and analysis, one cannot simply apply criteria established for all of these other types of research to a single action research study. Therefore, criteria specific to action research have been proposed.

Creswell (2003) poses the following questions as guidelines for evaluating action research:

- Does the study clearly address a problem or issue in practice that needs to be addressed?

- Did the researcher develop a logical plan and collect data in a systematic, valid way?
- Were different types of data triangulated or compared?
- Did the researcher collaborate with others who had an interest in the problem?
- Did the research lead to a change or a solution to a problem that made a difference? Did it improve the lives of others or empower them to make changes in their lives?
- Did the plan of action contribute to the researcher's ability to reflect on his or her professional activities?

Chapter Summary

Educational researchers are increasingly recognizing the value of collecting both quantitative and qualitative data. One advantage of using mixed methods is that it combines the strengths of both qualitative and quantitative research to provide an in-depth look at context, processes, and interaction as well as precise measurement of attitudes, and outcomes. A major disadvantage of mixed methods is that a researcher has to be competent in both types of methodology. There are several different designs for mixed-methods research. The explanatory design is the most common design where data are collected in two phases, with quantitative data collected first, followed by qualitative data collected at a later date. Exploratory design also includes two phases. Qualitative data are collected in phase one, followed by quantitative data afterward. The triangulation design gathers both quantitative and qualitative data simultaneously. Action research is a type of research typically conducted by practitioner-researchers for the purpose of enacting immediate changes in an educational setting. There are two types of action research, critical action research and practical action research. Action research is fluid and flexible, so it is inappropriate to prescribe a set sequence of steps to follow. In general, action researchers reflect on practice, identify a problems, engage in several cycles of data collection, collaborate with others, and develop and implement action plans.

Key Concepts

mixed-methods research design

action research

explanatory design

exploratory design

triangulation design

critical action research

critical pedagogy

practical action research

Discussion Questions or Activities

1. Discuss how quantitative and qualitative methods might be combined to study the educational experiences of students with severe physical disabilities. Discuss the types of quantitative and qualitative data that might be collected and provide a rationale for why both are needed. Which mixed-method design would be best suited to your study? How would the steps in conducting the research and the data analysis differ from using only one approach?

2. Plan an action research study examining the literacy strategies used by middle school or high school teachers. Discuss several types of data you might collect, what your role in the research would be, how you might manage your role as a practitioner and researcher, and who might be your collaborators. What do you think are the advantages and barriers to this type of research?

Suggested Readings

Anderson, G. L., Herr, K., & Nihlen, L. S. (1994). *Studying your own school: An educator's guide to quality practitioner research*. Thousand Oaks, CA: Corwin Press.

Creswell, J. (1999). Mixed-method research: Introduction and application. In C. J. Cizek (Ed.), *Handbook of educational policy* (pp. 455–472). San Diego: Academic Press.

Wadsworth, Y. (1998, Nov.). What is participatory action research? *Action Research International*. Paper 2. Retrieved Sept. 10, 2004, http://www.scu.edu.au/schools/gcm/ar/ari/p-ywadsworth98.html.

Sample Mixed-Methods Research Studies

Eckman, E. W. (2002). Woman high school principals: Perspectives on role conflict, role commitment, and job satisfaction. *Journal of School Leadership, 12*(1) 57–77.

Martin, B., & Newcomer, S. (2002). A descriptive study of gender equity in rural secondary classroom situations. *Rural Educator, 23*(3), 37–46.

Sample Action Research Studies

Hashey, J. M., & Connors, D. J. (2003). Learning from our journey: Reciprocal teaching action research. *The Reading Teacher, 57,* (3), 224–232.

Short, D. J., & Echevaria, J. (1999, Dec.). *The sheltered instruction observation protocol: A tool for teacher-researcher collaboration and professional development.* (EDO-FL-ii-09) Reston, VA: ERIC Clearinghouse on Languages and Linguistics.

CHAPTER THIRTEEN

ORGANIZATION AND ANALYSIS OF QUALITATIVE RESEARCH DATA

Chapter Objectives

After reading this chapter, you should be able to

1. Identify the processes involved in analyzing qualitative data, including data coding, description, identification of themes, hypothesis testing, and reporting and interpretation of data
2. Discuss how a qualitative researcher goes about establishing themes and generating hypotheses
3. Apply the process of qualitative data analysis to simple data samples

Research Vignette

Jualita is a fifth-grade social studies teacher who has collected several types of qualitative data about her students' understanding of democracy. She has copies of student papers; three months of journal entries in which she recorded her thoughts about class discussions, activities, and individual student comments to her; tapes of class discussions; and field notes and photographs from the field trips that her class took to government buildings and historical sites. Jualita also has records of the diverse family and social backgrounds of the 20 students in her class, which includes 10 students whose parents emigrated to the United States from Central American or Asian countries, 4 African American students, 5 students who maintain strong ethnic affiliations with their Italian and Irish roots, and 1 student who has a mixed racial background. Jualita's initial question that guided her data collection was, "How do students with different life experiences come to understand the concept of and processes involved in democracy?" She has recorded her thoughts about what her data have shown regarding this question as research memos in her journal throughout the process of data collection. However, she now wants to do a more systematic and comprehensive analysis of her data. She sits looking at the boxes of data on her desk, wondering how she will make sense of all of this information!

Overview of Qualitative Data Analysis

Jualita is not alone in feeling overwhelmed by her data. Most qualitative researchers amass mounds of information in the course of their studies. Like all good qualitative researchers, Jualita did not wait until all of the data were collected to analyze her data. She reviewed her data as she collected and recorded them and wrote up her hunches, initial analyses, and questions in the form of research memos in her journal. As we noted in Chapter Eleven, this is part of the emergent nature of qualitative research. Unlike quantitative research in which data analysis comes after the study has been completed, with qualitative research analysis of data occurs throughout the study and guides the ongoing process of data collection.

Data collection and analysis in qualitative research are inductive processes. As you may recall from previous chapters, this means that numerous small pieces of data are collected and gradually combined or related to form broader, more general descriptions and conclusions. Although the steps involved in qualitative data analysis will vary according to the research questions asked and the type of approach taken, the steps listed below are common to most studies:

1. Preparing and organizing the data
2. Reviewing and exploring the data
3. Coding data into categories
4. Constructing descriptions of people, places, and activities

5. Building themes and testing hypotheses
6. Reporting and interpreting data

Note that there may be some back-and-forth movement between the steps. One might need to review data initially before deciding how to organize it. The process of coding might also lead one to reorganize some of the data. However, the steps tend to flow in this general direction. In this chapter, we examine the procedures involved in each of these steps in depth and also discuss how qualitative research is evaluated.

Preparing and Organizing the Data

The first task for data analysis is to make sure that data are in a form that can be easily analyzed. Depending on the time and resources available, researchers may aim for different levels of depth in preparing their data. If interviews were tape-recorded, preparation involves transferring the information from the recorded interviews into a written form. The quickest and least accurate approach involves listening to tapes with written notes from the interview and recording the general issues or ideas that are reported using participants' own words as much as possible. Possible illustrative quotes are also noted and recorded. This type of transcription actually involves data analysis as well as preparation, and it is not suitable for complex research questions or beginning qualitative researchers. By analyzing the data at the same time that one is preparing and organizing it, the researcher's biases are more likely to influence the study's findings.

Most qualitative researchers prefer to separate the process of data preparation and analysis by transcribing interviews verbatim. Verbatim transcription is time–consuming: typically a one-hour interview will take six to eight hours to transcribe. The exact words of the participants are recorded, along with some aspects of nonverbal communication, such as pauses, laughter, interruptions, changes in vocal tone or emotion, and places where the tape is inaudible or not understandable. These nonverbal aspects of an interview are usually noted inside brackets, such as [laughter]. In group interviews, the person who is speaking would also be noted with the use of abbreviations to guard confidentiality. Group interviews often involve several interviewers, one of whom records observations of interactions among group members and other details that might not be captured on the tape. If the group observer records time intervals on the notes taken at the interview, notes from the verbal transcription and the observations can be examined side by side. See Box 13.1 for a sample of a transcription of an interview with a teacher. The interview was conducted as part of a case study of the youth referred to as "J" who helped another youth referred to as "M."

Box 13.1 Sample Interview Transcript

Interviewer: You mentioned that J gets along with everybody, so can you give me an example of how you see that in your class?

Teacher: I think [pauses as train goes by]. I think J could get to know the engineer on that train. [laughter]

Interviewer: Yeah, right.

Teacher: I think one of the, one of the best examples I have of J being able to talk to anybody and actually helping people who are really shy to come out of their shyness is, there is a student in the journalism class, M, who, umm [laughs], this is probably, probably not a good story. At the beginning of the year, I was trying to figure out why this kid wouldn't do anything. M was a big, big kid, a little older than most of them. And he just did nothing the first five weeks of school. So I looked up who his counselor was, and I went to the counselor and said, "I have a student, and I have real big problems getting him to do anything in my class." And she asked who the kid was, and I told her M. And she went [with exaggerated horror], "Oh, no! You don't have him in journalism, do you?" I said, "Yeah." She's like, "Oh, oh my God! You know some of the kids we say that they are very special. This one is just retarded." [Teacher shakes his head and looks at Interviewer with disbelief and disgust.]

This is coming from the kid's counselor! So she actually tried to get him out of the journalism class, but once I got the information that M has a severe learning disability I gave the kid things that he could do, and he was fine. And for a good part of the year, he would just quietly do those things. And I was the only person that he would talk to. But then J just took it on himself to start talking to M. When J was talking with a group, he would turn around and ask M a question. He would frequently invite him to help him edit his stories or ask him about ways to illustrate his stories. And now M just walks around the room and talks to everybody.

Other types of data preparation might include the development or enlarging photographs, labeling videotapes with identifying information (date, setting, or group), and making backup copies of data to store in a separate location (after months of data collection, you do not want to lose any data!). If computerized data analysis tools (discussed in more detail later) will be used, the data might also need to be put into a format compatible with the software program to be used.

Finally, the researcher must decide on a way to organize the large amount of data that a qualitative study typically yields. Data may be organized in many different ways, depending on the research questions and the method of qualitative research used. Following are some common methods for organizing data:

- *Site or location from which data were collected.* This method is common in studies where multiple sites or locations were observed.
- *Person or group studied.* Data may be organized by the individual person or group, or data from persons or groups with similar characteristics or backgrounds might be grouped together.
- *Chronological order.* Data might be organized into the time periods in which it was collected.
- *Type of data.* Interview transcripts might be assembled together, separate from field notes and journals.
- *Type of event or issue addressed.* If interviews focused on different issues or observations of different events were made, the data pertaining to each issue or event might be grouped together.

Although one does need to decide on an initial method for organizing the data, it is possible that data may be reorganized after the initial data analysis to look more closely at the categories and themes that emerge.

Reviewing and Exploring the Data

This step is a lot like jumping off the high–dive board at the swimming pool. Just like Jualita, a qualitative researcher might look with dread at the enormous pile of data waiting for analysis. However, all you can do is jump in and begin to explore by reading and looking through the various types of data collected. The initial review does not involve a careful reading for detail. Instead, one reads and examines data to get an overall sense of what is in them and whether enough data have been collected. Many researchers will begin to jot down words and phrases that capture important aspects of the data in this initial review. However, the real purpose is to immerse oneself in the data and gain a sense of their possibilities.

Because Jualita made notes to herself about the data as she collected them, she has already begun the process of reviewing the data. The initial review, however, is more comprehensive and involves examining all of the different sources of data together. Through the initial review, qualitative researchers seek to understand the scope of their data before they begin to divide them into more manageable chunks organized through codes. For many qualitative researchers, it is hard to say when the initial review stops and the coding begins because one process leads naturally to the next.

Coding Data into Categories

Coding is the process of identifying different segments of the data that describe related phenomena and labeling these parts using broad category names. It is an inductive process of data analysis that involves examining many small pieces of information and abstracting a connection between them. There is nothing mysterious about coding; Table 13.1 describes common code categories and examples of code names that Jualita might use in her analysis of her data. As you can see, the codes describe general categories that can be used to organize the information contained in the data. Any given segment might be viewed differently by two different researchers or even coded using more than one label by a given researcher. Therefore, qualitative researchers continually read, reread, and reexamine all of their data to make sure that they have not missed something or coded them in a way that is inappropriate to the experiences of the participants.

New codes are added as the researcher reviews the data. Most data sets use 30 to 40 codes initially, although complex studies might include more than this. The actual process of coding can be conducted by hand or by computer. When coding is done by hand, the researcher writes the code in the margin of the data source (which was duplicated before coding began) and then organizes the data into piles

TABLE 13.1 COMMON CODE CATEGORIES AND EXAMPLES OF CODE NAMES FROM A STUDY OF STUDENT UNDERSTANDING OF DEMOCRACY.

Code Category	Code Names
Setting or context	Classroom, field trip, lunchroom
Activities or actions	Group activity, instructional strategy, movie, class project, student questions
Events	State senate visit, guest speaker
Perspectives of participants	Student perspective, parent perspective, teacher perspective
Feelings, emotions of participants	Pride, fear, love, anger
Concepts, issues	Freedom of speech, voting, rights, citizenship
Relationships, social structure	Responsibility, community student groups, group differences, ethnic identity, social class
Cultural context	Sex, social class, race, ethnicity, immigrant status, personal history

with the same codes, cutting up data sheets as needed. When one has hundreds of pages of data, this can get messy. Most qualitative researchers reserve a part of their office or an entire room for data analysis, and one researcher we know who conducts extensive qualitative research even built an addition on her house for her research work! Exhibit 13.1 displays a portion of an interview transcript with codes from the study of allies to persons who are gay or lesbian by Kennedy and Voegtle (2000) that we introduced in Chapter Eleven.

Several computer programs are available to assist in the analysis and especially the coding of data, although we should emphasize that the computer is only a tool and the researcher still makes decisions about how to do the analysis and what the results mean. However, computer programs such as NUD*IST (Non-numerical Unstructured Data Indexing, Searching, and Theorizing) or Ethnograph can be used to combine files from different data sources, select and code the data, and organize data using codes or hypermedia links. Computer programs do facilitate the processes of applying multiple codes to the same segment, viewing data using different organizations of codes, and displaying data using different formats. For more in-depth information on using computer software for qualitative analysis, see Judy Norris's QualPage Web site at http://www.qualitativeresearch.uga.edu/QualPage/qda.html.

Whether the researcher uses a computer program or manual cutting and pasting, coding involves a process of continual refinement and abstraction from the

EXHIBIT 13.1 INTERVIEW TRANSCRIPT WITH CODES.

Interview Transcript with Codes

Friendship

Family background

Initial feelings

Acceptance

Social activism

Political beliefs

I had grown up with Allen. His parent's and mine were kind of progressive activists together and then he and I were progressive activists together later on. And so when he came out it was a huge impact on my life. I was stunned, amazed. The realization was very sudden for me because it was something I hadn't thought about before at all. The families were upset and shocked. It was a very radical period. It seemed very strange to me, I didn't quite know what to make of it but my ideology was a very radical ideology and I really figured that anything that was this unsettling to the status quo must be a good thing. Sort of my response was if it's this bad, it must be good.

data. The initial 30 to 40 codes are gradually combined and reduced to about 15 to 20, with the goal of eliminating overlap and producing a more coherent view of the patterns in the data. In the study by Kennedy and Voegtle (2000), codes used in interviews with different allies initially included Political Beliefs, Religious Beliefs, and Social Beliefs. These were later combined into a single code labeled Ideology as the researchers determined that the various belief systems guiding the allies' actions all functioned in similar manners. When the researcher is satisfied that the major ideas and issues in the data have been identified through codes, the next step is to use the codes to organize data and construct descriptions of the data.

Constructing Descriptions of People, Places, and Activities

Once the data have been coded, the researcher writes detailed descriptions of the people, places, and events in the study. The goal is to provide rich, in-depth descriptions, often referred to as **thick descriptions,** of the experiences, perspectives, and physical settings represented in the data. You may recall that we discussed thick description of field notes in Chapter Eleven. Descriptions in data analysis often involve expanding on one's field notes and combining notes and interviews with the same codes into more integrated descriptions of people, situations, and places. Exhibit 13.2 presents a sample of a thick description of the preschooler Max discussed in Chapter Eleven that combines data from classroom observations, school records, and interviews with Max and his teacher.

Writing good detailed descriptions of even the most ordinary aspects of everyday life is an essential part of qualitative research. Good qualitative research can make readers feel like they are actually living the experiences described. This is the real power of qualitative research.

Building Themes and Testing Hypotheses

Coding and description comprise the first two levels of qualitative data analysis. Deeper analysis in which explanation of the events and issues represented in the data occurs as the researcher continues the process of abstraction by identifying major and minor **themes** in the coded data. Themes are typically "big ideas" that combine several codes in a way that allows the researcher to examine the foreshadowed questions guiding the research. In other words, themes provide the organizing ideas that the researchers will use to explain what they have learned from the study. Like codes, themes are usually described using a few words or phrases, but they identify the major concepts or issues that the researcher will use to interpret and explain the data. The researcher then reexamines the data using the themes as organizational frameworks to see if they provide a deeper understanding of the data.

EXHIBIT 13.2 THICK DESCRIPTION.

Ms. Smith, the head teacher in Max's classroom, holds an advanced degree, as do all the head teachers at Max's preschool. As a group, these teachers have an average of 10 years of teaching experience. The preschool classroom is divided into two rooms, one essentially devoted to gross motor development and the other to the development of fine motor skills. Myriad toys and activities are always prepared for the children before they enter in the morning.

On a cold Tuesday morning in February the children enter the classroom and begin the long and arduous process of taking their coats, mittens and boots off. As more and more children come into the classroom, the noise and activity level quickly rises as they prepare for the school day. Max walks into class with his mom and goes right up to his "cubby" where he carefully places his winter items. Most of the children go directly to the circle area (which has a piano right in the middle) and excitedly greet each other. Max, however, goes to the book corner and begins to read a book. He kisses his mom goodbye and becomes focused in his reading. Ms. Smith calls all the children to circle time, but Max ignores the instructions. After several reminders, Max puts his book down and reluctantly joins the group. Max looks for a place in the circle to sit. He finds a spot in the circle and sits down. During this entire process he is ignored by his classmates.

Following circle time, the children are permitted to select from several different activities. Max selects the puzzle center. As he approaches the center several children sigh and one child says "oh no, here comes Max."

Max knows when he is not welcome in an activity. As he often does when he feels left out, Max growls at his classmates and as he tries to make his way into the puzzle activity. This makes his classmates more annoyed with him, and they try to ignore him. When this does not stop Max, the children turn to Ms. Smith and say, "Max is being a bad boy again."

Ms. Smith walks over and begins to talk to Max and the other children. She tries to find out what is going on with Max and the children in the puzzle activity. Max continues to growl and Ms. Smith tries to refocus his behavior and explain to the children that they should try to get along. In general, Ms. Smith's classroom is focused on cooperation and the development of self-control using a system of rewards and punishments. The children receive positive feedback whenever they are engaged in appropriate behavior. Negative feedback and time-out are often used to control and minimize undesirable behavior. When asked to describe Max, Ms. Smith says that he is an "adorable child," who is very bright (IQ score of 130 as measured by WIPPSI) and keenly aware of his surroundings. She indicates that he is very polite when he comes into school in the morning, greeting and saying hello to everyone. "He has very strong verbal skills; however, he is socially quite young," says Ms. Smith. "Furthermore, when he feels alone and isolated, he will respond by growling which further upsets his classmates." Most attempts to get Max to cooperate during play have thus far been unsuccessful. In fact, according to Ms. Smith, he has been "getting in the face of other children in an aggressive way."

Note: WPPSI = Wechsler Preschool and Primary Scale of Intelligence.

Different themes may also be combined to form specific hypotheses regarding the issues identified in the foreshadowed research questions. Unlike research hypotheses used in quantitative research, hypotheses in qualitative research emerge from the data analysis. They are not predictions about what will happen; rather, they are tentative explanations of the processes underlying what has been observed. Once a hypothesis has been formulated, data are then reexamined for both confirming and disconfirming evidence to test it. Confirming evidence is often obtained through triangulation, the process of comparing different sources of data (e.g., interviews and observations) or perspectives of different participants. Given the nature of qualitative research there are often times when participants offer conflicting perspectives. For example, in the case study involving Max, the researchers found that Max's teacher and mother disagreed regarding his readiness for kindergarten. Compare the descriptions of Max by his mother and his teacher in Exhibit 13.3 with the excerpt from Exhibit 13.2. What would you conclude regarding Max's readiness for kindergarten?

When conflicting perspectives are found, qualitative researchers must reexamine other data sources to see if the differences can be resolved. In some cases, if the differences cannot be resolved, they may decide to simply present the different perspectives. For example, in the final case study of Max the researchers simply described the differences in the mother's and teacher's views regarding his kindergarten readiness.

Researchers also seek out evidence that might disconfirm their hypotheses by continually reviewing their data or collecting new data to examine their hypotheses. If disconfirming evidence is found, the hypothesis is revised. Do you get the feeling that qualitative researchers read and reread their data obsessively? Well, as a matter of fact, they do! It is part of the inductive process of building hypotheses and theories from the ground up. And it often pays off. One of the researchers in the allies study reported that she was rereading her interview transcripts for the fourth time when she found a phrase that became a central hypothesis for the study. The ally described the process of becoming an ally as involving "friendship merging with ideology." Kennedy and Voegtle (2000) then reexamined their data to see if interviews with all of their allies supported the hypothesis that a combination of close friendships with persons who were gay, lesbian, or bisexual and an accepting ideological framework were necessary to support the social activism of all their allies. Eight of nine interviews did support the hypothesis, and the one ally whose ideological framework was crumbling was also retreating from her ally work. The phrase suggested by their participant actually became a part of the title of their study, which illustrates how qualitative researchers seek out and use their participants' own words to more accurately represent their views and experiences.

EXHIBIT 13.3 CONTRASTING PERSPECTIVES IN A CASE STUDY.

Mother's perspective: When talking about Max's social skills, Mom has some real concerns. She says that his "social skills are a little lacking with his peers." She believes that Max has difficulty initiating play activities with other children. He appears to "be rigid, and I just wish he would be more flexible," says Mom. He does not appear to want to compromise with his peers and wants his own way. Mom says that Max does have one good friend at school with whom he shares similar interests. They apparently play pretty well together until the little friend does something that Max doesn't want him to do. For the most part, Mom believes that Max is "kind of a loner, unless kids want to do what he wants to do." In the future, she hopes that Max will learn to compromise. She worries that he will be the kid who won't sit in his chair and is always in the principal's office because he wants to do what he wants to do. Mom feels very strongly that Max needs a structured classroom. "He needs to have a time to do one thing and a time to move on to something else." Mom does not believe that Max can get such a structured environment in a preschool setting. Given the fact that academically Max is so far ahead of his peers, Mom has been looking at different kindergarten programs despite the fact that his preschool teacher believes that Max is not ready to move on to a kindergarten classroom and needs one more year in preschool.

Teacher's perspective: One of the behaviors Ms. Smith is particularly concerned with is Max's tendency to "get into the faces" of other kids. He knows "exactly whose face to get into." She says that while she has tried various techniques to eliminate the behavior, nothing has seemed to work. She praises him when he is playing cooperatively with the other children. She has also tried a time-out when he is behaving inappropriately and verbally tells him that his behavior hurts others' feelings. She explicitly tries to tie the "in-your-face behavior" to the hurt feelings of others. Ms. Smith says that Max does not seem to care and that the reprimand does not appear to make any difference to him. While Ms. Smith believes that Max has made tremendous progress over the first several months of this year, she is concerned that socially he might not be ready for kindergarten. She believes that Max is clearly ready to do the academic work of kindergarten, but his social skills need to be further developed. She has recommended another year of nursery school, especially given the fact that he is just turning four.

Although we have described the processes of coding, description, theme building, and hypothesis testing through review of data as if they are separate steps, qualitative data analysis is actually an iterative process: the steps are repeated several times, with something new added in each iteration. The process is repeated until the researcher feels that the research questions have been answered and sufficient meaning extracted from the data. Figure 13.1 displays the iterative nature of the processes of coding, description, and theme identification.

FIGURE 13.1 PROCESSES IN QUALITATIVE DATA ANALYSIS.

```
                    ┌─────────────────────┐
            ┌──────▶│     Researcher      │◀──────┐
            │       │   organizes data,   │       │
            │       │     examines it     │       │
            │       └─────────────────────┘       │
            │                 │                    │
            │                 ▼                    │
            │       ┌─────────────────────┐        │
            │       │     Researcher      │        │
            │       │ reexamines data and │        │
            │       │   codes them with   │        │
            │       │  30 to 40 different │        │
            │       │        codes        │        │
            │       └─────────────────────┘        │
            │                 │                     │
            │                 ▼                     │
            │       ┌─────────────────────┐         │
            │       │      Codes are      │         │
            │       │    combined and     │         │
            │       │  reduced to 15 to   │         │
            │       │   20 categories;    │         │
            │       │      data are       │         │
            │       │    recoded with     │         │
            │       │      new codes      │         │
            │       └─────────────────────┘         │
            │           ╱           ╲                │
            │          ▼             ▼               │
  ┌─────────────────┐       ┌─────────────────┐
  │  Descriptions   │◀─────▶│ Major and minor │
  │  are generated  │       │  themes are     │
  │  summarizing    │       │ identified and  │
  │ data organized  │       │   hypotheses    │
  │    by codes     │       │     tested      │
  └─────────────────┘       └─────────────────┘
            ╲                   ╱
             ▼                 ▼
          ┌─────────────────────┐
          │  Final analysis and │
          │   interpretation    │
          │      of data        │
          └─────────────────────┘
```

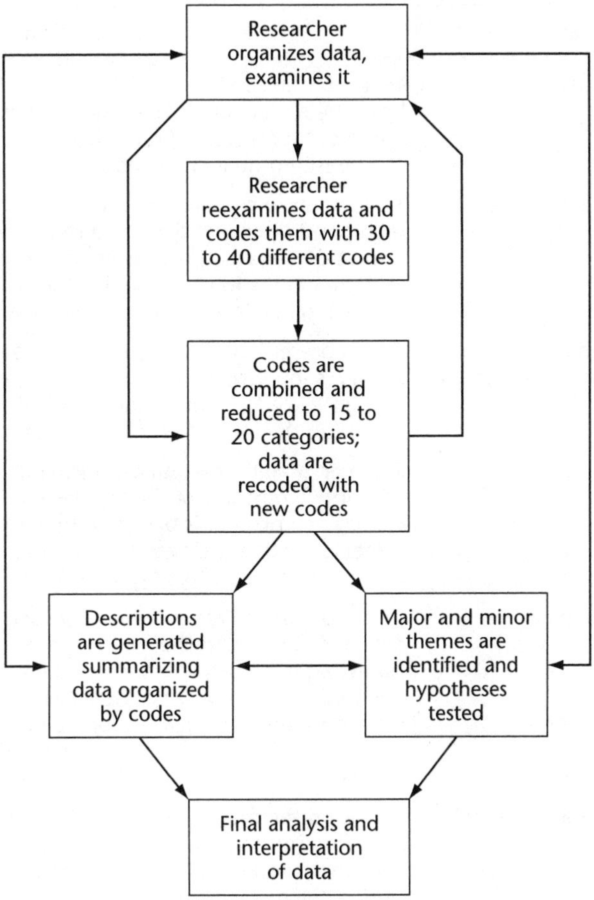

Reporting and Interpreting Data

The final step in qualitative data analysis is the actual writing of the research report, including the researcher's interpretations of what the data mean. Most qualitative research is reported in a narrative manner, which often makes it more enjoyable to read than quantitative research. The narrative may be organized using any of several different formats summarized in Table 13.2. The choice of format may be determined both by the results of the data analysis and by the researcher's philosophical framework and purpose in conducting the research. Many re-

TABLE 13.2 FORMATS FOR
WRITING THE TEXT OF QUALITATIVE REPORTS

Format	Description
Thematic	Text is organized in terms of discussion of themes that arise from the data analysis. This is a flexible format that fits a wide range of topics and is probably the most common method of presenting qualitative reports.
Natural history	Text structure parallels or "recreates" the process of exploration and discovery that occurred during fieldwork. This format conveys a strong sense of the people, the setting, and the interactions involved in the research although it makes it difficult to do theme analysis.
Alternative or performance-based	Text is presented using a performance-based format such as a story, song, dramatic performance, or highly personalized account called an autoethnography. This format is useful in capturing the intense emotionality of a setting or experience.
Amalgamation	Researcher analyzes data from several people and creates descriptive portraits of the "types" of persons involved in the study. Each portrait is based on multiple persons so that it protects confidentiality of the information. Activities may also be amalgamated into a "typical day or week."
Theoretical	Text is organized around a theory used throughout the report. A developed theory may serve as the framework for reviewing literature and collecting data, as in a theoretically oriented case study. Grounded-theory approaches organize writing in terms of the creation of a new theory that explains the data or the modification of an existing theory based on the data.
Traditional scientific	Text is presented in the traditional style of research reports including Introduction, Review of Literature, Method, Results, and Discussion sections. Results and Discussion sections include analysis of themes.

Source: From Creswell (2005), Denzin and Lincoln (2005), and Glesne (2006).

searchers include visual diagrams or images to represent the complex array of events, issues, or themes that emerged from their data analysis. For example, Spaulding, Lodico, Jones, and Gligora (2004) presented photographs taken by the youth in a summer camp academic enrichment program to illustrate the major findings of their research evaluating the program.

Reports of qualitative studies usually include extensive samples of quotes from participants. By using the participants' own words, researchers aim to build the reader's confidence that they are accurately representing the reality of the persons and situation studied. As in quantitative research, qualitative studies also report the methods used to collect and analyze data, but the criteria used to evaluate qualitative studies differ. (These criteria were discussed in Chapter Eleven.)

It is often difficult to distinguish between the reporting of findings in a qualitative study and the interpretation of the findings. According to Lincoln and Guba (1985), interpreting qualitative data involves making sense of the "lessons learned" by looking for their larger meaning. Interpretation might involve relating the findings to previous published studies or to a theoretical framework. For example, Kennedy and Voegtle (2000) related their findings on ally development to Allport's contact theory of racial prejudice (1955). Interpretation of qualitative data may also involve personal reflections by the researcher because the researcher has typically invested considerable time and emotional energy in collecting and analyzing the data. Researchers taking an emancipatory-liberatory approach will also discuss the implications for taking action suggested by the data analysis, especially if the data indicate that certain groups are being treated unfairly. Finally, as in quantitative studies, interpretation of the data in a qualitative study may also include discussion of the limitations of the study and ideas for future research.

Chapter Summary

Data collection and analysis in qualitative research are inductive processes. Like quantitative studies, qualitative studies have certain steps that the researcher has to conduct. The first step is preparation and organization of the data. Several levels of data collection from interviews are available, ranging from taking notes from tape-recorded interviews to full transcriptions being made from such tapes. Qualitative researchers try to keep data collection and preparation separate from data analysis. Data can be organized in several ways, for example, by site or location, person or groups being studied, or chronologically. The second step is the initial review and exploration of the data. As part of this process, the researcher initially reads through all data to get an overall sense of what are in the data and whether enough data have been collected. The third step is the coding of data into categories. To do this, qualitative researchers typically continually read, reread, and reexamine all of their data to make sure that they have not missed something or coded them in a way that is inappropriate to the experiences of the participants. Qualitative researchers use 30 to 40 codes, although complex studies may require more. Computer programs such as NUD*IST or Ethnograph are also used by qualitative researchers. Following this, the next step is constructing descriptions of people, places, and activities. Once the data have been coded, the researcher writes detailed descriptions of the people, places, and events in the study for the purpose of providing rich, in-depth descriptions, often referred to as thick descriptions. Building themes and testing hypotheses comprise the next step. Themes are big ideas that combine several codes in a way that allows the researcher to examine foreshadowed questions guiding the research. Researchers also seek out evidence that might disconfirm their hypothesis by continually reviewing their data or collecting new data to examine their hypothesis. Reporting and interpreting data are the last step in the qualitative research process.

Key Concepts

coding

thick descriptions

themes

Discussion Questions or Activities

1. Select a movie that depicts classroom interactions between a new teacher and students (e.g., *Stand and Deliver* works well), and with your class, identify three research questions that you can use to guide qualitative data collection. View the film, and record field notes on what you observe. Combine the field notes with those of other students, and identify common themes that you see. Based on your initial themes, formulate a hypothesis that could be examined through further data collection.

2. Discuss how the criteria for evaluating qualitative studies differ from those used in quantitative research and why different criteria are needed for each type of research. Select one qualitative study that you have read this semester, and discuss how it did or did not provide strong evidence to support its conclusions. What did you find convincing or not convincing when reading the results of the qualitative study?

Suggested Readings

Merriam, S. B. (1998). *Qualitative research and case study applications in education*. San Francisco: Jossey-Bass.

Morse, J. M., & Richards, L. (2005). *README FIRST for a user's guide to qualitative methods*. Thousand Oaks, CA: Sage Publications.

Schensul, J. J. (1999). *Analyzing and interpreting ethnographic data (Ethnographer's Toolkit, Vol. 5)*. Lanham, MD: AltaMira Press.

CHAPTER FOURTEEN

PROGRAM EVALUATION IN EDUCATION

Chapter Objectives

After reading this chapter, you should be able to

1. Define program evaluation and note several characteristics that separate program evaluation from educational research
2. List several differences between formative and summative evaluation and describe the purpose of each
3. Define the role of an internal and external evaluator and describe some of the benefits and challenges that an evaluator working in these two different methods would encounter
4. Describe the approaches to program evaluation and discuss the similarities and differences in the approaches' characteristics

Research Vignette

An urban school district receives a three-year grant to implement an after-school program to improve student academic achievement. As they start to implement the program, the district administrator realizes that an evaluation of the program is required. The district administrator also realizes that such work requires the expertise of someone from outside the district, and the superintendent, with permission from the school board, hires an external evaluator from a local college. After reviewing the grant, the evaluator conducts an initial review of the program's curriculum and activities. Next, the evaluator develops an evaluation plan and presents it at the next school board meeting. The evaluation plan overviews the objectives that the evaluator has developed and the tools that he will use to collect the data. As part of the data collection process, the evaluator discusses how the plan will provide two different types of feedback: formative and summative evaluation. Formative evaluation will be used to address issues as the program is happening. A sample question might be: Are all the participants aware of the program and its offerings? Summative evaluation will be used to answer the overall evaluation question: Did students in the after-school program have a significant increase in their academic achievement over those students who did not participate? The board approves the plan, and the evaluator spends the next month collecting data for the formative and summative portions of the project.

At the next board meeting, the evaluator presents some of the formative evaluation and reports that there is a need to increase communication with parents. He suggests that the program increase the number of fliers that are sent home, update the school Web site, and work more collaboratively with the parent council. In addition, he notes that there is a wide variation in parental education levels within the district and that a large number of parents speak Spanish as their native language. The evaluator recommends that phone calls be made to parents and that all materials be translated into Spanish.

At the end of project year 1, summative findings are presented in a final report. The report shows that the lack of parental communication is still a problem. In addition, there is little difference in the scores on the standardized measures used to gauge academic achievement for those students who participated in the program versus comparable students who did not participate.

Based on the evaluation report, district officials decide to make modifications to the program for the upcoming year. A parent center, which was not part of the original plan, was added, based on the belief that this would help increase parental involvement. In addition, the administration decided to cut back on the number of extracurricular activities the after-school program was offering and to focus more on tutoring and academic interventions, hoping that this would increase academic achievement in year 2.

What Is Program Evaluation?

A common distinction used to separate program evaluation from research is that *program evaluation* is used for decision-making purposes whereas *research* is used to build our general understanding and knowledge on a particular topic and to inform practice. In general, program evaluation examines programs to determine their worth and to make recommendations for programmatic refinement and success. Although such a broad definition makes it difficult for those who have not been involved in program evaluation to get a better understanding, hopefully the above vignette highlights some of the activities unique to program evaluation. Let us look a little more closely at some of those activities in continuing this comparison between program evaluation and research.

What Is a Program?

One distinguishing characteristic of program evaluation is that it examines programs. A **program** is a set of specific activities designed for an intended purpose with quantifiable goals and objectives. Although a research study could certainly examine a particular program, most research tends to be interested in either generalizing findings back to a wider audience (e.g., quantitative research) or discussing how the study's findings relate back to the literature (e.g., qualitative research). Most research studies, especially those that are quantitative, are not interested in knowing how just one after-school program functioned in one school building or district. However, for those conducting program evaluations, this is seen as precisely the purpose.

Programs come in many different shapes and sizes and, therefore, so do the evaluations that are conducted. Educational programs can take place anytime during the school day or after school. For example, programs can include a morning breakfast-nutrition program, a high school science program, an after-school program, or even a weekend program. Educational programs do not necessarily have to occur on school grounds. An evaluator may conduct an evaluation of a community group's educational program or a program at the local YMCA (Young Men's Christian Association) or Boys and Girls Club.

Accessing the Setting and Participants

Another characteristic that sets program evaluation apart from research is the difference between how the program evaluator and the researcher gain access to the project and program site. As described in the vignette, the program evaluator was hired by the school district to conduct the evaluation of its after-school program. In general, a program evaluator enters into a contractual agreement directly or indirectly with the group whose program is being evaluated. This individual or group is often referred to as the **client.**

As a result of this relationship between the program evaluator and the client, the scope of what the evaluator wishes to look at could also be restricted by the client. To have the client dictate what one would investigate would be unusual for a research study, but not for program evaluation. For example, because of the nature of qualitative research, a qualitative researcher who enters a school system to do a study on school safety may find a gang present in the school and choose to observe students as they try to leave the gang. If a program evaluation was conducted in the same school, the evaluator may be aware of the gang and students trying to get out of the gang. This might strike the evaluator as an interesting phenomenon, but it would not be pursued unless the client perceived it as an important aspect of school safety or unless gang control fit into the original objectives of the program.

Collecting and Using Data

As demonstrated in the vignette, program evaluation often collects two different forms of evaluation data: **formative** and **summative.** The purpose of formative data is to "change" or "make better" the thing that is being studied (at the very moment in which it is being studied). This is something that is typically not found in most applied research approaches. Rarely would a researcher have this "reporting relationship" where formative findings were being reported back to stakeholders or participants for the purposes of immediately changing the program. A further discussion about formative and summative evaluation is presented later in this chapter.

Changing Practice

Although program evaluation uses the same methods as research to collect data, program evaluation is different from research in its overall purpose or intent and the speed at which it changes practice. For example, in the previous chapters, the overall purpose of applied research (e.g., correlational, case study, experimental) was to expand our general understanding or knowledge about the topic and to ultimately inform practice. This is certainly a main purpose of applied research, but empirical evidence supporting a new method or approach does not necessarily mean that people will suddenly abandon what they have been doing for years and switch to the research-supported approach.

Notice how in the vignette, change occurred much more rapidly through the use of program evaluation. Based on the evaluation report, administrators, school board members, and project staff decided to reconfigure the structure of the after-school program and to provide parents with a center in the hopes of increasing parental involvement. In addition, it was also decided that many of the extracurricular activities would be done away with and that the new focus would be on the tutorial component of the program—hoping to see even more improvement in students' academic scores in the coming year.

Take, for example, applied research in the area of instructional methods in literacy. In the 1980s, the favored instructional approach was whole language (Weaver, 1994); however, a decade of research began to support another approach called phonics (Slavin, 2000). Despite the mounting evidence in favor of phonics, it took about a decade for practitioners to change their instruction. In the early 1990s, however, researchers began to examine the benefits of using both whole language and phonics in what is referred to as a "blended approach." Again, despite substantial empirical evidence, it took another 10 years for many practitioners to use both approaches in their classrooms. Although this is a simplified version of what occurred, the purpose here is to show the relationship between applied research and practice and the speed (or lack of it) with which systems or settings change based on applied research.

Although there are certainly many program evaluations that do not lead to change as swiftly (or at all), one difference between program evaluation and research is the increased emphasis program evaluation places on such change occurring. In fact, philosophies and approaches in program evaluation emphasize the use of evaluation findings to the extent that they believe if the evaluation report and recommendations are not used by program staff to make decisions and changes to the program, then the entire evaluation was a waste of time, energy, and resources (Patton, 1997).

Reporting Findings and Recommendations

Another unique feature of program evaluation that separates it from research is the way that program evaluation findings are presented. In conducting empirical research, researchers commonly write a study for publication, preferably in a high-level refereed journal. In program evaluation, and as in the vignette, the findings are presented in what is commonly referred to as the "evaluation report" and not *published in a journal.* In addition, most evaluation reports are given directly to the group or client that has hired the evaluator to perform the work and are not made available to others.

Formative and Summative Evaluation

Both quantitative and qualitative data can be collected in a program evaluation. Depending on the purpose and the audience of the evaluation, an evaluator may choose to conduct an evaluation that is solely quantitative or qualitative or a mixed-methods approach. In addition to using quantitative and qualitative data, a program evaluator also has the option of providing summative and formative evaluation within a project (Figure 14.1). As this figure shows both summative and formative evaluation may proceed simultaneously.

FIGURE 14.1 PROCESSES INVOLVED IN A PROGRAM EVALUATION.

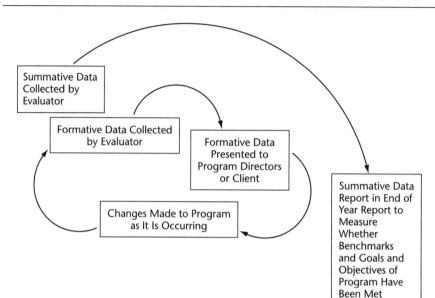

Summative and formative evaluations are not exclusively dictated by whether the evaluator collects quantitative or qualitative data. Many people have the misperceptions that summative evaluation uses exclusively quantitative data and that qualitative data are used for formative evaluation. This is not always the case. Whether evaluation feedback is formative or summative depends on what type of information it is and when it is provided to the client (see Figure 14.1).

Data for summative evaluation are collected to measure outcomes and to determine how those outcomes relate to the overall judgment of the program. As demonstrated in the vignette, summative findings are provided to the client at the end of the project or at the end of the project year or cycle. Typically, summative data include student scores on standardized measures such as state assessments, intelligence tests, and content-area tests. Surveys and qualitative data gathered through interviews with stakeholders may also serve as summative data if the questions or items are designed to elicit participant responses that summarize their perceptions of outcomes or experiences.

For example, an interview question in which participants are asked to discuss any academic or behavioral changes that they have seen in students as a result of participating in the after-school program will gather summative information. This information would be reported in an end-of-project-year report. However, an interview question that asks stakeholders to discuss any improvements that *could be made* to the program to better assist students in reaching those intended outcomes would be formative.

Formative data are different from summative in that instead of collecting data from participants at the end of the project to measure outcomes, formative data are collected and reported back to project staff as the program is taking place. Data gathered for formative evaluation need to be reported back to the client in a timely manner. There is little value in a formative evaluation when the evaluator does not report such findings to the client until the project is over. A formative evaluation can be reported through the use of memos, presentations, or even phone calls. The important role of formative feedback is to identify and address the issues or serious problems in the project. Imagine if the evaluator in our vignette did not report back formative findings regarding parental communication. Imagine how many students might not have been able to participate in the after-school activities. One of the roles of the evaluator is to identify these program barriers and inform program staff so that changes can occur. When programs are being implemented for the first time, formative feedback is especially important to developers and staff. Some programs require several years of intense formative feedback to "get the kinks out" before the program can become highly successful.

Formative feedback and the use of that information to change or improve the program are something that separates program evaluation from most types of applied research approaches that were discussed in earlier chapters. Remember back to the experimental or quasi-experimental research approaches and how the researcher tries to control extraneous variables so that only the independent variable can affect the dependent variable. An important aspect of experimental research is a clear definition of the different treatments or levels of independent variable. If the program is the treatment variable, it must be designed before the study begins. An experimental researcher would consider it disastrous if formative feedback were given because the treatment was changed in the middle of the study. By contrast, program evaluators, while trying to keep the independent variables or treatment constant, realize that it is better to make modifications to the program, even if it "distorts" the lines of causality, than to deliver a substandard program consistently for the entire school year.

Training in Program Evaluation

How do evaluators get involved in program evaluation, and where do they receive their training? These are both good questions. Although program evaluation today is certainly a more recognized field, it is made up of those who have formal training in program evaluation theory and practices as well as those who have been less formally trained. In reality, no specialized degree or certification is required for people to call themselves evaluators. Today, a number of colleges and universities offer course work in program evaluation as well as advanced degrees in this area. Whereas course work will vary by institution, most course work focuses on quantitative and qualitative methods, program evaluation theory, and ethics as well as a practicum experience.

As in any field, program evaluators come from a wide range of backgrounds and experiences as well as from different philosophical and methodological perspectives. Many times faculty at colleges and universities serve as program evaluation consultants working with area school districts, agencies, nonprofit and not-for-profit programs, and other institutions of higher education. Private evaluation consulting companies also exist and hire evaluators. Furthermore, public agencies at both the state and federal levels also hire program evaluators for full-time positions to conduct internal evaluations within the setting and to conduct single-site and multisite evaluations.

The American Evaluation Association is an international organization devoted to improving evaluation practices and methods, increasing its use, promoting evaluation as a profession, and supporting evaluation to generate theory and knowledge. This organization has about 4,000 members and representatives from 50 states and 60 foreign countries. Each year the association hosts an annual conference in the United States that focuses on a theme such as collaboration, methodology, or utilization (http://www.eval.org/News/news.htm). The association also comprises special interest groups that specialize in certain areas or topics (e.g., teaching program evaluation or environmental evaluation).

Internal or External Evaluators

The proximity of an evaluator to what is being evaluated plays a critical role in both the access to information, collection of that information, and the reporting and use of that information to promote change. Just like a waiter at a restaurant has a different perspective of the food and the management from that of a food critic who comes to dine and to write up a review for the local newspaper, an evaluator's perspective and his or her relationship to the setting or program is something that needs to be considered. In the field of program evaluation, this perspective is often addressed by what are referred to as internal and external evaluators. An **external evaluator** is someone from outside the immediate setting who is hired to "come in" and evaluate the program. Because this person has no obligations, he or she would in theory have no immediate biases for or against the program or any one of the stakeholder groups involved in the project. Most programs that receive federal, state, or foundation funding require an external evaluator to be present.

On the other hand, many companies, agencies, institutes of higher education, school districts, and other groups also employ internal evaluators. An **internal evaluator** is typically someone who is an employee of the company, agency, or group who is responsible for carrying out duties that pertain to evaluation. For example, many school districts now have a program evaluator on staff. The responsibilities of this person are to establish and work with databases to maintain student academic and behavioral data and to use data to assist staff and administration in improving practice. Internal evaluators at districts provide expertise in working with the state testing and accountability data and monitor programs that the school is currently implementing.

There are many strengths and barriers to both internal and external evaluators. As mentioned earlier, the main reason that many funding agencies require an external evaluator to be present is to increase the objectivity of the data that are being collected. However, while this may or may not be true, the role of the external evaluator also has some challenges. External evaluators are often faced with the difficulty of establishing trust with the stakeholders involved in the program that they are evaluating. Even though the external evaluator is collecting data on the program and not specifically on the performance of program staff, this stakeholder group may not welcome the evaluator with open arms. Stakeholders may, and often do, see the evaluator as a threat, someone whose job it is to find "holes" in the program. They may see the evaluator's work as a direct threat to their livelihood. In some cases, the stakeholders may feel that the external evaluator "really doesn't know them . . ." or "doesn't know what they are all about . . ." In some cases, they may feel that the evaluator does not know enough about the setting or the context of how things work in that setting to be able to gather in-depth data that would pertain to them and be meaningful for evaluation purposes. In many cases, stakeholders who are unsure and uncertain about this evaluator are likely to avoid the evaluator altogether, not returning phone calls to set up interviews and not returning surveys. Entering a foreign setting, establishing trust with the various groups involved in the program, and providing meaningful feedback to participants for programmatic improvements can be daunting and often difficult challenges for even the most seasoned program evaluators.

On the contrary, internal evaluators typically do not have to deal with establishing trust from stakeholders, as external evaluators do. In addition, internal evaluators also know the setting, how to access needed data, and the "language" that each group uses. In some cases, there might be both an internal and external evaluator. If an internal evaluator is already present in a school system or program, then an evaluation plan should encompass the work of both evaluators to optimize the breadth and depth of data that are collected and to hopefully ensure the overall success of the program. In such situations, the internal evaluator would be responsible for collecting certain types of data that the external evaluator would not have to access. In turn, the external evaluator would collect additional data to ensure the authenticity and objectivity of the evaluation effort and its findings. For a more in-depth description of how an external evaluator works with clients, the following case example illustrates an evaluator's experience with expanding a science program to another state.

Role of the Program Evaluator in Delivering Bad News

A program evaluator was hired by a group of curriculum developers to evaluate the expansion efforts of an inquiry-based science program for high school students. For the past three years, the developers had been piloting their program on the East Coast through a grant they received from a national sponsor. As part of the grant requirements, the developers hired a program evaluator who had worked with them to provide both formative evaluation and annual summative reports that they have used to steadily improve the program. During that time, the developers had to restructure the process for recruiting teachers into the program and refine some of the materials used for the three-week summer training of teachers. At the end of the program pilot, the developers felt confident that all the kinks were out of the program and received an additional grant to expand their efforts to a state in the midwest. The following summer, the developers held a three-week training for 30 teachers in the expansion state. The program evaluator arrived during the last few days of training to observe, administer a survey, and hold several focus groups with the teachers. The purpose of the site visit was threefold: to document the training, to gather teachers' perceptions about the quality of the training, and to document if the teachers felt prepared to implement the program in their school that coming fall. From implementing the programs on the East Coast, the developers and evaluator had learned that teachers who do not feel prepared to implement the program at the beginning of the school year typically fail to keep the program going once it has started. Following a break in the training, the evaluator administered the survey to the teachers-in-training, and later, during lunch, the evaluator quickly scanned the surveys and, much to his surprise, discovered that all the teachers indicated that they would not be implementing the program that coming fall. This was a surprise to the evaluator, especially because in the past, all teachers had indicated that they would be implementing the program following the training. Believing that surely teachers had misread the question, the evaluator adds this item to his interview protocol. During the three focus groups, all the teachers validate the survey finding and reaffirm that they are not going to be implementing the program that school year. Confused, the evaluator asks the teachers why they were not going to implement and found out that under their state education department, all new curriculum adopted by school districts has to undergo a yearlong review. This was not the case on the East Coast, where school districts could adopt any curriculum desired by the administration. The evaluator then asked the teachers if they had relayed any of this information to the developers during the past three weeks. The teachers said that they had not told the developers because they thought they were nice people and did not want to upset them. At the end of the day, the evaluator broke the bad news to the developers. The developers were shocked; they could not believe that the teachers were not going to implement the program and had sat through the training without telling them. Having learned this, the developers changed the last day of the training to focus on what teachers could do to get ready for the program over the next year. The teachers found the switch by the developers to be helpful because it eased their bad feelings about not being able to do the program in the fall, and all teachers implemented the program the following year with great success. The developers and evaluator learned an important lesson: not to assume that what works well in one setting will automatically work the same way in another, despite how similar the two settings may appear to be on the outside.

Types or Models of Program Evaluation

Just like there are many types of applied research approaches described in the previous chapters, there are several approaches that program evaluators can use. The most common approach to program evaluation is the **objective-based approach,** which uses objectives written by both the creators of the program and the evaluator. Evaluation objectives are written statements that depict the overarching purpose of the evaluation and clearly state the type of information that will be collected. Many times these objectives are also supported through the use of **benchmarks.** A benchmark is more detailed than an objective in that it specifically states what quantitative goals the participants in the program need to reach for the program to be successful. Presented in Box 14.2 is an evaluation objective followed by a program benchmark.

Box 14.2 Examples of an Evaluation Objective and Benchmark

Evaluation Objective: To document middle school student changes in academic achievement, particularly in the area of reading-literacy skills

Benchmark: Students in grades 5 through 8 will show a 10% gain on the English Language Arts state assessment in year 1 and a 20% increase in the number of students passing the ELA in program years 2 and 3.

Many times evaluators will start with the objectives for the evaluation and build evaluation data-collecting activities from those objectives. Evaluation objectives may guide either formative or summative data collection. Either way, quantitative or qualitative data (or both) would be collected, and findings are compared with the project's objectives. Although objectives are helpful in shaping the evaluation, one of the problems is that evaluators may become so focused on the objectives that they lose sight of other unanticipated outcomes or benefits to participants as a result of the program.

Although objectives assist in guiding an evaluation, the **goal-free evaluation** approach is another method that does not prescribe using evaluation objectives. This approach is guided by the perspective that many findings and outcomes do not fall within the "tightly packaged" goals and objectives established by both the project directors and the evaluator. Those who practice goal-free evaluation believe that the unforeseen outcomes are more important perhaps than outcomes that the program developers employ. One of the difficulties in conducting a goal-free evaluation is that projects that receive funding are required to show specific outcomes based on objectives. If the outcomes are not included in the evaluation, the appropriate data may not be collected.

The **expertise-oriented evaluation** approach is noted for being one of the oldest and most utilized methods of program evaluation, employing the evaluator to be a content expert and to serve a role more as judge than evaluator (Fitzpatrick, Sanders & Worthen, 2004). Agencies that grant accreditation to institutions, programs, or services would send program evaluators to these sites to conduct an expertise-oriented evaluation. In these situations, data are typically not collected by the evaluators but are "presented" by the participants being judged or seeking accreditation. The evaluators under this approach would judge the program or service based on an established set of criteria as well as their own expertise in the area. An example of this type of evaluation is the National Council for Accreditation of Teacher Education. Colleges and universities who train teachers often seek national accreditation to demonstrate the quality of their programs.

Participant-oriented evaluation approaches take a different perspective on program evaluation than the other approaches that have been described so far. Where the focus of the above approaches has been on the program and examining different aspects of the program, the participant-oriented evaluation approach is ultimately interested in those whom the program serves. Under this model, an evaluator would want to involve program participants in the actual evaluation of the program. In some cases, the participants would develop instruments, collect data, analyze data, and report findings.

Chapter Summary

Although program evaluation uses the same quantitative, qualitative, and mixed-methods approaches as in applied research, program evaluation is typically used for decision-making purposes. A main difference between program evaluation and research is in how each accesses the settings and works with participants. Whereas researchers might look at subgroups or individuals in a particular setting, program evaluators are generally hired or contracted by a group to judge the worth or merit of a particular program as a whole. Program evaluators also rely on summative and formative evaluation. Summative evaluation focuses on gathering specific kinds of outcome data, such as test scores and final results to determine whether the project met its overall goals. Summative data are provided to the client or group that commissioned the evaluation work at the end of the project. Formative data are collected by the evaluator as the program is occurring and are used to modify or refine program activities to improve program quality before the program has been completed. Because of the speed at which formative evaluation needs to be presented back to the client, formative findings can be presented in oral reports, memorandums, or scheduled conference calls between the evaluator and the client. Summative findings are typically presented in a more formal evaluation report at the end of the project.

Internal evaluators are persons who already are employed or associated with the group that is having an evaluation conducted. An external evaluator is someone who is hired from outside the group to conduct an evaluation. Because internal evaluators are already associated with the group that is conducting the evaluation, they are aware of how the group functions, its processes, language, and politics. Not being a part of these systems, many times external evaluators have to work to establish trust with the group that they are evaluating. There are several evaluation approaches that evaluators today use. Objective-based, goal-free, expertise-oriented, and participant-oriented evaluations are examples of different approaches, each geared to focus on different aspects of the evaluation, each with different intentions driving their methods.

Key Concepts

client

formative

summative

benchmarks

programs

internal evaluators

external evaluators

objective-based approach

goal-free evaluation

expertise-oriented evaluation

participant-oriented evaluation

Discussion Questions or Activities

1. An external program evaluator has been hired to examine the science program at a suburban high school and to show how the program affects students' future success in college. The high school, however, already has a staff member who serves as an "informal" internal evaluator collecting data on student performance. Discuss what expertise these two evaluators can bring to the project and what data possibilities each can collect.
2. A program evaluator is working on a project and is having difficulty building trust with the client. The client fears that the evaluator is interested only in digging up bad stuff about the client and things that the client is not doing with the program. Provide an overview of the differences between formative and summative evaluation findings, and then discuss how the evaluator might go about using these two approaches to improve the rapport with the client.
3. Discuss some possible issues that program evaluators might face on a regular basis, particularly because of the close working relationship that exists between them and their clients.

Suggested Readings

Cousins, J. B., & Earl, L. M. (1992). The case for participatory evaluation. *Education Evaluation and Policy Analysis, 14*(4), 397–418.

MacNeil, C. (2002). Evaluator as steward of citizen deliberation. *American Journal of Evaluation, 23*(1), 45–54.

Patton, M. Q. (2002). *Qualitative research and evaluation methods.* Thousand Oaks, CA: Sage Publications.

CHAPTER FIFTEEN

EDUCATIONAL RESEARCH CAN MAKE A DIFFERENCE

Chapter Objectives

After reading this chapter, you should be able to

1. Discuss important researchers whose work has had an impact on teaching and learning
2. Determine the type of research used by these researchers
3. Recognize the importance of research in an educational or social setting

Researchers Who Have Made a Difference

As we have tried to stress throughout this book, research in education adds to the body of educational knowledge but can and should influence and change practice. These changes should not only improve teaching and learning but in some way enhance the lives of those we touch. What better way to prove this than to share with you the work of researchers who have made a difference in the lives of many. Some of these names you will recognize; others you likely will not. These famous researchers have made significant contributions to the field of education, and as such, we should celebrate their accomplishments. However, the not-so-famous people, in our minds, are equally important to highlight because they also demonstrate the role that research can play in improving practice. All of these researchers serve as models for all of us and, in their unique ways, have made our profession a better one. Using these individuals as examples, we hope to demonstrate that with an understanding of the research process and a commitment to our profession, you can engage in research that may one day prove to make a difference.

Researchers Working at Colleges and Universities

There are many researcher we might have selected as people whose research has made a difference in the field of education. Following are six whose work we respect and admire.

Diana Baumrind. University of California psychologist Diana Baumrind's research on parenting style represents years devoted to the exploration of the relationship between parenting and children's social, emotional, and cognitive development. In what is now a classic piece of observational research, Baumrind (1967) observed the daily activities and behavior of nursery school children. From these observations, she identified three patterns of child behavior. Specifically, she identified children as energetic or friendly, conflicted or irritable, and impulsive or aggressive. Following the observational portion of the study, Baumrind conducted interviews and observations of the parents and children interacting in the home and in a laboratory setting. Her research found that there were clear links between the style of parenting and children's behavioral outcomes. These styles of parenting and their connection to child development were described by Baumrind as follows:

- *Authoritarian.* In this style of parenting, parents stress the importance of their authority and focus attention on conformity and obedience to rules. Through their parenting, they attempt to control and shape the behavior of their children. There is little verbal negotiation of rules, and if rules are broken, authoritarian parents believe in punitive behaviors. Baumrind's research revealed that this type of parenting style produced children who lacked initiative, curiosity, and social competence.
- *Authoritative.* Unlike authoritarian parents, authoritative parents encourage conversation and discussion of rules or decisions and create a reciprocal relationship with their children. They set high standards for behavior but are more likely to use reasoning than physical punishment when children do not follow the rules. Children are encouraged to be independent and to be good problem solvers and decision makers. Authoritative parenting leads to self-reliant, socially competent, and happy children.
- *Permissive.* Permissive parents are undemanding and exhibit less control than both authoritarian and authoritative parents. They tend to overindulge their

children, believing that "kids will be kids." Although there is a lack of expectations of their children, permissive parents tend to develop a loving relationship between the child and the parent. However, the children often exhibit impulsivity and immaturity.

A fourth type of parenting, uninvolved parenting, was added to Baumrind's theory by Maccoby and Martin (1983). Uninvolved parents are indifferent or neglectful of their children. These parents are self-centered and focus on their own needs and not the needs of the child. Children raised by uninvolved parents often are moody, insecurely attached, and lack the skills for social and academic pursuits.

Baumrind's research has led numerous other researchers to examine parenting and its relationship to child and adolescent development. Furthermore, it has been the focus of many parental education programs designed to improve parenting skills and the kind of interactions that occur between parent and child. However, her research is not without criticism. Most of her original research was conducted on predominately white middle-class preschoolers. Questions have been raised about the generalizability of these findings to other ethnic or cultural groups and those of different socioeconomic backgrounds. These questions are important ones and have led to a new series of research studies examining parenting styles in different ethnic and socio-cultural contexts.

Myra and David Sadker. *Failing at Fairness: How Our Schools Cheat Girls* (1995) summarizes the extensive research conducted by Myra and David Sadker in elementary and secondary schools and college classrooms. The Sadkers' research has had a significant impact on teaching, learning, and teacher preparation. The Sadkers met in the late 1960s and began a life and career together. Their professional lives were highly influenced by their training at the University of Massachusetts at Amherst, where there was a commitment to educational equity and where the focus of the curriculum was on issues of multiculturalism and race. Although both Sadkers were interested in these important issues, they became increasingly concerned about educational equity and gender.

The research question that drove much of their work was, "What happens to girls in schools?" With funding from the National Institute of Education (followed by two decades of federal dollars), they collected data from urban, suburban, and rural multiracial classrooms and observed multiracial teachers in a variety of content areas. In general, their observations revealed the pervasiveness of sex bias. Specifically, at all grade levels, teachers interacted more with boys than girls. Furthermore, boys were given more time to talk in class. Teachers helped boys more, gave them more attention, and punished them more (a form of attention) than girls. Perhaps equally as troubling was that many of these educators were unaware

of the existence of gender bias in their own classrooms, and in fact, many es-
poused views supporting gender equity.

Based on this study and numerous others like it, the Sadkers documented the
inequities in the treatment of boys and girls in the classroom. Their findings
demonstrated the need to educate teachers about gender bias and gender equity
in the classroom. In fact, their research has led directly to training programs for
teachers that are designed to increase teacher sensitivity to gender bias and include
activities that teachers can use to promote more gender-equitable classrooms.

Myra Sadker was professor of education and dean of the School of Education at American University in Washington, DC, until 1995, when she died of
breast cancer. Her work continues through the Myra Sadker Advocates. David
Sadker continues his work as professor at American University. Current reform
movements to promote equity in teaching are a legacy to the work of Myra and
David Sadker.

Paulo Freire. As mentioned in Chapter Twelve, the work of Paulo Freire is often
credited in part with the move to politicize practical action research and transform it into critical action research. Freire was born September 19, 1921, in north-
eastern Brazil and died in 1997. His family suffered severe financial loss during
the Great Depression, and he grew up poor and hungry. These early experiences
with poverty influenced his beliefs and professional focus.

As Freire's family circumstances improved, he eventually completed secondary
school and was able to enter Recife University, where he studied law, philosophy,
and the psychology of language. During this time, he found employment working as an instructor of Portuguese in a secondary school. On graduation from Recife, Freire worked for a short time as a lawyer (in fact, he left the profession just
after he passed the bar exam) and then continued his teaching career. His interest in adult education grew, and he went to work as a welfare official and later as
the director of the Department of Education and Culture, a governmental agency.
His experiences as a government official brought him into close contact with the
poor and politically disenfranchised. During his years as director, he became interested in adult education and literacy. In 1959 he was awarded a doctoral degree from the University of Recife.

In the early 1960s, Freire became the first director of the University of Recife's Cultural Extension Service where he was responsible for bringing literacy
programs to the poor of Brazil. In fact, Freire and his literacy teams successfully
improved the adult literacy rate. The foundation of his literacy program was that
teaching reading and writing as decontextualized or isolated skills was ineffective.
Rather, Freire believed that to motivate the poor to learn to read and write, they
should be shown how the development of these skills would result in their in-

creased participation in the political process. His goal was not only to increase literacy but also to empower the poor to take control over their lives and become part of the political process. As one would imagine, those in political power were threatened by this, and Freire was jailed for what was termed "subversive activities." It was in jail that he began to write his first major educational work, *Education as a Practice of Freedom* (1967/1976), which was finished in Chile following his expulsion from Brazil.

While in Chile, Freire continued his work in literacy among the poor and became even more committed to the important role that literacy played in bringing freedom to oppressed groups. It was during this time that he engaged in what he called "thematic" research projects. These research projects were highly inductive, involved the participants in the research, and promoted a high degree of interaction and respect between the researchers and those being studied. In addition, the goal of these research projects was to encourage social action that would lead to an improvement in the lives of the people being studied. His work is often credited with the politicizing of action research.

Toward the end of the 1960s, Freire became an invited lecturer at Harvard University. It was during this time that he wrote his most famous book, *The Pedagogy of the Oppressed* (1970). In this book Freire explained the importance of education to the liberation of all people. First, people must become *conscientized*, meaning that they become constantly aware of the existence of oppression in their lives. Second, *praxis* (informed action linked to values) should transform schools, communities, and societies so that all can be liberated. According to Freire, teachers can play a critical role in this transformation. By engaging in respectful dialogue, developing an understanding of community from within, and developing collaborative relationships between the student and the teacher and the teacher and the communities, real change can occur and oppressed people can develop their own voice and power.

John Uzo Ogbu. As a professor of anthropology at the University of California at Berkeley, John Uzo Ogbu focused his research on examining the historical treatment of minorities in the social, economic, and political domains. Born in a small village in Nigeria in 1939, Ogbu obtained a bachelor's degree in anthropology in 1965, his master's degree in 1969, and his doctorate in 1971. He began teaching in 1970 at the University of California, Berkeley, and became a full professor in 1980. He died of a heart attack at age 64 and was buried in his native Nigeria.

Much of Ogbu's research was ethnographic and conducted in minority communities. His research findings stirred controversy when he reported that African American students did not live up to their academic potential because of the fear of being perceived as "acting white" (Ogbu, 1986). He went on to argue that the gap in test scores between blacks and American-born Latinos and whites and Asians was rooted in collective identities and attitudes that were highly influenced by historical and cultural experiences. Collective identity, a "we feeling," for African Americans is formed in the context of slavery and oppression by white society. Furthermore, African Americans and Latinos born in the United States are "involuntary minorities" who live in a country with a history of racial and ethnic discrimination. These experiences influence minority students' attitudes toward schools, which are typically negative. Schools are viewed by these minorities as being "white" and doing well in school as acting white.

In a book, *Black American Students in an Affluent Suburb: A Study of Academic Disengagement* (2003), Ogbu wrote that black students' cultural attitudes should be considered when planning strategies to improve academic performance. These strategies should be developed by members of the community. Although the school can and should develop programs to demonstrate that academic success and excellence can be experienced by all, the community must play a role in developing positive attitudes toward achievement as well.

Robert E. Slavin. What kind of learning environment enhances learning? Should students quietly engage in their own work? Should they carefully follow the direct instruction provided by the teacher? Should they actively engage in discussions with their peers? Finding answers to these questions has been Slavin's life work. One researcher who believes strongly that students should be encouraged to discuss, interact, teach, and debate while working collaboratively with each other is Robert E. Slavin. Slavin is the codirector of the Center for Research on the Education of Students Placed at Risk at Johns Hopkins University in Baltimore and is chair of the Success for All Foundation. He graduated from Reed College in Portland, Oregon, in 1971 and received a doctoral degree from Johns Hopkins University in 1975.

Slavin and his colleagues have authored numerous journal articles and books about the benefits of such activities and have become vocal proponents of cooperative learning. Cooperative learning is a classroom strategy that supplements a teacher's instruction where students are given an opportunity to construct and discover information while working in groups with their peers. To demonstrate the positive effects of cooperative learning, Slavin has conducted many types of research that have focused on many different variables. For example, numerous experimental studies have investigated the effect that cooperative learning activities have on academic achievement. These experimental designs compared the effects of cooperative learning with those of traditional classroom learning (teacher directed). In many of these studies (Slavin, 1990), teachers were randomly assigned to the cooperative learning and traditional learning groups, and extraneous student variables were carefully controlled. Although some of the studies vary in their results, most of these studies demonstrated that cooperative learning significantly improves academic performance as long as students clearly have common goals and all are held accountable (Slavin). Furthermore, cooperative learning has been found to be effective for all types of students, urban, suburban, and rural, and with students from different ethnic groups (Slavin & Oickle, 1981). Slavin's research has also demonstrated the positive effects of cooperative learning on many other important variables such as self-esteem, interethnic cooperation, and friendship, to name just a few.

These studies, in addition to research conducted by others, have resulted in the widespread use of cooperative learning in elementary and secondary schools as well as in colleges and universities. Clearly, as demonstrated by the research, cooperative learning has led to improved teaching and learning.

Researchers Working in Schools and Community Organizations

Following are descriptions of educators we have known as students or colleagues. They may not be as famous as the researchers at colleges and universities, however, they are also excellent examples of persons who have used research to make a difference.

Maria Smith. Maria Smith is the director of a prekindergarten child care center in a major city. Most parents the center serves come from a Spanish-language culture and speak Spanish as their primary language. As part of her duties, Smith constructed a survey in Spanish to ask parents what they thought about the program, what they liked and did not like, and what aspects of the program they saw as being beneficial. When Smith got the results of the study back, she was surprised to see that most of the parents indicated that they believed the children in the program played too much during the day. Smith examined the literature to get another perspective and found that in many Spanish-language cultures, the idea of "play" is not something that is valued or believed to be associated with learning. The parents reported that they believed the curriculum at the center needed to be more academically rigorous. Based on this evidence, Smith decided to change how parents were initially introduced to the center. The center revamped their brochures and materials, emphasizing the importance of play and how the children were being assessed and taught through play. In addition, Smith worked one-on-one with parents, describing the kinds of outcomes that were being measured and how a youngster learns through play. Slowly parents came to understand better the use of play at the center, and later Smith heard many parents report that they now encouraged much more play at home.

Inge Miller. Inge Miller is the director of support services for a Board of Cooperative Education Services (BOCES) organization in Albany, New York. BOCES is a state-funded organization that provides technical assistance, training, programming, and resources to schools to better meet the needs of their students. As director of support services, Miller sets up teacher trainings and consults with schools on the development of new programs. She uses her training in research methods "all of the time" to assess the activities of her organization. Miller has designed surveys to monitor parent and student satisfaction with programs. She also collects data on student outcomes and helps schools use these data to identify areas in which they need to add services or make modifications. Miller says that research is essential to the day-to-day operations of her organization and has enabled her to better target its services to meet the needs of the students, parents, teachers, and administrators in her district.

Joe Zapoli. Joe Zapoli is a sports trainer for athletes at a small private college. He works with coaches and athletes to set up training programs for strengthening and also for rehabilitation of injuries resulting from participation in sports. Zapoli observed that the athletes often had intense emotions following a serious injury, and he wanted to learn more about their experiences. He used surveys and interviews to explore the range of feelings they experienced in the months following their injuries. Although the experiences were often unique, for many athletes, the emotions changed over time in a manner that paralleled the process of grieving. Zapoli examined the similarities and differences between the athletes' coping processes and those described in models of grieving. He said that his research has helped him to better understand the emotional processes that athletes with serious injuries experience and how he can better motivate them to persist in their rehabilitation programs.

Tracy Sullivan. Tracy Sullivan teaches home economics courses at a middle school and was recently recognized as a Teacher of the Month by a local television station. (Teachers of the Month are nominated by their students.) With action research as an ongoing component of her teaching, Sullivan uses student journals and interviews to obtain student feedback about her assignments and her methods of teaching. She looks at teaching from a critical action point of view, frequently planning lessons with her students and inviting them to assess themselves and their classmates. She even invited her students to critique her final presentation for her graduate studies programs and modified her presentation based on their feedback. Her energy and creativity enliven both her teaching and her research, which are so intertwined that it is sometimes hard to know where one begins and the other ends. Sullivan says that research has provided an additional means for her to engage her students in teaching and learning and share her passion for both with them.

Marty Owen. Marty Owen, a middle school math teacher in a large rural school district, decided to conduct an action research project in his district. Students in the five middle schools had failed to reach benchmarks on the state's annual math assessment. Examining the assessment, Owen realized that most of the test focused on problem-based items that required students both to do math computations and to work within an open-ended question that had several possible answers. Owen had discussions with several colleagues and his building principal about inquiry- and problem-based learning, and he got conflicting perceptions. Based on what he found initially, Owen decided to survey all middle school teachers and administrators regarding their perceptions on inquiry- versus problem-based learning. He found that teachers within buildings, as well as principals, disagreed or had misperceptions about what these instructional approaches entailed. Owen presented his findings to the administration, and it was determined that the district would have a workshop on problem-based learning and instruction at the next superintendent's day. Following the training, Owen discovered several of his colleagues who teach at different grade levels working together to better sequence how they introduce and teach using problem-based learning experiences. Teachers continued to work for the remainder of the school year on their course sequencing. The following year, the district experienced a notable increase in their students' performance on the math assessment. According to the state's educational department, however, the district will have to maintain these changes for another year to consider them true outcomes. The district is hopeful, and members believe that addressing this issue from a grassroots approach was an effective method to school change.

Chapter Summary

We hope that we have provided you with a glimpse of the impact that just a few researchers have had on students, their families and communities, and society in general. We would like you to notice that there was no one research approach used by these researchers. Slavin preferred the experimental method, Ogbu used ethnography, and Owen and Sullivan used practical action research. Zapoli used a mixed-methods approach, Miller and Smith used survey research, Freire used critical action research, and Baumrind and Sadker and Sadker used observational research. Although you now know that under No Child Left Behind, there is pressure on the educational community to focus on experimental research, we hope that by reading the research of the individuals we included in the final chapter of this book, you, too, will recognize the importance of using multiple approaches to solve the problems facing education today.

Seeing research in a context and how it can improve lives hopefully will create in you a desire to become researchers or incorporate it into your practice.

Discussion Questions or Activities

1. What other researchers do you believe have made a real difference in the field of education? What types of research approaches did they use?
2. What do you see as a future direction for educational research? What topics or research questions still need to be addressed? What new types of research approaches remain to be tried?

REFERENCES

Allport, G. (1955). *The nature of prejudice*. Cambridge, MA: Addison-Wesley.

Andersen, R. E., Crespo, C. J., Bartlett, S. J., Cheskin, L. J., & Pratt, M. (1998). Relationship of physical activity and television watching with body weight and level of fatness among children. *Journal of the American Medical Association, 279*(12), 938–943.

Anderson, G. L., Herr, K., & Nihlen, A. S. (1994). *Studying your own school: An educator's guide to qualitative practitioner research*. Thousand Oaks, CA: Corwin Press.

Bandura, A., Grusec, J. E., & Menlove, F. L. (1966). Observational learning as a function of symbolization and incentive set. *Child Development, 37*(3), 499–506.

Baumrind, D. (1967). Child care practices anteceding three patterns of preschool behavior. *Genetic Psychology Monographs, 75*(1), 43–88.

Bell, J. H., & Bromnick, R. D. (2003). The social reality of the imaginary audience: A grounded approach. *Adolescence* [Online version], *38*(150), 205–219.

Bracht, H. G., & Glass, V. G. (1968). The external validity of experiments. *Journal of the American Educational Research Association, 5*(4), 437–474.

Brady, M. P. (1989). Differential measures of teachers' questioning in mainstream classes: Individual and classwide patterns. *Journal of Research and Development in Education, 23*(1), 10-17.

Brookhart, S. (n.d.). Review of Iowa Test of Basic Skills. In O. K. Burros (Ed.), *Mental measurement yearbook on-line*. Retrieved May 10, 2005, from Silverplatter database: http://spweb.silverplatter.com.

Campbell, D. T., & Fiske, D. W. (1959). Convergent and discriminant validation by the multitrait-multimethod matrix. *Psychological Bulletin, 56*, 81–105.

Campbell, D. T., & Stanley, J. S. (1971). *Experimental and quasi-experimental designs for research*. Boston: Houghton Mifflin.

Case, R. (1992). Neo-Piagetian theories of child development. In R. J. Sternberg & C. A. Berg (Eds.), *Intellectual development* (pp. 161–196). New York: Cambridge University Press.

Centers for Disease Control and Prevention. (1996, June). *HIV/AIDS Surveillance Report, 8*, Table 7.

Chalk, J. C., Hagan-Burke, S., & Burke, M. D. (2005). The effects of self-regulated strategy development on the writing process for high school students with learning disabilities. *Learning Disability Quarterly, 28*(1), 75–87.

Ciechalski, J. E. (n.d.). Review of Mathematics Self-Efficacy Scale. In O. K. Burros (Ed.), *Mental measurement yearbook on-line*. Retrieved May 10, 2005, from Silverplatter database: http://spweb.silverplatter.com.

Cochran-Smith, M., & Lytle, S. L. (1993). *Insider/outsider: Teacher research and knowledge* (Language and literacy series). New York: Teachers College Press.

Cohen, L., & Manion, L. (1994). *Research methods in education*. London: Routledge.

Cook, T. D., Campbell, D. T., & Peracchio, L. (1979). Quasi experimentation. In M. D. Dunnette & L. M. Hough (Eds.), *Handbook of industrial and organizational psychology* (2nd ed.) (pp. 491–576). Palo Alto, CA: Consulting Psychologists Press.

Creswell, J. W. (2003). *Research design: Qualitative, quantitative, and mixed methods approaches*. Thousand Oaks, CA: Sage.

Creswell, J. W. (2005). *Educational research: Planning, conducting, and evaluating quantitative and qualitative research*. Upper Saddle River, NJ: Merrill Prentice Hall.

Darling-Hammond, L. (2001). *The research and rhetoric on teacher certification: A response to "Teacher Certification Reconsidered."* (ERIC Document Reproduction Service No. ED 477 296). Retrieved July 14, 2005, from ERIC database.

Davies, R. D. (2003). *To prove or improve*. Paper presented at the American Evaluation Association, Reno.

Denzin, N. K. (1978). *The research act: A theoretical introduction to sociological method*. New York: Praeger.

Denzin, N. K., & Lincoln, Y. S. (Eds.). (2005). *Handbook of qualitative research* (2nd ed.). Thousand Oaks, CA: Sage.

Eisner, E. W. (1998). *The enlightened eye: Qualitative inquiry and the enhancement of educational practice*. Upper Saddle River, NJ: Merrill Prentice Hall.

Elkind, D. (1967). Egocentrism in adolescence. *Child Development, 38*, 1025–1034.

Erwin, E. J., Perkins, T. S., Ayala, J., Fine, M., & Rubin, E. (2001). "You don't have to be sighted to be a scientist, do you?": Issues and outcomes in science education. *Journal of Visual Impairment & Blindness, 95*(6), 338–353.

Fitzpatrick, B. L., Sanders, J. R., & Worthen, J. F. (2004). *Program evaluation: Alternative approaches and practical guidelines*. Boston: Allyn & Bacon.

Freire, P. (1970). *Pedagogy of the oppressed*. M. B. Ramos, Trans.) New York: Herder & Herder.

Freire, P. (1976). *Education as a practice of freedom*. London: Writers and Readers Pub. Cooperative (Original work published in 1967)

Gay, L. R., & Arasian, P. (2003). *Educational research: Competencies for analysis and application*. Columbus, OH: Prentice Hall.

Glaser, B., & Strauss, A. (1967). *The discovery of grounded theory*. Chicago: Aldine.

Glesne, C. (2006). *Becoming qualitative researchers: An introduction* (3rd ed.). Boston: Allyn & Bacon.

Go, C., & Murdock, S. (2003). To bully-proof or not to bully-proof: That is the question. *Journal of Extension, 41*(2). Retrieved January 18, 2005, from http://www.joe.org/joe/2003april/rbl.shtml.

Goetz, J. P., & LeCompte, M. D. (1984). *Ethnography and qualitative design in educational research.* New York: Academic Press.

Gold, R. L. (1958). Roles in sociological field observation. *Social Forces, 36,* 217–223.

Grissmer, D. W., Kirby, S. N., Rand, C., & Santa, M. (1991). *Patterns of attrition among Indiana teachers, 1965–1987.* 1991 (ERIC Document Reproduction Service No. ED 355 174). Retrieved July 12, 2005, from ERIC database.

Harter, S., & Pike, R. (1984). The pictorial scale of perceived competence and social acceptance for young children. *Child Development, 55*(6), 1969-1982.

Jones, L., & Kafetsios, K. (2005). Exposure to political violence and psychological well-being in Bosnian adolescents: A mixed method approach. *Clinical Child Psychology & Psychiatry, 10*(2), 157–177.

Jordan, L.,& Hendricks, C. (2002). Increasing sixth grade students engagement in literacy Learning. *Networks, 5*(1). Retrieved March 24, 2004, from http://uscs.edu/faculty/gwells/Networks/Vol5%282%29.2002/march/Jordan.htm.

Kennedy, J., & Voegtle, K. (2000). Friendship merging with ideology: The process of becoming an ally. *Initiatives* [Online serial], Sept. 2000. Retrieved January 2001 from http://nawe.org/members/journal/59.4/kennedy.htm.

King, B. (1990). *Creating curriculum together: Teachers, students, and collaborative investigation.* Paper presented at the annual meeting of the American Educational Research Association, Boston. (ERIC Document Reproduction Service No. ED 322 111). Retrieved March 16, 2005, from ERIC database.

Kozol, J. (1995). *Amazing grace: The lives of children and the conscience of a nation.* New York: HarperCollins.

Kozol, J. (2000). *Ordinary resurrections: Children in the years of hope.* New York: Crown Publishers.

Krejcie, R. V., & Morgan, D. W. (1970). Determining sample size for research activities. *Educational & Psychological Measurement, 30*(3), 607-610.

Larson, R. (1989). Beeping children and adolescents: A method for studying time use and daily experience. *Journal of Youth and Adolescence, 18*(6), 511-530.

LeCompte, M. D., & Schensul, J. J. (1999). *Designing and conducting ethnographic research.* Walnut Creek, CA: AltaMira Press.

Lewin, K. (1948). *Resolving social conflicts; selected papers on group dynamics.* Gertrude W. Lewin (Ed.). New York: Harper & Row.

Lincoln, Y. S. (1995). In search of students' voices. *Theory into Practice, 34*(2), 88–93.

Lincoln, Y. S., & Guba, E. G. (1985). *Naturalistic inquiry.* Newbury Park, CA: Sage.

Linn, R. L. (2003). Performance standards: Utility for different uses of assessment. *Education Policy Analysis Archives, 11*(31). Retrieved August 1, 2005, from http://epaa.asu.edu/epaa/v11n31/.

Maccoby, E. E., & Martin, J. A. (1983). Socialization in the context of the family: Parent-child interaction. In P. H. Mussen (Ed.), *Handbook of child psychology.* (Vol. 4) (pp. 1–101). New York: Wiley.

Marcia, J. E. (1966). Development and validation of ego-identity status. *Journal of Personality & Social Psychology, 3*(5), 551–558.

Merriam, S. B. (1998). *Qualitative research and case study applications in education.* San Francisco: Jossey-Bass.

Miles, M. B., & Huberman, A. M. (1994). *Qualitative data analysis: An expanded sourcebook* (2nd ed.). Thousand Oaks, CA: Sage.

Mills, G. E. (2000). Action research: Accountability, responsibility and reasonable expectations. *Educational Researcher, 32*(7), 3–13.

Mills, L. J., & Daniluk, J. C. (2002). Her body speaks: The experience of dance therapy for women survivors of child sexual abuse. *Journal of Counseling & Development, 80*(1), 77–86.

Neuman, S. (2002). *Proven methods: Scientific based research. (Seminar transcripts).* Retrieved December 1, 2004, from http://www.ed.gov/nclb/methods/whatworks/research/index.html.

Newman, D. L., & Spaulding, D. T. (1997). *Research in the high schools: National Science Foundation.* State University of New York, Albany: The Evaluation Consortium.

Ogbu, J. U. (1986). Black students' school success: Coping with the burden of "acting white." *The Urban Review, 18*(3), 176-206.

Ogbu, J. U. (2003). *Black American students in an affluent suburb: A study of academic disengagement.* Mahwah, NJ: Lawrence Erlbaum.

On-Line Learning Center (2005). *Cooperative learning lesson.* Retrieved May 12, 2005, from http://olc.spsd.sk.ca/DE/PD/instr/strats/coop/lesson.pdf.

Pasko, M. (2004). Curriculum connections: Linking literature and math. *Networks, 7*(2). Retrieved October 10, 2004, from http://education.ucsc.edu/faculty/gwells/networks/journal/Vol.7(2).2004may/Pasko.html.

Patton, M. Q. (1990). *Qualitative evaluation and research methods* (2nd ed.). Thousand Oaks, CA: Sage.

Patton, M. Q. (1997). *Utilization-focused evaluation: The new century text.* (ERIC Document Reproduction Service No. ED 413 355). Retrieved July 7, 2005, from ERIC database.

Perkins, T. S., Ayala, J., Fine, M., & Erwin, E. J. (n.d.). *Ethnographic study of "Playtime Is Science" for children who are blind or visually impaired: "You don't have to be sighted to be a scientist, do you?"* Retrieved April 29, 2005, from Educational Equity Center Web site: http://www.edequity.org/ethnographicstudy.pdf.

Phillips, D. C., & Burbules, N. C. (2000). *Positivism and educational research.* Lanham, MD: Rowan & Littlefield.

Proctor, M. H., Moore, L. L., & Gao, D. (2003). Television viewing and change in body fat from preschool to early adolescence: The Framingham children's study. *International Journal of Obesity & Related Metabolic Disorders, 27*(7), 827–833.

Raider Open Door Academy (n. d.). *Literacy skills checklist.* Retrieved May 12, 2005, from http://nettleton.crsc.k12.ar.us/~ncovey/Literacy%20Skills%20Checklist.htm.

Reichardt, C. S., & Rallis, S. F. (1994). The qualitative-quantitative debate: New perspectives. *New Directions for Program Evaluation, 61*, 5-11.

Sadker, D., & Sadker, M. (1995). *Failing at fairness: How our schools cheat girls.* New York: Touchtone Press.

Schmitt-Rodermund, E., & Vondracek, F. W. (1998). *Breadth of interests, exploration, and identity development in adolescence.* (ERIC Document Reproduction Service No. ED 420 445). Retrieved July 8, 2005, from ERIC database.

Seashore, H. G. (1980). Method of expressing test scores, In *Test service notebook 148.* New York: Psychological Corporation.

Shablak, S., Cavino, H., & Spaulding, D. T. (2005). *State improvement grant (SIG): Evaluation Report.* Syracuse, NY: Syracuse University.

Slavin, R. E. (1990). Learning together. *American School Board Journal, 177*(8), 22–23.

Slavin, R. E. (2000). *Educational psychology: Theory and practice.* Boston: Allyn & Bacon.

Slavin, R. E., & Oickle, E. (1981). Effects of cooperative learning teams on student achievement and race relations: Treatment by race interactions. *Sociology of Education, 54*(3), 174–181.

Spaulding, D. T., & Lodico, M. G. (2004). *Proposal for a feasible study for a Nativity/San Miguel model middle school.* Unpublished manuscript. The College of Saint Rose, Albany, NY.

Spaulding, D. T., Lodico, M. G., Jones, K., & Gligora, M. (2004, April). *Is a picture really worth a thousand words? Using student generated photographs and journals to document experiences in a summer enrichment program for at-risk youth.* Paper presented at the American Educational Research Association Conference, San Diego.

Stigler, J. W., & Perry, M. (1990). Mathematics learning in Japanese, Chinese, and American classrooms. In J. W. Stigler & R. A. Shweder (Eds.), *Cultural psychology: Essays on comparative human development.* New York: Cambridge.

Swanson, C. B. (2003). *Keeping count and losing count: Calculating graduation rates for all students under NCLB accountability.* (ERIC Document Reproduction Service No. ED 480 915). Retrieved July 8, 2005, from ERIC database.

University of Oregon (2004). Dynamic indicators of basic early literacy skills. *Official DIBELS Homepage.* Retrieved May 3, 2004, from http://dibels.uoregon.edu.

U.S. Department of Education (2005a). *No Child Left Behind: A new era in education presentation.* Retrieved December 28, 2005, from http://www.ed.gov/nclb/overview/intro/presentation/index.html.

U.S. Department of Education (2005b). *Resources + Reforms = Results.* Retrieved October 28, 2005, from http://www.ed.gov/about/offices/list/ods/resources-reform/index.html.

Weaver, C. (1994). *Reading process and practice: From socio-psycholinguistics to whole language.* Portsmouth, NH: Heinemann.

SAMPLE QUALITATIVE PROPOSAL

Running Head: HIGH-STAKES TESTING

High-Stakes Testing in New York:

Are High-Stakes Graduation Requirements Changing Instruction?

Student's Name

The College of Saint Rose

Introduction

Standardized testing has become a familiar scene throughout the United States. From second grade through high school, students all over the country can be found filling in bubbles with their No. 2 pencils. Many of the tests that students are taking are termed "high-stakes," and states are using them as monitoring systems that guarantee a basic quality level of education (Natriello & Pallas, 1998). Policymakers contend that these tests will help improve instruction and the overall education that students receive. As this testing wave takes over our schools, it is essential that we continue to examine the classrooms to find out if the goal of educational improvement is actually achieved.

According to the American Educational Research Association (AERA), tests qualify as high stakes if they "carry serious consequences for students or for educators" (AERA, n.d.,¶ 2). In other words, schools, teachers, and students are being either rewarded or punished on the results of their test scores. Perhaps the most visible assessment with stakes attached is high school graduation exams, which students have to pass to receive a diploma. As of 2002, 18 states use graduation exams, and more states are in the process of implementing exams (Amrein & Berliner, 2002). Teachers are now being asked to incorporate these tests into their curriculum and to produce results. Because the testing movement is rapidly progressing, it would be helpful to determine how teachers view the changes and how it is affecting their instruction and their morale.

The quality of education in the United States came under scrutiny in 1983 when the National Commission on Education published an influential report titled *A Nation at Risk*. The report noted that America's position in the world was in jeopardy, and consequently the commission called for educational reform that included a high-stakes testing movement that would raise the nation's standards and expectations in the schools. Over the past two decades, the use of high-stakes testing has increased throughout the country, with an emphasis on holding schools accountable for results. The government took a stand in support of the movement when President Bush signed the No Child Left Behind Act of 2001. According to the U.S. Department of Education, the new law requires "annual academic assessment" that will be aligned with each state's curriculum and academic standards. The government feels that "standards should drive the curriculum, which, in turn, must drive instruction" (U.S. Department of Education, n.d., ¶ 9). With the equality gaps and illiteracy problems in this country, this seems to be a step in a positive direction; however, by adding high-stakes and emphasizing standardized testing, are we really improving instruction in the schools?

According to the research on high-stakes testing, teachers do not fully support the idea that their instruction is improving. The positive effects of high-stakes testing that have been reported include increased learning opportunities, the identification of struggling students, and teacher collaboration (Firestone, Mayrowetz, & Fairman, 1998; Grant, 2000; Schleisman, 1999). However, the majority of research demonstrates that the negative effects seem to

High-Stakes Testing   4

outweigh the positive. Some of the noted concerns include teaching to the test, cultural and class biases, and emphasis on remediation (Costigan, 2002; Cunningham & Sanzo, 2002; Grant, 2000; Kohn, 1999; Wright, 2002). In addition, high-stakes tests are causing teachers to feel doubt, frustration, uncertainty, and a loss of power (Costigan, 2002; Grant, 2000; Wright, 2002). There seems to be a serious discrepancy between the negative research results and the increasing use of high-stakes testing.

Because each state has its own curriculum requirements and its own testing policies, it is difficult to determine the national effect of high-stakes assessment. This research proposal will focus on the state of New York. New York is an interesting state because it has just recently implemented brand new requirements for students to receive a high school diploma. According to the New York State Education Department, "students entering ninth grade in 2001 will be the first class of students who must take and pass five Regents examinations with a score of 65 in order to graduate" (Kadamus, 1998, p. 3). Before the implementation of these requirements, Grant (2000) explored New York teachers' responses to state-level testing in terms of changing pedagogical ideas and practices. What he discovered was that although teachers were not opposed to change, they were concerned about the nature of the proposed changes and professional development opportunities available to them to learn about the changes. Now that the requirements and tests are in use and the 2001 freshman classes are in tenth grade, Grant's findings and teacher perceptions on high-stakes testing need to be further investigated.

Statement of Purpose

Therefore, the purpose of this study is to explore experienced teachers' perspectives on how the high-stakes graduation requirements are changing instruction in New York State high schools. Areas that will be discussed include instruction, student-teacher interaction, educational quality, and teacher morale. The initial question to be explored in this qualitative study is how do teachers think high-stakes graduation requirements affect both the quality of education and educational processes in New York high schools?

Review of Literature

High-stakes testing is currently a hot topic in education that has led to a large amount of anecdotal literature for both sides of the argument. However, the actual research studies, both quantitative and qualitative, show little evidence that high-stakes testing programs are improving instruction (Amrein & Berliner, 2002; Groves, 2002; Klein, Hamilton, McCaffrey & Stecher, 2000; Wright, 2002). With accountability the main rationale for using these tests, it is essential to determine how high-stakes tests influence instruction.

Although instruction is the focus of this study, it is important to acknowledge what the test scores are telling us. Policymakers are hoping that attaching high stakes to tests will improve education in our country. If this does result, then students who do well on their state test should do equally well on tests that measure the same areas of knowledge. Amrein and Berliner (2002)

High-Stakes Testing 6

performed an extensive analysis in 18 states to see if the testing programs were affecting student learning. The goal was to determine if students who take high-stakes exams can demonstrate transfer of learning to other exams, or if their test scores are simply a result of being trained for the test. The four measures that were used in the study were scores from the American College Test (ACT), the Scholastic Aptitude Test (SAT), the National Assessment of Educational Progress (NAEP), and the Advanced Placement (AP) exams. In contrast to policymakers' hopes, the research produced no evidence of an overall transfer of learning to the other tests. For example, in New York, student achievement actually decreased on all exams except the AP exams after high stakes were attached in 1999 (Amrein & Berliner, 2002).

Test scores also show that instead of lessening the equality gap in education, it is possible that high-stakes tests are helping to increase it. Natriello and Pallas (1998) reported that students from ethnic minorities in Texas, New York, and Minnesota did not perform as well as their majority-group peers in all cases. Similar studies have noted that race and socioeconomic status are factors in determining test scores, and therefore the stakes are not equal for everyone (Cunningham & Sanzo, 2002; Klein et al., 2000). This evidence shows that schools and teachers with minority and low–socioeconomic status populations are dealing with the greatest challenges.

The research mentioned above used a quantitative approach to look at actual test results, but the greater part of the research in this field uses a qualitative approach to examine the effects that high-stakes testing programs are having on schools. An example of the qualitative approach is the case study done by Wright (2002), who chose to focus on one school and, by doing so, gave in-depth insight into how the tests are affecting teachers and students. Wright examined an elementary school in southern California in a low-socioeconomic inner-city neighborhood with a large English-language-learner (ELL) popula-tion. Formal interviews were conducted with five second-grade teachers whose students were preparing to take the SAT-9. From his interviews, observations, and artifact examinations, Wright concluded that "the SAT-9 is having harmful effects on the teachers and the students" (p. 31). Some of these effects include stress, pressure to teach to the test, and disempowerment. The teachers believed that the emphasis on the test was too high and that teaching and learning were not improving. The teachers in the school also noted the additional stress of "being compared to higher socioeconomic schools with significantly smaller numbers of ELL students and being blamed for their students' low scores" (p. 31). The significance of these feelings was that the teachers were now be-ginning to question if they should stay in the profession. As one teacher put it, "this is not what I signed on for" (p. 28). Although Wright was previously a teacher at this school, he argued that his assessment was not biased; instead, he said that his experience gave him the ability to look at the overall picture.

To truly determine the effects of testing on a school, some researchers have witnessed and analyzed a school before and after high-stakes tests were implemented. For example, McNeil (2000) observed the unwilling transfor-mation of three unique magnet schools in Texas during the policy changes of the 1980s. In her book, *Contradictions of Reform: Educational Costs of Standardized Testing,* McNeil makes it clear that the policymakers, not the educators, were the ones who decided what would be best for the schools, and the students and teachers consequently suffered from those decisions.

> The data from the magnet schools demonstrate compellingly that these "reforms," ostensibly meant to improve education, reduced what was taught, constrained teachers in the ways they could teach, and as a result, set in motion dynamics in which teachers would have to choose between course content they felt to be valid and content that was required by the state. They would have to choose between creating lessons that were meaningful and engaging for all their students, students of varying ability and cultures and learning styles, or lessons that would earn them, the teachers, high ratings on their own annual performance evaluations (p. 190).

McNeil also points out that one of the reform goals was to improve the "bad" teachers; yet, the standardized reform is hurting some of the best teachers by "forcing them to teach watered-down content" (p. 192). A well-known author against high-stakes testing, McNeil criticizes the dominant role that the government has taken in reforming education.

McNeil's statements are supported by additional studies, such as that by Groves (2002), who also witnessed the implementation of a high-stakes testing program. From her interviews and observations, Groves determined that the testing actually worsened teaching and learning in one elementary school in North Carolina. The research was conducted over two school years. The first year of observation took place before the implementation of the program titled the "ABCs of Public Education," and then for the second year, the school was fully operating with the new ABC program. In the first year of her study, Groves observed an urban school that was thriving with a program that emphasized creativity and student engagement and maintained high levels of teacher satisfaction. Unfortunately, once the ABC program began the following year, these positive and successful characteristics were left behind, and the focus of the school was now on the North Carolina End of Grade (EOG) tests. To get the students to pass EOGs, the school erased its creative atmosphere and removed many nontested subjects such as social studies, science, art, and drama and instead used only instructional practices that would raise test scores. So yes, the school is no longer labeled "low performing," but are the students realistically benefiting from this? After witnessing this transformation, Groves concluded that a school cannot be judged merely on test scores and that high-stakes tests "actually worsen conditions of teaching and learning and push imperative principles of equity and democracy to the margins" (p. 15).

As Groves reveals, schools are taking whatever measures necessary to produce high test scores, and policymakers will flaunt them when they occur, but research shows that teachers do not have the same pride in these scores. Flores and Clark (2003) did an ethnographic study that focused on the voices and opinions of teachers. They used threaded e-mail journals and observational

High-Stakes Testing   10

journals to give teachers an opportunity to voice their feelings and opinions on the Texas Assessment of Academic Skills (TAAS) in Texas. The study revealed six notable themes about the testing program:

1. Teachers are not against accountability; rather, they view assessment as distinct from high-stakes testing.
2. Teachers posit that an overemphasis on testing results in an unbalanced curriculum and inappropriate instructional decisions.
3. Teachers suggest that excessive pressure is placed on particular grade levels.
4. Teachers are having second thoughts about pursuing or remaining in the teaching profession.
5. Teachers propose that test results should not be used to make high-stakes decisions.
6. Teachers have observed that test emphasis affects students negatively and is manifested as physical, psychological, or emotional symptoms. (p. 8)

These findings are comparable to those of Costigan (2002), who interviewed six first-year elementary school teachers in New York City and heard similar sentiments from them. They felt that the testing has a "highly negative impact on their students and their classroom practice" (p. 7). They also found themselves unprepared, powerless, and unable to be creative because testing was always the primary focal point, which contributed to occupational distress.

Both of these findings demonstrate that when schools are observed and teachers' voices are heard, the negative implications seem to always outshine the positive ones. In fact, this would lead one to ask, are there any positive effects from high-stakes testing?

Policymakers and proponents of high-stakes testing argue that high-stakes tests help teachers and students know what is important to learn, they motivate teachers to do better because they are being held accountable, and they push students to work harder. Proponents also assume that the tests are a good measure of the curricula and that they provide an equal playing field (Amrein & Berliner, 2002). Unfortunately, the majority of the research illustrates that many times, the opposite effects occur and that these supportive statements are only true some of the time. One example of supportive research is that of Schleisman (1999), who investigated the school- and district-level changes in policies due to the implementation of the Minnesota Basic Standards Test. Using open-ended semistructured interviews focusing on key informants, Schleisman reported some positive results, such as that the tests helped schools identify the needs of some students who may have otherwise "slipped through the cracks" (p. 9). The schools also mentioned an increased focus on reading and only hinted at the narrowing of the curriculum. Another supportive study was done by Firestone et al. (1998), who observed eighth-grade math teachers in Maine and Maryland. The research found the negative effects of high-stakes testing in both states to be overrated. There was no change in instructional methods besides the order of when the content was taught. However, Firestone et al. do point out that these tests are also not doing anything to promote teacher improvement or increase opportunities to do so. Although this study is limited to one grade and one subject, it does point out that not all teachers are feeling a burden.

Teachers' perceptions and opinions on instruction are the focus of this research, yet it is difficult to generalize regarding the national effect of high-stakes testing because the states are using different tests. Rather than trying to reach general conclusions, it may be more useful to examine high-stakes testing within a more limited context. The purpose of this research is to narrow the lens of the effects of high-stakes testing by viewing the effect on New York State high schools. The research will also build on the previous work of Grant (2000), who did a qualitative study to determine how New York teachers respond to state-level testing. Grant conducted focus groups made up of a cross-section of educators from urban, suburban, and rural elementary and high schools with a variety of experiences. The focus groups took place over a two-year period before the full required changes were implemented in 2001. In this transition phase, the teachers did not view standardized testing as black and white but rather as a mixed bag and said that they were feeling an "uneasy combination of hope and fear, anticipation and dread" (p. 8). The group did point out possible pedagogic consequences such as reductive forms of teaching and learning, an increased emphasis on remediation, and the use of drill sessions on the tested material. The teachers understood the need for change but were mostly concerned with the nature of the changes and the professional development opportunities that were available to them to learn about these changes. Perhaps the most significant point from Grant—and many of the other researchers concur—is that "teachers are not passive participants and must not be designed around" (2000, p. 22). If the purpose of high-stakes testing is to improve the quality of education, one might think that teachers would have a say in the reform and that there is certainly not a one-size-fits-all solution for all schools (Popham, 1999).

Because most previous research has emphasized the need to consider teacher perspectives and also differences due to location, the present study will explore teacher perspectives regarding the impact of high-stakes testing on instruction in New York high schools. As stated earlier, the primary research question to be examined in the proposed study is, How do teachers think high-stakes graduation requirements affect both the quality of education and educational processes in New York high schools? Because the study will examine the ongoing emphasis on testing and accountability in New York, several foreshadowed questions will guide the research: Is instruction different now from what it was in previous years? If yes, how is it different? Are students getting a better or worse education, or has the quality remained unchanged? How are students benefiting or not benefiting from the new graduation requirements? How do teachers feel about the quality of instruction since high–stakes tests were introduced? Is teacher morale different? Is student-teacher interaction different? Answers to these questions will hopefully give us an insight into what is actually happening in the New York high schools.

High-Stakes Testing   14

Method

Participants

As a qualitative phenomenological research design, this study will use three focus groups of key informants to explore the effects of high-stakes testing on instruction. The key informants will be teachers from three high schools in the Hudson Valley region of New York who were chosen using a criterion-based purposive sampling strategy. Teachers to be selected will be those who have taught at their current school for at least ten years. The reason for this criterion is to ensure that each participant has been able to witness the full transformation of the Regents' testing requirements. It will be necessary to use volunteers for the focus group because the group will have to meet after school hours to accommodate their schedules.

Using teachers from multiple schools allows a variety of opinions and perceptions to be solicited about how the tests have affected their instruction. In addition, having teachers from multiple schools may enhance the transferability to other high schools in New York.

To locate volunteers and establish the focus group, a meeting will be set up with an administrator from each school to determine which teachers have been at the school for ten years or more. A meeting with the prospective teachers will then take place to explain the study and the time commitment. Once a list of volunteers is established, the group will be narrowed down based on grade levels and subject areas. The key informant group will represent four grades, including at least one resource room teacher and all five Regents exam subjects, which include English, math, global studies, U.S. history, and the sciences.

The Hudson Valley is an ideal location to conduct this focus group because it contains a wide range of urban and suburban communities with significant differences in both ethnicity and socioeconomic status among the schools. The schools that will be contacted are located in Dutchess County and Ulster County. No more than 12 teachers will be used from each school with about equal numbers from each grade level.

Role of the Researcher

The researcher has been a high school social studies teacher for five years and is currently enrolled in a graduate class in educational research. As part of this class, she is learning to conduct qualitative interviews, including focus group interviews. Her instructor will listen to tapes of the interviews and provide guidance on her interviewing skills throughout the duration of the study.

As a high school teacher at a school in New York, the researcher has experienced firsthand the changes occurring as a result of high-stakes testing. This experience provides insight and understanding that should enhance the ability of the researcher to relate to the teachers being interviewed while she is conducting the interviews. However, the researcher also has formed some of her own ideas about the impact of high-stakes testing. Specifically, she believes that testing has reduced the quality of teaching at her school and has nar-

High-Stakes Testing   16

rowed the curriculum. To control for bias and potential problems due to previous relationships with teachers, no teachers will be selected with whom the researcher has a prior acquaintance. Also, the researcher will record reflective field notes about her feelings about the interview sessions after each interview. Her instructor will serve as a peer debriefer by reviewing these notes with her and listening to the tape-recorded interviews for possible instances of bias.

Methods of Data Collection

As noted above, the primary method of data collection will be focus group interviews with the teachers. The reason for choosing a focus group is to promote interaction and discussion among teachers about their experiences with high-stakes testing. In addition to the teachers, the focus group will include a moderator and a research assistant who will tape-record each session and take field notes. Participants will be assured that all comments will be kept confidential and that their participation is voluntary. In appreciation for their participation in the study, each teacher will be given a gift certificate to a local store where teaching supplies may be purchased.

A topic will be identified for each session, and open-ended questions will be presented to initiate discussion. The moderator will ask additional questions to encourage participants to expand on their answers or to more fully explore differences in the responses by different teachers. The initial session outline is as follows but is subject to change:

High-Stakes Testing   17

Session I: Now Versus Then

- How is instruction different now from what it was 10 years ago?
- Do you feel you are providing a better education? Why or why not?
- Do you feel your teaching style has changed? If so, for the better?

Session 2: The Students

- How do students react toward the testing? Have student-teacher interactions changed?
- Are students benefiting from the new requirements?

Session 3: Teacher Morale

- Has teacher morale changed in your school?
- Are the tests changing what it means to be a teacher?
- Do you enjoy teaching more or less now that these requirements are in place?

Session 4: Professional Development

- Do you feel the professional development opportunities are adequate to handle the new requirements?
- Do you feel your opinions are being heard?

Session 5: Miscellaneous

The content of the session will be determined by reviewing the notes from preceding sessions and formulating questions to follow up on the issues raised. This session will also cover any unfinished topics or unheard perspectives.

Each teacher will receive a copy of the transcribed notes to review and will be invited to make additions or corrections to more accurately represent their feelings. In addition, member checks will be conducted in which participants will receive a copy of the write-up of the study's conclusions and invited to provide feedback regarding its accuracy and completeness.

Procedures

The focus groups for this study will be made up of 10 to 12 teachers. The group will meet five times throughout the school year at a central location that is to be determined. The sessions will be two hours long, and they will be held in September, November, February, April, and June. The regents exams are given twice a year in January and June, so these staggered meetings will ideally generate a variety of discussions before, during, and after the exams are given.

The goal of this study is to explore teachers' perspectives on how the regents graduation requirements are changing instruction in New York high schools, but the term *instruction* includes a variety of ideas such as daily operations, student-teacher interaction, morale, curriculum planning, and so forth. Because of this multitude, each focus group session will highlight a specific aspect of instruction. The sessions will be semistructured with some monitored questions, although the goal of the questions is to lead to an open discussion. Because high-stakes tests are a controversial topic, attempts will be made to ensure that the discussion stays on task and that participants probe their feelings deeply rather than simply complaining about required activities.

Following each session, the data will be transcribed and sent to participants for comments or additions. The researcher will review the transcripts from each session and identify issues or themes that need further discussion. These will be presented at the start of the following session. After each session, the researcher will also record her reflections in a journal. She will review this journal and discuss entries with her peer debriefer as they examine the transcripts for possible bias that might influence the teacher responses. After the five sessions are completed in June, then follow-up interviews will be conducted with a few individual teachers to ensure triangulation. The teachers will be shown the data in a summarized form to confirm that the research findings portray the essence of the focus group discussions.

Benefits and Limitations

By asking teachers these questions and giving them an opportunity to discuss their experiences, the researcher will attempt to shed light on how teachers feel that instruction has changed because of high-stakes testing. This exploratory study is not looking to determine if high-stakes tests are beneficial but instead asks what changes are occurring because of them? Answers to these questions and the others that are generated from the discussion will hopefully produce insight into what is actually happening in the schools.

The strength of this study is that there will be limited observer bias because the research is being conducted in a focus group setting and the researcher's interactions are being reviewed and critiqued by a peer debriefer.

High-Stakes Testing   20

Also, using representatives from multiple schools will bring in a variety of teaching experiences from all grades and all regents subject areas. One weakness of this study includes a limited amount of transferability because only three schools are being used; however, this is not the goal of the study. Another possible weakness is the potential of subject motivation, where the teachers are responding in certain ways that they think are desired by the researcher. However, because it is a focus group with multiple people, this should be able to be avoided. In addition, the individual interviews will provide an opportunity for participants to express feelings that they may not have felt comfortable revealing in the group. Ideally, this study will provide an in-depth look at how the state requirements are changing instruction and experiences in several high schools. It also gives a voice to teachers who are one of the groups most affected by the state requirements. If research gives teacher perspectives the attention that they deserve, their experiences may begin to influence the formation of policies for educating students.

References

American Educational Research Association (n.d.). *AERA position statement concerning high-stakes testing in preK-12 education.* Retrieved January. 22, 2003, from http://www.aera.netlabout/policy/ stakes.htm.

Amrein, A. L., & Berliner, D. C. (2002 Mar. 28). High-stakes testing, uncertainty, and student learning. *Education Policy Analysis Archives, 10*(18). Retrieved February 2, 2003, from http://epaa.asu.edu/epaa/v10n18.

Costigan, A. T. III (2002). Teaching the culture of high stakes testing: Listening to new teachers. *Action in Teacher Education, 14*(23), 28–34. Retrieved January 22, 2003, from WilsonWeb database.

Cunningham, W. G., & Sanzo, T. D. (2002 June). Is high-stakes testing harming lower socioeconomic status schools? *NASSP Bulletin, 86,* 62–75.

Firestone, W. A., Mayrowetz, D., & Fairman, J. (1998). Performance-based assessment and instructional change: The effects of testing in Maine and Maryland. *Education Evaluation and Policy Analysis, 20*(2), 95–113.

Flores, B. B., & Clark, E. R. (2003, March 3). Texas voices speak out about high-stakes testing: Preservice teachers, teachers, and students. *Current Issues in Education, 6*(3). Retrieved March 13, 2003, from http://cie.ed.asu.edu/volume6/number3.

Grant, S. G. (2000, February 24). Teachers and tests: Exploring teachers' perceptions of changes in the New York State testing program. *Education Policy Analysis Archives, 8*(14). Retrieved February 2, 2003, from http://epaa.asu.edt!L ~aa/v8n14.html.

Groves, P. (2002). "Doesn't it feel morbid here?" High-stakes testing and widening of equity gap. *Educational Foundations, 16*(2), 15–31. Retrieved January 22, 2003, from Wilson Web database.

Kadamus, J. A. (1998, February). *Update on the learning standards and state assessment system.* Retrieved Jan. 27, 2003, from http://www.emsc.nysed.gov/ciai/testing/ assesspubs/updatelearnstand.pdf.

Klein, S. P., Hamilton, L .S., McCaffrey, D. F., & Stecher, B. M. (2000 Oct.
    26). What do test scores in Texas tell us? *Education Policy Analysis
    Archives, 8*(49). Retrieved Feb. 6, 2003, from http://epaa.asu.edu/
    epaa/v8n49.

Kohn, A. (1999). *The schools our children deserve.* New York: Houghton Mifflin.

McNeil, L. M. (2000). *Contradictions of school reform: Educational costs of stan-
    dardized testing.* New York: Routledge.

Natriello, G., & Pallas, A. M. (1998). *The development and impact of high stakes
    testing.* Retrieved January 29, 2003, from Columbia University Web site:
    http://www.Columbia. edu/~gin6histake.html.

Popham, J. (1999). Why standardized testing won't measure educational
    quality. *Educational Leadership, 56*(6), 8–17.

Schleisman, J. (1999). *An in-depth investigation of one school district's responses
    to an externally-mandated, high-stakes testing program in Minnesota.* Min-
    neapolis: Annual meeting of the University Council for Educational Ad-
    ministration. (ERIC Document Reproduction Service No. ED 440465).

U.S. Department of Education (n.d.). *Testing for results.* Retrieved January 27,
    2003, from http://www.ed.gov/nclb/testingforresults.

Wright, W. E. (2002 June 5). The effects of high stakes testing in an inner-city
    elementary school: The curriculum, the teachers, and the English lan-
    guage learners. *Current Issues in Education, 5*(5). Retrieved Jan. 23,
    2003, from http://cie.ed.asu.edu/volume5/number5.

SAMPLE QUANTITATIVE PROPOSAL

Kindergarten and Social Behavior   1

Running Head: KINDERGARTEN AND SOCIAL BEHAVIOR

The Effect of Full-Day and Half-Day

Kindergarten Programs on Student Social Behavior

Student Name

Institution's Name

Full-Day and Half-Day Kindergarten Programs and Social Behavior

Friedrick Froebel established the first kindergarten in 1837 in Germany. Froebel's ideas influenced the development of kindergarten in the United States. Kindergarten began as a full day but was shortened to a half day during World War II as a result of a teacher shortage and growing birthrate (Oelerich, 1979). Today over 3.3 million children attend kindergarten in the United States. In 1993 about 54% of kindergarten teachers taught full-day classes and 45% of the kindergartners attended full-day programs (Karweit, 1990).

Kindergarten scheduling has been steadily becoming a growing area of controversy in private and public school systems today (Clark, 2001). This controversy has developed as a result of the options for the kindergarten programs themselves. School systems have the choice of establishing a full-day program, in which the students would attend a regular school day as they would in, for example, a first grade class. Or, they have the option of establishing a half-day program. In a half-day program the kindergarten students would be separated into two groups. One of the groups would attend kindergarten in the morning and the other would attend in the afternoon. The decision-making process is often based on availability of funds, the professional opinion of the administrators and teachers, as well as the opinions of the parents of the students involved (Clark, 2001).

Some school districts base their decisions on prior research conducted to examine the effectiveness of each of these scheduling options. Most of the research conducted has focused on the later development of academic achievement and reading abilities in children who attended kindergartens with different schedules. Early studies found that children who are exposed to a full-day educational environment were likely to be better readers than children in half-day programs (Gullo, 1990). It was also found that most full-day kindergarten programs had literacy at the center of their curriculum and the children were being exposed to more literature than they would be if they were participating in a half-day program (da Costa & Bell, 2001). However, later research has supported the idea that a full-day program would consistently increase achievement scores for children who are at risk but would do nothing for other children who do not meet the "at risk" criteria (Clark, 2001). Fusaro (1997), however, found that all children attending a full-day kindergarten schedule manifested significantly greater achievement overall, signaling that these findings could be solely based on the mere structure of these classrooms.

Statement of Purpose

Although research on full-day and half-day programming has focused its attention on student academic achievement, research that has investigated the role such programming has played in student social behavior has gone somewhat unexplored. Therefore, the purpose of this study is to examine the effect of the type of kindergarten class on students' social-emotional development. For the purposes of this study, the independent variable will be the two types of kindergarten class: full-day and half-day programs. The dependent variable

Kindergarten and Social Behavior   4

in this study will be defined as student scores on a social-emotional development inventory.

Review of Literature

The studies examining the effects of a full-day kindergarten program as compared to a half-day program are inconclusive. Some studies found beneficial
effects of a full-day kindergarten program on student achievement as opposed
to half-day kindergarten, while other studies failed to find any difference in
achievement between the two at all (Fusaro, 1997).

Holmes and McConnell (1990) found no significant differences in overall academic achievement in kindergarten students based on their enrollment
in a half-day or a full-day kindergarten program, although they did find differences in math scores. After conducting an experimental study they supported
the idea that it is a "matter of speculation" as to why students enrolled in the
full-day program had scored significantly higher on the mathematics portion
of the California Achievement Test than children enrolled in a half-day program. They speculated that the difference was due to the lack of parental help
in mathematics for both groups. The full-day students were able to make up
for this lack of parental help in mathematics through the additional time for
practice at school. Because parents provided activities in other areas of the curriculum, no differences occurred between the two groups. The speculation by
the authors with no supporting data might lead the reader to believe that this
study is biased. The authors reported no significant differences in the results

Kindergarten and Social Behavior   5

but emphasized a nonsignificant advantage for full-day kindergarteners in their discussion. The explanation offered by Holmes and McConnell is consistent, however, with the hypothesis that the children who are defined as at-risk would benefit from a full-day program. This hypothesis is also supported by several other studies (Clark, 2001; da Costa & Bell, 2000, 2001; Elicker, 1997).

Clark (2001) suggested that because the number of single parent and dual-income families has been steadily increasing, the need for an all-day kindergarten program is two-fold. The caregivers of these kindergarteners are usually full time in the workplace and having their child in school all day provides the child with a sense of stability as well as providing support for the caregiver. A full-day program would also better prepare children for their future academic careers. Clark, however, does not address the potential extraneous variable of parental backgrounds. This may also produce differences between the assessments of the two programs. Elicker (1997) and da Costa and Bell (2000, 2001) have all based their research on that same theory. Their research supports the idea that all-day kindergarten programs provide positive social and learning benefits for children. Clark (2001) concluded that parents and educators must remember that how children are spending their time at school is most important rather than how long they are actually there. However, Hildebrand (2000) found quite the opposite. Hildebrand conducted an experiment to discover the effects of all-day kindergarten and half-day kindergarten programming on academic achievement. She concluded that it was not the quality of time spent in the classroom but rather the quantity of time spent in the classroom that enable the students to perform better on achievement tests. An analysis of covariance showed the all-day kindergarten group scored significantly higher on reading scores than a half-day group after merely being exposed regularly to an environment that supported learning, such as school. Children who participate in a half-day program, according to Hildebrand, are missing out on half of the experience of simply being in the classroom and developing schemas. One main concern with this study is the lack of control for the type of curriculum presented in the research. Also, Hildebrand did not control for parental background.

However, Gullo (1990) and Olsen and Zigler (1989) support the idea that an all-day kindergarten is simply too much too soon, and they contend that, despite the test scores, this type of stressful environment is inappropriate for children of this age. These authors question the conclusions by Hildebrand (2000) supporting a longer kindergarten day to ensure more exposure of educational material to the kindergarteners. Elicker (1997) tested the theory that full-day kindergarten is stressful with his study observing a full-day kindergartener's experience at school. Elicker's main goal was to assess the stress and pressure the students in an all-day program were feeling and he discovered that there was none. According to Elicker, the students did not seem stressed by the all-day experience. In fact, Elicker noted that the students and the teacher appeared to benefit from all of the time they had allotted to them in a given day to complete all of the required material. The results showed actually that a full-day kindergarten program would be less stressful than a shorter schedule because there is more time to do the work. This study, however, did not follow up with achievement scores or discuss its comparison to other kindergarten programs. Elicker's study also neglected to address the ways in which time was used during the kindergarten day.

Fusaro (1997) attempted to provide statistical evidence to settle the debate by conducting a meta-analysis on the differences in achievement between students who had attended a half-day kindergarten program and those who had attended a full-day program. The results indicated that overall the students who had attended a full-day kindergarten program scored significantly higher in achievement. Fusaro admitted that meta-analyses were prone to "potential contaminating effects" such as the file-drawer problem. This problem occurs when the results are tucked away (in a file drawer) to ensure that the results lean toward full-day kindergarten programs. However, he described his procedures for selecting studies carefully to avoid this problem and still found an advantage for full-day programs. Again, throughout this study only test scores were examined, not the quality of time spent in the classroom as far as structure and organization of activities.

However, some more recent research raises questions about Fusaro's conclusions. Alber-Kelsay (1998) hypothesized that children who had participated in a full-day kindergarten program would not show significant academic achievement in first grade when compared to those students who had participated in a half-day kindergarten program. The results of this study supported the hypothesis. Her conclusion was that children need to be at school every

Kindergarten and Social Behavior   8

day; however, they also need regular at-home time throughout the day and that this is best accomplished with a half-day schedule. In this study the examiner only looked at one school in a small midwestern city. This limits the generalizability of the results of this study since the sample is nonrepresentative of the population. Alber-Kelsay also never disclosed what the children were doing and where they were when they were not at school. The children were also from a higher socioeconomic status than in other studies, and these children attending the half-day program could have been continuing with their learning outside of the classroom with a tutor or at an academically driven day care center.

The above studies were mostly concerned with standardized test scores even though young children's test performance tends to be unreliable because they are sensitive to environmental factors (Pellegrini & Glickman, 1990). Few studies have looked at students' peer interactions skills, which are an important part of learning in kindergarten (Waters & Sroufe, 1983).

Behavior outcomes were examined in a study by Gullo, Bersani, Clements, and Bayless (1986). Classroom behaviors of students in full-day and half-day kindergartens were rated using the Hahnemann Elementary Behavior Rating Scale. No significant differences were reported in the teacher ratings although significant differences in academic achievement favored the full-day schedule.

Cryan, Sheehan, Wiechel, and Bandy-Heddan (1992) also examined peer interactions and children's social skills. They found that teachers rated children in full-day programs as better behaved, more original, more involved, more likely to be independent and less likely to be shy than children in half-day

programs. Pellegrini and Glickman (1990) point out that academic achievement and peer relations are both predictors of later first grade achievement.
Pellegrini demonstrated this in a study in which he observed 35 children on
their playground at social recess for two years. Classroom teachers also assessed the children with two standardized tests: the Metropolitan Readiness
Test and the Georgia Criterion-Referenced Test in first grade. The results indicated that the standardized tests alone accounted for 36% of the variance in
children's first grade achievement scores. However, when the behavioral data
was added, the two variables accounted for 75% of the variance in first grade
achievement. This demonstrates the importance of assessing social as well as
academic achievement.

   In sum, research has shown that an all-day experience is not harmful to
five-year-old students and may have academic benefits. There is some indication that children may benefit socially as well from a full-day schedule. Gullo
(1990) points out that half-day teachers typically have 20 to 25 students per session for a total of 40 to 50 per day while full-day teachers typically have only 20
to 25 students total. Therefore, teachers in full-day programs have more time to
spend with each student and may be able to get to know each student better.
However, the research on social behaviors is limited and some studies have
failed to control for family background or teacher training or have used un-
representative samples. Because social behaviors are a strong predictor of later
academic achievement and are important in their own right, a study examin-

ing whether there are differences in social behaviors between children attending full-day and half-day kindergartens is needed.

It is hypothesized that children who participate in an all-day program that is developmentally appropriate will demonstrate more positive behaviors than children who participate in a half-day program that is developmentally appropriate. *Developmentally appropriate* is defined as a practice in which the activities and materials should take into account individual appropriateness and are age appropriate. Teachers and parents will receive training on curriculum that is developmentally appropriate prior to the start of the study. The all-day program will be 30 hours per week of instruction and the half-day program will consist of 15 hours per week of instruction. Behavior of the children will be measured by the Hahnemann Elementary Behavior Rating Scale.

Method

Participants

The study will involve teachers, parents, and students from 10 school districts in upstate New York. The school districts will be chosen based on the following criterion: The kindergarten schedule (half-day or full-day) used in the school districts will have been in place for at least three years because differences in student achievement could be a result of teachers' inexperience with the schedule.

Five of the 10 school districts will be districts that are currently using a full-day schedule and five will be districts that are currently using a half-day schedule. These 10 districts will all be within a 100 mile radius from Albany, New York, and each school district will represent an urban, rural, or suburban environment. A multiple stage random cluster sampling procedure will be used to select the 10 districts and then to select 200 children from these districts. Districts and children will be selected using methods to control for possible extraneous variables. The 10 districts will first be defined as rural, urban, or suburban based on information from the U.S. Census. An equal number of districts from urban, suburban, and rural areas will be selected for the full-day and half-day schedules. The next step will be to select students who are matched based on gender. Homogeneous grouping will be used to select students for full-day and half-day kindergarten classes who are equal in parental employment status, family income, and previous preschool experience. This information will be obtained from the school districts. Parent permission for participation in the study and for obtaining demographic information will also be obtained from all parents in both groups.

Teachers will also be involved in this study. Each schedule will include five classrooms with five teachers who will attend a training session on using age appropriate materials that each district will be given. A total of 10 teachers will be recruited as volunteers: five for the full-day schedule and five for the half-day schedule. All 10 teachers will have been teaching their assigned schedule for at least three years and they will all be expected to attend the training sessions prior to the study.

Instrument

The children's behaviors will be measured by the Hahnemann Elementary Behavior Rating Scale (HESB) (Spivak & Swift as cited by Gullo, Bersani, Clements, and Bayless, 1986). The HESB was designed to identify certain classroom behaviors in elementary school children. The instrument includes 15 behaviors that are rated by the teacher. The students are rated on a scale from one to five or one to seven, depending on the category. The score is an indication of how much of that factor the child is perceived as having. Therefore, a high score illustrates that the child is exhibiting more of that factor in the classroom.

The following is a list of the 15 behaviors (factors). The first behavior is originality, which includes a description of the level of curiosity and imagination that is displayed. The second behavior is independent learning. This category shows how a child is able to guide his or her own learning and think for him-self or herself. Involvement is the third behavior measured by HESB. This cat-egory assesses how a child uses other classmates to enrich his or her learning. The fourth behavior measures how well a child works with peers. The next be-havior is a child's intellectual dependency on peers. This factor describes how much children are influenced by their peers and how much they depend on them for direction. The sixth behavior is failure anxiety and the seventh is un-reflectiveness, which assesses the degree of cognitive impulsivity. Irrelevant talk is the eighth measurement. Disruptive behavior is the next factor mea-sured. The tenth behavior is negative feelings, which includes helplessness and criticism of others. The extent to which the children hold back from class-room activity is the next measurement of behavior. The twelfth factor is criti-cal-competitiveness which assesses the tendency to dominate and compete with peers. Blaming others is also measured as the thirteenth behavior. The fourteenth factor measured is approaching the teacher and the last behavior measured is inattention, which is measuring the limitations of attentiveness.

The HESB was chosen as the instrument used to measure social behav-iors because it covered many of the age-appropriate behaviors that are experi-enced in a kindergarten classroom. Another reason for using this test is that it looks at both positive and negative behaviors. The validity of the test has been demonstrated by examining the relationship of factor scores from the HESB and teacher grades and measured I.Q. A significant relationship has been found between the HESB and both of these measures. Factor scores have also

Kindergarten and Social Behavior   14

been found to significantly differentiate between different diagnostic groups of children with emotional disturbances (Spivak & Swift as cited by Gullo, Bersani, Clements, and Bayless, 1986).

No information has been given on reliability. To ensure for interrater reliability in this study teachers will be trained in the use of the instrument and a trained observer will also observe each classroom. The ratings of the teachers and the trained observer will be compared and the degree of agreement between the ratings will be determined.

Design and Procedure

The study will use a causal comparative approach. The independent variable is the length of school day for the children in kindergarten—either full day or half day. The dependent variable is the score on the Hahnemann Elementary School Behavior Rating scales.

Teachers will be asked to volunteer for the study. They will also be required to attend a training program and they will also be involved in rating the children's behavior using the Hahnemann Elementary School Behavior Rating Scale. Teachers who teach the full-day schedule will have three years experience teaching this schedule prior to the study and teachers teaching the half-day schedule will also have had three years prior experience teaching half-day kindergarten. All teachers participating will have been teaching in school districts that have been chosen based on their environments, so that urban, rural, and suburban areas are all represented equally. Threats to external validity are being controlled because the teachers are coming from a diverse range of environments and the children are randomly selected to represent a variety of backgrounds. Before the teachers are asked to participate permission from the school principals will be obtained and school policies regarding research will be followed for each school throughout this study. Parent permission will also be obtained before the study begins.

Once the teachers have volunteered, training classes will begin. One training class will be held prior to the start of school in September. The training class will give the teachers information on the study, age-appropriate materials, and training on how to complete the Hahnemann Elementary School Behavior Rating Scale. The teachers will be expected to rate each student's behavior at the beginning of the school year and again at the end.

The training on age-appropriate behavior will be the same for both schedules and will be delivered by an early childhood educator from a nearby university. This training will concentrate on the importance of providing children with experiences and activities that are meaningful for children in kindergarten. The training will also highlight the importance of seeking a balance between child- and teacher-initiated activities, as well as recognizing the importance of time for play in the kindergarten schedule.

During the first week of school the parents will attend a two-hour informational meeting. This meeting will highlight the importance of this study and outline the purpose and procedures of the study. Parents could affect the results of this study as an external influence; therefore, it is important that they

Kindergarten and Social Behavior   16

know what to expect from the study. Parents will also be briefed on age-appropriate behavior, because often parents will put pressure on their children to exceed at tasks they are not ready for. At this time parents will also be given the option to have their child not participate in the study.

Children chosen to participate will be assigned to teachers randomly in their school. Children who are in a school district with the full-day schedule will remain in that district and children in districts with the half-day schedule will remain in those districts as well.

To control for observer bias, trained researchers will be assigned to the different schools to rate children's behavior using the Hahnemann Elementary School Behavior Rating Scale. The researchers will be asked to rate the children at the same time that the teachers are. Children will be rated during the first month of school and during the last month as well. The reason for both observations is to provide pretest information so that possible threats to internal validity, maturation and history, can be controlled. The first observation will help to control for possible developmental differences among children as they enter kindergarten.

Throughout the year the researchers will periodically visit the classrooms to ensure that the teachers do not have any questions and to make sure that the quality and delivery of instruction is equal in all the classes. To ensure that the teachers are teaching comparative programs, reviews will be conducted of the lesson plans, topics to be studied, and posted schedules.

At the end of the year students will be observed and rated using the Hahnemann Elementary School Behavior Rating Scale once again. After the results have been calculated the principals, teachers, and parents will be invited to hear the results, and questions concerning the study can be addressed.

The threat of children dropping out will be controlled by the pretest observation. The researcher will know the pretest scores in the beginning of the year and that can be taken into consideration at the end of the year if children drop out of the study.

Another threat to the internal validity is differential selection of subjects. The pretest controls for this by providing a measure to compare the groups' similarities or differences prior to kindergarten.

A threat to external validity that may occur due to this experimental design is pretest-treatment interaction, which refers to the tendency for subjects to react differently to a treatment because they have been pretested. However, in this study that does not appear to be a threat because the observers will be in the room for both the pre- and postobservations and the children will also not know that they are being observed. Also, the young age of the children and the length of time make it unlikely that they will react to the pretest.

Benefits and Limitations

This study was designed to investigate the effect of kindergarten schedules on children's social behavior. Previous studies have made it difficult to make conclusive statements regarding kindergarten schedules effects on children's academic and social achievement. This study focused on social behaviors because

previous studies focused on academic achievement rather than peer interactions, which are an important predictor of later achievement.

In order to determine if there were differences in classroom behavior,
the results from the 15 Hahnemann Elementary School Behavior scales will
be analyzed by calculating means and standard deviations for the two different schedules. It is expected that significant differences between the two schedules will be found for intellectual dependency, productivity with peers,
involvement in the classroom, independent learning, and approaching the
teacher. In all of these categories children participating in full-day programs
are expected to be rated higher than the children participating in half-day programs. In addition, full-day kindergarten students are expected to be rated
lower on the negative category of being withdrawn. If obtained these results
would be similar to the results found in a study by Cryan, Sheehan, Wiechel,
and Bandy-Heddan (1992).

From these results one might conclude that children who attend a full-
day schedule have more time in school to practice different social skills. However, another possibility is that teachers in the "all-day" kindergarten have half
as many children to deal with than the teachers that taught the "half-day"
schedule and get to know these children better. Therefore, the children in the
full-day schedule might show more social skills due to this closer relationship
rather than the time alone. Future studies might explore whether the degree
of closeness to the teacher is related to either children's social skills or the type
of kindergarten schedule.

It is also possible that children in the half-day program spend a greater percentage of their time in teacher-led large groups and less time in play than children in full-day programs. This may also be the reason for teachers rating children in the full-day program higher in some of the behaviors; that is, the children have more time to develop their social skills through participating in free play. Early childhood professionals, such as Olsen and Zigler (1989), have feared that if full-day schedules are adopted in districts children will be exposed to more academic programs and less time to play. Although the current study is expected to show that children in full-day schedules have high levels of social skills, it did not directly measure the time spent in play. Researchers have stated that the most reliable assessment of children's social behavior is observing them in free play, because they are more comfortable and have opportunities to exhibit their skills (Pellegrini & Glickman, 1990). Therefore, it is possible that teachers in the full-day schedule had more opportunities to observe positive social behavior than those teachers who taught the half-day schedule.

Children in the full-day program were expected to be seen by their teachers to be significantly better behaved in areas valued by educators. Full-day children were expected to be more involved, show more originality and independent learning, and be less shy and withdrawn than the children in the half-day program.

Unlike many of the previous studies, participants were randomly selected for this study from multiple school districts. This enhances the external valid-

Kindergarten and Social Behavior   20

ity of this study because a random sample is supposed to be more representative of the greater population, which in this study would be children in school districts within 100 miles of Albany, NY.

Although the findings in this study are more generalizable than earlier studies because of random selection, other factors such as teacher and community attitudes could also be examined. It would be interesting to study these two schedules on a select population, such as children from low-income families in a rural environment.

This study is expected to indicate that there are some advantages to the full-day schedule for children attending kindergarten. Children in the full-day program may have a greater chance of developing positive social behaviors. Added to previous research the findings would suggest that children gain both academic and social benefits from full-day kindergarten.

Social and economic changes sending more than 50% of the mothers into the workforce dictate a growing need for full-day kindergarten (Gullo, 1990). Many educators are wondering if the full-day schedule is beneficial to children or just convenient to the parents. This study along with previous studies would show that full-day programs do not cause any harm to five-year-olds. In fact, children in the full-day program can benefit from the longer school day. Policymakers should also keep in mind what is developmentally appropriate for five-year-olds in a full-day program. Lengthening the school day does provide more opportunities for learning, but the actual use of time is still the critical issue.

Kindergarten and Social Behavior   21

References

Alber-Kelsay, K. (1998). *Full-day versus half-day kindergarten: The outcomes of first grade reading achievement.* Elizabeth, NJ: Kean University. (ERIC Document Reproduction Service No. 417380).

Clark, P. (2001). Research on all-day kindergarten. *ERIC Digest.* Champaign, IL: ERIC Clearinghouse on Elementary and Early Childhood Educa-tion. (ERIC Document Reproduction Service No.543982). Retrieved February 2, 2003, from ERIC database.

Cryan, I., Sheehan, R., Wiechel, J., & Bandy-Redden, I. G. (1992). Success-ful outcomes of full-day kindergarten: More positive behavior and increased achievement in the years after. *Early Childhood Research Quarterly, 7,* 187–203.

da Costa, J. L., & Bell, S. (2000). *Full-day kindergarten at an inner city elemen-tary school: Perceived and actual effects.* Paper presented at the annual Meeting of the American Educational Research Association. New Orleans. (ERIC Document Reproduction Service No. 440751).

da Costa, J. L., & Bell, S. (2001). *A comparison of the literacy effects of full-day versus half-day kindergarten.* Paper presented at the annual Meeting of the American Educational Research Association. Seattle. (ERIC Document Reproductions.

Elicker, J. (1997, November). *Full day kindergarten may ease stress on students.* West Lafayette, IN: Purdue University. Retrieved on January 30, 2003,

Kindergarten and Social Behavior 22

from http://www.purdue.edu/uns/html4ever/9711.elicker.
kindergarten.html.

Fusaro, J. A. (1997). The effect of full-day kindergarten on student achievement: A meta-analysis. *Child Study Journal, 27*, 269–272.

Gullo, D. (1990). The changing family context: Implications for the development of all-day kindergartens. Young Children, *45*, 35–39.

Gullo, D., Bersani, C., Clements, D. H., & Bayless, K. M. (1986). A comparative study of all-day, alternate day and half-day schedules: Effects on
achievement and classroom social behaviors. *Journal of Research in
Childhood Education, 1*, 87–94.

Hildebrand, C. (2000). *Effects of all-day and half-day kindergarten programming on reading, writing, math, and classroom social behaviors.* (ERIC
Document Reproduction Service No. 495906). Retrieved February 12,
2003, from ERIC database.

Holmes, C. T., & McConnell, B. M. (1990, April). *Full-day versus half-
day kindergarten: An experimental study.* Boston: Paper presented
at the Annual Meeting of the American Educational Research
Association. (ERIC Document Reproduction Service No. ED
382418).

Karweit, N. (1990). The kindergarten experience. *Educational Leadership, 62*,
82-86.

Oelerich, M. L. (1979, April). *Kindergarten: All day, every day?* St. Louis, MO:
Paper presented at the National Conference of the Association for

Childhood Education International. (ERIC Document Reproduction Service No. ED 179282).

Olsen, D., & Zigler, E. (1989). An assessment of the all-day kindergarten movement. *Early Childhood Research Quarterly, 4,* 167–185.

Pellegrini, A. D., & Glickman, C. D. (1990). Measuring kindergartner's social competence. *Young Children, 42,* 40–44.

Waters, E., & Sroufe, L. (1983). Social competence as a development construct. *Developmental Review, 3,* 79–97.

CALCULATION OF THE STANDARD DEVIATION

There are two formulas for calculating the standard deviation. The first, referred to as the definitional formula, clearly shows what the standard deviation represents, but the second (calculation) formula is easier to calculate. Both yield the same result. The definitional formula follows.

Definitional Formula of Standard Deviation

$$\text{Standard deviation} = \sqrt{\frac{\Sigma (X - \overline{X})^2}{N - 1}}$$

where X means each score,
$\overline{X}$ means the mean, and
N means the number of scores.

Step One

List the scores in the distribution and calculate the mean.

20
19
17
16
16
15
14
12
10
 8

Total of scores = 147
Mean = total of scores divided by the number of scores:
147/10 = 14.7

Step Two

Subtract the mean from each score. See the middle column below.

X	$X - \bar{X}$	$(X - \bar{X})^2$
20	+5.3	28.09
19	+4.3	18.49
17	+2.3	5.29
16	+1.3	1.69
16	+1.3	1.69
15	+0.3	0.09
14	−0.7	0.49
12	−2.7	7.29
10	−4.7	22.09
8	−6.7	44.89

Step Three

Square (multiply times itself) the result of each score minus the mean. $(X - \bar{X})^2$. See the right-hand column above.

Step Four

Add up the numbers in the right-hand column, so

$\Sigma (X - \overline{X})^2 = 28.09 + 18.49 + 5.29 + 1.69 + 1.69 + 0.09 + 0.49 + 7.29 + 22.09 + 44.89 = 130.1$

Step Five

Divide the number in step four by $N - 1$ or $10 - 1 = 9$.

$$\frac{[\Sigma (X - \overline{X})^2]}{(N - 1)} = \frac{130.1}{9} = 14.46$$

Step Six

Take the square root of 14.46. The resulting number is the standard deviation.

$$\sqrt{\frac{\Sigma (X - \overline{X})^2}{N - 1}} = \sqrt{14.46} = 3.8026$$

Calculation Formula for Standard Deviation

$$\text{Standard deviation} = \sqrt{\frac{\Sigma X^2 - \frac{(\Sigma X)^2}{N}}{N - 1}}$$

where X means each score and
N means the number of scores.
So using the same data as above, the steps in the calculation would be as follows:

Step One

Square each score (multiply it times itself) and then add up the squares of the scores. This is the ΣX^2 part of the formula.

X	X^2
20	400
19	361
17	289
16	256
16	256
15	225
14	196
12	144
10	100
8	64

$\Sigma X^2 = 400 = 361 + 289 + 256 + 256 + 225 + 196 + 144 + 100 + 64 = 2291$

Step Two

Add up the scores in column one to obtain the ΣX.

$\Sigma X = 20 + 19 + 17 + 16 + 16 + 15 + 14 + 12 + 10 + 8 = 147$
$(\Sigma X) = 147$

Step Three

Square the ΣX by multiplying 147 by itself. Then divide this number by the number of scores (10).

$$\frac{(\Sigma X)^2}{N} = \frac{(147 \times 147)}{10} = \frac{21609}{10} = 2160.9$$

Step Four

Subtract $[(\Sigma X)^2/N$ from ΣX^2 and then divide that number by $N-1$ or 9

$$\frac{\Sigma X^2 - \{[(\Sigma X)^2]/N\}}{N-1} = \frac{(2291 - 2160.9)}{(10-1)} = \frac{130.1}{9} = 14.46$$

Step Five

Take the square root of 14.46. The resulting number is the standard deviation.

$$\sqrt{\frac{\Sigma X^2 - \{[(\Sigma X)^2]/N\}}{N-1}} = \sqrt{14.46} = 3.8026$$

INDEX